What readers are saying about Newcomer's Handbooks:

I recently got a copy of your Newcomer's Handbook for Chicago, and wanted to let you know how invaluable it was for my move. I must have consulted it a dozen times a day preparing for my move. It helped me find my way around town, find a place to live, and so many other things. My only suggestion is a more detailed map of the area. It's just a small gripe however, as your book helped me so much. Thanks.
—Mike L.
Chicago, Illinois

Excellent reading (Newcomer's Handbook for San Francisco and the Bay Area) ... it seems balanced and trustworthy. One of the very best guides if you are considering moving/relocation. Way above the usual tourist crap.
—Gunnar E.
Stockholm, Sweden

I was very impressed with the latest edition of the Newcomer's Handbook for Los Angeles. It is well organized, concise and up-to date. I would recommend this book to anyone considering a move to Los Angeles.
—Jannette L.
Attorney Recruiting Administrator for a large Los Angeles law firm

I recently moved to Atlanta from San Francisco, and LOVE the Newcomer's Handbook for Atlanta. It has been an invaluable resource – it's helped me find everything from a neighborhood in which to live to the local hardware store. I look something up in it everyday, and know I will continue to use it to find things long after I'm no longer a newcomer. And if I ever decide to move again, your book will be the first thing I buy for my next destination.
—Courtney R.
Atlanta, Georgia

In looking to move to the Boston area, a potential employer in that area gave me a copy of the Newcomer's Handbook for Boston. It's a great book that's very comprehensive, outlining good and bad points about each neighborhood in the Boston area. Very helpful in helping me decide where to move.
~~~~ given (online submit form)

TABLE OF CONTENTS

CONTENTS

THIS BOOK IS DEDICATED TO THE PROPOSITION THAT IT IS AS rewarding to live in New York City as it is to work here. However, the transition from newcomer to New Yorker isn't necessarily achieved without some discomfort. To minimize the difficulties involved in moving to New York, we have written the *Newcomer's Handbook® for Moving to New York City*, which has been continually updated since its 1980 inception in order to keep up with change in this fastest-paced of cities. On September 11, 2001, as this edition was going to press, the World Trade Center disaster devastated part of Lower Manhattan, killing thousands and stunning the world. Even as it stumbled, a resilient New York City set about restoration and rebuilding. The task will take months, years, so portions of this book which refer to the World Trade Center area will need updating in later editions. What about the possibility of future terrorism here? Risk may be greater in the immediate future, but few New Yorkers consider leaving. This book is addressed to them and to the determined newcomer.

Whether you are looking for the right neighborhood or the right health club, the right synagogue or simply a quiet, green oasis, these chapters will guide you, the newcomer, in your search.

The 1990s brought a boom in two pillars of the New York economy: the stock market and tourism. These resurgent industries, plus a lower crime rate and an upbeat feeling created a tight real estate market, especially in the more desirable neighborhoods. A softened economy in 2001 brought an easing of rents, but the quest for a good, affordable apartment is still difficult. Use this handbook as a tool in that quest and in making your life in New York more rewarding once you've landed.

In addition to regular updating and detailed descriptions of neighborhoods in the city and New Jersey, this 19th edition includes timely information on renting or buying a home in **Finding a Place to Live**, as well as a survey of services for seniors in **Helpful Services**, and a new chapter, **Moving and Storage**. Throughout the book, wherever available, we've included web sites for locations, institutions, and establishments that are mentioned. We've also added information on getting around the city by bicycle and by car in the **Transportation** chapter, as well as an extended list of **Useful Phone Numbers and Web Sites**.

As usual, we welcome readers' suggestions and comments on the tear-out page at the back of the book.

We hope that the information presented on the following pages will help you establish a New York City residence smoothly and speedily. We also hope that once you select your neighborhood and settle in, the book will help you get on with the pleasure part: enjoyment of the city's myriad and unrivaled resources.

FROM THE WIND-WHIPPED CORNER OF EAST END AVENUE ON AN icy January evening Greenwich Village seems as accessible as Alaska. So you cancel plans to meet a Village acquaintance downtown, call a friend on East 85th and get together at an uptown bistro instead. Clearly, the neighborhood in which you live affects what you do and who you see in New York City. The cachet of shared space in the Upper East Side (or another of Manhattan's established communities) usually has more allure for the neophyte than space of one's own in the boroughs or a recently gentrified enclave. It takes time, familiarity with the city, and a certain street-honed sophistication to be totally at ease in distant or just-emerging districts. Still, unless money is no object, today's rental market often requires compromises, not only in the way you live but also in the neighborhood you choose. But wherever you settle, once established, you're likely to become rooted in your own special area.

Not for nothing are New Yorkers neighborhood proud. More than just an address or a source of necessary services, neighborhoods provide residents with identification and a sense of belonging, which in turn provides sufficient sustenance and heart for daily confrontations with the city's size and pace. Most New Yorkers feel fairly chauvinistic about their area and delight in extolling its virtues—and its faults as well.

Manhattan neighborhoods are listed clockwise (picture an exceedingly elongated clock) starting with Yorkville, continuing south along the East River downtown around the tip of the island and then uptown along the Hudson ending with Washington Heights/Inwood. Descriptions of communities in The Bronx, Brooklyn, Queens, and Staten Island, as well as five in New Jersey follow Manhattan. No description, however, can substitute for your own experience. You are strongly encouraged to visit the neighborhoods that interest you and talk to residents before signing a lease.

(Among other things, it is an excellent way to get leads on apartments that might otherwise escape your attention.) Resources and city services within each neighborhood are included in order to facilitate orientation once you're settled.

For newcomers who might wish to look further afield, to the suburbs for example, we have listed additional communities worth investigating in Brooklyn, Queens, and Staten Island, as well as suburban towns in New Jersey, Connecticut, Westchester County, NY, and Long Island, none more than an hour's commute from Manhattan.

Suggestions on how to go about finding an apartment and how best to enjoy the city come after **Neighborhoods** in **Finding A Place to Live** and in other sections.

FORMULAS FOR FINDING STREET AND AVENUE ADDRESSES ABOVE 14th Street are described below. Crosstown street numbers follow a more-or-less set pattern; not so, avenue street numbers. In a town where 950 Amsterdam Avenue is at 107th Street, 950 Broadway at 23rd, 950 5th at 76th, and 950 Third at 57th, the somewhat elaborate system used to discover the location of an avenue address is worth knowing.

EAST AND WEST SIDE AVENUES

To determine the cross street for an address on an avenue, proceed as follows: first, take off the last digit of the building number; second, divide the remainder by two; third, add or subtract the number given in the column below.*

Avenues A,B,C,D . . . . + 3
1st Ave. . . . . +3
2nd Ave. . . . . +3
3rd Ave. . . . . +10
4th Ave. . . . . +8
5th Ave.
    Up to 200 . . . . +13
    Up to 400 . . . . +16
    Up to 600 . . . . +18
    Up to 775 . . . . +20
    From 775 to 1286
      (Cancel last figure) . . . . −18
6th Ave.
    (Ave. of the Americas) . . . . . . −12
7th Ave.
    Below 110th St. . . . . +12
    Above 110th St. . . . . +20
8th Ave. . . . . +10
9th Ave. . . . . +13
10th Ave. . . . . +14
Amsterdam Ave. . . . . +60
Broadway
    Above 23rd St. . . . . −30
Columbus Ave. . . . . +60
Convent Ave. . . . . +127
Lenox Ave. . . . . +110
Lexington Ave. . . . . +22
Madison Ave. . . . . +26
Manhattan Ave. . . . . +100
Park Ave. . . . . +35
West End Ave. . . . . +60

EAST SIDE CROSSTOWN STREETS

5th to Madison & Park 1-99
Park to Lexington 100-139
Lexington to 3rd 140-199
3rd to 2nd 200-299
2nd to 1st 300-399
1st to York 400-499

WEST SIDE CROSSTOWN BELOW 58TH

5th to Ave. of Americas 1-99
Ave. of Americas to 7th 100-199
7th to 8th 200-299
8th to 9th 300-399
9th to 10th 400-499
10th to 11th 500-599

WEST SIDE CROSSTOWN ABOVE 58TH

Central Park West
to Columbus 100-199
Columbus to Amsterdam . . 200-299
Amsterdam to West End . . 300-399
West End to Riverside 400-499

*Central Park West and Riverside Drive do not fit into this formula. Divide the house number by 10 and add 60 to find the cross street on Central Park West; for Riverside Drive, divide the house number by 10 and add 72.

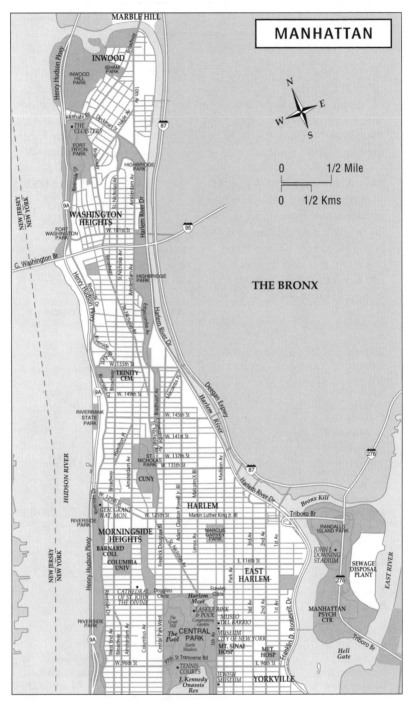

(North)

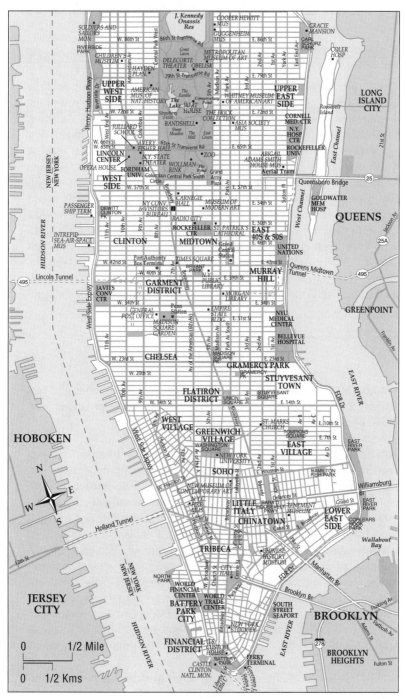

(South)

MANHATTAN

"New York, New York, it's a wonderful town/The Bronx is up and the Battery's down," goes the song. That'll do for a start. Like the rest of the world, when New Yorkers say New York they mean Manhattan. And from Manhattan, The Bronx is up (north), and the Battery is the southern-most tip of this long, skinny island. You need to know, further, that most of Manhattan is laid out in a grid, streets running east and west, avenues stretching north and south, except below 14th Street, where the street pattern is irregular. Much of this grid is bisected by Fifth Avenue, with streets designated east or west. Hence, West 25th Street runs west of Fifth Avenue, East 25th stretches east from Fifth. Building numbers begin at Fifth, so 15 West 15th Street is in the first block west of Fifth Avenue. North to south there are 20 city blocks to a mile; cross town blocks are longer, but not uniformly. The longest avenue in Manhattan, and the oldest, Broadway follows an old Indian trail from the Battery north through the top of the island into The Bronx.

YORKVILLE

Boundaries and Contiguous Areas: North: East 96th Street and East Harlem; **East**: East River; **South**: East 79th Street and Upper East Side; **West**: Lexington Avenue and Upper East Side

What distinguished Yorkville from its Upper East Side surroundings until recently was the character imbued by immigrants from Germany and Eastern Europe. Now, however, you'll find more co-op signs and health clubs than residents of Hungarian or Czechoslovakian ancestry. In the 1980s, a co-op, condo, and rental apartment boom finished off what World War II started: the erosion of Yorkville's old-world ethnicity. Old walkups were first leveled in the late 1940s to make way for new apartment buildings attractive to professionals—white-collar types who, once drawn to the neighborhood, began replacing the immigrants in the remaining railroad flats. Only traces of Yorkville's European heritage remain, and while Yorkville is still the most accessible part of the Upper East Side, what began as a scattering of stolid brick apartment buildings in mid-century is now an area chockablock with living space in a forest of ever-more-fanciful towers and fortresses.

Eighty-sixth Street, from Lexington to First avenues, has been attempting to redefine itself into a pricier shopping strip. However, the hoped for stability has not entirely materialized. Large residential projects such as the 17-story Park Avenue Court (really on Lexington) and the Colorado luxury apartment building are offering prime retail space (and lots of it) that has been attracting upscale, international stores.

Yorkville was a pleasant rural community when the first wave of German and Irish immigrants arrived on these shores in the 1850s. Tranquil pastures surrounded river estates owned by wealthy merchants, many of whom were of German origin. In the 1880s the completion of the Second and Third Avenue elevated lines opened the area to settlement, and German immigrants, many attracted by jobs in the developing breweries, moved north from the Lower East Side. Irish immigrants followed and then, as they grew more prosperous, Hungarians, Czechs and Slovaks. Today, the second and third generations are more likely to be found in Queens and Westchester than in Yorkville, and it is a dwindling, elderly Middle European population that patronizes the few remaining ethnic bakeries, butcher shops, and restaurants. Not that these stores are empty; customer ranks have been swelled by appreciative young professionals who now dominate the area.

The inviting mix of buildings, old and new, that characterizes Yorkville, as well as the community's relatively low crime rate and good public schools, makes it an attractive destination for the determined apartment seeker. After a six-year hiatus in the early 90s, housing construction is again active, with luxury rentals designed for young professionals rising between East 86th and 96th streets. Traditionally north of 96th Street has been considered beyond the Pale, but in a crowded, affluent Manhattan market that barrier has fallen and renovation and construction push north on Third to 100th Street, at slightly lower rents. Sunday *Times'* Real Estate Section is thick with ads drumming those amenity-laden new Yorkville buildings as well as less expensive, shareable one-bedroom apartments in newly renovated brownstones and tenements between Third Avenue and York.

For a refreshing pause, explore Carl Schurz Park bordering the East River at 86th Street and East End Avenue, where you can also spy the mayor's residence, graceful Gracie Mansion built in 1799. Jutting over F.D.R. Drive, this semi-sylvan oasis recalls Yorkville of yore and affords a spectacular view of the East River, its islands, boats, and barges. Astors, Rhinelanders and Schermerhorns had their estates here, and this quiet neighborhood is still Yorkville's most coveted roost and home to two of the city's best private girls' schools, not to mention the Asphalt Green sports/community center and adjacent AquaCenter.

Upscale new apartment towers have attracted a tide of young professionals to the upper northeast reaches of Yorkville, and with them food and convenience stores, not to mention the coffee bars that have Seattlized Manhattan. Streets once sparsely peopled are now alive with baby strollers and dogs.

Web Site: official New York City site, www.nyc.gov

Area Codes: 212, 646

Post Offices: Yorkville Station, 1617 Third Avenue, NYC 10128, at 91st Street, 212-369-2747; Gracie Station, 229 East 85th Street, NYC 10028, 212-988-6682

Zip Codes: 10128, 10028, 10021

Police Precinct: Nineteenth, 153 East 67th Street, NYC 10021, 212-452-0600

Emergency Hospitals: Mt. Sinai Hospital, Fifth Avenue at 100th Street, NYC 10029, 212-241-6500; Metropolitan Hospital, 1901 First Avenue, NYC 10029, 212-423-6262; Beth Israel Medical Center—North Division, 170 East End Avenue, NYC 10128, 212-870-9197

Library: Yorkville Branch, 222 East 79th Street, NYC 10021, 212-744-5824

Public School Education: School District #2 (see **Chelsea**).

Community Resources: 92nd Street Y, (Young Men's and Young Women's Hebrew Association), 1395 Lexington Avenue, NYC 10128, 212-427-6000

Transportation—Subway: #4, #5, #6 Lexington Avenue at 96th Street, 86th Street (Exp), 77th Street, 68th Street, 59th Street (Exp)

Transportation—Bus: Crosstown 96th Street (#19); Crosstown 86th Street (#86); Crosstown 79th Street (#79); Crosstown 72nd Street (#72); Crosstown 66th/67th Street (#66); Crosstown 57th Street (#57, #58); Uptown First Avenue-Downtown Second Avenue (#15); Uptown Third Avenue-Downtown Lexington Avenue (#98, #101, #102)

THE UPPER EAST SIDE

Boundaries and Contiguous Areas: North: East 96th Street to Lexington Avenue and Yorkville, East Harlem: **East:** the East River and Lexington Avenue, 79th to 96th streets; **South:** 59th Street and the East Forties and Fifties; **West:** Fifth Avenue

The affluent heart of the Upper East Side—that quadrant caught between Fifth, 79th, Lexington and 59th Street and the panhandle stretching from 79th along Fifth to 96th Street—has landmark status and as a result may remain ever thus. But this does not mean that Manhattan's most popular neighborhood for the wealthy and the upwardly mobile is completely homogeneous. Each avenue that traverses the area, from Fifth east to York, has a distinctive character all its own.

Fifth Avenue, flanking Central Park, glitters with some of the city's most magnificent museums, most exclusive cooperatives, and some of its most glamorous relics, those wonderfully ornate mansions which so clearly reflect the tastes and fortunes of our turn-of-the-century millionaires. Fricks, Dukes, Carnegies, Whitneys—their copies of palaces, chateaux, and Gothic castles established the avenue as highly fashionable. Dominating Fifth physically and artistically in the East 80s, the Metropolitan Museum is also the site of one of the liveliest street scenes in town. Its sprawling stone steps, while providing access to the museum, offer seats and a meeting place from which to watch the mimes, musicians, and street vendors who use the sidewalk around the entrance as performing space.

Madison Avenue between 60th and 86th streets is a veritable gauntlet of classy international boutiques and fine arts galleries. This solid wall of chic was pepped up some with the addition of The Limited, Ralph Lauren, Timberland, and Barneys. Around 81st Street and P.S. 6 (Public School #6), the premier elementary school on the Upper East Side, a number of trendy designers have set up shop. Above 86th Street, where Andrew Carnegie built the elaborate mansion that now houses the Cooper-Hewitt Museum, most of the other palatial beaux-arts residences constructed in the early 1900s have been acquired by schools, consulates, and cultural institutions. Today these grand buildings, interspersed with bow-fronted, brick Georgian homes and solid pre-World War II apartment buildings, form an exceedingly harmonious neighborhood.

On Park, the handsome center strip of year-round greenery and sea-sonal plantings make the stately square cooperative buildings that proceed shoulder to elegant shoulder up the avenue more gracious still.

Lexington Avenue has largely taken over from Madison as purveyor of quality produce to Upper East Siders. Immaculate, and imaginative, shops harboring fishmongers and florists, greengrocers and bakers are crowded into the ruddy, rustic brick buildings that line the street.

The area from Third Avenue east to the river, once the province of the "el" and tenements, has been Trumped up. Today, sleek glass and granite shafts intersperse postwar brick apartment blocks that loom over the once characteristic, and now disappearing, five-story walkups. Turn-of-century building along First through Third avenues is aimed at young professionals. And turnover is a constant among the clubs, bars and restaurants catering to east-of-Third singles.

Web Sites: www.uppereast.com; www.uppereastside.about.com; www.decny.com/cb8; official New York City site, www.nyc.gov
Area Codes: 212, 646
Post Office: Lenox Hill Station, 217 East 70th Street, NYC 10021, 212-879-4401; nearby: Gracie Station, 229 East 85th Street, NYC 10028, 212-988-6681
Zip Codes: 10128, 10028, 10021, 10022

Police Precinct: Nineteenth, 153 East 67th Street, NYC 10021, 212-452-0600

Emergency Hospitals: Lenox Hill Hospital, 100 East 77th Street, NYC 10021, 212-434-2000; New York Hospital-Cornell Medical Center, 525 East 68th Street, NYC 10021, 212-746-5454; Manhattan Eye, Ear and Throat Hospital, 210 East 64th Street, NYC 10021, 212-838-9200; nearby: Mt. Sinai Hospital, Fifth Avenue at 100th Street, NYC 10029, 212-241-6500

Libraries: 96th Street Branch, 112 East 96th Street, NYC 10128, 212-289-0908; Webster Branch, 1465 York Avenue between 77th and 78th streets, NYC 10021, 212-288-5049; The New York Society Library, 212-288-6900, a private institution with membership dues $135 per year and 250,000 volumes, is an outstanding resource located at 53 East 79th Street, NYC 10021.

Public School Education: School District #2 (see **Chelsea**).

Adult Education: Marymount Manhattan College, 221 East 71st Street, NYC 10021, 212-517-0400; Hunter College, 695 Park Avenue at 68th Street, NYC 10021, 212-772-4000

Community Resources: 92nd Street Y (Young Men's and Young Women's Hebrew Association) 1395 Lexington Avenue, NYC 10128, 212-427-6000; the Cooper-Hewitt Museum, 2 East 91st Street, 212-849-8300; the International Center of Photography (ICP), 1130 Fifth Avenue at 94th Street, 212-860-1777; the Jewish Museum, 1109 Fifth Avenue at 92nd Street, 212-423-3200; the Solomon Guggenheim Museum, 1071 Fifth Avenue at 89th Street, 212-423-3500; the Whitney Museum of American Art, 945 Madison Avenue at 75th Street, 212-570-3676; the Metropolitan Museum of Art, Fifth Avenue at 82nd Street, 212-535-7710 for recorded information, 212-879-5500 for assistance; the Frick Collection, 1 East 70th Street, 212-288-0700; The Asia Society, 725 Park Avenue (at 70th Street) 212-517-ASIA; the Center for Inter-American Relations, Park Avenue and 68th Street; the China Institute, 125 East 65th Street, 212-744-8181; Society of Illustrators, 128 East 63rd Street, 212-838-2560, and numerous other societies, museums, galleries and auction houses.

Transportation—Subway: #4, #5, #6 Lexington Avenue at 96th Street, 86th Street (Exp), 77th Street, 68th Street, 59th Street (Exp)

Transportation—Bus: Crosstown 96th Street (#19); Crosstown 86th Street (#86); Crosstown 79th Street (#79); Crosstown 72nd Street (#72); Crosstown 66th/67th Street (#66); Crosstown 57th Street (#28); Uptown Madison Avenue (#1, #2, #3, #4); Downtown Fifth Avenue (#1, #2, #3, #4)

ROOSEVELT ISLAND

Located off 59th Street in the East River

Roosevelt Islanders have always had an unusual commute: a silent aerial float to and from 59th Street and Second Avenue in Manhattan (every 5 to 15 minutes for $1.50) up and over the East River with the city's skyline first at eye level and then, incredibly, beneath your feet. Small wonder that the trams find favor with tourists and day-trippers. Residents used to be reduced to taking cabs or a roundabout bus ride through Queens to Manhattan when the funicular occasionally faltered. Now, however, the city's Transit Authority has a subway line (the Q train) connecting the island with Queens (at 21st Street and 41st Avenue) and Manhattan (at 63rd and Lexington Avenue).

An appealing small-town quality pervades this island community of modern apartment buildings. It's quiet. Automobile access is limited, and a red minibus (25¢) provides regular service between the tram terminal and high rises lining relatively spotless streets where strolls with baby carriages and street corner chats are ritual—a sort of time zip back to the 1940s. Sunbathers crowd the greensward on a warm afternoon, joggers pad silently along the Promenade, and the contemplative sit, observing sailboats and barges floating past Manhattan's skyline. Roosevelt Island has extensive recreational facilities and stores supplying the basic needs, if not the exotic or ethnic ones. Built by early farmers in 1796, the Manor House is preserved at the foot of Main Street. The Octagon Lighthouse has recently been restored. Schools go up to the eighth grade and are part of District #2 (information in the **Chelsea** section).

Inauguration of the long-awaited subway line in 1989 came not a moment too soon: the red brick five-building **Manhattan Park** development on an eight-acre site just north of the original concrete buildings added 1,100 units to the housing stock and some 2,500 inhabitants to the island's existing population of 5,200. Manhattan Park attracts upper middle class families (no studios) with stunning views and concierges at prices about 25% below comparable Manhattan rents. Ground was broken in 2001 for the first three of the nine buildings that will comprise **Southtown**, between existing **Northtown** and the Queensborough Bridge. Residents hope these changes and the future development of the island's south point will do nothing to disturb the peaceful, low-crime character of the narrow, two-and-a-half-mile island.

Manhattan Park buildings are managed by Grenadier Realty Corp., 212-773-7990, with a rental office in Building 2 at 30 River Road. The Roosevelt Island Housing Management Corp., 212-838-4747, at 552 Main

Street manages the rental units and subsidized apartments (for which there are specified income limits) in the original buildings; co-ops are managed by Rose Assoc. Inc., 212-308-7271. **Note**: If you own a dog, Roosevelt Island isn't for you; dogs are *verboten* on the narrow 2 1/2-mile-long island.

Web Sites: www.rooseveltisland.org; www.decny.com/cb8; official New York City site, www.nyc.gov
Area Codes: 212, 646
Post Office: Island Post Office, 694 Main Street, 212-752-5564
Zip Code: 10044
Police Precinct: One Hundred and Fourteenth, 34-16 Astoria Boulevard, Astoria, New York 11103, 718-626-9311
Public School Education: School District #2 (see **Chelsea**).
Emergency Hospital: Goldwater Memorial Hospital, Roosevelt Island, 212-318-4315
Library: Roosevelt Island Community Library, 524 Main Street, NYC 10044, 212-308-6243
Transportation: Tramway (59th Street and Second Avenue); Bus: Queens (Q32); Subway: 63rd Street (B, Q)

EAST FORTIES AND FIFTIES

Boundaries and Contiguous Areas: **North**: 59th Street and the Upper East Side; **East**: East River; **South**: 42nd Street and Murray Hill; **West**: Lexington Avenue

In the 18th century, this urbane neighborhood in the shadow of the United Nations was known as Turtle Bay Farm. The mid-19th century brought industrialization and the "el" rumbling over tenements built along the East River. A construction boom in the 1920s left the heart of **Turtle Bay** much as you see it today: handsome, tree-shaded blocks of carefully maintained brownstones interspersed with relatively small apartment buildings. But not until the 1940s, when the squalid slaughterhouses that had replaced the riverside slums were razed to make room for the United Nations, and the 1950s, when the "el" came tumbling down, did Turtle Bay become eminently respectable from Lexington Avenue clear to the East River. Now the area is one of the most prestigious—and one of the safest—in town; a self-assured place with tony restaurants and charming cul-de-sacs such as Amster Yard on 49th Street, Greenacre Park on 51st and the private, somewhat secret, garden enclosed by twenty Italianate townhouses in which Katharine Hepburn and E.B. White once lived.

Apartment prices, as befits a neighborhood embracing exclusive Sutton Place, Beekman Place, the two glass towers at United Nations Plaza, and the latest and tallest Trump tower, are among the highest around. For the least rarefied rates look along First and Second avenues and the side streets in between.

Tudor City lies southwest of Sutton Place and somewhat downscale. Bounded by 40th and 43rd streets, this huge complex of Tudor-style buildings between First and Second avenues includes a hotel, church, and private parking area. Unfortunately for would-be tenants, eleven of the twelve buildings completed in 1930 have been converted to cooperatives.

The opening, in 1999, of the long awaited Bridgemarket in the extraordinary Gustavino-tile-vaulted hall beneath the Queensboro Bridge at 59th Street, between First and York avenues, is probably the most exciting development in this otherwise sedate neighborhood since the building of the UN. Designed originally in 1914 as an open-sided marketplace, the 24 to 44-foot high, domed bays house a market-style food emporium, two restaurants operated by Sir Terence Conran, and a high-end Conran home furnishings store. Predictably, the completion of this project has stimulated new residential development in the neighborhood. A half-mile to the south Donald Trump's 72-story Trump World Tower is making its own waves— not to mention a long shadow—throughout the area. The next waves will radiate from the contemplated development of the large ConEd site along First Avenue south of Tudor City.

Web Sites: official New York City site, www.nyc.gov; www.turtlebay-ny.org; www.tudorcity.com

Area Codes: 212, 646

Post Office: Tudor City Station, 5 Tudor City Place, NYC 10017, 212-697-8656

Zip Codes: 10022, 10017, 10016

Police Precinct: Seventeenth, 167 East 51st Street, NYC 10022, 212-826-3211

Emergency Hospital (nearest): New York Hospital-Cornell Medical Center, 525 East 68th Street, NYC 10021, 212-746-5454; New York University Hospital and Medical Center, 550 First Avenue, NYC 10016, 212-263-7300

Libraries (nearest): 58th Street Branch, 127 East 58th Street, NYC 10022, 212-759-7358; Mid-Manhattan, 455 Fifth Avenue, NYC 10016, 212-340-0833

Public School Education: School District #2 (see **Chelsea**).

Adult Education: Turtle Bay Music School, 244 East 52nd Street, NYC 10022, 212-753-8811

Community Resources: Young Men's Christian Association of Greater

New York, Vanderbilt Branch, 224 East 47th Street, NYC 10017, 212-756-9600; YWCA of the City of New York, 610 Lexington Avenue, NYC 10022, 212-755-2700; Japan Society, 333 East 47th Street, NYC 10017, 212-752-3015; Phillip Morris branch of the Whitney Museum of American Art, 120 Park Avenue, NYC 10017, 917-663-2453

Transportation—Subway: Crosstown 42nd Street Shuttle (S), Lexington Avenue; Crosstown (#7) Lexington/Third Avenues; #4, #5, #6 Lexington Avenue at 59th Street (Exp), 51st Street, 42nd Street (Exp).

Transportation—Bus: Crosstown 49th/50th streets (#27, #50); Crosstown 42nd Street (#42); Uptown Madison Avenue (#1, #2, #3, #4); Uptown Third Avenue—Downtown Lexington Avenue (#98, #101, #102); Uptown First Avenue—Downtown Second Avenue (#15)

MURRAY HILL

Boundaries and Contiguous Areas: **North**: 42nd Street and the East Forties and Fifties; **East**: East River; **South**: 34th Street and the Gramercy Park Area; **West**: Fifth Avenue

Murray Hill is the kind of neighborhood where you can walk into a compact, ground-floor apartment, open a back door and have access to a garden larger than the flat. Time was when the great mansions of Fifth and Madison avenues—lastingly elegant buildings such as J.P. Morgan's magnificent McKim, Mead and White-designed library—conferred social status on the houses highest on the hill. Below these were the stables and carriage houses serving them, and in the shadow of the old Third Avenue "el," tenements. The tenements are gone now, and as Fifth Avenue became more commercial, residential Murray Hill shifted east and the carriage houses proved to be fashionable—indeed, charming—homes. The streets are a mix of tranquil landmarks such as Sniffen Court, a private mews at 150-158 East 36th Street, nondescript brick apartment buildings, and postmodern fantasies such as the undulating, 57-story Corinthian. And brownstones: these solid and unpretentious turn-of-the-century buildings are nonetheless elegant and lend a particularly substantial quality to life.

The neighborhood takes its name from a Quaker merchant, Robert Murray, who built a farmhouse at what is now the corner of 37th Street and Park Avenue. Grand Central stands on what was his cornfield. Murray's wife and daughters played a minor role in the Revolutionary War by detaining General Howe and his officers at tea while Washington and his troops escaped their pursuit. Among the historic buildings in the area is the slender brownstone at 125 East 36th Street where Franklin and Eleanor Roosevelt first lived. An active neighborhood association guards the quiet residential character of Murray Hill. Their next challenge is the proposed sale of four acres of Con Edison industrial sites along the East River. Intensive residential development there will impact significantly on the neighborhood.

University and Bellevue Hospitals and related New York University medical facilities are a major presence just to the south, and the casual, inviting shops and restaurants crowding Second and Third avenues play to a youthful audience. Housing possibilities include proliferating high rises on the flatlands east of Third as well as brownstones and carriage houses on Murray Hill itself.

Web Sites: Murray Hill Neighborhood Association, www.murrayhill.org; official New York City site, www.nyc.gov

Area Codes: 212, 646

Post Office: Murray Hill Station, 115 East 34th Street, NYC 10016, 212-689-1124

Zip Code: 10016

Police Precinct: Seventeenth, 167 East 51st Street, NYC 10022, 212-826-3211

Emergency Hospitals (nearest): New York University Medical Center, 550 First Avenue (at 33rd Street), NYC 10016, 212-263-7300; Bellevue Hospital Center, 462 First Avenue (at 27th Street), NYC 10016, 212-562-4141

Library: Kips Bay Branch, 446 Third Avenue, NYC 10016, 212-683-2520; the New York City Science, Industry and Business Library (SIBL), 188 Madison Avenue at 34th Street, NYC 10017, 212-592-7000

Public School Education: School District #2 (see **Chelsea**).

Adult Education: American Academy of Dramatic Arts, 120 Madison Avenue, NYC 10016, 212-686-9244; Stern College, Yeshiva University, 245 Lexington Avenue at 35th Street, NYC l0016, 212-340-7700

Community Resources: Pierpont Morgan Library, 29 East 36th Street, NYC 10016, 212-685-0008, an exquisite edifice housing an extraordinary collection of rare books, including three Gutenberg Bibles, manuscripts, and works of art; Murray Hill Neighborhood Association, 36 East 36th Street, NYC 10016, 212-886-5867, www.murrayhill.org.

Transportation—Subway: Crosstown 42nd Street Shuttle (S), Lexington Avenue; Crosstown (#7) Lexington/Third Avenues; #4, #5, #6 Lexington Avenue at 42nd Street (Exp), 33rd Street

Transportation—Bus: Crosstown 34th Street (#16, #34); Uptown Madison Avenue (#1, #2, #3, #4); Uptown Third Avenue—Downtown Lexington Avenue (#101, #102); Downtown Second Avenue (#15)

GRAMERCY PARK AREA

Boundaries and Contiguous Areas: **North**: 34th Street and Murray Hill; **East**: First Avenue and Stuyvesant Area; **South**: East 14th Street; **West**: Park Avenue South/Chelsea and the Flatiron District

The Gramercy Park is a verdant, block-square, fenced and locked enclave to which only residents of the surrounding buildings hold keys. With its lovely old trees, squirrels, flowering spring plantings and the occasional nanny, the park is reminiscent of a quiet London square. But it wasn't the work of a homesick Brit; a real estate developer, to increase the value of 66 lots he owned nearby, laid out the private park in 1831. That this strategy was successful is evidenced by the quality of the ornate later-19th century buildings that still surround the square—elaborate structures such as The Players Club (Edwin Booth's former home) and the National Arts Club (designed in a Gothic Revival style by Calvert Vaux).

The air of dignified elegance which permeates Gramercy Park and sets such a pleasant tone for the neighborhood as a whole is reinforced by historic Stuyvesant Square (located four blocks to the southeast at 15th Street) with its lovely brick Friends Meeting House and brownstone St. George's Church, where J.P. Morgan worshipped. In general, this is an enclave of small townhouses and rows of trim brickfronts interspersed with renovated tenements, modest apartment houses and an occasional high-rise.

North of the park the **Kips Bay** neighborhood stretching from Lexington Avenue to the East River houses a fairly middle class populace, including medical personnel from the hospitals along First Avenue, in corner high-rises and side-street brownstones. Subsidized rental complexes include the highly desirable **Waterside** between 23rd and 28th streets, overlooking the East River and **Henry Phipps Plaza** along Second Avenue in the 20s.

To the west, Lexington Avenue in the 20s, redolent with the spices of the Indian restaurant strip known locally as "Curry Hill" (a play on adjacent Murray Hill), is recently gentrified. Apartment buildings there have been upgraded, making the area worth a look. Convenient take-out is a bonus.

Renovation of the once-again handsome Madison Square Park and Union Square Park has coincided with the resurgence of Park Avenue South as a commercial office market and a dining destination, attracting residents, many from the fashion and publishing fields, to newly available housing. On Second Avenue, and in the 20s and low 30s, new condos have sprouted like field mushrooms after a warm fall rain. Pricey rentals are available at the Rutherford Place apartments overlooking Stuyvesant Square.

Gramercy Park is a desirable place to live, but you probably have a better chance of finding an apartment in one of the newer high rises that ring the neighborhood than in one of the townhouses adjacent to the park itself. In any event, the Gramercy area is relaxed and neighborly, and it pays to walk through the community talking with doormen and building super-intendents when searching for an apartment here.

Web Site: official New York City site, www.nyc.gov

Area Codes: 212, 646

Post Offices: Murray Hill Station, 115 East 34th Street, NYC 10016, 212-689-1124; Madison Square Station, 149 East 23rd Street, NYC 10010, 212-673-3771

Zip Codes: 10016, 10010, 10003

Police Precincts: Seventeenth (above 30th Street), 167 East 51st Street, NYC 10022, 212-826-3211; Thirteenth, 230 East 21st Street, NYC 10010, 212-477-7411

Emergency Hospitals (nearest): New York University Hospital Medical Center, 560 First Avenue at 33rd Street, NYC 10016, 212-263-7300; Bellevue Hospital Center, First Avenue at 27th Street, NYC 10016, 212-562-4141; Cabrini Medical Center, 227 East 19th Street, NYC 10003, 212-995-6000; Beth Israel Medical Center, 16th Street at First Avenue, NYC 10003, 212-420-2000; New York Eye and Ear Infirmary, 310 East 14th Street, NYC 10003, 212-979-4000

Library: Kips Bay Branch, 446 Third Avenue, NYC 10016, 212-683-2520; Epiphany Branch, 228 East 23rd Street, NYC 10010, 212-679-2645

Public School Education: School District #2 (see **Chelsea**).

Adult Education: Stuyvesant Adult Center, 345 East 15th Street, NYC 10003, 212-254-2890; School of Visual Arts, 209 East 23rd Street, NYC 10010, 212-592-2000; Baruch College of Adult and Continuing and Professional Studies, 19 Lexington Avenue, Room 920, NYC 10010, 212-802-5600

Community Resources: The Players, 16 Gramercy Park South, between Irving Place and Park Avenue South, NYC 10003, 212-228-7610, con-tains important collections of letters, playbills, prompt books, plays and materials relating to 19th century British and American theater which can be seen by appointment. Theodore Roosevelt House, 28 East 20th Street, NYC 10003, between Broadway and Park Avenue South, 212-260-1616; a National Park, Roosevelt's exuberantly Victorian birthplace contains letters, books and objects collected from his many trips.

Transportation—Subway: Crosstown 14th Street (L) at Union Square, Third Avenue; #4, #5, #6 Lexington Avenue at 33rd Street, 28th Street, 23rd Street, 14th Street/Union Square (Exp)

Transportation—Bus: Crosstown 34th Street (#16, #34); Crosstown 23rd Street (#23); Crosstown 14th Street (#14); Uptown Madison Avenue (#1, #2, #3, #4); Uptown Third Avenue—Downtown Lexington Avenue (#101, #102); Downtown Second Avenue (#15)

STUYVESANT TOWN AND PETER COOPER VILLAGE

Boundaries and Contiguous Areas: North: 23rd Street; **East:** FDR Drive; **South:** 14th Street and the East Village; **West:** First Avenue and Gramercy Park Area

Two of the oldest and best known housing developments in New York City, **Stuyvesant Town**, 14th to 20th streets, and its upscale (larger apartments and rents) little brother, **Peter Cooper Village**, 20th to 23rd streets, are easier to penetrate now than formerly, but at a price. Waiting lists for the rent-regulated apartments are closed, and the two developments are in the process of gradually renovating and converting to market-rate status as regulated apartments are vacated. With a total of 11,250 apartments in the two enclaves, the process of deregulation is expected to take a couple of decades. But now market-rate apartments are available with a relatively short wait for those who meet the income requirements. What makes these developments so desirable is their resolutely middle-class, family-oriented population, relative safety and—after 50 years' growth of trees, flowers, ivy and climbing hydrangea against the otherwise unrelieved brick walls—unpretentious attractiveness. So, if you care to pursue the matter, apply at the renting office for both developments, which are owned by Metropolitan Life Insurance Co., the Peter Cooper Management Office, at 629 East 14th Street, NYC 10009, 212-780-1300, and get in line, or "on line," as we say in New York.

The community surrounding Peter Cooper and Stuyvesant includes luxury buildings as well as owner-occupied brownstones and upgraded tenements. When scouting the area (First Avenue west to Lexington), try the side streets. The neighborhood is a comparison shopper's dream, with major supermarkets and many ethnic food stores (especially south on First Avenue), clothing shops and decorating showrooms along First and Second avenues vying for your dollars. There are large, quiet tree-shaded parks for breaks between apartment visits, and in warm weather the renovated public swimming pool at 23rd Street and Asser Levy Place is available for a cooling few laps. (In fact, look for this turn-of-the-century stone Roman bath even if you can't swim; it's a beauty.) And if you're beset by hypochondria, this neighborhood, with five top hospitals within walking distance, merits serious consideration.

Web Site: official New York City site, www.nyc.gov
Area Codes: 212, 646
Post Office: Peter Stuyvesant Station, 432 East 14th Street, NYC 10009, 212-677-2112; Madison Square Station, 149 East 23rd Street, NYC 10010, 212-673-3771

Zip Codes: 10010, 10009

Police Precinct: Thirteenth, 230 East 21st Street, NYC 10010, 212-477-7411

Emergency Hospitals: New York University Hospital Medical Center, 560 First Avenue at 33rd Street, NYC 10016, 212-263-7300; Bellevue Hospital Center, First Avenue at 27th Street, NYC 10016, 212-562-4141; Cabrini Medical Center, 227 East 19th Street, NYC 10003, 212-995-6000; Beth Israel Hospital Medical Center, 16th Street and First Avenue, NYC 10009, 212-420-2000; New York Eye and Ear Infirmary, 310 East 14th Street, NYC 10003, 212-979-4000

Libraries: Epiphany Branch, 228 East 23rd Street, NYC 10010, 212-679-2645; Kips Bay Branch, 446 Third Avenue, NYC 10016, 212-683-2520

Public School Education: School District #2 (see **Chelsea**).

Adult Education: Stuyvesant Adult Center, 345 East 15th Street, NYC 10003, 212-254-2890; School of Visual Arts, 209 East 23rd Street, NYC 10010, 212-592-2000; Baruch College of Continuing and Professional Education, 17 Lexington Avenue, Room 920, NYC 10010, 212-802-5600

Transportation—Subway: Crosstown 14th Street (L) at Lexington Avenue, Third Avenue, First Avenue; #4, #5, #6 Lexington Avenue at 23rd Street, 14th Street/Union Square (Exp)

Transportation—Bus: Crosstown 34th Street (#16) goes across 34th Street and down Second Avenue, then east across 23rd Street and uptown to 34th Street along F.D.R. Drive; Crosstown 23rd Street (#26); Crosstown 14th Street (#14); Uptown First Avenue—Downtown Second Avenue (#15)

EAST VILLAGE

Boundaries and Contiguous Areas: North: 14th Street and the Stuyvesant Area; **East**: East River; **South**: Houston Street and the Lower East Side; **West**: Broadway and Greenwich Village

Once again this colorful neighborhood is in the process of reinventing itself. Time was when it was best described as the upper Lower East Side, both geographically and socio-economically. But sometime in the 1960s, perhaps in an attempt to bestow a bit of cachet, this largely immigrant neighborhood with an emerging avant-garde colony was dubbed the East Village. Attracted by low rents, a lively arts scene and street life, boutiques on the cutting edge of fashion, a burgeoning restaurant and club life, college students flocked east, followed by affluent young professionals. It became one of the most desirable alternative neighborhoods in town. An ethnic population which includes Italians, Poles, Ukrainians and Latinos, along with the bakeries, butcher shops, restaurants and cultural institutions they nurtured, adds diversity as well as depth to the neighborhood.

The retaking of **Alphabet City**—A, B, C, and D avenues east of First Avenue—from the control of drug dealers and junkies was a major factor in the gentrification of the East Village since the 1980s. "There are still some rough blocks," says one realtor, "but it has changed from a low-income to a trendy, hip area for young people." Rents have escalated as tenements are upgraded, and new buildings have shot up, condos and co-ops included, to attract a young and affluent populace. Some innovative public schools have recently evolved to serve their children. In the middle of it all a nicely restored Tompkins Square remains the East Village's leafy back yard.

To the west, the **Astor Place** area bubbles with student life centered around Cooper Union and nearby NYU, the ever-lively Joseph Papp Public Theater, and good buys in books, booze and youthful clothing along Broadway. Connecting Astor Place with the Second Avenue heart of the East Village is St. Mark's Place, actually part of 8th Street, where hippies and flower children frolicked, the Electric Circus drew limousines from uptown, and W.H. Auden lived. St. Mark's is a bit quieter now, visually and audibly, but little changed. Nearby on East Seventh, Ninth and Stuyvesant streets clusters of Japanese restaurants, shops, and saki bar/cafes cater to the area's young Japanese ex-pats.

To the south the area between the Bowery and Broadway, where once Vanderbilts and Astors lived, has re-acquired a bit of its old chic—if not its elegance—and the tag **NoHo** (for **No**rth of **Ho**uston Street). Clubs, cafes, and restaurants abound, attracting upscale singles and the hip, and while there's a rapid turnover of conventional rentals and walk-ups, they don't come cheap. Plan to walk for groceries; there's nary a supermarket. Lofts in the brick and cast-iron industrial buildings fetch lofty prices, but much of NoHo is legally reserved for certified artists. Prospective residents should check with the City Loft Board, 212-788-7610, to determine their eligibility and to be sure the particular building is in compliance with the Loft Law.

East of NoHo the next neighborhood happening is the **Cooper Square** mixed used development, scheduled for occupancy late in 2002. Straddling East Houston Street between the Bowery and Second Avenue, the development will comprise some 618 rental apartments, a quarter of which will be filled by lottery from applicants of limited means, while the remainder will be market-rate. Hitherto dingy East Houston moves up.

Although condo conversions are multiplying in the East Village, be prepared for walk-ups; most of the housing stock consists of improved tenements. Start your apartment search by studying ads in *The Village Voice*, then check Cooper Union and NYU bulletin boards, walk the streets and talk to people who live here.

Web Site: official New York City site, www.nyc.gov

Area Codes: 212, 646

Post Offices: Cooper Station, 93 Fourth Avenue, NYC 10003, 212-254-1389; Peter Stuyvesant Station, 432 East 14th Street, NYC 10009, 212-677-2112; Tompkins Square Station, 244 East Third Street, NYC 10009, 212-673-6415

Zip Codes: 10003, 10009

Police Precinct: Ninth, 321 East Fifth Street, NYC 10003, 212-477-7811

Emergency Hospitals: Beth Israel Hospital Medical Center, 16th Street and First Avenue, NYC 10009, 212-420-2000; New York Eye and Ear Infirmary, 310 East 14th Street, NYC 10003, 212-979-4000

Libraries: Ottendorfer Branch, 135 Second Avenue, NYC 10003, 212-674-0947; Tompkins Square Branch, 331 East 10th Street, NYC 10009, 212-228-4747

Public School Education: School District #1: Community School Board, 80 Montgomery Street, NYC 10002, 212-602-9700

Adult Education: Third Street Music School Settlement, 235 East 11th Street, NYC 10003, 212-777-3240; Stuyvesant Adult Center, 345 East 15th Street, NYC 10003, 212-254-2890, offers a wide variety of inexpensive evening adult education courses, from languages to sewing.

Community Resources: La Mama Experimental Theater Club, 74A East Fourth Street, 212-475-7710, on the cutting edge of avant-garde theater for over two decades, and PS (Performing Space) 122, 150 First Avenue, 212-477-5288, a reclaimed public school, to say nothing of the Joseph Papp Public Theater, 425 Lafayette Street, 212-598-7100, indicate the lively state of this neighborhood's arts. Second Avenue was the Yiddish rialto until 1940. Now the Theater for the New City performs new plays in a converted city market building at 155 First Avenue, 212-254-1109, and CSC Repertory Theater has been successfully producing classics at 136 East 13th Street, 212-677-4210, for nearly 20 years. The Third Street Music School (see above) also offers concerts and recitals, and Cooper Union at 51 Astor Place, 212-353-4195, has frequent exhibits, concerts and lectures. Theater and opera thrive even on the Bowery: classics at the Jean Cocteau Repertory, at 330 Bowery, 212-677-0060, and Italian opera at The Amato Opera Theater at 319 Bowery, 212-228-8200.

Transportation—Subway: Crosstown 14th Street (L) at Union Square, Third Avenue, First Avenue; #6 at 14th Street/Union Square, Astor Place and Bleecker Street; F at Broadway/Lafayette Street and Houston Street/Second Avenue; N and R at 14th Street/Union Square and 8th Street/Broadway

Transportation—Bus: Crosstown 14th Street (#14); going East: Crosstown West 10th Street/West Eighth Street (#13); going West:

Crosstown West Ninth Street/Christopher Street (#13); Uptown Third Avenue/Lexington—Downtown Lexington/Third Avenue (#101, #102); Uptown First Avenue—Downtown Second Avenue (#15)

LOWER EAST SIDE, LITTLE ITALY AND CHINATOWN

Boundaries and Contiguous Areas: North: Houston Street and the East Village; **East**: East River; **South**: Downtown; West: Broadway and SoHo

"Give me your tired, your poor…" wrote Emma Lazarus, and when they arrived, many of them, it was to the Lower East Side. Between 1870 and 1920, wave upon wave of immigrants from Italy, Bohemia, China, and the ghettos of eastern Europe poured into the warren of fetid tenements on Mulberry, Elizabeth, Hester and Division streets. Here they lived and worked until able to move up and out to the suburbs, or at least The Bronx, leaving room for the next wave.

Public housing, especially along the easternmost strip of the Lower East Side, alleviated crowding and let in some light and air, and along Grand Street, from Essex to the river, 28 co-op buildings with *riv vus* provided affordable housing for the middle class. The Grand Street co-ops now sell at market rates their previous owners could not have imagined. And the grandchildren of immigrants are claiming renovated tenement apartments for their homes at near-market rentals. It began along the fringes, where the young and impecunious—artists, students and the like—established beachheads. Formerly vacant tenements have been renovated to attract more affluent young adults. Along East Houston (pronounced how-ston) and grungy Ludlow Street clubs, trendy restaurants and boutiques are unmistakable signs of gentrification.

Actually, at least three lower east sides exist, with imprecise and constantly changing borders: (1) to the east, the old Jewish **Lower East Side**, now largely Latino and Chinese; (2) **Chinatown** in the southwest portion, which continues to expand inexorably northward into (3) **Little Italy**. Colorful Orchard Street is still chockablock with little stores and Yiddish-speaking shopkeepers, many of them bearded, black-hat-wearing Hasidim. The shop owners live elsewhere, and at night all that remains of a once vibrant Jewish community are forlorn old synagogues, deserted or converted to Pentecostal churches. But the buildings above the shops, formerly vacant, house young professionals in $3,000-a-month studios. Antique shops and young designer boutiques have crept in among the dusty menswear shops.

A wave of recent arrivals have burst Chinatown's traditional seams past East Broadway into the old Jewish enclave and north over Canal Street into

Little Italy, which is now two-thirds Asian. Housing is impossibly crowded, and sweatshops abound. But walking the almost impassable sidewalks of Chinatown on a Saturday, one would think this area existed solely to satisfy the city's insatiable appetite for Chinese food.

Little Italy, between Canal and Houston streets, has a vanishing Italian population but an expanding selection of Italian restaurants and cafes. Along Mulberry Street on a warm spring evening the combined hisses of uncountable cappuccino machines sound like a locomotive gathering steam. The neighborhood seems destined to become a restaurant district operated increasingly from Long Island, Staten Island, and New Jersey. And, although frozen dim sum take the place of frozen ravioli in innumerable small stores, a bit of the old Southern Italian character still remains. As well, the community's reputation as a don't-mess-with-us, low-crime neighborhood with strong ethnic ties around the old, original St. Patrick's on Mulberry Street near Houston. But here on the northern edge of Little Italy, galleries, boutiques, and cafes are filling the once-vacant storefronts, and the neighborhood has acquired the name **Nolita** (for **No**rth of **Li**ttle **Ita**ly).

Infiltration of the Lower East Side by the middle class is no longer news. In 1984, intrepid souls brave enough to sign leases on The Bowery, Rivington or Pitt streets were featured in *The New York Times*. In 2001 ground was broken for a new, 66-apartment doorman building at 199 Bowery. Most notably, the refurbished Police Building at 240 Centre Street, a granite Renaissance Revival palazzo built in 1909, reopened with crystal chandeliers and 54 luxury condos behind a statuary-cluttered facade in the heart of Little Italy. Rents in the neighborhood move ever upward, and the unmonied and creative have moved on. Still, apartment listings are sparse. Best to talk to someone who lives in the neighborhood, and do walk around, looking (carefully) block by block.

Web Site: official New York City site, www.nyc.gov

Area Codes: 212, 646

Post Offices: Knickerbocker Station, 128 East Broadway, NYC 10002, 212-227-0089; Chinatown Station, 6 Doyers Street, NYC 10013, 212-267-3510

Zip Codes: 10012, 10013, 10002

Police Precincts: Fifth, 19 Elizabeth Street, NYC 10013, 212-334-0711; Seventh, 19 Pitt Street, NYC 10002, 212-477-7311

Emergency Hospital (nearest): New York Downtown Hospital, 170 William Street, NYC 10038, 212-312-5000

Libraries: Hamilton Fish Park Branch, 415 East Houston Street, NYC 10002, 212-673-2290; Seward Park Branch, 192 East Broadway, NYC 10002, 212-477-6770

Public School Education: School District #1: Community School Board,

80 Montgomery Street, NYC 10002, 212-602-9700; School District #2 (see **Chelsea**).

Community Resources: The Henry Street Settlement is actually a variety of resources, with its Abrons Arts Center, Settlement Playhouse and New Federal Theater at 466 Grand Street, NYC 10002, 212-598-0400. The Lower East Side Tenement Museum, 90 Orchard Street, NYC 10002, 212-431-0233, includes exhibits in three buildings (one of which has been "unrestored" to illustrate life as it was) as well as neighborhood walking tours. The recently renovated and renamed Museum of Chinese in the Americas, 70 Mulberry Street, NYC 10013, 212-619-4785, offers historical walking tours as well as exhibits and video documentaries.

Transportation—Subway: #6 Lafayette Street at Spring Street, Canal Street (Exp); F at Houston/Second Avenue, Delancey Street; B and D at Grand Street (Exp); N and R at Broadway and Canal; J, M, Z at Canal, Bowery and Essex Street

Transportation—Bus: Crosstown West-East Houston (#21); Uptown First Avenue—Downtown Second Avenue (#15); Uptown Bowery/Third Avenue—Downtown Third Avenue/Bowery (#101, #102)

DOWNTOWN

Boundaries and Contiguous Areas: North: Chambers Street and Tribeca; **East**: East River; **South**: Upper New York Bay; **West**: Hudson River

The streets of downtown New York are so convoluted and irrational in design that even natives sensibly carry maps. It is an area which encourages the visitor to look up—to the top of the World Trade Center, where television transmitters hover like rocket launchers; up at the four limestone sculptures (of Asia, America, Europe and Africa) emerging from the granite palace which was once the US Customs House at Bowling Green and Bridge Street; up at the delicate spire of Trinity Church (Broadway and the beginning of Wall Street), where lunchtime crowds gather for concerts at noon and munch sandwiches while walking among the historic tombstones; up at the masts of ships docked at the South Street Seaport Museum alongside the Fulton Fish Market and the Rouse Development Corporation's South Street Seaport renewal.

Consisting of renovated Schermerhorn Row, museum shops, the Fulton Market, and a shopping Mecca on Pier 17, the Seaport edges the East River at Fulton Street and, like sister developments in Boston and Baltimore, is a pleaser. Crowds browse craft stands and upscale boutiques, stroll and nosh their way through a tantalizing assortment of ethnic snack bars, queue for the multimedia show at the Trans-Lux Theater, and dine in the glamorous, glass-enclosed pavilion shimmering over East River waters.

Visitors downtown also look up at old wholesale houses, offices, and bank buildings in the process of conversion to residential use and new structures going up expressly for that purpose. Downtown is slowly adjusting to the fact that people live (as opposed to just work) here, 24-hours a day, seven-days a week. The 1970 census showed only 7,000 residents in the oldest part of Manhattan; you could take tea in the middle of Wall Street on a Sunday afternoon—if you could find some tea to take. An estimated 25,000 people live Downtown now, serviced by dry cleaners where there were none, day care centers, a few supermarkets and food specialty shops (stocked with tea) along the western edge. Residents of the **Wall Street** area are still under-served, especially at night and on weekends, but an Amish Market on Cedar Street brings some relief. It's a neighborhood in the making, with its own handsome Public School 234, several hotels, a branch library, and a weekly newspaper, *Downtown Express*, which also serves Tribeca and SoHo.

Battery Park City, built between West Street and the Hudson River on landfill excavated from the World Trade Center site, is the largest development ever constructed in Manhattan. With a third of its 92 acres reserved for parks, plazas and esplanades, the development comprises a collection of architecturally diverse residential and financial complexes managed by the Battery Park City Authority. The World Financial Center—four stunning, copper-topped buildings fastidiously designed by Cesar Pelli—faces the World Trade Center and, along with the Mercantile Exchange, forms Battery Park City's hub. At its center like an imperial gateway to the city, the soaring, glass and polished-steel Winter Garden with sixteen California palms set in gleaming marble provides an elegant site for free concerts edging the North Cove Yacht Harbor. Surrounding the Winter Garden throughout the ground floor of the World Financial Center, upscale shops and restaurants beckon. The beautifully landscaped Esplanade—connecting the Winter Garden with South Cove and Rockefeller Park—constitutes the spine of the development as it stretches over a mile along the Hudson River. Battery Park City is a work in progress nearing completion. About 9,000 people, mostly young professionals who work in Lower Manhattan, live in its 6,000 mixed high- and low-rise condos and upscale rental apartments. Construction of another 2,000 units, including three-bedroom apartments to attract families will be completed by 2003, as will a Ritz-Carlton Downtown Hotel and Skyscraper Museum, and an addition to the Museum of Jewish Heritage and Holocaust Memorial. Some 25,000 people will live, another 40,000 work, within sight of the Statue of Liberty when the mammoth project is completed. The whole is even now surrounded by parks and sculpture-filled plazas and connected by ferry service to New Jersey and by climate-controlled walkways to the World Trade Center, public transportation, and the Financial District.

The size and splendor of this mega-project should not, however, obscure the presence in Lower Manhattan of other residential possibilities. For example, small, architecturally distinguished condominiums such as Greenwich Court have sprung up on the West Side below Chambers Street, and conversions are rife throughout lower Manhattan. Tax incentives have quickened the pace of conversion from commercial to residential use, and today many of the handsome turn-of-the-century office towers near Wall Street contain nary a brokerage firm but, rather, families in rentals, condos, and co-ops, lofts even. And in a tight real estate market these pioneers are paying less than they would pay for comparable space uptown.

Web Sites: www.downtownny.com; www.worldfinancialcenter.com; www.cb1.org; www.batteryparkcity.org; official New York City site, www.nyc.gov

Area Codes: 212, 646

Post Offices: Church Street Station, 90 Church Street, NYC 10007, 212-330-5313; Peck Slip Station, 1-19 Peck Slip, NYC 10038, 212-964-1055; Bowling Green Station, 25 Broadway, NYC 10004, 212-363-9490

Zip Codes: 10007, 10038, 10047/48 (World Trade Center), 10006, 10004, 10005, 10041, 10280, 10281, 10282

Police Precinct: First, 16 Ericsson Place, NYC 10013, 212-334-0611

Emergency Hospital: New York Downtown Hospital, 170 William Street, NYC 10038, 212-312-5000

Library: New Amsterdam Branch, 9 Murray Street, NYC 10007, 212-732-8186

Public School Education: School District #2 (see **Chelsea**).

Adult Education: Pace University, 1 Pace Plaza, NYC 10038, 212-346-1200; New York Institute of Finance, 2 Broadway, 5th Floor, NYC 10004, 212-390-5020, www.nyif.com

Community Resources: South Street Seaport Museum, Fulton and Water streets, NYC 10038, 212-748-8600; American Numismatic Society (display on the history of money), 140 Watts Street, NYC 10038, 212-964-3886; National Museum of the American Indian, Alexander Hamilton US Customs House, 1 Bowling Green, NYC 10004, 212-514-3700; the Museum of Jewish Heritage, 1 Battery Park Plaza, NYC 10004-1484, 212-968-1800; Trinity Church, Broadway at Trinity Place, 10006, 212-602-0800, houses a museum and offers mid-day concerts on weekdays, as does St. Paul's Chapel up Broadway at Fulton. Concert information is available at 212-602-0874. Also see **Tribeca**.

Transportation—Subway: #1/#9, #2, #3 Varick/Greenwich streets at Chambers (Exp), Cortlandt, Rector, South Ferry/Battery Park, Park Place/Broadway, Fulton (Exp), Wall (Exp); A, C, E at the World Trade Center; N and R at Broadway/Nassau (Exp), City Hall, Cortlandt, Rector,

Whitehall; #4, #5, #6 at Brooklyn Bridge, Fulton (Exp), Wall (Exp), Bowling Green (Exp); J, M Fulton (Exp); Broad (Exp); PATH (to New Jersey) World Trade Center

Transportation—Bus: Crosstown Chambers/West/Vesey/Park Row to Madison Street (#22); Uptown Church/Hudson/Eighth Avenue—Downtown Seventh Avenue/Varick/West Broadway (#10); Uptown Church/Sixth Avenue—Downtown Broadway (#6); Uptown and Downtown Grand Central Terminal—Wall Street Express (#X25) weekdays only

TRIBECA

Boundaries and Contiguous Areas: North: Canal Street and SoHo; **East**: Broadway; **South**: Chambers Street and Downtown; **West**: Hudson River

South of Canal Street, where the island of Manhattan narrows toward its tip, Greenwich Street angles to intersect West Broadway, leaving in its wake not only the loft district dubbed Tribeca (**tri**angle **be**low **Ca**nal) but triangular blocks and crossroad parks unique in the city. Felicitous little Duane Park, the most charming of the lot, breathes into an area composed of 19th century brick and cast iron structures, sprawling warehouses and commercial space, an air of peace and tranquillity rare in the Big Apple.

Before becoming Tribeca-ized, the area consisted of a warren of scruffy walkups that housed the city's wholesale fruit, vegetable and flower district, the Washington Market, as well as the butter and egg district. Most of the market was razed and sent packing to The Bronx in the late 1960s, to be replaced in part by the ponderous brick Independence Plaza project at 40 Harrison Street, but a few vestiges of the produce district remain. A row of Federal houses was left tucked under Independence Plaza's angular wing, and only two-block Staple Street—an alley actually—remains as a vestige of the produce district. There are no staples there.

Tribeca is also home to a number of elegantly sculptural cast-iron buildings—the first built not far from Duane Park by James Bogardus in 1849. The noticeably cleaner of the arched and colonnaded facades front residential lofts and cooperatives skillfully adapted from commercial space, as well as the galleries and offices of the avant-garde establishment (the pioneering fringe has moved to the Lower East Side and across the East River into Queens and Brooklyn). Loft living with amenities is now an accepted urban lifestyle, and Tribeca has changed radically from the quiet backwater it remained throughout the 1970s. It is a prime destination for those who like their buildings wide and their spaces open. Antique and design stores cluster along Franklin and Duane streets, catering to their tastes.

The vaunted, often vaulted warehouses just south of the Holland Tunnel sheltered the clubs responsible for Tribeca's dominant position on the late-night-life scene during the 1980s. Restaurants that the disco devotees haunted feed a more staid clientele these days. Tribeca hosts a kaleidoscopic range of restaurants—Ethiopian, trattorias, French cafes, and some of the best three-stars in Manhattan—for the hip, the chic and the up-and-coming; midday they nourish Wall Street suits and rumpled denizens of City Hall.

Competing pressures—southbound from booming SoHo, from 10,000 students at Manhattan Community College in its midst, and most insistently from affluent, ever-expanding Battery Park City to the south—are transforming Tribeca into a thriving, cohesive, mixed-use community. And despite a nervous Wall Street in 2001, the conversion of former warehouses and factories to handsome, upscale residential lofts continues, selling at seven-digit prices hitherto associated with the Upper East Side. A growing population of children where once there were none, an attractive neighborhood school (P.S. 234) and now a small-town newspaper, *The Tribeca Trib,* along with unimpeded bike riding on weekends, the architecture and night life, are among the attractions of living in Tribeca. Drawbacks? Few grocery stores.

Web Sites: www.cb1.org; official New York City site, www.nyc.gov
Area Codes: 212, 646
Post Office: Canal Street Station, 350 Canal Street, NYC 10013, 212-925-3378
Zip Code: 10013
Police Precinct: First, 16 Ericsson Place, NYC 10013, 212-334-0611
Emergency Hospital (nearest): New York Downtown Hospital, 170 William Street, NYC 10038, 212-312-5000; St. Vincent's Hospital and Medical Center, 153 West 11th Street (at Seventh Avenue), NYC 10011, 212-604-7000
Library (nearest): New Amsterdam Branch, 9 Murray Street, NYC 10007, 212-732-8186
Public School Education: School District #2 (see **Chelsea**).
Adult Education: Borough of Manhattan Community College, Office of Continuing Education, Room S763, 199 Chambers Street, NYC 10007, 212-346-8000, offers a variety of inexpensive evening and weekend courses ranging from computer to business to self-improvement. Concerts and theater are also presented regularly in the College's Triplex Theater.
Community Resources: Tribeca quarters alternative spaces displaying works for and by the avant-garde much as upper Madison Avenue houses deluxe galleries catering to the establishment. These include Artists

Space, 38 Greene Street, 3rd Floor, NYC 10013, 212-226-3970; Franklin Furnace, 45 John Street, Suite 611, NYC 10038, 925-4671; and The Clocktower (Institute for Art and Urban Resources), 108 Leonard Street, 13th floor, NYC 10013, 212-233-1096. Also, Borough of Manhattan Community College, 199 Chambers Street, NYC 10007, 212-346-8000.

Transportation—Subway: A, C, E at Canal Street (Exp), Chambers Street (Exp); #1/#9, #2, #3 Varick Street at Canal Street, Franklin Street, Chambers Street (Exp)

Transportation—Bus: Crosstown Madison & Chambers Street/West Street & Grand Street (#22); Uptown Hudson Street/Eighth Avenue—Downtown Seventh Avenue/Varick Street (#10); Uptown Sixth Avenue (#6); Uptown and Downtown Grand Central Terminal—Wall Street Express (X25) weekdays only

---

SOHO

Boundaries and Contiguous Areas: **North**: West Houston Street and Greenwich Village; **East**: Broadway and Lower East Side; **South**: Canal Street and Tribeca; **West**: Sixth Avenue

SoHo's cast iron buildings are justifiably famous and a visual delight. Look up to appreciate the beauty of the patterns—columnar shapes, Greek Revival capitals and other architectural embellishments—pressed into the cast iron facades. Windowsill house plants, paintings and some of the city's most colorful walls reveal the loft residences which now occupy most of what was manufacturing space. Behind these slightly grimy fronts live some of New York's trendiest setters, often in 4,000-square-foot spreads.

The structures are based on a technique perfected by James Bogardus around 1850. Forerunners of today's "curtain wall" skyscrapers, these cast iron buildings are supported by interior columns, obviating the need for thick walls and allowing the use of much more glass than was previously possible. As a result, the graceful windows, many of them arched, nicely complement the strong, solid buildings, and the whole is extremely harmonious. The buildings are also exceedingly attractive to the city's artists, ever on the lookout for good light and space. In the early 1960s they began to move into the area, just as industry had previously moved into what had been the city's red light district a century before; loft living became legal in 1971. With the subsequent discovery of SoHo by the affluent, high prices have driven many of the original artists to less costly neighborhoods. But art galleries and audacious boutiques remain to prosper and proliferate.

The popularity of SoHo has in no way diminished. On the contrary, monied arrivistes commingle with painters and sculptors on the upper floors of the converted cast iron structures while at street level, hard-edged, minimalist (whatever the fashion-of-the-moment) showrooms spread their plate glass windows far and wide. "An international marketplace for style and design," *The New York Times* calls it, attracting shoppers from Jersey to Germany. "This feels like the world's greatest shopping mall," exclaims a merchant of upscale linens. Just so. You can buy the latest in wearable art, Japanese designer clothes, French prêt-à-porter, exquisite antique blouses and accessories, antique or art deco furniture, and more. Take a shopping break in a chic eatery along West Broadway's restaurant row. Bring money. And if you live here, don't venture out on the weekend. It's packed.

What has changed in recent years is the eastern edge of SoHo. Galleries, clothing shops, and even offices have spread east from West Broadway past Wooster, Greene and Mercer to Broadway and beyond. Once drab and lifeless, Broadway has undergone a personality change as faux marble and hand-grained surfaces replace the tatty showrooms of fabric wholesalers. The relocation of Dean and DeLuca's extraordinary food emporium to a vast, white space resembling an edible art gallery was a sure sign of the Broadway revival. Then along came Armani, The Nature Store, Louis Vuitton, Williams-Sonoma. As SoHo crawls ever eastward, the boundary between SoHo and Little Italy is blurring.

While loft living is legal in many buildings, and you need not necessarily qualify as an artist to rent or sublet SoHo space, caution is advised in taking over a lease or paying key money for a loft or apartment. Check with the New York City Loft Board for the status of legal rents and living situations (see **Lofts** in **Finding a Place to Live**). Many artists sublet when they go on sabbatical or receive grants that take them out of town. If you're not in the market for a condo, the best line on housing availability down here is by word-of-mouth (and conversation is lively at the local art galleries and show openings, which anyone can attend) and bulletin boards. Try the one outside the Broome Street Bar.

Web Sites: www.artseensoho.com; official New York City site, www.nyc.gov
Area Codes: 212, 646
Post Office: Prince Street Station, 103 Prince Street, NYC 10012, 212-226-7868
Zip Codes: 10012, 10013
Police Precinct: First, 16 Ericsson Place, NYC 10013, 212-334-0611
Emergency Hospitals (nearest): St. Vincent's Hospital and Medical Center, Seventh Avenue and 11th Street, NYC 10011, 212-604-7000; New York Downtown Hospital, 170 William Street, NYC 10038, 212-312-5000
Libraries (nearest): Jefferson Market Branch, 425 Avenue of the Americas, NYC 10011, 212-243-4334; Hudson Park Branch, 66 Leroy Street, NYC

10014, 212-243-6876 has an excellent film program for children.

Public School Education: School District #2 (see **Chelsea**).

Adult Education: The French Culinary Institute, 462 Broadway, NYC 10013, 212-219-8890, offers a variety of professional and non-professional cooking courses (lunch and dinner too at their restaurant, L'Ecole, 212-219-3300 for reservations); Pratt Manhattan, the local branch of Brooklyn's Pratt Institute, 295 Lafayette Street, NYC 10012, 212-461-6000, has extensive evening and weekend course offerings in the arts and professional areas.

Community Resources: New Museum of Contemporary Art, 583 Broadway, NYC 10012, 212-219-1222; Guggenheim SoHo, 575 Broadway, NYC 10012, 212-423-3500; Museum for African Art, 593 Broadway, NYC 10012, 212-966-1313; the Fire Museum, 178 Spring Street, NYC 10012, 212-691-1303. The district is crammed with great and small gallery spaces—investigate them at leisure. Most are closed Sunday and Monday. A scan of *Art Now's Gallery Guide*, available in galleries throughout the city, gives a total picture of the area's resources and current shows. For weekly guides to arts events in SoHo see *The Village Voice*, the "Weekend" section on Friday, and the "Arts and Leisure" section on Sunday in *The New York Times, Time Out New York,* and *The New Yorker* magazine's "Goings on About Town" section, *New York* magazine's "Cue" section, as well as the *NY Press*, a free weekly covering and available mainly downtown. Nearby Tribeca also offers opportunities to explore the more avant-garde side of the arts, as does the East Village, from which, amoeba-like, galleries have spread throughout the Lower East Side.

Transportation—Subway: A, C, E Sixth Avenue at Spring Street, Canal Street (Exp); B, D, F, Q at Broadway/Lafayette; N, R at Prince Street, Canal Street; #4, #6 at Bleecker Street, Spring Street, Canal Street

Transportation—Bus: Crosstown West-East Houston (#21); Uptown Sixth Avenue—Downtown Fifth Avenue (#5); Downtown Seventh Avenue/Broadway (#10); Uptown Sixth Avenue—Downtown Broadway (#6)

GREENWICH VILLAGE

Boundaries and Contiguous Areas: North: 14th Street, Chelsea and Flatiron District; **East:** Broadway and the East Village; **South:** West Houston Street and SoHo; **West:** Hudson River

Greenwich Village is the kind of community where neighbors look after each other's plants and pets and where people do call the police or fire department if they notice something amiss. Residents still tend to be arts-oriented, and more liberal and politically active than most, particularly when it comes to incursions, real or threatened, on the free-wheeling life style adopted by some or on the hallowed six-story maximum building limit. It was the Village's great good fortune to have its streets laid out along the original 18th century farm lanes and property lines before city planners superimposed the grid pattern on most of Manhattan. The crooked streets that intersect major arteries at askew angles prevent the standardization, through traffic, and large buildings (not to mention urban boredom) that mar other neighborhoods.

Since the 19th century, the brick, Federal-style structures along these crooked streets have housed more than their share of the city's talented and creative. Writers came first: Edgar Allan Poe in 1837, later Mark Twain, Henry James, and Walt Whitman. Artists and intellectuals followed. A handful of people and institutions played key roles in the evolution of the Village as a magnet for those in the vanguard of the arts and letters. Gertrude Vanderbilt Whitney opened her first studio here, exhibiting and encouraging the artists who subsequently became the nucleus of the "Ashcan school" of social realist painters. Mabel Dodge's famed literary salon was on Washington Square, and the Provincetown Players established an early experimental theater on Macdougal Street in 1916. New York University was founded on Washington Square in the 1830s, the New School on West 12th Street in the 1920s. By then the local populace included John Dos Passos, e.e. cummings, Willa Cather, Henry Miller and Edna St. Vincent Millay, and the Village was the avant-garde capital of the nation.

After WW II, abstract expressionists, method actors, controversial novelists and muckraking journalists all coexisted, bringing creative vitality to the area. Only as recently as the early 1970s and the advent of spiraling rents has the Village's appeal lessened as a haven for artists and writers. These days there are probably more appreciators around than doers, but the charm of the Village, with its pleasing proportions and special kind of peacefulness, remains.

Greenwich Village contains a balanced mix of high-rise elevator buildings, older, rent-stabilized apartments, lofts, renovated tenements, and brownstones (a harmonious ensemble threatened, in the West Village at least, by the emergence of several buildings above the prescribed height limit to obtain Hudson River views). New, pricey rental apartments and condos in the handsome conversions in the wholesale antiques district bordering University Place and in the now-fashionable converted warehouses lining West and Washington streets are widely advertised.

The meat market district in the far-west Village, south of 14th Street continues to heat up as a trendy restaurant/gallery/upscale-clothing mecca, and luxury housing seems sure to follow. Further additions to

Village housing stock will be found on lower Hudson Street and along the river on West Street, where new rentals and condos continue to rise, offering upscale *riv vus* outside the landmarked district.

Because the area is essentially an assembly of small communities—the predominantly Italian **South Village**, the central **Washington Square** neighborhood, and the **West Village** bounded by Seventh Avenue and the Hudson River—searching for rentals is best done on foot and through reliable real estate agents.

Web Sites: www.greenwich-village.com; official New York City site, www.nyc.gov

Area Codes: 212, 646

Post Offices: Patchin Station, 70 West 10th Street, NYC 10011, 212-475-2534; West Village Station, 527 Hudson Street, NYC 10014, 212-989-9741; Cooper Station, 93 Fourth Avenue, NYC 10003, 212-254-1389; Village Station, 201 Varick Street, NYC 10014, 212-989-9741

Zip Codes: 10014, 10011, 10012, 10003

Police Precinct: Sixth, 233 West 10th Street, NYC 10014, 212-741-4811

Emergency Hospital: St. Vincent's Hospital and Medical Center, Seventh Avenue and 11th Street, NYC 10011, 212-604-7000

Libraries: Jefferson Market Branch, 425 Avenue of the Americas, NYC 10011, 212-243-4334; Hudson Park Branch, 66 Leroy Street, NYC 10014, 212-243-6876

Public School Education: School District #2 (see **Chelsea**). Greenwich Village has two elementary schools. P.S. 41 offers "traditional" public school education, while P.S. 3 with an "open corridor" program is more experimental.

Adult Education: Parsons School of Design, 2 West 13th Street, NYC 10011, 212-229-8900; New School University, 66 West 12th Street, NYC 10011, 212-229-5600; The Cooper Union for the Advancement of Science and Art, Third Avenue and 7th Street, NYC 10003, 212-353-4195; Greenwich House Music School, 46 Barrow Street, NYC 10014, 212-242-4770; Greenwich House Pottery, 16 Jones Street, 212-242-4106; New York University, 50 West 4th Street, NYC 10003, 212-998-1212

Community Resources: The District Office of Community Planning Board No. 2 has a resource directory of all Greenwich Village associations, service organizations and cultural agencies. The directory is up-to-date and free (3 Washington Square Village, Suite 1A, NY 10012, 212-979-2272).

Transportation—Subway: Crosstown L at Eighth Avenue, Sixth Avenue, Broadway/Union Square; A, C, E at Eighth Avenue and 14th Street (Exp), West 4th/8th Street (Exp); #1/9, #2, #3 at Seventh Avenue and 14th Street (Exp), Christopher Street/Sheridan Square, Houston Street;

F, D, B, Q at 14th Street, West 4th/8th Street (Exp); #4, #5, #6 at 14th Street/Union Square (Exp), Astor Place, Bleecker Street at Lafayette; N, R at 14th Street/Union Square (Exp), 8th Street/NYU; PATH (between New Jersey and 33rd Street) Christopher Street at Hudson, 9th and 14th Streets at Sixth Avenue

Transportation—Bus: Crosstown 14th Street (#14); Going East: Crosstown West 10th Street/West 8th Street (#13); Going West: Crosstown West 9th Street/Christopher Street (#13); Uptown Greenwich Street/Tenth Avenue—Downtown Ninth Avenue/Hudson Street (#11); Uptown Hudson Street/Eighth Avenue—Downtown Seventh Avenue (#10); Uptown Sixth Avenue (#5, #6, #7); Uptown University Place—Downtown Fifth Avenue (#2, #3)

FLATIRON DISTRICT

Boundaries and Contiguous Areas: **North**: 23rd Street and Madison Square; **East**: Park Avenue South and Gramercy Park Area; **South**: 14th Street; **West**: Sixth Avenue and Chelsea

Thanks to the famous wintry photograph by Edward Steichen, the thrusting nose of the Flatiron Building is familiar, even to out-of-towners. The triangular structure at the convergence of Broadway and Fifth Avenue at 23rd Street was a wonder, a skyscraper, when completed in 1902. The 21-story steel-frame edifice was also at the apex of the Ladies' Mile, New York's elegant shopping district. Macy's, Tiffany, Lord & Taylor, and other luxurious emporiums now forgotten cut a fashionable swath down Broadway, Fifth and Sixth avenues in the late 19th century.

But just as the rumbling Sixth Avenue elevated had stimulated the development of the Ladies' Mile, so the city's booming economy caused the great stores to move uptown. The elegant buildings with rhythmic cast iron fronts, elaborate mansard roofs, Byzantine columns and Gothic finials were abandoned to a dim and sooty half-life as manufacturing lofts and warehouses. The 1990s saw a reawakening south of 23rd Street, and the wedge-shaped Flatiron Building has lent its name to the neighborhood. Andy Warhol was, perhaps, the first to set up in the Flatiron District when he established his notorious Factory on **Union Square**. Professional photographers began moving bed-and-tripod into the neighborhood's vast manufacturing lofts in the 1970s. Photo supply houses and model agencies came next, followed by publishing houses, advertising agencies and, most recently, internet and multi-media startups. Lower Fifth Avenue is experiencing a retail renaissance, led by such fashion heavyweights as Armani, Paul Smith, and Matsuda. The abandoned palaces of the Ladies Mile on

Sixth Avenue have re-opened as mega-stores selling books, housewares, office supplies, and clothes. On Broadway home furnishing stores cluster around the feet of ABC Carpet and Home. Young cyber whizzes working in hi-tech computer studios have earned a new name for the area: Silicon Alley. On and off the avenues, trendy restaurants proliferate like chanterelles after a rain, as have fitness clubs of every persuasion. So you can lunch among the literati and leggy lovelies in sprawling theme restaurants, furnish your kitchen at Williams-Sonoma, work up a sweat, shoot billiards till dawn, and boogie the night away, all in the Flatiron District. The neighborhood even has its own weekly, the *Flatiron News*.

There are rentals in the handsome Zeckendorf Towers set back from Union Square with airy, teal pyramid points atop the brick towers and a 24-hour supermarket downstairs. Madison Green, overlooking restful **Madison Square Park**, is among the notable modern condominiums. And a sleek new apartment tower, 1 Union Square South, rises above the new Circuit City. Building and renovation along the 14th Street corridor between Third and Seventh avenues is adding housing stock to the area, much of it for NYU, as well as a much improved streetscape. More typical of the Flatiron District, however, are the elegant, converted living lofts hidden away in the stolid manufacturing buildings that darken the side streets. Consult a real estate broker for the occasional sublet that comes on the market when the owner's away shooting photos in Crete. Besides a prime location with good public transportation, you'll have the graceful, green breathing space that is now Union Square for a front yard. The four-day-a-week greenmarket (see **Greenmarkets** in the **Shopping for the Home** chapter) is the Square's *pièce de résistance*. Manhattanites trek year round to the northwest corner at East 16th and Broadway for fresh produce, fish, sausages, cheese, pretzels, breads, honey—oh, endless edibles.

Web Sites: www.cb1.org; www.unionsquaresouth.com; official New York City site, www.nyc.gov
Area Codes: 212, 646
Post Offices (nearest): Cooper Station, 93 Fourth Avenue, NYC 10003, 254-1389; Madison Square Station, 149 East 23rd Street, NYC 10010, 212-673-3771
Zip Codes: 10003, 10010, 10011
Police Precinct: Thirteenth, 230 East 21st Street, NYC 10010, 212-477-7411
Emergency Hospitals (nearest): Cabrini Medical Center, 227 East 19th Street, NYC 10003, 212-995-6000; St. Vincent's Hospital and Medical Center, Seventh Avenue and 11th Street, NYC 10011, 212-604-7000
Libraries (nearest): Muhlenberg Library, 209 West 23rd Street, NYC 10011, 212-206-5480; Epiphany Branch, 228 East 23rd Street, NYC 10010, 212-679-2645

Public School Education: School District #2 (see **Chelsea**).
Adult Education: School of Visual Arts, 209 East 23rd Street, NYC 10010,
    212-679-7350; Baruch College of Continuing and Professional Studies,
    17 Lexington Avenue, Room 920, NYC 10010, 212-802-5600
Community Resources: Tibet House, 22 West 15th Street, NYC 10011,
    212-807-0563
Transportation—Subway: Crosstown L on 14th Street at Sixth Avenue,
    Union Square; #4, #5, #6 at 23rd Street, 14th Street/Union Square
    (Exp); N, Q, R at 14th Street/Union Square (Exp); PATH (between New
    Jersey and 33rd street) at 14th and 23rd Streets at Sixth Avenue
Transportation—Bus: Crosstown 23rd Street (#23); Crosstown 14th
    Street (#14); Uptown Park Avenue South/Madison Avenue (#1, #2, #3);
    Uptown Sixth Avenue (#5, #6, #7); Downtown Park Avenue South (#1);
    Downtown Fifth Avenue (#2, #3, #5); Downtown Broadway (#6, #7)

CHELSEA

Boundaries and Contiguous Areas: North: 34th Street and Clinton; **East**:
Sixth Avenue and Flatiron District; **South**: 14th Street and Greenwich
Village; **West**: Hudson River

Residential Chelsea is a sunny community renowned for peace, quiet, and
four- and five-story brownstone row houses, but its origins date back to
1750, when Capt. Thomas Clarke's farm encompassed the area. In the
1830s, Clarke's grandson, Clement Clarke Moore, began developing
Chelsea as a highly desirable suburb. Moore donated land for the block-
square General Theological Seminary just down the street from the Gothic
Revival style St. Peter's Episcopal Church, where he read his "A Visit from
Saint Nicholas" to family and parishioners. The tree-shaded Seminary Close
is still a neighborhood oasis.

To the west, the Hudson River Railroad attracted slaughterhouses,
breweries and shanties, and in 1871 Chelsea was darkened by the city's first
elevated railroad, on Ninth Avenue. Successive decades saw the brief emergence of West 23rd Street as the city's theater district; the raising of vast
cast iron structures on Sixth Avenue to house fashionable emporiums such
as the original B. Altman's, and in the 1920s and 1930s a thriving vice district; the beginning of the nation's movie industry; and the opening of one
of the city's first cooperative apartment houses, now the Chelsea Hotel,
home over the years to artists and writers. Urban renewal in the 1950s and
1960s spurred the restoration of many fine townhouses and made way for
two low-income housing projects and the middle-income International
Ladies Garment Workers cooperative between Eighth and Ninth avenues.

Sharing the side streets with restored one- and two-family houses are the occasional apartment house and tenement, not to mention formidable **London Terrace**, 405 West 23rd Street, with 14 buildings, four of which are co-ops. The lofts in the photography, flower, fur and fashion districts (roughly 15th to 30th streets between Fifth and Eighth avenues, which includes the Flatiron District) were discovered by artists in the 1950s and now increasingly attract young families and professionals.

In 1982 the down-at-the-heels Elgin, a 1930s movie house on Eighth Avenue, was transformed into the exuberantly deco Joyce Theater, the first theater in the dance capital of the world to be specifically designed for small and medium-sized dance troupes. Since then Chelsea has become something of a dance and performance district. Way west, nightclubs offer do-it-yourself dance in between auto-repair shops and factories.

Eighth Avenue, between 14th and 23rd streets, is Main Street, Chelsea. With a lively restaurant scene and boutiques punctuating the relatively unobtrusive condos and co-ops, Eighth Avenue caters to a youthful, substantially gay, population. Chelseaites and Villagers shop Chelsea Market for quality foods in the imaginatively recycled Nabisco factories on Ninth Avenue and 15th Street. The most recent wave to hit Chelsea is the art scene; more than 100 trendily stark galleries cluster near the pioneering Dia Center for the Arts on 22nd Street and along the western corridor between 17th and 27th streets. Ninth and Tenth Avenue eateries feed the gallery crowd.

Simultaneously anchoring the western edge of Chelsea is the extraordinary 1.7 million square-foot Chelsea Piers Sports and Entertainment complex in four piers over the Hudson River, stretching between 17th and 23rd streets. The movie industry returned to Chelsea in the new film and television studios housed in the pier-head, through which once streamed passengers from some of the world's great ocean liners. In the handsome complex stretched out behind the studios, workout devotees strain and sweat on state-of-the-art equipment while others run, ice skate, in-line pirouette, play league hockey, soccer, lacrosse and basketball, scale a climbing wall, bowl, refine gymnastic skills or drive balls to target greens on a 200-foot Astroturf fairway under nightlights. Others watch and hang out at one of several restaurants. This $100 million entry into Chelsea's westernmost, hitherto industrial neighborhood is transforming it into a destination once again.

North of the piers and looming over the Hudson, the vast industrial Starrett-Lehigh Building, long semi-vacant, attracts high-profile tenants now, including art galleries, film studios and new media groups, not to mention Martha Stewart. And much of that industrial neighborhood is becoming luxury lofts. It's the new SoHo.

Chelsea's hot now; housing here is much in demand and expensive.

The new frontier, less attractive but accessible, is Sixth, Seventh, and Eighth avenues, from 23rd to 31st streets, where a zoning change now allows construction of apartment buildings in a previously industrial zone. Some 300 studio to two-bedroom apartments became available at market rates in 2000, with 20% of these reserved at subsidized rates for low-income tenants. Expect more.

Web Site: official New York City site, www.nyc.gov

Area Codes: 212, 646

Post Offices: General Post Office, Eighth Avenue at 33rd Street, NYC 10001, 212-967-8585, open 24 hours; London Terrace Station, 232 Tenth Avenue, near 24th Street, NYC 10011, 212-242-8248; Old Chelsea Station, 217 West 18th Street, NYC 10011, 212-675-2415; Port Authority Station, 76 Ninth Avenue, NYC 10011, 212-929-9296

Zip Codes: 10001, 10011

Police Precincts: Midtown South, 357 West 35th Street, NYC 10001, 212-239-9811; Tenth, 230 West 20th Street, NYC 10011, 212-741-8211

Emergency Hospitals (nearest): St. Clare's Hospital and Health Center, 415 West 51st Street, NYC 10019, 212-586-1500; St. Vincent's Hospital and Medical Center, Seventh Avenue and 11th Street, NYC 10011, 212-604-7000

Library: Muhlenberg Branch, 209 West 23rd Street, NYC 10011, 212-206-5480; Library for the Blind and Physically Handicapped, 40 West 20th Street, NYC 10011, 212-206-5400

Public School Education: Chelsea is in the NYC Board of Education's School District #2, one of the best in Manhattan; School Superintendent, 330 West 18th Street, NYC 10011, 212-330-9400; Committee on the Handicapped, District Manager, P.S. 33, 281 Ninth Avenue, NYC 10011, 212-244-6426. Bayard Rustin High School for the Humanities, 351 West 18th Street, 212-675-5350, is the city's newest college preparatory high school.

Adult Education: Fashion Institute of Technology, 227 West 27th Street, NYC 10001, 212-217-7999, classes plus art gallery open to the public.

Community Resources: McBurney YMCA, 215 West 23rd Street, NYC 10011, 212-741-9210; the Joyce Theater, 175 Eighth Avenue at 19th Street, NYC 10011, 212-691-9740; Dance Theatre Workshop, 219 West 19th Street, NYC 10011, 212-924-0077; The Kitchen, 512 West 19th Street, NYC 10011, 212-255-5793; Dia Center for the Arts, 548 West 22nd Street, NYC 10011, 212-989-5566; Atlantic Theater Company, 336 West 20th Street, NYC 10011, 212-645-1242, and galleries galore

Transportation—Subway: Crosstown (L) at Eighth Avenue and 14th Street (crosses 14th Street and continues into Brooklyn); #1, #2, #3 at 34th Street/Penn Station (Exp), 28th Street, 23rd Street, 18th Street,

14th Street (Exp); A, C, E at Sixth Avenue and 34th Street (Exp), 23rd Street, 14th Street (Exp); PATH (between New Jersey and 33rd Street) 14th, 23rd and 33rd streets on Sixth Avenue

Transportation—Bus: Crosstown 34th Street/Ninth Avenue (#16); Crosstown 23rd Street (#23); Crosstown 14th Street (#14) also down Avenue A and Avenue D; Uptown Tenth Avenue—Downtown Ninth Avenue (#11); Uptown Eighth Avenue—Downtown Seventh Avenue (#10)

MIDTOWN

Boundaries and Contiguous Areas: **North**: 59th Street (Central Park South) and Central Park; **East**: Lexington Avenue and East 40s and 50s, Fifth Avenue (south of 42nd Street) and Murray Hill; **South**: 34th Street and Chelsea; **West**: Eighth Avenue and Clinton

For all that it contains within its bounds, Midtown is not a neighborhood. Some 700,000 people work here, but few call it home. Not since the mansions of the mighty—the Rockefellers, the Havemeyers, the Vanderbilts—were left to the wrecker's ball and commercial development around the turn of the 20th century has Midtown felt like a neighborhood. This core of the core of the city throbs and bustles daily with industry in the garment district, commerce between Lexington and Sixth Avenue (or Avenue of the Americas, officially speaking but rarely spoken), with shoppers from Macy's to Bergdorf Goodman to Bloomingdale's, and with tourists everywhere. Except in the theater district, the 40s and 50s west of Sixth Avenue, Midtown is quiet at night, all but deserted in some areas.

There are no supermarkets here, no children's playgrounds (or children to speak of either) and but one city park, the elegantly renovated Bryant Park, one block square and a little bit of Europe, behind the New York Public Library at 42nd Street. What there is, is almost all of the city's legitimate theater, ballet at City Center, music at Carnegie Hall and smaller venues, museums, restaurants of every conceivable persuasion, Rockefeller Center, major art galleries along 57th Street, and shopping till you're dropping from K-Mart to Tiffany. Not to mention that perhaps your job is here.

You *can* live in Midtown. On the high side in Trump and other glassy towers along Fifth and Park avenues and Central Park South, in some fine pre-war (WW II, that is) apartment buildings between Sixth and Eighth avenues in the 50s, and just a bit more modestly in modern doorman buildings. The occasional brownstone is a side-street surprise west of Fifth. Affordable apartments may be found in the 40s between Broadway and Eighth Avenue; explore the area first and talk to residents in order to be sure about location.

The ongoing transformation of Times Square and West 42nd Street has attracted major law firms, publishing houses, investment firms and new family entertainment to the glassy new towers and renovated theaters in this throbbing, neon-lit "crossroads of the world." Tourists and New Yorkers use a comprehensive array of services at the Times Square Visitor's Center and at the city's official Visitor Information Center. This transformation is driving the development of a formerly shabby Eighth Avenue in the 50s as a new frontier of upscale modern apartment living. Where once the peep shows and XXX theaters huddled, gleaming apartment towers rise offering marble baths and health clubs at East Side prices, no fee; see the Sunday *New York Times* for their ads. Between these towering newcomers housing will continue to be spotty but increasingly less shabby. The search here is best made with the help of reliable real estate agents. Watch the ads in the Sunday *Times* and *The Village Voice* to find agents handling properties in the area. You may also find the list of brokers in **Finding a Place to Live** helpful.

Web Sites: official New York City site, www.nyc.gov; www.timessquare.org
Area Codes: 212, 646
Post Offices: Grand Central Station, 450 Lexington Avenue, NYC 10017, 212-330-5733; Midtown Station, 221 and 223 West 38th Street, NYC 10018, 212-967-8585 and 212-944-6597; Rockefeller Center Station, 610 Fifth Avenue, NYC 10020, 212-265-3854; Bryant Station, 23 West 43rd Street, NYC 10036, 212-279-5960; Murray Hill Station, 115 East 34th Street, NYC 10016, 212-679-9127; Station #138 Macy's, 151 West 34th Street, NYC 10001, 212-695-4400, ext. 2688
Zip Codes: 10001,10016,10017,10018, 10019, 10020, 10022, 10036
Police Precincts: Midtown North, 306 West 54th Street, NYC 10019, 212-767-8400; Midtown South, 357 West 35th Street, NYC 10001, 212-239-9811
Emergency Hospital (nearest): St. Luke's-Roosevelt Hospital Center, 1000 Tenth Avenue, NYC 10023, 212-523-4000
Libraries: The Mercantile Library, 17 East 47th Street, NYC 10017, 212-755-6710, a membership library; General Society Library, 20 West 44th Street, NYC 10036, 212-921-1767, a membership library; Donnell Library Center, New York Public Library, 20 West 53rd Street, NYC 10019, 212-621-0618; Fifty-Eighth Street Branch, 127 East 58th Street, NYC 10022, 212-759-7358; Mid-Manhattan Branch, 455 Fifth Avenue, NYC 10016, 212-340-0863; New York Public Library, Fifth Avenue and 42nd Street, NYC 10018, 212-869-8089; the new Science, Industry and Business Branch (SIBL) in the former B. Altman building, 188 Madison Avenue at 34th Street, NYC 10016, 212-592-7000.
Public School Education: School District #2 (see **Chelsea**).

Adult Education: Graduate School and University Center, City University of New York (CUNY), 33 West 42nd Street 10018, 642-1600

Community Resources: International Center of Photography (ICP) Midtown, 1133 Avenue of the Americas at 43rd Street, NYC 10036, 212-768-4682; Museum of Modern Art, 11 West 53rd Street, NYC 10019, 212-708-9400; Museum of Television and Radio, 25 West 52nd Street, NYC 10019, 212-621-6800; American Craft Museum, 40 West 53rd, NYC 10019, 212-956-3535; City Center Theater, 130 West 55th Street, NYC 10019, 212-581-1212; Carnegie Hall and Weill Recital Hall, 154 West 57th Street, NYC 10019, 212-903-9600; NYC's Official Visitor Information Center, 810 Seventh Avenue, 212-397-8200, www.nycvisit.com; Times Square Visitor's Center, 1560 Broadway between 46th and 47th streets, NYC 10036, 212-869-1808, www.timessquarebid.org

Transportation—Subway: S train (shuttle), 42nd Street from Times Square to Grand Central; #7, 42nd Street at Times Square, Fifth Avenue, Grand Central; A, C, E, Eighth Avenue at 34th Street (Exp), 42nd Street (Exp), 50th Street, 59th Street (A, C), 50th Street at Seventh, Fifth and Lexington avenues (E); #l/9, #2, #3, Seventh Avenue at 34th Street (Exp), 42nd Street (Exp), 50th Street and Broadway, 59th Street and Broadway; B, D, F, Q, Sixth Avenue at 34th Street (Exp), 42nd Street (Exp), 47-50th Street (Exp), 57th Street (B, Q), 53rd Street at Fifth Avenue and Lexington Avenue (F); #4, #5, #6, Lexington at 42nd Street (Exp), 51st Street, 59th Street

Transportation—Bus: Crosstown 34th Street (#34); Crosstown 42nd Street (#42, #104); Crosstown 49/50th streets (#50); Crosstown 57th Street (#57, #31); Uptown Eighth Avenue—Downtown Seventh Avenue (#l0); Uptown Sixth Avenue—Downtown Fifth Avenue (#5); Uptown Sixth Avenue—Downtown/Seventh Avenue and Broadway (#6, #7); Uptown Madison Avenue—Downtown Fifth Avenue (#2, #3, #4, #18); Uptown Madison Avenue—Downtown Fifth Avenue and Park Avenue (#1); Uptown Lexington Avenue—Downtown Third Avenue (#101, #102, #98)

CLINTON

Boundaries and Contiguous Areas: North: 59th Street and Lincoln Center; **East**: Eighth Avenue and the Theater District; **South**: 34th Street and Chelsea; **West**: Hudson River

Not so long ago Clinton was "Hell's Kitchen," the neighborhood—and it *is* a real neighborhood—which produced gangster Owney Madden and inspired *West Side Story*. Traditionally a poor workingman's district with often-squalid tenements and rooming houses, Clinton still has a few Irish and Puerto Rican gangs and raunchy blocks catering to transients. Reason enough to explain why this area, so close to midtown that developers are calling it "Midtown West," remained something of a backwater until the incursion of desirable living space brought respectability.

Upgrading began in the 1970s when Manhattan Plaza, 400 West 43rd Street, with its two towers, pool and tennis courts, was built. People with enough money to pay the high rents originally charged for the apartments were disinclined to live in the neighborhood, so the buildings were converted to subsidized housing for long-time residents displaced by the complex and for people in the performing arts. This new population helped found and now supports the thriving off-Broadway Theater Row on the south side of 42nd Street, a bonanza for New York's theater-going public, not to mention the theater world. The new respectability is firmly anchored on far-west 42nd Street by 1 River Place, a vast luxury rental building zig-zagging across a whole block on the city's western edge. Now in an area once characterized by sleaze and depression, there are good restaurants, more theaters, blocks of spiffed-up townhouses, and handsome co-op renovations such as the Piano Factory. Clinton's new frontier is Tenth Avenue, where The Foundry, a 222-apartment mixed-income rental complex rose over a parking lot and a taxi garage in 2000. The gentrification of Clinton continues.

The transformation of **West 42nd Street** from the tawdry "Deuce" that it once was to a safe, family-oriented entertainment/business center is in full swing, especially now that the Disney organization is firmly committed to the location. The giant stock-market ticker at 47th Street in Times Square proclaims Morgan Stanley's confidence in this redevelopment, which is also driving change in Clinton.

One Worldwide Plaza, a 49-story tower capped by an ever-so-fashionable nouveau mansard roof, is both a symbol and a powerful instrument of change in Clinton. Prestigious law firms and ad agencies now serve a classy clientele at Eighth Avenue and 50th Street, where the shabby, old Madison Square Garden once squatted, and winos, hookers, and pushers roamed. A plaza separates the office spire in the mixed-use Zeckendorf development from the residential area, which is located to the west in the block-square complex. There a 39-story high rise and a series of attractive brick low rises contain some 650 condo units. Eighth and Ninth avenues and the adjoining side streets are moving up.

One mammoth presence that has profoundly effected Clinton is the Jacob K. Javits Convention Center, 655 West 34th Street. Now, where there had been a nondescript patch of garages, warehouses, and parking lots, a mini-neighborhood springs forth, dubbed **TunJav** (for Lincoln Tunnel, which empties here, and Javits Center, which it adjoins) by the *Times*. A few artists, designers, architects, and others have carved homes out of these industrial buildings. The ethnic food shops and tantalizing fruits and vegetables along Ninth Avenue feed them. Further development in this area, wherever there are parking lots, is a foregone conclusion. The addition of a contemplated sports stadium adjacent to the Javits Center, if realized, will impact profoundly on the area. To get a sense of the neighborhood, visit its feisty web site, www.hellskitchen.net.

Because the neighborhood is in the midst of radical transformation, any apartment hunting here should be done block by block on foot. Besides the possibility of lucking into a reasonable rental on a decent block. Consult the weekly *Chelsea Clinton News* as an informative neighborhood reference, 212-268-2552.

Web Sites: www.hellskitchen.net; www.clintoncommunitygarden.org; official New York City site, www.nyc.gov

Area Codes: 212, 646

Post Offices: Midtown Station, 223 West 38th Street, NYC 10018, 212-944-6597; Times Square Station, 340 West 42nd Street, NYC 10036, 212-502-0420

Zip Codes: 10019, 10036, 10018

Police Precincts: Midtown North, 306 West 54th Street, NYC 10019, 212-767-8400; Midtown South, 357 West 35th Street, NYC 10001, 212-239-9811

Emergency Hospitals: St. Luke's Roosevelt Hospital Center: The Roosevelt Hospital at 428 West 59th Street, NYC 10019, 212-523-4000; St. Clare's Hospital and Health Care Center, 415 West 51st Street, NYC 10019, 212-586-1500

Libraries: Columbus Branch, 742 10th Avenue, NYC 10036, 212-586-5098

Public School Education: Clinton falls within Community School District #2 (see **Chelsea**).

Adult Education: John Jay College of Criminal Justice, 445 West 59th Street, NYC 10019, 212-237-8000

Community Resources: St. Clement's Episcopal Church, 423 West 46th Street, NYC 10036, 212-246-7277, has a special mission to the arts community, and its services are as likely to consist of theatrical performances as liturgy. The Intrepid Sea-Air-Space Museum, Pier 86 at West 46th Street and 12th Avenue, 212-245-0072, is housed in and around the aircraft carrier Intrepid and contains, among other permanent and changing exhibits, the USS Growler submarine and the USS Edson destroyer.

Transportation—Subway: #1/#9, #2, #3 Broadway at 59th Street, 50th Street, 42nd Street (Exp), 34th Street (Exp); A, C, E at 59th Street (Exp), 50th Street, 42nd Street (Exp), 34th Street (Exp)

Transportation—Bus: Crosstown 57th Street (#57, #58); Crosstown 49th/50th streets (#27, #50); Crosstown 42nd Street (#42); Crosstown 34th Street (#16, #34); Uptown Tenth Avenue—Downtown Ninth Avenue (#11); Uptown Eighth Avenue—Downtown Seventh Avenue (#10); Downtown Broadway (#104) to 42nd Street and then crossing to the East Side along 42nd Street.

LINCOLN CENTER AREA

Boundaries and Contiguous Areas: North: 72nd Street and the Upper West Side; **East**: Central Park West; **South**: 59th Street and Clinton; **West**: Hudson River

This neighborhood, dubbed **Lincoln Square**, is a prime example of the change a major new facility can effect in a marginal New York location. Construction in 1960 of the glass and travertine Lincoln Center complex with theaters, opera and ballet houses, concert halls, library, and the Juilliard School transformed a dreary stretch of rundown tenements and warehouses. Now it seems every other pedestrian carries a musical instrument or moves with the marked grace of a ballet dancer, and limousines queue up where once trucks double-parked.

Columnar apartment and office buildings rise above the cafes, restaurants, and boutiques lining Broadway, Columbus and Amsterdam avenues. Fordham University's West Side Campus and ABC/Capital Cities are also firmly planted in the neighborhood. The whole adds a boost to the renaissance of Columbus and Amsterdam avenues, which cater to the food, drink, and clothing needs of the West Side's relatively affluent young residents.

Condo spires and columns have shot up south and west of the culture complex, even on barren Tenth Avenue, which may be the new frontier of Lincoln Square. Tall white brick luxury buildings compose most of Lincoln's Square's housing. Breaking that mold, 35-story twin towers on a stone base, designed to appeal to families with dogs, opened to renters on West End Avenue between 64th and 65th streets in 2000. The builder chose that neighborhood, he was quoted in the *Times* as saying, because "it's young, vibrant, and cultural, blends the old New York with the new... and appeals to a broad range of people."

And now we have Trump Place, the much-heralded river-front project known in the planning stages as **Trump City**. That is, we have the beginning. When Donald Trump (New Yorkers know him as The Donald) purchased the site of the now-defunct railroad yards fronting the Hudson River between 59th and 72nd streets, plans for the development of an enormous housing, shopping and business complex to the west of Lincoln Center received a boost. But resistance to the Trumping of Lincoln Square solidified among residents and community planners, and future development is likely to be less dense, less grandiose than the original Trump model. For now, three structures housing condos and luxury rentals tower alone over the Hudson River, not to mention (and the ads don't) the noisy West Side Highway. More to come.

Web Site: official New York City site, www.nyc.gov; www.trumpplace.com

Area Codes: 212, 646

Post Office: Columbus Circle Station, 27 West 60th Street, NYC 10023, 212-265-7858

Zip Codes: 10023, 10019

Police Precinct: Midtown North, 306 West 54th Street, NYC 10019, 212-767-8400

Emergency Hospital (nearest): St. Luke's-Roosevelt Hospital Center: The Roosevelt Hospital at 428 West 59th Street, NYC 10019, 212-523-4000

Library: Library of the Performing Arts at Lincoln Center, 111 Amsterdam Avenue, NYC 10023, 212-870-1630

Public School Education: School District #3, 300 West 96th Street, NYC 10025, 212-678-2800; Committee on Special Education, 122 Amsterdam Avenue, NYC 10025, 917-441-3600

Adult Education: Fordham University, 113 West 60th Street, NYC 10023, 212-636-6000; The Juilliard School, Lincoln Center Plaza, NYC 10023, 212-799-5000; Art Students League of New York, 215 West 57th Street, NYC 10019, 212-247-4510; The Elaine Kaufman Cultural Arts Center, 129 West 67th Street, 212-362-8060, offers courses in music, dance, art and the theater.

Community Resources: For the plethora of cultural events, theaters, library, shops, restaurants, exhibits, and tours at Lincoln Center, consult the telephone directory; Merkin Hall, 129 West 67th Street, 212-501-3340, presents a variety of concerts, primarily ethnic and chamber music; Museum of American Folk Art, 2 Lincoln Square, NYC 10023, 212-595-9533.

Transportation—Subway: #1/9 Broadway at 66th Street, 59th Street; #1/9, #2, #3 Broadway at 72nd Street (Exp); A, B, C, D at 59th Street (Exp)

Transportation—Bus: Crosstown 72nd Street (#72); Crosstown 66th/67th streets (#66); Crosstown 57th Street (#57, #58); Uptown Tenth Avenue—Downtown Columbus Avenue (#11); Uptown Eighth Avenue—Downtown Central Park West/Seventh Avenue (#10)

THE UPPER WEST SIDE

Boundaries and Contiguous Areas: North: 110th Street and Morningside Heights; **East**: Central Park West; **South**: 72nd Street and Lincoln Center; **West**: Hudson River

For decades large sprawling apartments and an active community life have been luring writers, musicians, intellectuals, psychiatrists—in general, those seeking an alternative to the Upper East Side's more constrained life-style—to the West Side. Indeed, the city's first large apartment buildings, with lofty ceilings, thick walls and space to waste, were built here around the turn of the century. Grand structures rose first along Central Park West (note the famed Dakota at 72nd Street), claimed by some aficionados to be the most architecturally elegant avenue in New York; next on Broadway (the neoclassical Ansonia between 73rd and 74th streets and the block-square Apthorp between 78th and 79th are particularly grand), which was to be Park Avenue West but isn't; and then on West End Avenue and Riverside Drive.

Most buildings along the apartment-lined avenues—with the notable exception of **Columbus** and **Amsterdam**, which have only recently emerged from the Dickensian 19th to enter the trendiest century—managed to remain sufficiently attractive to hold the middle class. But the rows of brick, limestone, and brownstone townhouses built for the newly affluent on the cross streets during the early 1900s declined into squalid tenements and SRO (single room occupancy) rooming houses. Not until the 1960s, when an ambitious urban renewal plan spurred building and renovation, did this veritable architectural museum again become an address for affluent achievers. Today, the typical brownstone houses the owner's family on the garden or parlor floors and tenants on the original bedroom floors above.

A golden ghetto was never the goal of West Side planners. They have fought long and hard to keep the neighborhood diverse and representative of the city as a whole. However, the vogue-ish and often short-lived gourmet emporiums, bijou boutiques, clothing shops featuring somber Japanese designs, and fashionable hangouts decorating Columbus and Amsterdam avenues attest to the fickle wants of the upwardly mobile.

Ranks of condo towers have shot up along Columbus and, more recently, Amsterdam between 87th and 97th streets—just outside the boundaries of the Central Park West Historic District. These svelte and pricey (though cheaper than Lincoln Square) condominiums provide residents with plenty of play space: health clubs, pools, rooftop gardens, party rooms, and in-house parking are standard. Meanwhile, **Upper Broadway** is being transformed as high rises are slotted, sleek cheek by shabby jowl, among the wearier old-timers between 97th Street and Columbia University. A short-term rental in one of these buildings offers the undecided newcomer an opportunity to try out the neighborhood before making a long-term commitment.

Most of the handsome stone buildings fronting Central Park—the San Remo, the Beresford, the Majestic, etc—are cooperatives now, and as sought after and as pricey as those on Fifth Avenue across the park. Just south of 96th Street a few condos and rentals are to be found, and north of 96th in the area known as **Manhattan Valley** a mix of condos, co-ops and rentals makes Central Park West (CPW) more accessible north to 110th Street. The vast apartment co-ops lining **West End Avenue** and curving along Riverside Drive have enduring appeal. Pioneers stake their claims in Manhattan Valley east of Broadway in the upper 90s and 100s, and west of Broadway between 96th and 110th streets. For the less adventurous and thicker of purse, existing rental apartments are well worth pursuing, if only to live between Manhattan's greenest playgrounds, Central and Riverside parks, and near one of its cultural stalwarts, the massive Museum of Natural History, which devotes almost 25 acres of floor space to some of the finest scientific collections in the world.

While CPW looks east over Central Park, where its denizens find their recreation, Riverside Drive, stretching less exclusively from 72nd Street to 165th Street, looks west over Riverside Park, the Hudson River, and stunning sunsets over the Jersey Palisades. Market rate rental apartments are mostly between 92nd and 96th streets, the rest being largely co-ops whose boards tend to be less snobbish than in some other neighborhoods. Broadway is two blocks away, with its addictive gourmet food markets. But it is the park that gives the neighborhood its sense of community. Residents raise their children there, walk their dogs, play and dream there. Says one, "With its many levels it is a wonderful place to walk and stroll, sit and read, and have a sandwich—even in the colder months."

Web Site: official New York City site, www.nyc.gov
Area Codes: 212, 646
Post Offices: Cathedral Station, 215 West 104th Street, NYC 10025, 212-662-9191; Planetarium Station, 131 West 83rd Street, NYC 10024, 212-873-3701; Ansonia Station, 178 Columbus Avenue, NYC 10023, 212-362-7486
Zip Codes: 10025, 10024, 10023
Police Precincts: Twenty-fourth, 151 West 100th Street, NYC 10025, 212-678-1811; Twentieth, 120 West 82nd Street, NYC 10024, 212-580-6411
Emergency Hospital (nearest): Both branches of the St. Luke's-Roosevelt Hospital Center: The Roosevelt Hospital at 428 West 59th Street, NYC

10019, and St. Luke's Hospital, 114th Street and Amsterdam Avenue, NYC 10025, both 212-523-4000

Libraries: Bloomingdale Branch, 150 West 100th Street, NYC 10025, 212-222-8030; St. Agnes Branch, 444 Amsterdam Avenue, NYC 10024, 212-877-4380; Riverside Branch, 127 Amsterdam Avenue, NYC 10023, 212-870-1810

Public School Education: School District #3 (see **Lincoln Center Area**).

Adult Education: Bank Street College of Education, 610 West 112th Street, NYC 10025, 212-875-4400

Community Resources: Central Park, stretching from 59th Street over 840 acres up to 110th Street. For literary events, Gilbert and Sullivan, live jazz, Afro-Cuban rhythms and the new modern directions: Symphony Space, 2537 Broadway at 95th Street, 212-864-5400. For a multiplicity of musical styles, played live: the Beacon Theater, Broadway and 74th Street, 212-496-7070. American Museum of Natural History and the Rose Center for Earth and Space, Central Park West from 79th Street to 81st Street, museum information: 212-769-5100; the Bard Graduate Center for Studies in the Decorative Arts, 18 West 86th Street, NYC 10024, 212-501-3000; Nicholas Roerich Museum, 319 West 107th Street, NYC 10025, 212-864-7752; Children's Museum of Manhattan, 212 West 83rd Street, NYC 10024, 212-721-1234.

Transportation—Subway: #1/9, Broadway at 110th Street, 103rd Street; #1/9, #2, #3, 96th Street (Exp); #1/9, 86th Street, 79th Street; #1/9, #2, #3, 72nd Street (Exp); B, C at Central Park West and 110th Street, 103rd Street, 96th Street, 86th Street, 81st Street, 72nd Street

Transportation—Bus: Crosstown 96th Street (#19); Crosstown 86th Street (#86); Crosstown 79th Street (#79); Crosstown 72nd Street (#72); Crosstown 66th/67th streets (#66) ending at Central Park West and 72nd Street; Uptown Riverside Drive—Downtown Riverside Drive (#4, #5); Uptown Amsterdam Avenue—Downtown Columbus Avenue (#7, #11); Uptown Broadway—Downtown Broadway (#104)

MORNINGSIDE HEIGHTS

Boundaries and Contiguous Areas: **North**: 125th Street and Harlem; **East**: Morningside Drive; **South**: 110th Street and Upper West Side; **West**: Hudson River

Academia amidst a gritty urban-scape, this lively community occupying the formerly rocky slopes of northern Manhattan is dominated—physically, economically and socially—by Columbia University, one of the nation's oldest, richest, and largest educational institutions. In addition, Barnard

College as well as two important religious seminaries, the Manhattan School of Music, a large teaching hospital, and two major churches share the Heights with a mixture of students, professors, professionals, and urban poor. Up here next to the granite bulk of Ulysses S. Grant's pompous tomb, upper west side gray is relieved by Riverside Park, used extensively by residents as a front yard, and by Morningside Park, until recently avoided as unsafe. Spearheaded by the Morningside Area Alliance, efforts to clean up the park have involved the Parks Department, Columbia students and a new "Friends of Morningside Park"; daytime strollers, dog-walkers and joggers use the park now. Safe at night? Maybe not.

Work on its massive towers has halted indefinitely, but if they are ever completed, the Episcopal Cathedral Church of St. John the Divine will literally tower over the community; now spireless, the world's largest Gothic cathedral just looms. (The tall Gothic church tower you do see rising northwest of Columbia belongs to Riverside Church, the Rockefellers' non-denominational gift to the city.) St. John caters to cultural as well as spiritual needs, sponsoring a particularly rich and wide-ranging series of concerts from chamber music through liturgical works to jazz and other events including poetry readings, craft fairs and dance programs. The church dedicates a side altar to victims of AIDS.

Broadway, Morningside Heights' main street, showcases bookstores, coffee shops, all night fruit stands, student bars cum jazz joints, boutiques, and restaurants ranging from fast food to ethnic and elegant. In recent years Columbia has actively promoted the transformation of the ten blocks south of the campus between Broadway and Amsterdam, and this once-desolate area now appeals to a more sophisticated crowd than heretofore. The lively street life that continues late makes the neighborhood relatively safe and certainly interesting.

As owners of one-third of the community's housing stock, over half of which is occupied by tenants affiliated with the university, Columbia University is the Heights' biggest landlord. However, an occasional rental does hit the open market, and sometimes space becomes available when Columbia-connected roommates separate (graduate, marry or move) leaving behind an empty room and half the monthly rent bill. Co-ops, keenly sought now, escalated steeply in price during the 1990s but still represent good value, if not a bargain, when compared to Upper West Side prices.

Web Sites: www.morningsideheights.net; official New York City site, www.nyc.gov

Area Codes: 212, 646

Post Office: Columbia University Station, 534 West 112th Street, NYC 10025, 212-864-1874

Zip Codes: 10027, 10026, 10025

Police Precinct: Twenty-sixth, 520 West 126th Street, NYC 10027, 212-678-1311

Emergency Hospital: St. Luke's-Roosevelt Hospital Center: St. Luke's Hospital, 114th Street and Amsterdam Avenue, NYC 10025, 212-523-4000

Library: 115th Street Branch, 203 West 115th Street, NYC 10026, 212-666-9393; Columbia Branch, 514 West 113th Street, NYC 10025, 212-864-2530

Public School Education: School District #3 (see **Lincoln Center Area**).

Adult Education: Barnard College, 3009 Broadway, NYC 10027, 212-854-5262; Columbia University, Broadway and 114th Street to 120th Street, NYC 10027, 212-854-1754; Union Theological Seminary, Broadway and 120th Street, NYC 10027, 212-662-7100; Bank Street College of Education, 610 West 112th Street, NYC 10025, 212-875-4400; Jewish Theological Seminary, 3080 Broadway, NYC 10027, 212-678-8000; Manhattan School of Music, 120 Claremont Avenue, NYC 10027, 212-749-2802

Community Resources: Cathedral Church of St. John the Divine, West 112th Street and Amsterdam Avenue, NYC 10025, 212-316-7540, also has on its large grounds a Biblical Garden with plantings inspired by the Old Testament; north of St. John the Divine, Riverside Church, 400 Riverside Drive (at West 120th Street), NYC 10027, 212-870-6700, offers educational and cultural programs in addition to religious services.

Transportation—Subway: A, B, C, D at 125th Street (Exp), 116th Street, 110th Street

Transportation—Bus: Crosstown 116th Street (#20); Uptown Riverside Drive—Downtown Columbus Avenue (#11); Uptown Broadway—Downtown Broadway (#104)

THE HARLEMS

Boundaries and Contiguous Areas: *East Harlem*: **North** and **East**: Harlem River; **South**: 96th Street, Upper East Side and Yorkville; **West**: Central Park; *Harlem*: **North**: 155th Street and Washington Heights; **East**: Harlem River; **West**: Hudson River; **South**: 125th Street and Morningside Heights

This neighborhood, rich in culture, remains the spiritual focus of black America. Although Harlem pockets some of the worst poverty and crime in New York City, many of its high-stooped, row-house-lined streets are perfectly safe. And a strong economy in the 1990s into the new millennium stimulated renovation of its brownstones and abandoned apartment buildings, increased national chain retailers in its business district and ignited the rebirth of a lively restaurant and nightlife. The result has been an influx of middle class and professional people, black and white, to Harlem.

Originally settled in 1636 by Dutch tobacco farmers, Harlem blossomed into a prosperous suburb in the 1800s. Around 1900, black New Yorkers began settling into an abundance of apartment buildings left empty when real estate developers' plans for a white middle class neighborhood failed to materialize. In addition to brand new housing stock, Harlem offered its first black residents a less racially hostile environment than in other parts of the city.

Harlem in the 1920s is synonymous with the Harlem Renaissance. Musicians, playwrights, and novelists flocked to the neighborhood bursting with jazz clubs and casinos.

Since the 1930s, prominent African-American Harlemites have lived on Striver's Row, on West 138th and 139th streets, between Seventh and Eighth avenues. Dominated by brownstones now part of the **St. Nicholas Historic District**, Abyssinian Baptist Church, New York's oldest Black church, is located at 132 West 138th Street. Equally appealing to professionals, and to City College professors, is the **Hamilton Heights** area just north of the college, in particular Hamilton Terrace, with its handsome, landmarked brownstones. Vacancies are rare.

A little more affordable perhaps are the brownstones in the **Mount Morris Park Historic District**, 119th to 124th streets west of rocky Mount Morris/Marcus Garvey Park. More affordable yet and attracting pioneering professionals is the area known as **West Central Harlem**, or Manhattanville, stretching from 110th Street north to 125th, between Morningside Park and Adam Clayton Boulevard. Under the city's Homeworks program, developers were allowed to buy abandoned brownstones for renovation, and buyers who can qualify for a market rate mortgage can buy these shells at bargain rates and supervise their renovation. Rentals here are well below the market. City-sponsored renovation of abandoned apartment buildings has recently created affordable condos across from Morningside Park. Thorough exploration and the help of a good realtor are essential here. Further north, **Sugar Hill** with its mixture of high rise and pleasing brownstone apartments in the 140s and 150s between St. Nicholas and Edgecombe Avenues, has an enduring appeal, as does **Riverside Drive**, a racially mixed area housing professionals, middle- and low-income people.

In the heart of Harlem at Lenox Avenue (Malcolm X Boulevard) and West 135th Street is the Schomburg Center for Research in Black Culture, which houses the world's largest collection of Black history. On West 135th Street is the facility's outdoor sculpture garden; the outdoor amphitheater is on West 136th. Another neighborhood treasure at its western extreme is the splendid Riverbank State Park—28 acres of landscaped greenery with spectacular sunset views over the Hudson at 145th Street. Completed in 1993 atop an award-winning waste treatment plant, the recreational complex comprises indoor and outdoor swimming pools, a gym and fitness room, softball fields, basketball, tennis and handball courts outdoors, an indoor theater and an amphitheater, an ice and roller skating rink. Admission is free, open daily from 6 a.m. to 11 p.m., with a fee for the use of tennis courts and a nominal fee for the pool (see **Sports and Recreation**).

Harlem's east side is known as **Spanish Harlem** or El Barrio. Here you'll find mostly tenements and housing projects. Above 100th Street, newcomers should take care and know where they're going. La Marqueta, a Latino produce, meat, and houseware market keeps things bustling along El Barrio's busiest street, East 116th to Park Avenue.

Harlem celebrates its past and present history each August by hosting a one-week African-American and Hispanic festival. Call the Manhattan Chamber of Commerce, 212-479-7772, for details.

Class and racial tensions have kept Harlem somewhat isolated from the rest of Manhattan, but many say it is entering a second Renaissance. Indeed, with new families restoring many of Harlem's brownstone buildings and a thriving cultural scene (see **Cultural Resources** below), this neighborhood is pumping with life round the clock now. Tourism has increased, restaurants and jazz clubs have proliferated, and if the good life is defined by the availability of lobster, French cheeses, and filet mignon, Harlem has that too now and at competitive prices. The vast Fairway market on Marginal Street right on the Hudson between 132nd and 133rd streets has it all, seven days a week. But it's not all brie; along with milk, juice, chittlins and collards, there's a Kosher butcher and fish department. With all this and free parking too, Manhattan is beating a path to Harlem. And on the east side, Pathmark recently opened the city's largest supermarket at 125th Street and Lexington Avenue. Twenty-five aisles, with a wide array of products for Hispanic shoppers, a Chase bank branch, a pharmacy and rooftop parking, all this will transform the neighborhood.

Designation as an "Empowerment Zone" has brought Federal seed money flowing into Harlem. First, the ambitious Harlem USA complex on West 125th Street and Frederick Douglass Boulevard (Eighth Avenue), where a 6,000-square-foot Disney store and entertainment complex anchors a glassy structure containing a Chase bank, a cineplex, restaurants, stores, and a skating rink. Next in line is the development of Harlem's neglected Hudson River waterfront between 125th and 133rd streets, an area known as the Harlem Piers, though the piers are long gone. Competing proposals include a 450-room hotel, a sports complex located on two parallel barges, floating piers for a marina and community use, and a waterfront park.

Start your search for Harlem housing in the *Amsterdam News*, 212-932-7400, Real Estate section.

Web Sites: www.hometoharlem.com; official New York City site, www.nyc.gov

Area Codes: 212, 646

Post Offices: Hamilton Grange Station, 521 West 146th Street, NYC 10031, 212-281-8401; Manhattanville Station, 365 West 125th Street, NYC 10027, 212-662-1901; Hell Gate Station, 153 East 110 Street, NYC 10029, 212-860-3557; Triborough Station, 167 East 124th Street, NYC 10035, 212-534-0865; College Station, 217 West 140th Street, NYC 10030, 212-283-2235

Zip Codes: 10026, 10027, 10029, 10030, 10031, 10032, 10035, 10039

Police Precinct: Twenty-third, 162 East 102nd Street, NYC 10029, 212-860-6411; Twenty-fourth, 151 West 100th Street, NYC 10025, 212-678-1811; Twenty-fifth, 120 East 119th Street, NYC 10035, 212-860-6511; Twenty-eighth, 2271 Eighth Avenue, NYC 10027, 212-678-1611; Thirtieth, 451 West 151st Street, NYC 10032, 212-690-8811; Thirty-second, 250 West 135th Street, NYC 10030, 212-690-6311

Emergency Hospital: Harlem Hospital, 506 Lenox Avenue at 135th Street, NYC 10037, 212-939-1000, includes a crisis intervention center for battered wives, children and rape victims; Mount Sinai Hospital, 101st Street and Madison Avenue, NYC 10029, 212-241-6500.

Library: A regional branch of the New York City Public Library, Countee Cullen, is located at 136th Street and Lenox Avenue, NYC 10037, 212-491-2070. The Schomberg Center for Research In Black Culture, 515 Malcolm X Boulevard (135th Street at Lenox Avenue), NYC 10037, 212-491-2200, houses the city's African-American archives and presents local artists' works.

Public School Education: East Harlem: District #4, 319 East 117th Street, NYC 10035, 212-860-5885; further West: District #5, 433 West 123rd Street, NYC 10027, 212-769-7600; high schools include the Manhattan Center for Science and Mathematics, FDR Drive and 116th Street, NYC 10029, 212-876-4639; and A. Phillip Randolph Campus, Convent Avenue and 135th Street, NYC 10031, 212-926-0113.

Adult Education: City College, City University of New York (CUNY) 138th Street and Convent Avenue, NYC 10031, 212-650-7000; Boricua College, a private Hispanic liberal arts college, 3755 Broadway at 155th Street, NYC 10032, 212-694-1000

Community Resources: Apollo Theater, 253 West 125th Street, NYC 10027, 212-749-5838; Harlem Third World Trade Center on 163 West 125th; Studio Museum in Harlem, 144 West 125th Street, NYC 10027, 212-864-4500; Hamilton Grange, 287 Convent Avenue, NYC 10031, 212-283-5154; The Museum of the City of New York, Fifth Avenue at 103rd Street, NYC 10029, 212-534-1672; El Museo del Barrio at Fifth Avenue and 104th Street, NYC 10029, 212-831-7272, (art, culture, heritage of Puerto Rico and Latin America); Dance Theater of Harlem, 466 West 152nd Street, NYC 10031, 212-690-2800 (see **Dance** section); Harlem School of the Arts, 645 St. Nicholas Avenue between 141st and 145th streets, NYC 10030, 212-926-4100.

Transportation—Subway: #4, #5, #6, Lexington Avenue at 125th (Exp), 116th, 110th, 103rd Street and 96th Streets; #1/#9 at 157th, 145th, 137th, 125th, 116th, 110th, 103rd Street and 96th Street (Exp), all on Broadway; #2, #3, Lenox Avenue Terminal (Exp), Lenox Avenue at 145th Street (Exp), 135th (Exp), 125th (Exp), 116th and 110th Street (Exp), Central Park West at 103rd Street, Broadway at 96th Street (Exp); A (as in "Take the A Train"), B, C, D, St. Nicholas/8th avenues at 155th, 145th (Exp), 135th, 125th (Exp), and 116th, Central Park West at 110th, 103rd, and 96th Street

Transportation—Bus: Crosstown 96th Street (#19); Crosstown 116th Street (#20); Uptown Riverside Drive—Downtown Columbus Avenue (#11); Uptown/Downtown Broadway (#7, #100,#104); Uptown/Downtown St. Nicholas Avenue (#3); Uptown/Downtown Amsterdam Avenue (#101)

WASHINGTON HEIGHTS-INWOOD

Boundaries and Contiguous Areas: North: Harlem River and Riverdale; **East**: Harlem River; **South**: 155th Street and Harlem; **West**: Hudson River

Up here, where outcroppings from the Hudson riverbed rise to form Manhattan's highest ground, the tawny stone arches rhythmically lining the central courtyard at The Cloisters are echoed by the exceptionally graceful curve of the steel suspension cables looping the twin towers of the silvery George Washington Bridge. Long before John D. Rockefeller, Jr. gave the city the magnificent medieval Cloisters Museum as well as Fort Tryon Park, George Washington headquartered Revolutionary forces on the strategic terrain now called Washington Heights.

Six hundred acres of parkland, almost all of it in Fort Tryon Park and rocky, wooded Inwood Hill Park, refresh and beautify one of the most densely populated, and narrowest, sections of New York. On the map, the top of Manhattan looks like a knobby finger pointing across the Harlem River at The Bronx, from the elongated fist of Manhattan. **Washington Heights** and **Inwood** are all "West Side"; the Harlem River lops off the "East Side" at 138th Street.

Narrow as it is, this finger of Manhattan contains many neighborhoods, only two of which, along the western edge, we describe here. Commercial Broadway cuts through the area on a north-south bias, dividing the almost solidly Hispanic, mostly low-income Harlem River (eastern) half from the more middle-income, Hudson River (western) half. The western section contains the most coveted housing—solidly constructed one- and two-bedroom apartments, many with pleasing river and park views—situated in square, five- to ten-story buildings. The clusters of yellow, buff, and occasionally red brick Art Deco buildings clumped along a rocky spine above the river in the **Hudson Heights** section of Washington Heights have special appeal. Half-timbered Hudson View Gardens, between 183rd and 185th streets, and Castle Village with its gardens and panoramic Hudson River views nearby, two of the most desirable complexes, are cooperatives, as are many of the neighborhood buildings. Sublets, where you can get them, are still well below rentals further downtown, as are the co-op prices.

In previous years a violent drug trade made parts of Washington Heights, the West 150s and 160s in particular, a dicey neighborhood despite its solidly middle class population and the presence of prestigious New York Presbyterian Hospital. Most recently, however, crime is way down here, and though rentals and co-op prices are up, they remain at about 40% to 50% of prices for comparable properties further downtown. There are brownstones and large apartments in pre-war buildings, well worth a look, especially along Riverside Drive West and Fort Washington Avenue and the connecting streets.

For another dimension, travel up to Inwood and stroll the grassy fields of Inwood Hill Park near 218th Street and Indian Road. Ahead of you to the north the Harlem River sweeps under the soaring Henry Hudson Bridge, beyond which you can see the Jersey Palisades. To your immediate right are Columbia University's Baker Field, the only college stadium in Manhattan, the college boathouse and tennis bubble. And straight ahead, one of the city's loveliest and least-known parks, with wetlands, rolling greens and six miles of footpaths rising into rocky woods in which there are Indian caves to be seen. It's quiet, except for an astonishing variety of birds. The man jogging past is as likely to be an opera singer or an artist as he is to be a broker or a police officer.

If you find the friendly unassuming neighborhood attractive, plan to search, and search hard, on foot, questioning supers and building managers. It's a small neighborhood of pleasing pre-war brick apartment buildings located between the park and Broadway, north of 207th Street, which are Inwood's two main streets. No trendy restaurants, lively after-hours clubs or art film houses here. But the cost of a sunny one-bedroom (or two or three) on the park, if you can find one to rent, will make you giggle if you've been looking downtown. Prices have risen here on the end-century rising tide, but this is a neighborhood where a middle-class couple can afford to buy two apartments and combine them. Certainly, check with a reputable local real estate agent. Have a beer and a burger at the Piper's

Kilt, 4944 Broadway at 207th Street, and pick up a copy of the *Washington Heights and Inwood Report*, www.thereport.net.

Web Site: official New York City site, www.nyc.gov

Area Codes: 212, 646

Post Offices: Audubon Station, 511 West 165th Street, NYC 10032, 212-568-3311; Washington Bridge Station, 555 West 180th Street, NYC 10033, 212-568-7601; Fort George Station, 4558 Broadway, NYC 10040, 212-942-0052; Inwood Station, 90 Vermilyea Avenue, NYC 10034, 212-567-3032

Zip Codes: 10034, 10040, 10033, 10032

Police Precinct: Thirty-fourth, 4295 Broadway, NYC 10033, 212-927-9711; Thirty-third, 2120 Amsterdam Avenue, NYC 10032, 212-927-3200

Emergency Hospital: Columbia-Presbyterian Medical Center, 622 West 168th Street, NYC 10032, 212-305-2500

Libraries: Fort Washington Branch, 535 West 179th Street, NYC 10033, 212-927-3533; Washington Heights Branch, 1000 St. Nicholas Avenue, NYC 10040, 212-923-6054; Inwood Branch, 4790 Broadway, NYC 10034, 212-942-2445

Public School Education: School District #6: Community School Board, 4360 Broadway, NYC 10033, 212-795-4111

Adult Education: Yeshiva University, 500 West 185th Street, NYC 10033, 212-960-5400; Inwood Community Services, 651 Academy Street (just north of Dyckman Street), NYC 10034, 212-942-0043

Community Resources: The Cloisters, division of the Metropolitan Museum of Art, Fort Tryon Park (193rd Street and Fort Washington Avenue), NYC 10034, 212-923-3700; Audubon Terrace Museum complex, Broadway between West 155th and 156th streets, NYC 10032, including the American Academy and National Institute of Arts and Letters, 1633 West 155th Street, NYC 212-368-5900; Yeshiva University Museum, 2520 Amsterdam Avenue at 185th Street, NYC 10033, 212-960-5390; The Hispanic Society of America, 613 West 155th Street, 212-926-2234, www.hispanicsociety.org, includes a library and museum; Morris-Jumel Mansion and Museum, 65 Jumel Terrace, NYC 10032, 212-923-8008, a colonial home in garden surroundings used by Washington during the Revolution and later redecorated by Eliza Jumel; Dyckman House, 4881 Broadway at 204th Street, NYC 10034, 212-304-9422, is a restored 18th century Dutch farmhouse-museum belonging to the city and well worth a visit.

Transportation—Subway: A, 207th, Dyckman, 190th, 181st, 175th, 168th (all Exp) 163rd streets: stops along Fort Washington Avenue, Broadway; B, C at 168th, 163rd, 155th streets on Amsterdam Avenue;

#1/#9 at 215th, 207th, Dyckman, 191st, 181st, 168th and 157th streets: all stops along St. Nicholas Avenue

Transportation—Bus: Crosstown 181st Street (#3, #11, #13, #35, #36, #38); Uptown/Downtown Fort Washington Avenue to Broadway (#4); Uptown/Downtown Broadway (#7, #100); Uptown/Downtown St. Nicholas Avenue (#3); Uptown/Downtown Amsterdam Avenue (#101)

THE BRONX

Poor The Bronx, a borough that's seldom mentioned without its article. The northernmost and smallest, though not by much, of New York City's five parts is more often celebrated for a rude cheer and for Fort Apache, the south central section that has begun to struggle back from dilapidation and worse, than for large verdant parks, colleges and top-flight high schools or for some singularly attractive neighborhoods. To set the record straight, then, you should know that The Bronx boasts all of these.

Just south of Westchester County, New England-esque City Island floats rather quaintly in placid Long Island Sound. And over on the Hudson shore, Riverdale shelters estates and sylvan lanes worthy of suburban Scarsdale. In between these two neighborhoods, apartment buildings embellished with Art Deco motifs line the once-elegant Grand Concourse.

Four of the city's finest high schools are situated in The Bronx: the prestigious public Bronx High School of Science, from which so many Intel (formerly Westinghouse) Science Award winners graduate, as well as private Fieldston, Horace Mann, and Riverdale Country Day School. Eight universities and colleges enhance the borough's scholastic character.

A wealth of public land is probably The Bronx's greatest asset; parkland accounts for almost a quarter of the 43-square-mile borough. Partially forested Van Cortlandt Park, a mecca for cross-country skiers in the winter, is the spot for soccer, rugby, and football in the summer. Even larger Pelham Bay Park, from which little City Island dangles, harbors Orchard Beach along its sandy shore. But the star is Bronx Park with 500 acres about equally divided between two of the city's most illustrious scientific institutions: the Bronx Zoo (officially renamed the New York Zoological Society's International Wildlife Conservation Park) and the New York Botanical Garden. The Haupt Conservatory, a sparkling crystal greenhouse complex, displays thousands of plant varieties in natural micro-climates and must be seen. Kids of all ages, naturalists and explorers too, frequent the zoo, using the tram-like Skyfari for an overview of the African exhibit as well as to commute between pavilions that include the World of Darkness and World of Birds.

While chunks of The Bronx do flourish, the loft buildings and brownstones so dear to middle-income colonizers in search of inexpensive digs are in short supply. Cooperatives and condominiums continue to replace rental

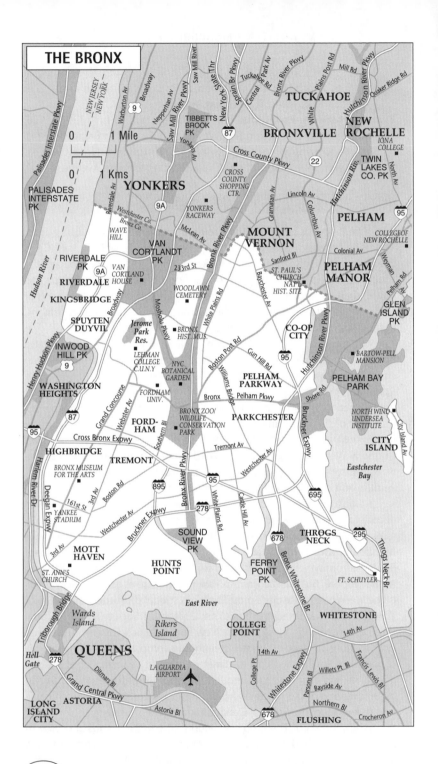

THE BRONX

NEW JERSEY / NEW YORK

TUCKAHOE

NEW ROCHELLE

IONA COLLEGE

BRONXVILLE

TWIN LAKES CO. PK

PALISADES INTERSTATE PK

0 ___ 1 Mile

0 ___ 1 Kms

YONKERS

CROSS COUNTY SHOPPING CTR.

Lincoln Av

PELHAM

COLLEGE OF NEW ROCHELLE

YONKERS RACEWAY

WAVE HILL

MOUNT VERNON

Colonial Av

PELHAM MANOR

VAN CORTLANDT PK

Sanford Bl

ST. PAUL'S CHURCH NAT'L HIST. SITE

GLEN ISLAND PK

RIVERDALE PK

VAN CORTLAND HOUSE

233rd St

WOODLAWN CEMETERY

RIVERDALE

KINGSBRIDGE

CO-OP CITY

BARTOW-PELL MANSION

SPUYTEN DUYVIL

Jerome Park Res.

BRONX HIST. MUS.

INWOOD HILL PK

LEHMAN COLLEGE C.U.N.Y

NYC BOTANICAL GARDEN

PELHAM PARKWAY

PELHAM BAY PARK

WASHINGTON HEIGHTS

FORDHAM UNIV.

Bronx

Pelham Pkwy

NORTH WIND UNDERSEA INSTITUTE

FORD-HAM

BRONX ZOO/ WILDLIFE CONSERVATION PARK

PARKCHESTER

CITY ISLAND

Cross Bronx Expwy

Tremont Av

Eastchester Bay

HIGHBRIDGE

TREMONT

BRONX MUSEUM FOR THE ARTS

Tremont Av

161st St

YANKEE STADIUM

Westchester Av

SOUND VIEW PK

THROGS NECK

MOTT HAVEN

HUNTS POINT

FERRY POINT PK

FT. SCHUYLER

ST. ANN'S CHURCH

East River

WHITESTONE

Wards Island

Rikers Island

COLLEGE POINT

Hell Gate

QUEENS

LA GUARDIA AIRPORT

LONG ISLAND CITY

ASTORIA

Astoria Bl

FLUSHING

apartments, but The Bronx has few neighborhoods that attract the younger singles in the fashion of Brooklyn and Hoboken. Bronx realtors are listed under **Apartment Hunting** in the **Finding a Place to Live** chapter.

RIVERDALE

Boundaries and Contiguous Areas: North: 263rd Street and Yonkers; **East**: Broadway and Van Cortlandt Park; **South**: West 239th Street and West 242nd Street, Spuyten Duyvil and Kingsbridge; **West**: Hudson River

The Riverdale that for most of its well-to-do length ridges the Hudson River seems more Westchester than New York. Call it a suburb in the city. It was mostly farmland, in fact, until the mid-nineteenth century, when a few wealthy souls moved out of smelly Manhattan, with its occasional cholera epidemics, and carved estates overlooking the river. Among these was Wave Hill (see below). With the completion of a railroad bridge across Spuyten Duyvil Creek (now known as the Harlem River) in 1853, Riverdale soon became a prosperous suburb, desirable for possessing the best of both rural and urban life. When in 1874 Riverdale was appended to New York City it took the objections of Frederick Law Olmsted, co-designer of Central Park, to prevent the re-mapping of the winding, wooded roads which make Riverdale so beguiling today. But no one could prevent Robert Moses from bisecting both Riverdale and Spuyten Duyvil with a clean slash of the Henry Hudson Parkway in the 1930s. Many of those mansions survive along the winding roads, often invisible behind ivy-crusted stone fences. One can buy a part of one, as many have been "condoed." Posh private schools attract kids who drive in from New Jersey and the suburbs as well as those who arrive by subway and bus from the boroughs. Shops are discretely curtailed to a few zones of mom and pop businesses. Supermarket complexes are built elsewhere. Riverdale's low, tree-shaded profile appeals to both affluent New York professionals and resident foreigners. The Russians built their white high-rise complex here, and many of the local estates house UN personnel and foreign executives.

Tall, red-brick apartment towers cluster in clumps along the potholed lanes in south Riverdale, built mostly in the 1960s and '70s and now almost all co-ops and condos. Spacious apartments, many with enviable views, sell at enviable prices by Manhattan standards and are a boon to young families looking for space and good schools. In north Riverdale, along the Yonkers border, brick and stucco houses on smallish lots can be had in a quiet neighborhood at fairly affordable prices. There are plenty of mini-mansions in Riverdale, too, although perhaps the single largest concentration of elegant single-family residences is located in adjoining **Fieldston**, a somewhat exclusive community with private streets. The urban grid and bustle so typical of New York is found on the flats below in **Kingsbridge**. If you're looking here, pick up a copy of the *Riverdale Review,* available in stores, lobbies and libraries or write for a copy to 6050 Riverdale Avenue, Riverdale, Bronx 10471.

For a great day in this country visit Wave Hill (call 718-549-2055 for directions; express buses run by Liberty Lines, 718-652-8400, provide direct service to West 252nd Street). The Hudson-side complex at 249th Street and Independence Avenue consists of two stone manor houses offering occasional chamber music, a greenhouse and 28 acres of perfectly gorgeous gardens, where in summer outdoor sculpture exhibits compete for your attention with lovely river views.

Web Sites: www.nypl.org/branch/bronx; official New York City site, www.nyc.gov

Area Codes: 718, 347

Post Offices: Riverdale Station, 5951 Riverdale Avenue, Bronx 10471, 718-549-7519; Kingsbridge Station, 5517 Broadway, Bronx 10463, 718-549-5500

Zip Codes: 10463, 10471

Police Precinct: Fiftieth, 3450 Kingsbridge Avenue, Bronx 10463, 718-543-5700

Emergency Hospital (nearest): Montefiore, 210th Street and Bainbridge Avenue, Bronx 10467, 718-920-4321

Library: Riverdale Public Library, 5540 Mosholu Avenue, Bronx 10471, 718-549-1212

Public School Education: School District #10: Community School Board, 1 Fordham Plaza, Bronx 10458, 718-584-7070

Adult Education: Manhattan College, Manhattan College Parkway and West 242nd Street, Bronx 10471, 718-862-8000; College of Mt. St. Vincent, Riverdale Avenue and West 263rd Street, Bronx 10471, 718-405-3267

Community Resources: Wave Hill, West 249th Street and Independence Avenue, Bronx 10471, 718-549-2055; Riverdale YM-YWHA, 5625 Arlington Avenue, Bronx 10471, 718-548-8200

Transportation—Subway: #1/#9 at 242nd and 238th streets (in Kingsbridge)

Transportation—Bus: commuters in Fieldston and Riverdale tend to use Liberty Line, 718-652-8400, express buses to mid-Manhattan and Wall Street, 45 minutes, $3 one way. Get a Bronx bus map for local MTA routes.

Transportation—Train: Metro-North Hudson line (212-532-4900), station at West 254th Street by the Hudson River, 25 minutes from Grand Central, $4.75 one way

SPUYTEN DUYVIL

Boundaries and Contiguous Areas: North: 239th Street and 242nd Street and Riverdale; **East**: Waldo and Johnson Avenues and Kingsbridge; **South**: Harlem River and Washington Heights-Inwood; **West**: Hudson River

Henry Hudson gazes off at his river from atop a 100-foot Doric column in Henry Hudson Memorial Park. Spuyten Duyvil (pronounced SPY ten DIE vul) has a southward pitch, so it seems to look back at Manhattan, but if you live here you're sure to look west to the spectacular sunsets, which blaze and bleed over the river.

There's little to distinguish Spuyten Duyvil from Riverdale, which abuts it to the north. Both are bisected by the Henry Hudson Parkway, and they share a rocky perch high over the Hudson River. But little Spuyten Duyvil, which has its own zip code and post office, feels like a village, despite being sliced and dotted with co-ops and condos. Perhaps it's charming little Edgehill Church, a country church, or the 19th century wood frame houses on a winding street below in the shadow of the Henry Hudson Bridge. The narrow streets are all jammed and tangled down here, wiggling around Spuyten Duyvil Shorefront Park, where strollers meander a gravel path that wanders down to the railroad station. Back up the hill joggers run along scenic Palisade Avenue above Riverdale Park and the Metro-North tracks.

Housing here is mostly in apartments, though there are houses occasionally on the market, especially east of the parkway. Both rentals and co-ops are considerably below Manhattan price levels, with the most expensive being those west of the highway with river views. Shopping is available along Johnson Avenue, east of the parkway, from 235th to 236th streets, and along Riverdale Avenue between 235th and 238th streets. There's also a shopping area conveniently located around the 231st Street subway stop. In any of these places you can pick up a copy of the *Riverdale Review* to get a sense of the community, or write for a copy (see above under **Riverdale**).

Any reason not to live here? Your friends can't pronounce it.

Web Sites: www.nypl.org/branch/bronx; official New York City site, www.nyc.gov

Area Codes: 718, 347

Post Office: Spuyten Duyvil Station, 562 Kapock Street, Bronx 10463, 718-601-1300

Zip Code: 10463

Police Precinct: Fiftieth, 3450 Kingsbridge Avenue, Bronx 10463, 718-543-5700

Emergency Hospital (nearest): Montefieore, 210th Street and Bainbridge Avenue, Bronx 10467, 718-920-4321

Library (nearest): Riverdale Public Library, 5540 Mosholu Avenue, Bronx 10471, 718-549-1212

Public School Education: School District #10: Community School Board, 1 Fordham Plaza, Bronx 10458, 718-584-7070

Adult Education: see **Riverdale**.

Community Resources: see **Riverdale**.

Transportation—Subway: #l/#9 at 238th, 231st and 225th streets (all in Kingsbridge)

Transportation—Bus: commuters tend to use Liberty Line, 718-652-8400, express buses to mid-Manhattan and Wall Street, $3 one way. Get a Bronx bus map for local MTA routes.

Transportation—Train: Metro-North Hudson Line, 212-532-4900, $4.75 one-way

You might also want to consider...

- **City Island**; it's not Nantucket, this unselfconscious island dangling off Pelham Bay Park, but boat fanciers and aquaphiles appreciate the thump of boats against pilings, the salty air, technicolor sunsets, and scruffy charm of this watery small town. It's fairly cheap though not altogether convenient living here, you can park your sailboat out back, and there's a decent French restaurant. (On the internet go to www.cityisland.com)
- **Pelham Parkway**; straddling the leafy parkway which stretches between Bronx Park and Pelham Bay Park in the central Bronx, this affordable neighborhood houses an ethnically and economically diverse populace in Art Deco and Tudor Style apartment buildings and detached houses along shady side streets convenient to the subway. "If you can't afford Riverdale, then you buy here," says one realtor. Community Board 11, 718-892-6282

BROOKLYN

"For safety and real rental value, Brooklyn beats Manhattan hands down." The chauvinistic local real estate broker might have added a qualifying "certain neighborhoods" in Brooklyn. But it is true that by crossing the East River to Long Island's westernmost purchase you can pay less for housing than you might in Manhattan. Even rents in staid, lovely old Brooklyn Heights are a bit cheaper than equally prestigious Manhattan locations. It follows that relative bargains can be found in the four and five-story row

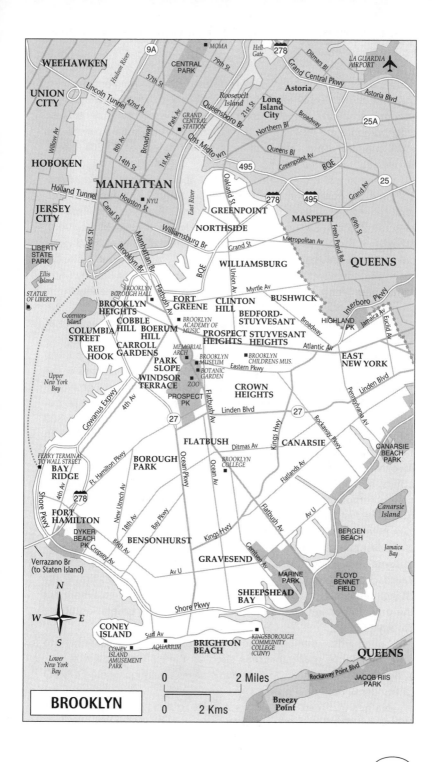

BROOKLYN

houses, more often than not lovingly restored by a Brooklyn brownstoner, that line the streets in less securely established communities such as Boerum Hill or Fort Greene/Clinton Hill. Among the salient features of these neighborhoods are the brick, clapboard and, yes, brownstone row houses representing a virtual catalog of architectural styles from 1820s Federal through 1910s late Victorian.

Other pluses? Brooklyn boosters boast about excellent subway transportation, the quality of the public schools in District 15, and the lively cultural climate engendered by the culture scene's Big Three: the Brooklyn Museum, Brooklyn Botanic Garden, and Brooklyn Academy of Music (BAM). Brooklyn, it is said, is a state of mind. To explore that state of mind visit a quirky, literate grab bag of a web site called *1010 President Street: A Brooklyn Home Page* at www.brooklyn.net, which has links to other Brooklyn sites worth meandering. For more about the history of the area check with the Brooklyn Historical Society, online at www.brooklynhistory.org.

The city's most populous borough is experiencing a renaissance of sorts, a transformation surely. Immigration, most recently from the countries of the former Soviet Union and from Asia have added to the population, especially in Sunset Park and in some of the further reaches of the borough. This and a buoyant economy are feeding commercial growth in Brooklyn. The year 1987 marked the beginning of the long-overdue revitalization of downtown Brooklyn. First, 1 Pierrepont Plaza opened, with 800 computer and back-office workers from Morgan Stanley. Metrotech, with 11 buildings the largest of several new mixed-use projects, headquarters Brooklyn Union Gas and some 6,000 Chase Manhattan workers, among others, in handsome quarters. Just across Jay Street, Renaissance Plaza houses corporate offices in a 32-story tower including a luxury Marriott Hotel, the first new hotel in Brooklyn in 50 years. A suburban-type mall with megastores along Flatbush Avenue at Atlantic marks the completion of the first phase of the Atlantic Center, with housing and office buildings to come. Rebuilding of the combination subway station and Long Island Railroad station there, long overdue, is underway. Besides drastically changing the face of downtown Brooklyn, these developments represent the most important change in Brooklyn since the completion of the Brooklyn Bridge.

Young artists, musicians, and writers from Manhattan come here to find affordable space in areas such as Park Slope, Fort Greene, Williamsburg, and, lately, in Brooklyn's newest neighborhood, DUMBO (see under **Brooklyn Heights**).

Names of Brooklyn realtors can be found under **Apartment Hunting** in **Finding a Place to Live**.

BROOKLYN HEIGHTS

Boundaries and Contiguous Areas: **North**: Fulton Ferry Landing and Cadman Plaza West; **East**: Cadman Plaza and Court Street; **South**: Atlantic Avenue and Cobble Hill; **West**: The Esplanade overlooking the East River and Brooklyn-Queens Expressway (BQE)

A *New York Times* article described two young lawyers walking home along Henry Street in the Heights one summer evening discussing cooperative apartments they had just bought. Not only did they estimate the purchase prices to be about 20% lower than comparable real estate in Manhattan, but they believed the location couldn't be topped professionally. And as generalizations go, that is a fair one. A large percentage of Heights residents have arrived, are established, and will continue to lead the good life in carefully restored 19th and early 20th century townhouses built by earlier generations of successful Manhattan professionals.

Robert Fulton's steamboat ferry service, inaugurated in 1814, spurred the development of the rural Brooklyn settlement. Newly accessible to lower Manhattan, and cooled by East River breezes, the Heights attracted merchants and lawyers, who built the substantial homes and noteworthy churches which characterize the community today. Brooklyn Heights boasts 684 pre-Civil War era houses alone, and more than a dozen mostly-Gothic Revival churches.

The opening of the Brooklyn Bridge in 1883 brought the Heights that much closer to Wall Street and provided its most spectacular landmark, the gossamer span flung from Gothic tower to Gothic tower over the busy East River. Wealth crossed the bridge to Brooklyn Heights and created one of the richest communities in the nation by the turn of the century. But the Depression wiped out many residents, the bankers and businessmen who worked on Wall Street, and blight came to the Heights.

In the 1950s and early 1960s, Brooklyn's first "brownstoners," attracted by the innate quality of the rundown housing stock, discovered Brooklyn Heights. These pioneers began a wave of renovation that, in the ensuing decades, has swept over row upon row of dilapidated Brooklyn townhouses. Today, the Heights' relatively cohesive population resides in stolid prewar apartment buildings and lovingly restored brownstones, as well as in striking warehouse conversions down at Fulton Ferry Landing. Besides the obvious, a five-minute subway zip to Manhattan; other commuting modes include the feet. Hearty residents stride briskly along the soaring raised center walkway of the Brooklyn Bridge to their jobs in Lower Manhattan.

From the start, accessibility to Wall Street attracted residents to the Heights, and the exceptional view of Manhattan and the harbor kept them there. The magnificent panorama brings a steady stream of day-trippers, who come to absorb the view while strolling the wide and gracious Esplanade and to enjoy the quiet, landmarked district with its informal restaurants and pleasant shops.

From the north end of the Esplanade continue down the hill past the pristine Watchtower complex to the foot of the hill and the great stone base of the Brooklyn Bridge. There beneath the bridge and beyond, along the water to the underbelly of the Manhattan Bridge, you are in Brooklyn's newest neighborhood, **DUMBO**, for **D**own **U**nder **M**anhattan **B**ridge **O**verpass. Some prefer to call it "Down Under," but the first moniker seems to have stuck as evidenced by the DUMBO Neighborhood Association now in existence. Artists, ever in search of affordable space, started moving into this somewhat spooky industrial area in the 1970s, despite the lack of services or other people. It's not exactly SoHo, and many of the pioneers there hope it won't ever be, but the Two Trees development company hopes to create a mixed use community, residential, retail, industrial and recreational, here beginning with high-end condos in the converted Clock Building, and following up with rental lofts and apartments in three consolidated buildings. Make no mistake about it, this is an area in transition. A historic district designation protects some of it, and from all of it the view of a sweeping East River beneath the soaring bridges with lower Manhattan beyond, is simply astounding.

Development of a proposed—and hotly contested—70-acre waterfront park with restaurants, a hotel and convention center, an amphitheater and recreation center along the East River from Atlantic Avenue north to Jay Street, should it come to pass, will have a powerful effect on the neighborhood.

Web Sites: www.brooklynheights-ny.com; www.southbrooklyn.net; www.brooklyn.org; official New York City site, www.nyc.gov

Area Codes: 718, 347

Post Offices: General Post Office, 271 Cadman Plaza East, Brooklyn 11201, 718-348-3000; Municipal Building Station, Municipal Building, 210 Joralemon Street, Brooklyn 11201, 718-596-7263

Zip Code: 11201

Police Precinct: Eighty-fourth, 301 Gold Street between Tillary and Johnson Streets, Brooklyn 11201, 718-875-6811

Emergency Hospital (nearest): Long Island College Hospital, 340 Henry Street at Amity Street, Brooklyn 11201, 718-780-1000

Libraries: The Business Library, 718-623-7000, and Brooklyn Heights Branch of the Brooklyn Public Library, 718-230-2100, share the same address: 280 Cadman Plaza West, Brooklyn 11201. The Brooklyn Historical Society's private library, 128 Pierrepont Street, Brooklyn

11201, 718-254-9830, houses excellent historical and genealogical collections open to the public for a nominal fee.

Public School Education: School District #13: Community School Board, 355 Park Place, Brooklyn 11238, 718-636-3204; and School District #15: Community School Board, 360 Smith Street, Brooklyn 11231, 718-330-9300

Adult Education: Long Island University, University Plaza, Brooklyn 11201, 718-488-1000; New York City Technical College, 300 Jay Street, Brooklyn 11201, 718-260-5000

Community Resources: Arts at St. Ann's, formerly housed in St. Ann's Church, now at 70 Washington Street, Brooklyn 11201, 718-834-8794, sponsors numerous concerts and other cultural events as well. Bargemusic, Ltd., Fulton Ferry Landing, Brooklyn 11201, 718-624-4061: chamber music concerts accompanied by gentle lapping from the East River. St. Francis College, 180 Remsen Street, Brooklyn 11201, 718-522-2300. The Brooklyn Arts & Culture Association, Inc. (BACA), 195 Cadman Plaza West, Brooklyn, 11201, 718-625-0080, coordinates and supports the efforts of a wide range of cultural programs within the borough; call to receive BACA's monthly *Calendar of Cultural Events*.

Transportation—Subway: #2, #3, Clark Street, Borough Hall; #4, #5, Borough Hall; A, C High Street/Brooklyn Bridge; N, M, R at Court Street

Transportation—Bus: stop by Brooklyn Transit Headquarters Information Center, 370 Jay Street, call 718-330-1234, or write the Metropolitan Transit Authority, 347 Madison Avenue, NYC 10017, for a bus map of Brooklyn.

COBBLE HILL

Boundaries and Contiguous Areas: **North**: Atlantic Avenue and Brooklyn Heights; **East**: Court Street and Boerum Hill; **South**: DeGraw Street and Carroll Gardens; **West**: Hicks Street

If it were possible to walk across the Mediterranean, a stroll starting at Atlantic Avenue down Court, Cobble Hill's main shopping street, to Carroll Gardens could be compared to a walk from Lebanon and the Middle East to Italy. Atlantic's famed Near and Middle Eastern spice and grocery stores and restaurants filter along Court south for a couple of blocks before meeting up with the pizzerias, Neapolitan bakeries, and shops selling Italian housewares, near the heavily Italian Carroll Gardens on Cobble Hill's southern boundary. This intriguing ethnic mix results in top-notch food sources that attract shoppers from all over Brooklyn.

The row upon row of brownstones—less expensive and not quite as grand as those in Brooklyn Heights—shaded by large, leafy trees (note particularly the sycamore trees that completely cover Clinton Street as it crosses Baltic, Veranda and Congress streets on the way to the Heights) attract a young professional crowd. Cobble Hill is probably the most homogeneous of all the Brooklyn brownstone communities, and award-winning Cobble Hill Park is a monument to neighborhood cohesiveness here. Apartment buildings and converted industrial properties have sprung up in Cobble Hill, notably The Henry Street Mews condos and One Tiffany Place, just west of the Brooklyn Queens Expressway. Other conversions include Cobble Hill Towers, the city's first low-income housing project when it was built in 1878, and the P.S. 78 condominiums, lodged in a late-19th century public school on Pacific Street.

It is no longer necessary to leave the neighborhood to find a good movie, a dress or a bistro meal. The Cobble Hill Cinema boasts five screens. And along Smith Street, where it moves down into Carroll Gardens, chic boutiques and restaurants cater to a young and prosperous clientele from the neighborhood and beyond.

Web Sites: www.southbrooklyn.net; www.brooklyncb6.org; www.brooklyn.org; official New York City site, www.nyc.gov

Area Codes: 718, 347

Post Office (nearest): Municipal Building Station, Municipal Building, 210 Joralemon Street, Brooklyn 11201, 718-596-7263

Zip Codes: 11201, 11231

Police Precinct: Seventy-sixth, 191 Union Street between Hicks and Henry Streets, Brooklyn 11231, 718-851-5611

Emergency Hospital: Long Island College Hospital, 339 Hicks Street, Brooklyn 11201, 718-780-1000

Library (nearest): Carroll Gardens Branch of the Brooklyn Public Library, 396 Clinton Street at Union Street, Brooklyn 11231, 718-237-7996

Public School Education: School District #15: Community School Board, 360 Smith Street, Brooklyn 11231, 718-330-9300

Adult Education: see **Brooklyn Heights** and **Boerum Hill**.

Community Resources: see **Brooklyn Heights** and **Boerum Hill**.

Transportation—Subway: #2, #3, #4, #5, Borough Hall; F, G, Bergen Street

Transportation—Bus: stop by the Brooklyn Transit Headquarters Information Center, 370 Jay Street, call 718-330-1234, or write Metropolitan Transit Authority, 347 Madison Avenue, NYC 10017, for a bus map of Brooklyn.

CARROLL GARDENS

Boundaries and Contiguous Areas: North: DeGraw Street and Cobble Hill; **East**: Gowanus Canal; **South**: Hamilton Avenue; **West**: Brooklyn-Queens Expressway

In Carroll Gardens singularly deep and lushly planted gardens front the four- and five-story row houses so characteristic of Brooklyn's brownstone neighborhoods. These splendid yards, with trees as tall as the high-stooped townhouses, form part of an eleven-block tract laid out in the 1850s. Verdant block fronts are, however, only part of the reason urban home-steaders began moving to Carroll Gardens in the 1970s. This predominant-ly Italian community has a lower crime rate than many other areas in Brooklyn. And furthermore, just like Cobble Hill, another "tight" neighbor-hood to the north, Carroll Gardens boasts better-than-average public ele-mentary and secondary schools.

Other pluses? Great food shopping. Shiny eggplants, peppers, and porcini—a veritable caponata—heap the Italian vegetable stands lining Court Street, where bulbous *pecorino* cheeses intersperse salamis and whole prosciuttos hanging from grocery store ceilings. Subway transporta-tion to Manhattan by F Train is fast and direct.

Less expensive, and less gentrified than the Heights and Cobble Hill, Carroll Gardens has long had limited housing stock. But apartment conver-sions from industrial buildings on the southern edge of Carroll Gardens have accelerated recently. On the eastern edge, an area in revival, the for-mer St. Agnes School has become the School House in Carroll Gardens, a 90-unit middle-income rental on DeGraw Street. The occasional low-rise condo appears.

Walk along Court and you'll still hear Italian spoken. The old men still play boccie in sweet little Carroll Park, where handsome brownstones along the north and graceful old trees make it feel like Washington Square. Heading north along Smith Street you can buy designer clothes in chic boutiques, eat Vietnamese, bistro French, or nouveau Italian in smart eater-ies. Use a real estate agent to find an apartment here, if after a stroll of the park-like streets you find the area appealing.

Another area to consider is the more affordable **Columbia Street Waterfront District**, adjacent to but separated from Carroll Gardens and Cobble Hill by the Gowanus Expressway. Its modest brick row houses were once the homes of the Irish, Italian, and Puerto Rican longshoremen who worked the thriving docks here, but the neighborhood declined when the expressway cut it off from its loftier neighbors. Revival began in the 1980s with the construction of the Columbia Terrace condominiums and the conversion of a former Tiffany lamp factory into condos on cob-blestoned Tiffany Place. There are no subway stations, schools, banks or supermarkets here, but from its quiet streets where on-street parking is easy the view across Buttermilk Channel to the Statue of Liberty and Lower Manhattan is stunning.

Web Sites: www.southbrooklyn.net; www.brooklyncb6.org; www.brook-lyn.org; official New York City site, www.nyc.gov
Area Codes: 718, 347
Post Office: Red Hook Station, 615 Clinton Street, Brooklyn 11231, 718-624-5632
Zip Codes: 11231
Police Precinct: Seventy-sixth, 191 Union Street, Brooklyn 11231, 718-851-5611
Emergency Hospital (nearest): Long Island College Hospital, 339 Hicks Street, Brooklyn 11201, 718-780-1000
Library: Carroll Gardens Branch of the Brooklyn Public Library, 396 Clinton Street at Union Street, Brooklyn 11231, 718-237-7996
Public School Education: School District #15: Community School Board, 360 Smith Street, Brooklyn 11231, 718-330-9300
Adult Education: see **Brooklyn Heights** and **Boerum Hill**.
Community Resources: see **Brooklyn Heights** and **Boerum Hill**.
Transportation—Subway: F, Carroll Street, Smith Street; G, Carroll Street, Smith Street
Transportation—Bus: stop by the Brooklyn Transit Headquarters Information Center, 370 Jay Street, call 718-330-1234, or write Metropolitan Transit Authority, 347 Madison Avenue, NYC 10017, for a bus map of Brooklyn.

BOERUM HILL

Boundaries and Contiguous Areas: North: Schermerhorn Street; **East**: Third Avenue; **South**: Wyckoff Street; **West**: Court Street and Cobble Hill

East and slightly downhill from sedate Cobble Hill and just south of bustling downtown Brooklyn, Boerum Hill seems lighter and more spacious along its blocks of three- and four-story brick and brownstone homes. Stately sycamores shade quiet streets such as Bergen, where children play untend-ed on sidewalks that line the flowering yards fronting set-back row houses. Ethnically more heterogeneous than its neighbors to the west, it is a com-munity of families, who shop along commercial Smith and Court streets.

The Boerum Hill Historic District, bounded roughly by Hoyt and

Nevins, Pacific and Wyckoff streets, contains an outstanding assemblage of pre-Civil War Italianate and Greek Revival row houses which constituted a fashionable district in the mid-19th century. Sidney Lanier lived here briefly, and literary visitors to the area included Washington Irving and James Fenimore Cooper. The neighborhood declined in later years, and today it is a monument to the efforts of new homeowners who in the early 1960s fought off a city effort to tear down the then-dispirited rooming houses to make way for urban renewal. Boerum Hill's turnaround—from near-slum to tight residential community—was achieved by a dedicated band of pioneers sophisticated enough to see the area's potential.

It was the construction of the Gowanus Canal beginning in 1845 that prompted the development of what is now Cobble Hill and Boerum Hill by draining the swamps south of Warren Street. In fact, that same canal might be said to have led to the brownstoning of all Brooklyn, since it made possible the shipping of New Jersey-quarried brownstone by barge into South Brooklyn.

Rentals in the handsome townhouses here are relatively affordable, when you can find one. Houses sell for about half of what comparable houses in Brooklyn Heights command. Co-ops and condos here are also a good buy.

Slicing across Boerum Hill from the waterfront, noisy Atlantic Avenue is somewhat blighted by the presence of the grim Brooklyn House of Detention and its surroundings, but from Hoyt Street eastward its concentration of inviting antique and Victorian bric-a-brac shops attracts shoppers from all over the city, while a few urbane eateries tend to other needs.

Web Sites: www.southbrooklyn.net; www.brooklyn.org; official New York City site, www.nyc.gov

Area Codes: 718, 347

Post Office: Times Plaza Station, 542 Atlantic Avenue, Brooklyn 11217, 718-875-7882

Zip Code: 11217

Police Precincts: Seventy-sixth, 191 Union Street between Hicks and Henry streets, Brooklyn 11231, 718-851-5611; Seventy-eighth, 65 Sixth Avenue between 6th and Bergen streets, Brooklyn 11217, 718-636-6411

Emergency Hospital: Long Island College Hospital, 339 Hicks Street, Brooklyn 11201, 718-780-1000

Library: Pacific Branch, 25 Fourth Avenue, Brooklyn 11217, 718-596-1531

Public School Education: School District #15: Community School Board, 360 Smith Street, Brooklyn 11231, 718-330-9300

Adult Education: Brooklyn YWCA, 30 Third Avenue, Brooklyn 11217, 718-875-1190, offers a health program plus a variety of adult classes.

Community Resources: New York Transit Museum (located in a former subway station), Boerum Place and Schermerhorn Street, Brooklyn, 718-243-8601.

Transportation—Subway: #2, #3, Hoyt Street, Nevins Street; #4, #5 Nevins Street; F, Bergen Street; G, Bergen Street, Hoyt/Schermerhorn streets; A, C, Hoyt/Schermerhorn streets

Transportation—Bus: stop by Brooklyn Transit Headquarters Information Center, 370 Jay Street, call 718-330-1234, or write Metropolitan Transit Authority, 347 Madison Avenue, NYC 10017, for a bus map of Brooklyn.

PARK SLOPE

Boundaries and Contiguous Areas: **North**: Flatbush Avenue; **East**: Prospect Park West; **South**: Windsor Place; **West**: Fifth Avenue

If Cobble Hill is the most homogeneous of Brooklyn's brownstone neighborhoods, Park Slope is the most heterogeneous, and proud of it. (It is also by far the largest of these communities.) The fact that the population is still economically, ethnically, and racially mixed appears, for a majority of residents, to be the neighborhood's most attractive attribute. Second place is probably a tie between the 526-acre Prospect Park, designed by Central Park' architects Frederick Law Olmsted and Calvert Vaux, and Park Slope's proximity to three of Brooklyn's cultural bastions: the Brooklyn Museum, the Central Library at Grand Army Plaza, and the Brooklyn Botanic Garden. A recent addition to Prospect Park is the re-opened Wildlife Conservation Center, a state-of-the-art children's zoo with a restored 1912 carousel (50¢ rides).

Park Slope's development paralleled that of Prospect Park in the 1880s. Sites with a park view were most highly prized, and small Victorian mansions line Prospect Park West. Closeness to the park and Grand Army Plaza determined the quality and appointments also of the Victorian bow-fronted townhouses that march row upon stolid row down the west-sloping streets. North Slope, nearest Prospect Park West and the Plaza, is considered the classiest part of the neighborhood. South Slope, below 9th Street, is the less expensive, still-developing section. Old industrial properties, such as the Ansonia Clock factory complex on 12th Street, once the country's largest clock works and now deluxe condominiums, have been converted to apartments and co-ops. Seventh Avenue, the principal shopping street and scene of a hugely successful fair each spring, reflects neighborhood needs: the boutiques, card shops, and unisex hair cutters once found exclusively at the North Slope end of Seventh have infiltrated blocks in South Slope as well. With the arrival of a Barnes & Noble the neighborhood is officially literate and upscale.

Without qualification Park Slope, together with Brooklyn Heights, has arrived as a suitable address for middle-class professionals, especially those with—or about to be with—families. P.S. 321, District 15's progressive, well-regarded elementary school, has served as an additional attraction to young families. But don't go looking for bargain basements; in real estate parlance, the neighborhood is "hot" (and has been for a while), especially along the park. Prices are lower down the slope and in adjoining **Windsor Terrace** and **Prospect Heights**, two revitalizing communities nicely situated near Prospect Park. (For more on these see below.) Down the slope west of Fifth Avenue around the Gowanus Canal artists and crafters have established homes and studios in a neighborhood known now simply as **Gowanus**. Cleaned up, if not yet pristine, the canal twists through a somewhat gritty area, which may yet become the Venice of Brooklyn. As you search, pick up a copy of the *Park Slope Courier*, 718-769-4400, to get a feel for the neighborhood.

Web Sites: www.southbrooklyn.net; www.brooklyncb6.org; www.brooklyn.org; official New York City site, www.nyc.gov

Area Codes: 718, 347

Post Office: Van Brunt Station, 275 9th Street, Brooklyn 11215, 718-768-6284

Zip Code: 11215, 11217

Police Precincts: Seventy-second, 830 Fourth Avenue between 29th and 30th streets, Brooklyn 11230, 718-965-6311; Seventy-eighth, 65 Sixth Avenue between 6th and Bergen streets, Brooklyn 11217, 718-636-6411

Emergency Hospital: Methodist Hospital, 506 6th Street between Seventh and Eighth avenues, Brooklyn 11215, 718-780-3000

Library: Brooklyn Central Library, Grand Army Plaza at Flatbush Avenue, Brooklyn 11238, 718-230-2100

Public School Education: School District #13: Community School Board, 355 Park Place, Brooklyn 11238, 718-636-3204; and School District #15: Community School Board, 360 Smith Street, Brooklyn 11231, 718-330-9300

Adult Education: Brooklyn Museum Art School, 200 Eastern Parkway, Brooklyn 11238, 718-638-5000; Brooklyn Botanic Garden, 1000 Washington Avenue, Brooklyn 11225, 718-623-7200, holds classes for plant enthusiasts. Brooklyn Conservatory of Music, 58 Seventh Avenue, Brooklyn 11217, 718-622-3300; St. John-St. Matthew Emmanuel Lutheran Church Community Center, 415 Seventh Street, between Sixth and Seventh avenues, Brooklyn 11215, 718-768-0528, allocates space to community educational and cultural groups.

Community Resources: Brooklyn Museum, 200 Eastern Parkway at Washington Avenue, Brooklyn 11238, 718-638-5000; behind the six Ionic columns of McKim, Mead and White's famed building are housed a number of exemplary collections as well as facilities for the cultural and educational programs sponsored daily by the museum; Brooklyn Arts Exchange, 420 Fifth Avenue at Eighth Street, 718-882-0018.

Transportation—Subway: with the exception of the A and C trains, subways stop near one part of Park Slope or the other. #2, #3, #4, #5 trains stop at Grand Army Plaza; F stops at Fourth Avenue, Seventh Avenue and 15th Street; D stops at Seventh Avenue and Atlantic Avenue; B, M, N, R stop along Fourth Avenue at Pacific Street, Union Street, 9th Street and Prospect Avenue.

Transportation—Bus: the Information Center at Brooklyn Transit Headquarters, 370 Jay Street, is the place to get a bus map of Brooklyn. Or call 718-330-1234 or write Metropolitan Transit Authority, 347 Madison Avenue, NYC 10017 to get a map.

FORT GREENE/CLINTON HILL

Boundaries and Contiguous Areas: **North**: Myrtle Avenue; **East**: Classon Avenue; **South**: Atlantic Avenue; **West**: Flatbush Avenue and Boerum Hill

"…Brooklyn's other fine residential district, the Hill…. abounded in churches and middle class houses, the majority of whose owners worked in New York." So wrote a Brooklyn historian of late 19th century Fort Greene and Clinton Hill. Despite a decline in the intervening years, that description is valid once again, except for the fringe areas to the north and east. What occasioned the turnabout? Historic designation and the brownstone revival, mainly.

Revival came late, in the 1970s, to **Fort Greene**. Even the once-elegant brownstones on the choice streets nearest Fort Greene Park had become dilapidated wino rows. But beneath the grime and neglect the original detailing remained, awaiting the attention of determined urban pioneers. Now, perfectly restored Anglo-Italianate brownstones line Washington Park, South Oxford Street, and South Portland Avenue. And sweeping 33-acre Fort Greene Park, the community's centerpiece designed by Olmsted and Vaux, has been restored to its rather English graciousness.

Homeowners are as likely to be black or Hispanic as they are white, as likely to be filmmakers or musicians as investment bankers. Fort Greene is integrated, both racially and socio-economically, and determined to stay that way. The throbbing cultural presence of the Brooklyn Academy of Music (BAM) helped stimulate the growth of a substantial community of black artists in Fort Greene. Plans to establish a cultural district in the area around BAM were advanced in 2001, when two major dance troops moved nearby, and this cultural enclave can be expected to expand substantially.

Clinton Hill, like Fort Greene, which it borders and from which it is barely distinguishable, contains an astonishing treasury of late 19th century urban architecture. The key word in this neighborhood is Pratt. Kerosene magnate Charles Pratt who built several handsome mansions on Clinton Avenue, including the present residence of the Bishop of Brooklyn. Charles Pratt also founded, built and, until his death in 1891, ran Pratt Institute, the focal point and cultural center of the community. And now it is the students, grads, and faculty of Pratt (art, design, architecture, engineering, computers and library sciences) who fill the streets and much of the local housing.

Clinton Hill has a few high rises and therefore a somewhat wider variety of housing than Fort Greene. But Clinton Hill has only one subway line, the sporadic G train, which requires a transfer to reach Manhattan. Many find the five-minute bus ride to downtown Brooklyn with a free transfer to a variety of trains more convenient. Fort Greene, on the other hand, is well tended by the subway system (see below). Both neighborhoods offer easy on-street parking.

Both the Metrotech commercial development to the west on Flatbush Avenue and the Atlantic Center mixed-use development nearly complete on the southeast edge of Fort Greene, have boosted the value and the cost of housing on the hill. Apartment hunting here is best done through a knowledgeable real estate agent.

Web Sites: www.brooklyn.org; official New York City site, www.nyc.gov

Area Codes: 718, 347

Post Offices: Pratt Station, 524 Myrtle Avenue, Brooklyn 11205, 718-622-8581; General Post Office, 271 Cadman Plaza East, Brooklyn 11201, 718-834-3000; Times Plaza Station, 542 Atlantic Avenue, Brooklyn 11217, 718-875-7882

Zip Codes: 11201, 11205, 11217, 11238

Police Precinct: Eighty-eighth, 298 Classon Avenue, Brooklyn 11205, 718-636-6511

Emergency Hospital: Brooklyn Hospital, 121 DeKalb Avenue, Brooklyn 11201, 718-250-8000

Libraries: Brooklyn Public Library, Clinton Hill Branch, 380 Washington Avenue, Brooklyn 11238, 718-398-8713; Walt Whitman Branch, 93 St. Edwards Street, Brooklyn 11205, 718-855-1508

Public School Education: School District #13, Community School Board, 355 Park Place, Brooklyn 11238, 718-636-3204

Adult Education: Pratt Institute, Continuing Education, 200 Willoughby Avenue, Brooklyn 11205, 718-636-3453; Medgar Evers Community College, 1150 Carroll Street, Brooklyn 11225, 718-270-4900; St.

Joseph's College, 265 Clinton Avenue, Brooklyn 11205, 718-399-0068

Community Resources: Brooklyn Academy of Music (BAM), 30 Lafayette Avenue, Brooklyn 11217, 718-636-4100; the borough's premier cultural resource, BAM contains four theaters of differing sizes presenting a spectrum of performances by artists from all disciplines and hosting the annual Next Wave Festival. Nearby: Long Island University, University Plaza, Flatbush at DeKalb avenues, Brooklyn 11210, 718-650-8114; and the Brooklyn Children's Museum, splendidly renovated, at 245 Brooklyn Avenue (Crown Heights), Brooklyn 11213, 718-735-4400.

Transportation—Subway: A, C, Lafayette Avenue; B, D at DeKalb Avenue; M, N, Q, R, DeKalb Avenue; #2, #3, #4, #5 at Nevins Street; G at Fulton Street, Clinton/Washington avenues

Transportation—Bus: the Information Center at Brooklyn Transit Headquarters, 370 Jay Street, is the place to get a bus map of Brooklyn. Or call 718-330-1234 or write Metropolitan Transit Authority, 347 Madison Avenue, NYC 10017 for a map.

GREENPOINT/NORTHSIDE, WILLIAMSBURG

Boundaries and Contiguous Areas: North: Newtown Creek and Queens; **East**: Newtown Creek and the Brooklyn-Queens Expressway (BQE); **South**: Grand Street; **West**: the East River

This northernmost portion of Brooklyn, protruding into the underbelly of Queens and just 20 minutes by subway from Manhattan, is one of Brooklyn's best-kept secrets, and that's just fine with **Greenpoint**. Or Greenpernt, as they pronounced it in the gangster movies of the 1930s. Just across the East River from 23rd Street in Manhattan, it might as well be another country. Modest two-, three-, and four-story houses, colorfully sided and impeccably tidy, line quiet streets. The feel is 1940-something small town. Housewives chat on front steps, and they are as likely to be speaking Polish as English.

Along Manhattan Avenue, Greenpoint's Main Street, *kielbasi* drape the butcher shops, restaurants offer *pierogi* and *golumpki,* and the travel agencies advertise Lot Airline flights to Poland. Italian restaurants, bodegas along Franklin Street, and the occasional shamrock define the ethnic composition of this largely blue-collar community. In the Historic District just west of Manhattan Avenue, Java and India streets with their handsome brownstones and churches recall the coffee and spice trade that once flourished along the docks here. And in the rather British-feeling Monsignor McGolrick Park a monument to the Civil War battleship Monitor, which was built here, memorializes Greenpoint's shipbuilding past as well.

Just to the south beyond McCarren Park and the stunning, copper-domed Russian Orthodox Cathedral of the Transfiguration lies **Northside, Williamsburg**, with nothing to mark the boundary between it and Greenpoint, so similar are the two communities. Numbered streets—declining from North 15th to Grand—cross Bedford Avenue, Northside's tidy, quiet Main Street. To the east traffic roars along the elevated Brooklyn-Queens Expressway. From the undeveloped waterfront area to the west comes the occasional scent of molasses from the Domino sugar plant and now and then of garbage from the processing concerns there. No sign now of the fashionable resorts which flourished here near the ferry landings until the Williamsburg Bridge and trolley service in 1905 brought immigrants streaming from the Lower East Side to make Williamsburg the most populous neighborhood in Brooklyn in 1920. But signs of change here are evident in the upscale cafes, the galleries, and an underground movie house with a candle-lit reflecting pool where a factory truck bay once stood. In fact, Williamsburg has had its own movie festival since 1998.

Young artists discovered the peace, quiet, and relatively low cost of living here, carving lofts out of former manufacturing space in Greenpoint in the 1980s and in Northside in the 1990s. Driven by rising rents in Manhattan, adventurous young professionals followed. There's talk of developing the waterfront, with its spectacular view of lower Manhattan. Meanwhile, you probably won't find a doorman in Greenpoint or Northside, nor a health club. Indoor pool, yes, but not in an upscale condo. After a $4.8 million restoration, the Metropolitan Pool and Bathhouse at Bedford and Metropolitan avenues is open again in all its rather Andalusian glory beneath a stunning copper-framed skylight. Accessible to the disabled, the pool and recreation center are operated by the Parks Department. A few blocks north, the 35 acres of McCarren Park includes ball-fields, tennis courts, a running track, and a fitness course.

Available housing, whether apartments or lofts in newly converted industrial space, is sparse. Though occasionally appearing among the rental listings in *The Village Voice*, available space is best found through local real estate agents. Expect few amenities and rents generally below the Manhattan rate for a small one- or two-bedroom. Allow six weeks to two months to find a suitable spot in this tight little community. Walk around to get a feel of the neighborhood, check the bulletin board outside the health food store on Bedford for a sublet or a share, pick up a copy of the weekly *Greenpoint Gazette*, 718-389-6067, for the apartment ads, and drop in on a real estate office.

Web Sites: www.brooklyn.org; official New York City site, www.nyc.gov
Area Codes: 718, 347
Post Office: Greenpoint Station, 66 Meserole Avenue, Brooklyn 11222,

718-389-5929; Williamsburg Station, 256 South 4th Street, Brooklyn 11211, 718-387-2459

Zip Code: 11222, 11211

Police Precinct: Ninety-fourth, 100 Meserole Avenue, Brooklyn 11222, 718-383-3879

Emergency Hospital (nearest): Woodhull Medical Center, 760 Broadway, Brooklyn 11206, 718-963-8000

Library: Brooklyn Public Library, Greenpoint Branch, 107 Norman Avenue, Brooklyn 11222, 718-349-8504

Public School Education: School District #14, 215 Heywood Street, Brooklyn 11206, 718-387-8698

Transportation—Subway: L, Bedford Avenue; G, Greenpoint Avenue, Nassau Avenue

Transportation—Bus: the Information Center at Brooklyn Transit Headquarters, 370 Jay Street, is the place to get a bus map of Brooklyn. Or call 718-330-1234 or write Metropolitan Transit Authority, 347 Madison Avenue, NYC 10017, for a map.

You might also want to consider...

- **Prospect Heights**, located uphill, but downscale in price, from Park Slope, Prospect Park, Brooklyn's major cultural institutions and accessible transportation. Its handsome brownstones, greystones and co-op apartments have attracted young, professional arrivals in recent years. Community Board 8, 718-467-5574.
- **Windsor Terrace**, a safe, old-fashioned community of small, detached houses, row houses and apartments nicely sandwiched between Prospect Park and beautiful, park-like Green-Wood Cemetery. Quiet, but for the birds. Call Community Board 7, 718-854-0003.
- **Stuyvesant Heights**, 12 landmarked blocks of exceptional brownstones along stately, tree-lined streets on the southern edge of Bedford-Stuyvesant houses a largely African-American professional community 25 subway minutes from Manhattan. Call Community Board 3, 718-622-6601
- **Flatbush**, fairly vast and varied, geographically and psychologically the heart of Brooklyn. Its most appealing neighborhoods are Prospect Park South and Ditmas Park, both of which feature lovely old Victorian homes along stately, tree-lined streets, and strong community spirit. Call Community Board 14, 718-859-6357
- **Bay Ridge**, way out by the Verazanno Bridge and overlooking the Narrows, studded with parks and restaurants. This conservative community with a Scandinavian and Italian heritage is peacefully 50 minutes by subway from Manhattan. Community Board 10, 718-745-6827

- **Fort Hamilton**, just beyond Bay Ridge around the base of the Verazanno Bridge, has more co-ops and condos among their one-family houses, with a similar perch on the Narrows and about an hour by subway to Manhattan. Community Board 10, 718-745-6827.
- **Red Hook** south of the Columbia Street Waterfront District on Upper New York Bay is still for pioneers. But a cluster of crafters—glassmakers, theatrical set builders, artists and artisans—have made homes and studios here, where rows of small houses intersperse the industrial landscape. Stunning views, a vast sky and water edged by historic stone warehouses are a draw. Community Board 8, 718-467-5574

QUEENS

"Queens is not New York!" exclaims a character in the film *Quiz Show*. Many Manhattanites would agree—but that is a Manhattan state of mind.

Among the five boroughs, Queens is the acknowledged bastion of New York's middle class. As skyscrapers identify Manhattan and brownstones Brooklyn, so solid brick buildings—free-standing, Tudor-inspired houses, semi-detached, two-, three-, and four-family dwellings, and six-story apartment blocks—define a good part of the largest borough in the city.

Until 1909 and the completion of the Queensborough Bridge, semi-rural Queens was a backwater connected only by ferry boat to Manhattan across the East River. But the bridge, followed almost immediately by train and then by subway service through new tunnels under the East River, opened the way for commuters and commerce. Great parcels of land were snapped up by developers, and 1908 saw the beginning of a building spree that continued, with few pauses, until World War II. While some communities are architecturally noteworthy—Forest Hills Gardens, a carefully designed 1909 enclave planned down to its English rustic street signs, and Malba, a charming melange of lawns, leafy lanes, and handsome, mostly 1920s homes nestled under the Whitestone Bridge—most of the housing is sturdy, unremarkable pre-World War II stock often laid out, suburban-style, in tracts.

Although many Queens neighborhoods are identified with various ethnic groups—Greeks gravitate to Astoria, Latin Americans to Jackson Heights, Russians to Rego Park, Asians to Flushing—a multi-national mix of businessmen, engineers, and other professionals continues to move into the area. Immediately across the river from Manhattan new life is being breathed into Long Island City, not only by artists attracted by P.S. 1, a highly successful alternative art, dance, and theater space, but also by the re-establishment of the enormous old Astoria movie studios, the new Silver Cup Studios, the Eaves-Brooks costume company and the gargantuan International Design Center, which contains more than 100 acres of show-

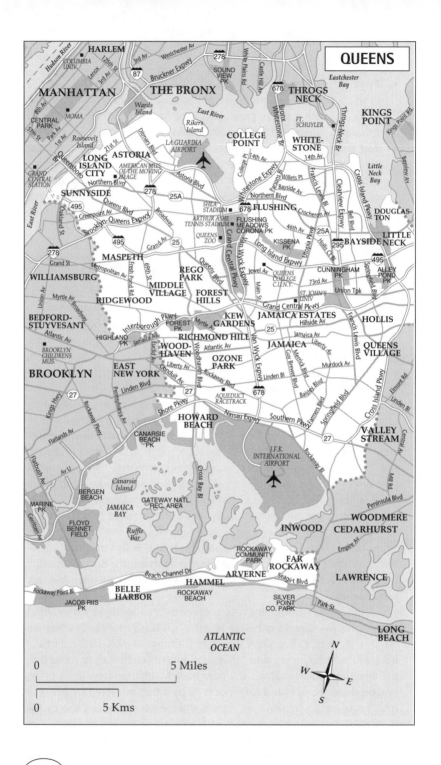

room space. Putting Long Island City ever more on the map was the marriage in 1999 between P.S. 1 and the prestigious Museum of Modern Art in Manhattan, making P.S. 1 not-so-alternative.

The 42-story, glass Citicorp spire, towering over these industrial surrounds like a giant among midgets, now dominates Long Island City. Just to the south in the Hunters Point section, the 42-story Citylights, with 522 co-op apartments, opened in 1997, the beginning of a long-planned residential/commercial development which will rise along the East River there. The Avalon Riverview tower opening alongside, in 2002, will contain another 372 rental units, with separate housing for the elderly on the same base. When completed, Queens West will comprise 6,385 tower and low-rise apartments, a hotel and office complex spread over a 74-acre waterfront site across from the United Nations and connected with it by passenger ferry.

New York magazine was perhaps premature in proclaiming Long Island City "The New Hot Neighborhood" a few years ago, at least as far as newcomers are concerned; although a number of artists are residents of this factory town, there is a paucity of houses and residential lofts. Astoria just to the north and Sunnyside to the southeast, both equally accessible to Manhattan, are moderately priced alternatives. Within subway reach, Rego Park, Forest Hills and Kew Gardens are popular established communities where one- and even two-bedroom apartments rent for about the same as a Manhattan studio. Further east, the new condominium units renting in big Bayside high rises seem to have appeal for those who don't find the trip by express bus or Long Island Railroad too daunting.

Names of Queens real estate brokers will be found in **Finding a Place to Live**. Local publications include the *Queens Chronicle*, 718-205-8000, www.queenschronicle.com, and the *Queens Courier*, 718-224-4400, www.queenscourier.com.

ASTORIA

Boundaries and Contiguous Areas: North: East River; **East**: Grand Central Parkway, Brooklyn-Queens Expressway and LaGuardia Airport; **South**: 35th Avenue and Sunnyside; **West**: East River

You don't have to be Greek (or Italian, Yugoslavian, or German either) to live in Astoria, but it can't hurt. And you needn't be Czech to lift a Pilsener over a plate of dumplings in the garden at Bohemian Hall here, the last beer garden in the city. A population that is nearly 60% Greek or Hispanic, gives this community a distinct old world feel. With and without belly dancers, the tavernas on Ditmars Boulevard and Broadway vibrate long and late to the keening of Greek dance music. The most recent wave of immigrants has brought an infusion of Irish, South Americans, Slavs, and Asians.

Urban professionals have discovered the apartments in the decently maintained but unprepossessing two-story houses and small apartment buildings bordering Astoria's relatively safe streets, in particular the area between Crescent and 35th streets, which is within walking distance of the N line and a 20-minute commute from Midtown. (A caveat: presumably Astorians have no problem with the improbably numbered streets, drives and avenues here; outsiders find them incomprehensible.)

The Olympic-sized city pool in spacious Astoria Park, just beneath the Triborough Bridge on the East River, is free, as is the un-crowded running space around the park. Condo living, with a free health club and unobstructed view of the Manhattan skyline, came to Astoria with the opening of the 405-unit Shore Towers in 1990 at the southern end of the park.

Astoria was the home of Paramount Studios from 1919 until the 1930s, when the business moved—lock, stock and W.C. Fields—to Hollywood. The movies are back, however, sharing with television the enormous, refurbished Kaufman Astoria Studios on 35th Avenue between 34th and 37th streets. The complex also houses the Museum of the Moving Image, the only museum in the country dedicated to movies, TV, and the interactive media. Several production facilities have sprouted nearby including Silvercup Studios, a maker of commercials and feature films. So it was hardly surprising when a new 14-screen cinema opened near the Kaufman Studios in 1999. The revitalization of southern Astoria's movie and television industry has suggested a new moniker for the area: Hollywood East.

Still, with the noteworthy exception of two extraordinary sculpture collections and the recent addition of a 750-seat public theater, colonnaded Athens Square in little Hellenic Park, cultural institutions and parks are in short supply in mainly blue-collar Astoria. Unlikely as it may seem, the prime showcase of Isamu Noguchi's sculpture—some 350 pieces by the famous artist—is located in the Noguchi Garden Museum on Vernon Boulevard at 33rd Road. And sculptor Mark Di Suvero organized the Socrates Sculpture Park, with a changing display of monumental abstract works in a vacant East River lot just across Vernon Boulevard. Could a branch of the Guggenheim Museum be next?

To get a further fix on life in Astoria and in greater **Long Island City**, go to www.licweb.com.

Web Sites: www.licweb.com; www.queens.nyc.ny.us; Queens Chamber of Commerce, www.queenschamber.org; official New York City site, www.nyc.gov

Area Codes: 718, 347

Post Offices: Astoria Station, 27-40 21st Street, Astoria 11102, 718-726-1005; Steinway Station, 43-04 Broadway, Astoria 11103, 718-726-1107; Woolsey Station, 22-68 31st Street, Astoria 11105, 718-274-5563; Broadway Station, 21-17 Broadway, Astoria 11106, 718-726-1007

Zip Codes: 11102, 11103, 11105, 11106

Police Precinct: One Hundred Fourteenth, 34-16 Astoria Boulevard at 35th Street, Astoria 11102, 718-626-9311

Emergency Hospital: Elmhurst Hospital Center, 79-01 Broadway, Elmhurst 11373, 718-334-4000

Library: Astoria Branch, Queens Public Library, 14-01 Astor Boulevard, Astoria 11102, 718-278-0601; Steinway Branch, 21-45 31st Street, Long Island City 11105, 718-728-1965

Public School Education: District #30, Community School Board, 49-05 20th Avenue, Jackson Heights, 11106, 718-777-4600

Community Resources: The Noguchi Garden Museum, 32-37 Vernon Boulevard, 718-204-7088; Socrates Sculpture Park, Broadway at Vernon Boulevard, 718-956-1819; Museum of the Moving Image, 36-01 35th Avenue, 718-784-4520; P.S. 1 Contemporary Art Center, 22-25 Jackson Avenue, Long Island City, 718-784-2084

Transportation—Subway: N, Queensboro Plaza, 39th Avenue, 36th Avenue, Broadway, 30th Avenue, Astoria Boulevard-Hoyt Avenue, Ditmars Boulevard; E, F, 23rd Street, Queens Plaza; G, R, Queens Plaza, 36th Street, Steinway Street and 46th Street; B, Q, 21st Street/Queens Bridge

Transportation—Bus: stop by the Queens Transit Headquarters Information Center, 124-15 28th Avenue, Flushing, for a bus map of Queens or call 718-330-1234 or write the Metropolitan Transit Authority, 347 Madison Avenue, NYC 10017, for a map.

SUNNYSIDE

Boundaries and Contiguous Areas: North: Barnett Avenue and the Sunnyside Conrail Yards; **East**: 52nd Street and New Calvary Cemetery; **South**: Long Island Expressway; **West**: 36th Street and Long Island City

This traditionally blue-collar community bounded by railroad yards, industrial tracts, cemeteries and the legendary LIE (the Long Island Expressway, known, among other sobriquets, as the world's longest parking lot) won't be the next "in" New York neighborhood. But the sensible, mostly-brick homes and apartments lining Sunnyside's residential streets, ten minutes by train from Manhattan, do attract young professionals, as well as immigrants from overseas, with more space for lower-than-Manhattan rents.

Newcomers are especially drawn to **Sunnyside Gardens**. "The Gardens," the first US development to be modeled on the English garden community, occupies 55 leafy acres north of bustling Queens Boulevard. Towering London plane trees shade the 650 one-, two- and three-family brick townhouses, which enclose long communal gardens. The effect is English village, with shrub-lined walks penetrating the landmarked blocks. "Like Greenwich Village and far more than Brooklyn Heights, it was a mixed community, in which one might mingle without undue intimacy with one's neighbors," recalls urban critic/historian Lewis Mumford, who lived in The Gardens from their inception in 1924 until 1936. They seem little changed.

There are private homes and rentals in greater Sunnyside as well, but most of the brick apartment blocks are non-rentable co-ops. The three main shopping thoroughfares are small-town Skillman Avenue at The Gardens' southern edge, Queens Boulevard in the shadow of the elevated IRT Flushing Line, and running diagonally southwest from the Boulevard, Greenpoint Avenue. There and on the side streets you can rent Korean movies, buy Irish imports, eat Italian, Middle European or Oriental, or lift a pint at Moriarty's Pub Restaurant. The city's longest established Spanish language theater, The Thalia on Greenpoint Avenue, plays to sellout crowds on weekends.

Thanks in large part to the efforts of the Sunnyside Foundation, whose staff works on planning and preservation issues, Sunnyside is an appealingly cohesive community, for all its ethnic diversity. Stop by the Foundation's office at 41-13 47th Street, 718-392-9139, for information, advice and a free copy of *The Sunnyside Herald* if you're thinking of moving here.

Web Sites: www.queens.nyc.ny.us; Sunnyside Chamber of Commerce, www.sunnysidechamber.org; official New York City site, www.nyc.gov

Area Codes: 718, 347

Post Office: Sunnyside Station, 45-15 44th Street, Sunnyside 11104, 718-729-1438

Zip Code: 11104

Police Precinct: One Hundred Eighth, 5-47 50th Avenue, Long Island City 11104, 718-784-5411

Emergency Hospital (nearest): Elmhurst Hospital Center, 79-01 Broadway, Elmhurst 11373, 718-334-4000

Library: Queens Public Library, Sunnyside Branch, 43-02 Greenpoint Avenue, Sunnyside 11104, 718-784-3033

Public School Education: School District #24, Community School Board, 43-31 39th Street, Sunnyside 11104, 718-417-2600

Transportation—Subway: #7 at 40th Street, 46th Street, 52nd Street

Transportation—Bus: stop by the Queens Transit Headquarters Information Center, 124-15 28th Avenue, Flushing, for a bus map of

Queens, or call 718-330-1234 or write the Metropolitan Transit Authority, 347 Madison Avenue, NYC 10017, for a map.

REGO PARK

Boundaries and Contiguous Areas: **North**: Queens Boulevard; **East**: Yellowstone Boulevard and Forest Hills; **Southwest**: Woodhaven Boulevard

What distinguishes Rego Park from neighboring Forest Hills and Kew Gardens, which it very much resembles, is the appreciably higher ratio of apartment buildings to private dwellings, slightly lower rents, somewhat older population and proportionately more recent immigrants. While the number of Indians, Pakistanis, and Asians has been increasing throughout the three communities, Rego Park has also attracted a sizable Russian population, a large Israeli group, and a nucleus of Iranians.

One of the borough's largest malls, the Queens Center housing Macy's, among others, with Stern's and Sears nearby, is quartered on the Rego Park stretch of Queens Boulevard. Smaller, more intimate shops line 63rd Drive.

It should be noted that the imposition of a rigid grid pattern was foiled in this part of Queens by circuitous streets laid out in "crescents" by the original developers. Wherever possible, each numbered thoroughfare has an Avenue, Road and Drive to its credit. For example, 63rd Avenue, 63rd Road, 63rd Drive in that order. The streets tend to be named, not numbered. Rego Park was first developed in 1923 and named for the company that built it: the Rego (for Real Good) Construction Company.

Web Sites: www.queens.nyc.ny.us; Queens Chamber of Commerce, www.queenschamber.org; official New York City site, www.nyc.gov

Area Codes: 718, 347

Post Office: Rego Park Station, 92-24 Queens Boulevard, Rego Park, NY 11374, 718-429-2696

Zip Code: 11374

Police Precinct: One Hundred and Twelfth, 68-40 Austin Street, Forest Hills, NY 11375, 718-520-9311

Emergency Hospital: St. John's Hospital, 90-02 Queens Boulevard, Elmhurst, NY 11373, 718-544-6464

Library: Queens Public Library, Rego Park Branch, 91-41 63rd Drive, Rego Park, NY 11374, 718-459-5140

Public School Education: Public School District #28 (see **Forest Hills**).

Adult Education: Queens College (see **Flushing**); St. John's University (see **Forest Hills**).

Transportation—Subway: R and G at Rego Park Station, 67th Avenue
Transportation—Bus: stop by the Queens Transit Headquarters
Information Center, 124-15 28th Avenue, Flushing, for a bus map of
Queens, or call 718-330-1234 or write the Metropolitan Transit
Authority, 347 Madison Avenue NYC 10017, for a map.

FOREST HILLS

Boundaries and Contiguous Areas: The neighborhood is shaped roughly
like a lower case "d." **North**: Long Island Expressway; **East**: Grand Central
Parkway and Corona Park; **South**: Union Turnpike and Kew Gardens; **West**:
Yellowstone Boulevard and Rego Park

Practical Queens Boulevard, a major shopping thoroughfare that sensibly
separates curbside businesses from through traffic with narrow cement
dividers, belies the charm of Forest Hills as it cuts through the heart of the
neighborhood. Bordering Corona Park northwest of the boulevard, the
"Cord Meyer" district consists of gracious, white-trimmed brick homes
begun in 1904 and large apartment buildings constructed later by the
Cord Meyer Development Co., which is still the largest landlord in the area.
South a block just off Austin, considered one of the most enticing shopping
streets in Queens, lies "The Gardens." Forest Hills Gardens, designed in the
eclectic tradition by an architect of the Beaux-Arts school and sponsored by
the Russell Sage Foundation, has few peers in the half-timbered world of
Victorian Tudor. Brick-fronted Cotswoldian houses face curving drives and
landscaped plots originally planned by Frederick Law Olmsted, Jr. Instantly
successful, the development spawned housing decorated with Tudor
clichés throughout central Queens.

Until 1977, when the US Open Tennis Championships moved to
Flushing, Forest Hills was the self-described "lawn tennis capital of the
Western Hemisphere." But the West Side Tennis Club, still occupying ten
acres next to the Gardens, continues to add luster to the community by
hosting the men's World Champion matches each spring, among other
tournaments. Shopping and noshing opportunities also add allure. In addition to the attractive Austin Street spots, appealing cafes and craft and
antique stores are cropping up on Metropolitan Avenue.

Old, established, and mostly—about 90% according to the last census—white, Forest Hills is becoming increasingly cosmopolitan. (A local
real estate agent reports a Japanese language map of Forest Hills on sale in
Tokyo bookstores.) And increasingly its brick apartment buildings have
gone co-op. The few six- to ten-story rental buildings congregating on
either side of Queens Boulevard and the IND/BMT subway lines, as well as

major arteries like Ascan, Metropolitan, and 108th Street, are worth pursuing for their quality pre-war construction as well as convenience to public transportation. Semi-detached apartments and units in private homes may require a slightly longer walk but offer landscaped lots and winding streets as dividends.

Web Sites: www.queens.nyc.ny.us; Queens Chamber of Commerce, www.queenschamber.org; official New York City site, www.nyc.gov

Area Codes: 718, 347

Post Office: Forest Hills Station, 106-28 Queens Boulevard, Forest Hills, NY 11375, 718-268-1696

Zip Code: 11375

Police Precinct: One Hundred and Twelfth, 68-40 Austin Street, Forest Hills, NY 11375, 718-520-9311

Emergency Hospitals: North Shore University Hospital, 102-01 66th Road, Forest Hills, NY 11375, 718-830-4000; Parkway Hospital, 70-35 113th Street, Forest Hills, NY 11375, 718-990-4100

Library: Queens Public Library, Forest Hills Branch, 108-19 71st Avenue, Forest Hills, NY 11375, 718-268-7934

Public School Education: School District; #28, 108-55 69th Avenue, Forest Hills, NY 11375, 718-830-8800

Adult Education (nearest): St. John's University, Grand Central and Utopia Parkways, Jamaica, NY 11439, 718-990-6161

Community Resources: West Side Tennis Club, 1 Tennis Place (bounded by Burns and Dartmouth streets and 69th and 70th avenues), 718-268-2300

Transportation—Subway: E, F, G and R, all to 71st and Continental Avenues, Forest Hills

Transportation—Bus: stop by the Queens Transit Headquarters Information Center, 124-15 28th Avenue, Flushing, for a bus map of Queens or call 718-330-1234 or write Metropolitan Transit Authority, 347 Madison Avenue, NYC 10017, for a map.

KEW GARDENS

Boundaries and Contiguous Areas: Northeast: Queens Boulevard; **South**: Metropolitan Avenue and Forest Park; **West**: Union Turnpike and Forest Hills

Bracketed by LaGuardia Airport and John F. Kennedy International, Queens is home to thousands of airline employees. Kew Gardens in particular is popular with flight crews, hence the nickname, "Crew Gardens." Real estate agents report more rentals available and more singles residing in Kew Gardens than in Forest Hills and Rego Park.

The neighborhood's oldest section dates to 1912, when the Kew Gardens Corporation was formed. The substantial Colonial and Tudor-accented private homes built on high, comparatively hilly ground between Maple Grove Cemetery and Forest Park have cachet even today. The blocks of red brick apartment buildings that ring Kew's center, the older ones especially, represent real value, though most are co-op. Austin Street and Metropolitan Avenue together with Lefferts and Queens boulevards make up Kew's main shopping area. There's a pleasingly small-town feel on Austin around the railroad station, and Forest Park (see **Greenspace and Beaches**), which bars cars, provides rustic peace and quiet.

Nevertheless, with the infusion of recent immigrants Kew Gardens has become a cosmopolitan community. Along Lefferts Boulevard a new Irish bar and restaurant, a Russian grocer, an Uzbekistan Cultural Center and a Caribbean nightclub suggest just a few of the ethnic components of this neighborhood. Good schools, including four Jewish schools, are another plus.

At its southeastern-most tip, Kew Gardens hosts not only the borough's newest commercial skyscraper, a tall, rectangular gray block with cutout circles at the corners, but also Queens Borough Hall just across the Van Wyck Expressway, a long bureaucratic brick and limestone structure usually filled with politicians and, occasionally, useful publications about the borough.

Web Sites: www.queens.nyc.ny.us; Queens Chamber of Commerce, www.queenschamber.org; official New York City site, www.nyc.gov

Area Codes: 718, 347

Post Office: Kew Gardens Station, 83-30 Austin Street, Kew Gardens, NY 11415, 718-847-1978

Zip Codes: 11415, 11375, 11365

Police Precinct: One Hundred and Second, 87-34 118th Street, Richmond Hill, NY 11418, 718-805-3200

Emergency Hospital (nearest): North Shore University Hospital, 102-01 66th Road, Forest Hills, NY 11375, 718-830-4000

Libraries: Queens Public Library, Lefferts Branch, 103-34 Lefferts Boulevard, Richmond Hill, 718-843-5950; Glen Oaks Branch, 25604 Union Turnpike, Forest Park, NY 11426, 718-831-8636

Public School Education: Public School District #28 (see **Forest Hills**).

Adult Education (nearest): Queens College, 65-30 Kissena Boulevard, Flushing NY 11367, 718-997-5411

Community Resources: Queens Borough Hall, 120-55 Queens Boulevard, Kew Gardens, NY 11424, 718-520-3220

Transportation—Subway: E, F, Kew Gardens/Union Turnpike

Transportation—Bus: stop by the Queens Transit Headquarters Information Center, 124-15 28th Avenue, Flushing, for bus map of Queens or call 718-330-1234 or write Metropolitan Transit Authority, 347 Madison Avenue, NYC 10017 for a map.

FLUSHING

Boundaries and Contiguous Areas: North: Cross Island Parkway and Whitestone; **East**: Utopia Parkway and Francis Lewis Boulevard and Bayside; **South**: Union Turnpike; **West**: Grand Central Parkway and Forest Hills

Middle class Flushing sprawls on either side of the Long Island Expressway, embraced by two great parks, at the center of thriving northern Queens. The nexus of multiple bus routes, rail lines and traffic arteries, downtown Flushing looks like the crossroads of the world as well. In recent years a strong influx of Asians—Chinese, Koreans, Indians, and Pakistanis—have revitalized commercial Flushing, enriched it culturally and changed its face. On weekends the colorful Chinese fish-fruit-and-vegetable venders, Muslim butchers, and sari shops along Main Street draw shoppers from outside the area. Religious observances are as likely to be in Korean, Hindi, or Mandarin as in English or Hebrew.

Away from commercial Main Street, Union Turnpike, and Northern Boulevard, the grid of shady residential streets has changed little, except perhaps to have become more presentable. The profusion of well-established trees, 2,000 varieties throughout Flushing, constitute a treasure and a living remnant of the nursery industry which flourished here from pre-Revolutionary times until recently. Another survivor, its back turned to Northern Boulevard, the austere Friends' Meeting House has been a place of worship since 1694, except during the Revolutionary War, when it was a British hospital, prison, and stable. Bowne House, built nearby in 1661, was an earlier site of Quaker worship and of the struggle for religious freedom in what was then a Dutch settlement. Down Bowne Street from this museum of colonial life, in a modest residential neighborhood, is an extraordinary Hindu temple covered with stone statues. That's Flushing.

Great tracts of green breathing space surround and bisect Flushing. Flushing Meadow Corona Park contains within its 1,200 acres the site of two world fairs, two lakes, a marina, the Queens Zoo, a botanical garden, the Queens Museum, Theatre in the Park, the New York Hall of Science, an indoor ice-skating rink, Shea Stadium, home of the New York Mets, and the USTA National Tennis Center, site of the annual US Open Tennis Championships. A green band connects this vast park with the more intimate and landscaped Kissena Park, which contains an appealing Nature

Center. The grassy stretches of Cunningham Park provide an outlet for all manner of amateur sports teams.

As might be expected, the presence of Queens College and the rich ethnic mix here support an unusually vibrant cultural life: music, art, literary pursuits and theater flourish here. The Flushing Branch of the Queens Borough Public Library on Main Street handsomely rebuilt in 1998 and the busiest branch of the busiest library system in the nation, is open daily. Holdings include books, periodicals, videos, and CDs in some 30 languages, computer WorldLinQ in Chinese, Korean, Russian, Spanish, and French, an Adult Learning Center, and a unique International Resource Center. Renovation of the subway station nearby has been a boon to the 100,000 commuters who use it, many of them transferring from the web of bus routes which cross here.

Besides the convenience of transportation and the physical amenities, what Flushing has to offer is more space at less-than-Manhattan rents. For luxury condos look elsewhere, Bayside perhaps. High-rise apartments cluster near downtown Flushing. The rest is two-story brick apartment enclaves, one and two-family houses, detached and semi-attached, all with on-street parking. Ads to sell or rent these properties are often placed in *Newsday* and *The New York Times* by their owners; consult these same pages and the list of realtors in **Finding a Place to Live** to find brokers who handle other properties.

Web Sites: www.queens.nyc.ny.us; Queens Chamber of Commerce, www.queenschamber.org; official New York City site, www.nyc.gov

Area Codes: 718, 347

Post Offices: Flushing Main Station, 41-65 Main Street, Flushing 11355, 718-670-4700; Fresh Meadow Station, 192-20 Horace Harding Expressway, Flushing 11365, 718-454-6647; Station "B," 136-50 Roosevelt Avenue, Flushing 11368, 424-2731; Pomonok Station, 158-05 71st Avenue, Flushing 11366, 718-591-6611; Utopia Station, 182-04 Union Turnpike, Flushing 11366, 718-380-0902; Station "A," 40-03 164th Street, Flushing 11358, 718-353-2819; Station "C," 75-23 Main Street, Flushing 11367, 718-544-0989; Linden Hill Station 29-50 Union Street, Flushing 11354, 718-461-1512

Zip Codes: 11354, 11355, 11358, 11365, 11366, 11367, 11368

Police Precincts: One Hundred and Ninth, 37-05 Union Street, Flushing 11354, 718-321-2250; One Hundred and Seventh, 71-01 Parsons Boulevard, Flushing 11365, 718-969-5100

Emergency Hospitals: New York Hospital Medical Center of Queens, Main Street at Booth Memorial Avenue, Flushing 11355, 718-670-1231; Flushing Hospital Medical Center, 4500 Parsons Boulevard, Flushing 11355, 718-670-5000

Libraries: Flushing Main Branch, Queens Public Library, 41-17 Main Street, Flushing 11355, 718-661-1200; Hillcrest Branch, 187-05 Union Turnpike, Flushing 11366, 718-454-2786; McGoldrick Branch, 155-06 Roosevelt Avenue, Flushing 11354, 718-353-0839; Mitchell-Linden Branch, 29-42 Union Street, Flushing 11354, 718-539-2330; Pomonok Branch, 158-21 Jewel Avenue, Flushing 11365, 718-591-4343; Queensboro Hill Branch, 60-05 Main Street, Flushing 11355, 718-359-8332; Vleigh Branch, 72-33 Vleigh Place, Flushing 11367, 718-261-6654

Public School Education: District #25, 70-30 164th Street, Flushing 11365, 718-281-7600; District #26, 61-15 Oceania Avenue, Bayside 11364, 718-631-6900

Adult Education: Queens College, 65-30 Kissena Boulevard, Flushing 11367, 718-997-5000

Community Resources: Queens Historical Society, Kingsland House, 143-35 37th Avenue, Flushing 11354, 718-939-0647; The Bowne House, 37-01 Bowne Street, Flushing 11354, 718-359-0528; Godwin-Ternbach Museum, Queens College, 65-30 Kissena Boulevard, Flushing 11367, 718-997-4747; Art Center, Benjamin S. Rosenthal Library, Queens College, 65-30 Kissena Boulevard, Flushing 11367, 718-997-5000; New York Hall of Science, 47-01 111th Street, Flushing Meadows-Corona Park, Flushing 11368, 718-699-0005; Queens Museum of Art, New York City Building, Flushing Meadows-Corona Park, Flushing 11368, 718-592-9700; Colden Center for the Performing Arts, Queens College, Long Island Expressway and Kissena Boulevard, Flushing 11367, 718-793-8080; Flushing Council on Culture and the Arts at Town Hall, 136-73 41st Avenue, Flushing 11355, 718-463-7700; Tung Ching Chinese Center for the Arts, 147-17 45th Avenue, Flushing 11355, 718-539-4682; Kissena Park Nature Center, Rose Avenue and Parsons Boulevard, 718-699-4202; Queens Botanical Garden 43-50 Main Street, Flushing 11355, 718-886-3800; Queens Theatre in the Park, Flushing Meadow Corona Park, Flushing 11368, 718-760-0064

Transportation—Subway: #7, Willets Point-Shea Stadium, Main Street; E, F, Union Turnpike-Kew Gardens

Transportation—Bus: stop by the Queens Transit Headquarters Information, 124-15 28th Avenue, Flushing, for a bus map of Queens; Queens Surface Corp., at the same address, 718-445-3100, offers express service on several routes to midtown Manhattan.

Transportation—Train: regular Long Island Railroad service from Main Street Station.

BAYSIDE

Boundaries and Contiguous Areas: North and **East:** Cross Island Parkway; **South:** Long Island Expressway; **West:** Francis Lewis Boulevard and Utopia Parkway

The bright barn-red Long Island Railroad station, white-trimmed and snappy, differentiates Bayside from other Queens stops. So does the concentration of pubs and restaurants—some dim and glitzy, others homey-comfortable with fireplaces—that surround the station. These places attract singles and have a bubbling atmosphere after work and on weekend nights. North of this Bell Boulevard and 41st Avenue junction one-and two-family homes re-establish that urban/suburban quiet which typifies residential Queens, until you reach **Bay Terrace**. Here, newer condominiums and co-oped garden apartment buildings again break the mold.

While the older, free-standing homes contain rental apartments, condominium rentals in the **Bay Club**, though expensive, are probably the biggest draw. The enormous development consists of 1,036 condominiums in two three-pronged towers, a glass-domed swim club, a health club and five tennis courts. The **Bay Bridge** condo development nearby, with some 2,000 luxury townhouses, is a shorefront village in itself. From the Bay Club windows, and from those in the older co-ops, you can see how the community got its name—Bayside is bounded on two sides by Little Bay and Little Neck Bay—and the Whitestone, Triborough and Throgs Neck bridges connecting Queens to The Bronx as well. An abundance of town parks and excellent schools have combined to make this a commuter favorite for decades.

Bayside has water views but no direct subway connection to Manhattan. Commuters have three public transportation choices: the Long Island Railroad, express buses, or Queens buses to Flushing's Main Street Station and the # 7 Flushing Line subway.

Web Sites: www.queens.nyc.ny.us; Queens Chamber of Commerce, www.queenschamber.org; official New York City site, www.nyc.gov
Area Codes: 718, 347
Post Office: Bayside Station, 212-35 42nd Avenue, Bayside, NY 11361, 718-229-0699
Zip Codes: 11360, 11361, 11364, 11357
Police Precinct: One Hundred and Eleventh, 45-06 215th Street, Bayside, NY 11359, 718-279-5200
Emergency Hospital: St. Mary's Hospital for Children, 29-01 216th Street, Bayside, NY 11360, 718-281-8800

Library: Queens Public Library, Bayside Branch, 214-20 Northern Boulevard, Bayside, NY 11361, 718-229-1834

Public School Education: Public School District #26, 61-15 Oceania Street, Bayside, NY 11364, 718-631-6900

Adult Education: Queensborough Community College, 222-05 56th Avenue, Bayside, NY 11364, 718-631-6262

Community Resources: Crocheron Park, 33rd Avenue and Little Neck Parkway, 718-762-5966, a 45-acre park; Queensborough Community College Gallery, 222-05 56th Avenue, Bayside, call 718-631-6396 for information.

Transportation—Train: regular LIRR service

Transportation—Bus: stop by the Queens Transit Headquarters Information Center, 124-15 28th Avenue, Flushing, for a bus map of Queens, or call 718-330-1234 or write Metropolitan Transit Authority, 347 Madison Avenue, NYC 10017, for a map.

You might also want to consider...

- **Richmond Hill**; with Victorian houses, golf and tennis in Forest Park, and a variety of ethnic stores, but less expensive than neighboring Kew Gardens and Forest Hills, for the most part. An easy commute by train or subway. Community Board 9, 718-286-2686; Richmond Hill Historical Society, www.richmondhillhistory.org
- **Douglaston**; an upper middle-class community on Little Neck Bay at the northeastern end of Queens, having mostly one- and two-family houses and co-ops, relatively low real estate taxes and lower prices than upscale Great Neck to the east. A 25-minute commute to Manhattan on the Long Island Railroad (LIRR); Community Board 11, 718-225-1054.
- **Whitestone**; on the East River between the Whitestone and Throgs Neck Bridges in northern Queens and 30 minutes on the #7 from Times Square (45 minutes by express bus). Mostly houses, co-ops and condos, few rentals. Includes exclusive Malba and Francis Lewis Park along the riverfront. Community Board 7, 718-359-2800
- **Jamaica Estates**; with its winding roads, shady streets, Tudor houses and English street names, 45 minutes by the E or F train to Manhattan. Expensive. Community Board 8, 718-591-6000
- **Middle Village** is mid-Queens, middle class and relatively affordable, with tidy one- and two-family houses and a scattering of condos housing a close-knit community of civic-minded people. Amenities include Juniper Valley Park, from which the Manhattan skyline is visible, good schools, Italian specialty stores and German bakeries. Community Board 5, 718-366-1834
- **Ridgewood**; a half-hour from Grand Central by subway, boasts a

German heritage, still apparent in its shops and restaurants, solid row houses, some of them landmarked, and a strong neighborhood feeling. Especially prized are the harmonious yellow-brick houses along Stockholm Street and two blocks of 69th Avenue, between Fresh Pond Road and 60th Street. Community Board 5, 718-366-1834

STATEN ISLAND

New York's least-populated borough is, for many, simply the turn-around point for New York's most beloved, and cheapest, boat ride. (Not that Staten Islanders mind.) The 400,000 residents would just as soon keep their 61-square-mile island off the coast of New Jersey to themselves. In fact, November 2, 1993, marked a red-letter day when islanders voted over-whelmingly to secede from New York City. Final word rests with Albany and this question is not likely to be settled soon.

Dreams of remaining far from the madding New York crowd were, in fact, conclusively shattered when the austerely beautiful Verrazano-Narrows Bridge connecting Staten Island with Brooklyn was opened in 1964. The island's semi-rural isolation ended once and for all as Brooklynites flocked across the longest single-span bridge in the world to take up residence in dozens of new tract developments.

Giovanni da Verrazano discovered hillocky Staten Island in 1524 but, until the dedication of his namesake bridge 440 years later, the island remained something of a backwater. Henry Hudson claimed *Staaten Eylandt* for the Dutch East India Company in 1609; however, Britain acquired Staten Island when the British took over New Amsterdam in 1644. Farming, and then oystering, flourished. By the mid-1800s, a railroad, trolley cars, and ferry service made the island's seashore and salubrious air accessible to the gentry.

The fickle fashionables had moved on though by the time Staten Island became part of New York City in 1898. Too bad, because the city improved the new borough's ferry service immeasurably: by 1904 there were a number of sturdy seaworthy boats running on schedule for the first time since young Cornelius Vanderbilt instituted ferry service to Manhattan around 1810. Today, three sunset-yellow ferries ply the choppy waters of the Upper Bay between St. George and the Battery during the rush hours. Off-peak, two modernized 1,200-passenger boats handle the immensely scenic 25-minute crossing. Now, not only do tracts and shopping malls flourish south of the Staten Island Expressway, straining the island's over-taxed infrastructure, but a modest renaissance is underway in communities within walking distance of the ferry landing. Wall Streeters cherish the office-to-ferry walk, as well as the uphill stroll home, almost as much as they cherish the fare: it's free.

Hills—precipitous slopes reminiscent of San Francisco—and stunning

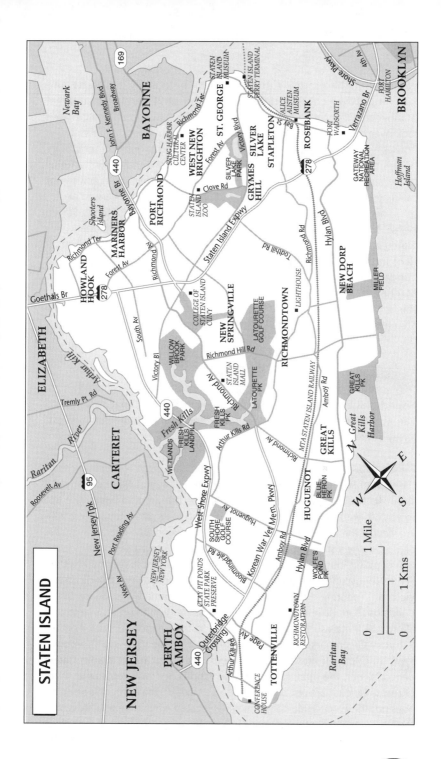

STATEN ISLAND

views from the craggy ridge that rises between St. George and Richmondtown characterize that portion of Staten Island nearest Manhattan. On leafy Todt, Emerson and Grymes hills, million-dollar homes look over the treetops to Brooklyn and Manhattan. Wood-frame Victorian houses, salted among the stucco mini-mansions and angular contemporary homes, are the darlings of homesteaders. You're more likely to find a rental apartment in a converted one-or two-family house than in an apartment building on Staten Island—although red brick apartment towers do exist.

The Staten Island Chamber of Commerce, 130 Bay Street, Staten Island, NY 10301, 718-727-1900, sells an excellent street map; the MTA's Staten Island Bus Map (free at the Chamber) is equally useful. Rental classifieds in the *Staten Island Advance* are more numerous on Saturday and Sunday but this afternoon paper publishes real estate ads every day. In Manhattan, pick up a copy of the *Advance* at the newsstand located inside the ferry terminal. *The Village Voice* is also a good source for listings. Some Staten Island realtors are listed in the section on Apartment Hunting.

ST. GEORGE

Boundaries and Contiguous Areas: North: Richmond Terrace and the Kill Van Kull; **East**: Bay Street; South: Victory Boulevard and Stapleton; **West**: Jersey Street and The Narrows

Flags a flap, the beguiling limestone and brick Borough Hall caps a rise to the right of St. George's ferry terminal. To the left as you exit the terminal a stunning structure, at once public sculpture, bridge, and lighthouse-like tower, crowns a plaza, inviting visitors to climb to its glassy top for a smashing view of the harbor and lower Manhattan beyond. The two are symbolic of St. George's struggle against blight. The downtown sector has defied gentrification, but uphill, within sight of the neo-Gothic spires of Curtis High School (between St. Mark's Place and Hamilton Avenue), you'll find restored Victorian, Tudor, and 1920s-stucco houses. Four formerly vacant apartment buildings there have been transformed into the Village on St. Marks with affordable rentals suitable for commuters to the Financial District. And the Saturday Greenmarket on St. Marks brings a village square feel to downtown St. George from May to December. In contrast to the maple-shaded period homes, the three converted grain and coffee warehouses that comprise Bay Landing are certainly up-to-date. Arguably the borough's trendiest housing, these waterside condominiums located a five-minute walk east of the ferry terminal are the first stage in a projected harbor front revival. Here, black pines and juniper separate the public marina, esplanade and the glass-enclosed Landing Cafe from the access road—shades of Sausalito.

New rentals, rare in Staten Island, are to be found in moderately-priced waterfront mid-rises at Harbor View. Come spring, fishing enthusiasts flock to the charter boats tied up at the Landing's pristine docks. The Joseph L. Lyons Pool, one of Staten Island's four municipal swimming pools, and the George Cromell Center, an indoor recreation center with tennis courts and a track situated on a pier, are both located near The Landing's complex. What's next in St. George? A minor league baseball stadium for the Staten Island Yankees on the shore near a renovated ferry landing and a national lighthouse museum to be built on the former Coast Guard base. Check the classifieds and our list of Staten Island real estate brokers in the **Finding a Place to Live** chapter for rentals, and after filing off the ferry, walk through the gradually reviving community of St. George.

Web Sites: www.statenislandusa.com, www.si-web.com; http://community.silive.com; official New York City site, www.nyc.gov

Area Codes: 718, 347

Post Office: St. George Station, 45 Bay Street, Staten Island, NY 10301, 718-981-1313; Ferry Terminal Station, St. George Ferry, Staten Island, NY 10301, 718-447-6443

Zip Code: 10301

Police Precinct: One Hundred Twentieth, 78 Richmond Terrace, Staten Island, NY 10301, 718-876-8500

Emergency Hospitals (nearest): Bayley Seton Hospital, 75 Vanderbilt Avenue (at Bay Street), Staten Island, NY 10304, 718-354-6000; St. Vincent's Medical Center of Richmond, 355 Bard Avenue, Staten Island, NY 10301, 718-876-1234

Library: St. George Library Center of the New York Public Library, 5 Central Avenue, Staten Island, NY 10301, 718-442-8560

Public School Education: School District; #31: Community School Board, 211 Daniel Low Terrace, Staten Island, NY 10301, 718-273-9559

Adult Education: College of Staten Island, St. George campus (part of the City University of New York), 130 Stuyvesant Place, Staten Island, NY 10301, 718-982-2000

Community Resources: Snug Harbor Cultural Center, 1000 Richmond Terrace, Staten Island, NY 10301, 718-448-2500, www.snug-harbor.org, is located in a clutch of handsome Greek Revival buildings on 80 arboreous acres. Once a haven for indigent sailors, the colonnaded buildings are now the locus of Staten Island's cultural rebirth. Concerts, art exhibits, and plays fill the high-ceilinged halls. Also on the grounds you'll find: The Staten Island Botanical Garden, 718-273-8200, and the Staten Island Children's Museum, 718-273-2060; the Staten Island Institute of Arts and Sciences, 75 Stuyvesant Place, Staten Island, NY

718-727-1135, a museum offering tours and cultural events.

Transportation—Train: the Staten Island Railway train costs $1.50 one way and provides service between the St. George Ferry Terminal and Tottenville at the southern tip of the 13.9-mile-long island. The second stop, Tompkinsville Station, is used for Bay Street Landing. Call 718-966-SIRT for information.

Transportation—Bus: local buses cost $1.50 one way. The #101, #42 bus leaves from and returns to the ferry terminal after circling northwestern St. George. Express buses to Manhattan via the Verrazano Bridge and Brooklyn Battery Tunnel cost $3 one way. Call 718-330-1234 for bus information.

Transportation—Ferry: free passenger ferries run every 15 or 20 minutes during rush hours, every half hour at other times, every hour from 11 p.m. to 6 a.m. Service is less frequent on holidays and weekends. Car ferry service is available between 4:30 and 11 p.m. and costs $3 per car. Call 718-815-2628 for information.

STAPLETON

Boundaries and Contiguous Areas: **North**: Victory Boulevard and St. George; **East**: Bay Street and Upper New York Bay; **South**: Canal and Broad Streets; **West**: Louis Street, Van Duzer Street and Grymes Hill

Bordering Bay Street, Stapleton boasts a batch of more-collectibles-than-antiques stores and a few somewhat upscale watering holes. These cafes, tarted up with Tiffany style lamps, polished brass and old-fashioned bottle vases, point to the presence of newcomers in Stapleton's craggy hills.

Located only two stops from the ferry terminal on the SIRT train, Stapleton for some time has attracted artists and young families looking for a third bedroom. Now, here come bankers and stockbrokers from Lower Manhattan. Sturdy 19th century homes characterize housing in **Stapleton Heights** and adjacent **Ward Hill**. Asphalt shingles sheath houses down on the flats near the gourmet takeout shops, the library and handsome Tappan Park. The Mud Lane Society, a group of community boosters, promotes Stapleton with an annual house tour.

Web Sites: www.statenislandusa.com, www.si-web.com; http://community.silive.com; official New York City site, www.nyc.gov

Area Codes: 718, 347

Post Office: Stapleton Station, 514 Bay Street, Staten Island, NY 10304, 718-727-2207; Rosebank Station, 567 Tompkins Avenue, Staten Island, NY 10305, 718-447-0787

Zip Code: 10304

Police Precinct: One Hundred Twentieth, 78 Richmond Terrace, Staten Island, NY 10301, 718-876-8500

Emergency Hospital (nearest): Bayley Seton Hospital, Bay Street and Vanderbilt Avenue, Staten Island, NY 10304, 718-354-6000

Library: New York Public Library, Stapleton Branch, 132 Canal Street, Staten Island, NY 10304, 718-727-0427

Public School Education: School District #31 (see **St**. **George**).

Adult Education (nearby): St. John's University, 300 Howard Avenue, Staten Island, NY 10301, 718-390-4545

Community Resources (nearby): The Jacques Marchais Center of Tibetan Art houses Tibetan monastery artifacts at 338 Lighthouse Avenue in Richmondtown, call for an appointment, 718-987-3500; the Richmondtown Restoration, a historic village comprised of 14 buildings operated by the Staten Island Historical Society at 441 Clarke Avenue, Staten Island 10306, 718-351-1617; The Conference House, a pre-Revolutionary manor house, at 7455 Hylan Boulevard, Staten Island 10307, 718-984-2086; Alice Austen House Museum and Garden, 2 Hylan Boulevard, Staten Island 10305, 718-816-4506.

Transportation—Train: the Stapleton Station is the third stop on the SIRT train (details under **St**. **George**).

Transportation—Bus: the #74, #76, and #51 travel Bay Street as far as Canal; the #78 runs along Van Duzer Street and St. Paul's Avenue in Stapleton Heights (details under **St**. **George**).

GRYMES HILL AND SILVER LAKE

Boundaries and Contiguous Areas: North: Louis Avenue; **East**: Stapleton, Van Duzer Street, and Vanderbilt Avenue; **South**: Clove Road and the Staten Island Expressway; **West**: Victory Boulevard

One blustery afternoon, a salty sea breeze rattled maple and birch branches, garnishing **Grymes Hill** with russet fall leaves. Save for the outline of Wall Street's mist-shrouded skyline, you could have been in Westchester. Interspersed with narrow blacktop lanes and imposing houses, the hills of Staten Island radiate a rustic sub-urbanity.

The higher you climb any one of the island's myriad hills, the more imposing the homes become. Four-hundred-foot high **Todt Hill**, the tallest of Staten Island's peaks, is the toniest. Grymes Hill, nearer the ferry terminal, is the most intellectual: St. John's University and Wagner College cluster its slopes; the College of Staten Island lies in an adjacent valley. Though 12-story Sunrise Tower is co-op, there are 475 two-and three-bedroom rental apartments in the Grymes Hill Apartments Complex, built by Donald Trump's father in the 1940s. In addition, rental apartments can be found in remodeled one-family homes.

Silver Lake combines with Clove Lakes Park to form a sylvan green-belt. There are tennis courts, bridle paths, ice skating rink, and a municipal golf course laid out around the reservoir, and between Clove Road and Broadway a small, accessible zoo with a first-rate reptile collection.

Web Sites: www.statenislandusa.com, www.si-web.com; http://community.silive.com; official New York City site, www.nyc.gov

Area Codes: 718, 347

Post Offices: St. George Station, 45 Bay Street, Staten Island, NY 10301, 718-981-1313; Stapleton Station, 514 Bay Street, Staten Island, NY 10304, 718-727-2207

Zip Codes: 10301, 10304

Police Precinct: 120th, 78 Richmond Terrace, Staten Island, NY 10304, 718-876-8500

Emergency Hospitals (nearest): Bayley Seton Hospital, Bay Street and Vanderbilt Avenue, Staten Island, NY 10304, 718-354-6000; St. Vincent's Medical Center of Richmond, 355 Bard Avenue, Staten Island, NY 10301, 718-876-1234

Library (nearest): New York Public Library, Stapleton Branch, 132 Canal Street, Staten Island, NY 10304, 718-727-0427

Public School Education: School District #31 (see **St. George**).

Adult Education: College of Staten Island, Sunnyside campus (nearby), 715 Ocean Terrace, Staten Island, NY 10301, 718-390-7733; St. John's University, 300 Howard Avenue, Staten Island, NY 10301, 718-390-4545; Wagner College (and Wagner College Planetarium), 631 Howard Avenue, Staten Island, NY 10301, 718-390-3100

Community Resources: Staten Island Zoo, 614 Broadway, Staten Island, NY 10310, 718-442-3100 (see also **Stapleton**).

Transportation—Train: A steep climb is required to reach Grymes Hill from Stapleton, the nearest stop on the SIRT line (details under **St. George**).

Transportation—Bus: The #74 bus traverses Van Duzer Street along the base of Grymes Hill; the #61, #62, #66, and #67 traveling Victory Boulevard connect with the #60 shuttle bus at Clove Road. The shuttle follows Howard Avenue as far as the St. John campus (details under **St. George**).

You might also want to consider...

• **West New Brighton** is a stable community across the Kill van Kull from New Jersey and southwest of the ferry. Here Victorian houses and apartments offer golf, tennis and extensive parkland in Silver Lake Park and Clove Lakes Park, which includes the Staten Island Zoo. The Snug Harbor Cultural Center is nearby. Bus to the ferry to the subway to work, about 50 minutes. Community Board 1, 718-981-6900, or Staten Island Chamber of Commerce, 718-727-1900

- **Port Richmond**, just south of West New Brighton on the Kill van Kull, offers reasonably priced housing, much of it pre-War, one- and two-family homes and a 50-minute commute by express bus or bus/ferry from Manhattan. Community Board 1, 718-981-6900, or Staten Island Chamber of Commerce, 718-727-1900

NEW JERSEY

FORT LEE AND EDGEWATER

Boundaries and Contiguous Areas: North: Englewood and Englewood Cliffs; **East:** Hudson River; South: Cliffside Park and West New York; **West:** Leonia and Palisades Park

Apartment towers in **Fort Lee** ride the Palisades above the Hudson like so many schooner masts, their rigging blown loose, flung across the river and fixed there as the lacy George Washington Bridge. Beneath these rocky cliffs, its back to the wall in fact, little Edgewater was virtually invisible until the mid-1980s, when low structures began to take shape, seemingly afloat on the river, and Manhattanites wondered "What's that over there?" For the most part, they're still wondering.

It was in what is now Edgewater that George Washington and his Continental Army landed in November of 1776, after the battle of Washington Heights. General Charles Lee had supervised the fortifications above on the site which bears his name, and their remnants are still to be found there. Fort Lee remained a sleepy little town with a ferry landing throughout most of the 19th century. Civil War gunboats used the volcanically formed Palisades for target practice, and these same cliffs provided the Belgian paving stones for the streets of Manhattan. In the late 1800s an amusement center and resorts flourished on The Bluffs, as they were known, but as business waned and ferry service finally ceased, Fort Lee declined.

The location of a nascent movie industry here from about 1910 into the 1920s offered a reprieve, but Hollywood won the climate competition, and the village languished. Completion of the George Washington Bridge in 1931 gave Fort Lee a suburban future. The tallest high-rise in Bergen County rose in Fort Lee in 1972. As rapidly and as large as they rose along Palisade Avenue, they filled up in this fastest growing town in Jersey's most

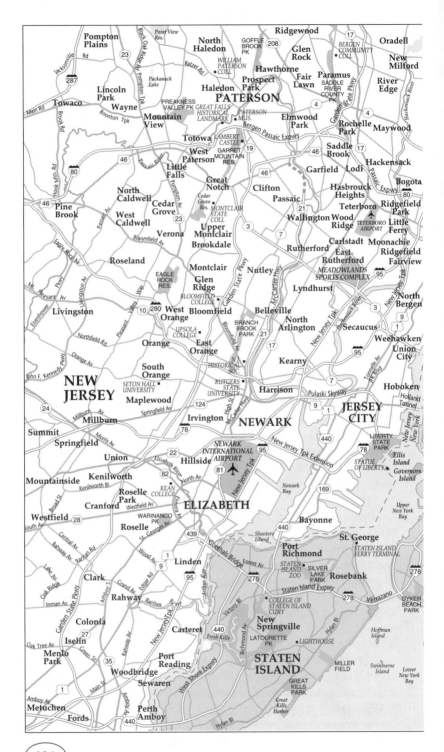

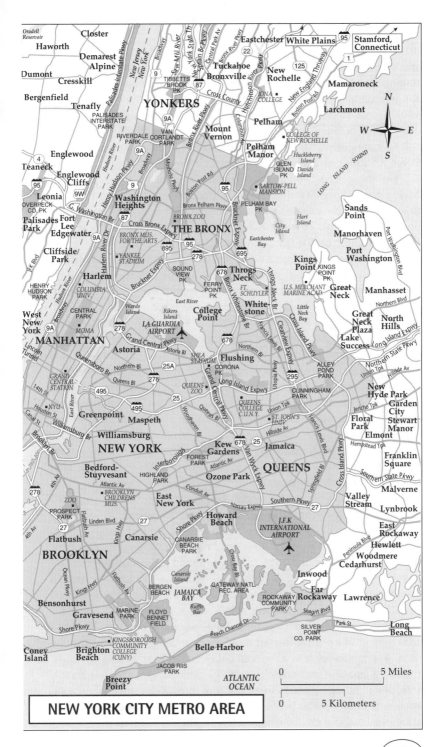

NEW YORK CITY METRO AREA

affluent county. Fort Lee straddles the approach to the bridge, but the most sought-after housing lies south of the bridge. An estimated 80% of the approximately 35,000 inhabitants commute to jobs in the city, largely by Jersey Transit to the Port Authority Bus Terminal in Manhattan. In recent years this population has included a strong infusion of affluent Japanese and Korean residents, as is evident in the store and office signs along Main Street. An appealing diversity of restaurants is the result.

No longer sleepy, Fort Lee has maintained a small-town feel, despite its having grown faster—and taller—than it could plan for. Along the quiet streets off Palisade Avenue tidy homes nearly fill their lovingly manicured postage-stamp lots (they're expensive, nonetheless). It's the view—Manhattan afloat on the Hudson—that determines the price of real estate and rentals. Apartments with a view fetch near-Manhattan prices, whether they are co-ops, condos, or rentals; but you use the same pool and health club at a lower rent without the view. Away from the edge, garden apartments and two-family houses are less expensive.

At the eastern, river end of Main Street in 33-acre Fort Lee Historic Park visitors trace the Revolutionary history of the area in the museum and discover the remnants of Continental Army dugouts. The park lies within the greater Palisades Interstate Park, a narrow strip of wooded land stretching for miles between the Hudson and the Palisades Parkway above, with marinas, picnic areas and a scenic drive known to few outside the immediate area. This constitutes an extraordinary recreation asset for residents of Fort Lee and Edgewater.

Main Street winds down the steep hill into River Road in **Edgewater**, one of the more unusual small towns in New Jersey. A blue-collar pocket with an industrial history, Edgewater hunches under the Palisades along steep, narrow streets, some of whose modest houses have recently been replaced by clutches of tidy condos. There's a somewhat funky feel to the town.

Construction of up-scale, high- and low-rise condo and rental developments along the river side of River Road has brought a wave of affluent young professionals, and change, to Edgewater and to the adjoining riverside towns directly to the south, North Bergen, West New York and Weehawken (see below). Sprawling handsomely at water's edge, or suspended over it on piles, these complexes with aquatic names such as Admiral's Walk, Mariner's Cove, and Jacob's Ferry offer all the amenities—tennis, pool, health club—and the view, at a price. Clustered about are cinemas, a supermarket, restaurants, a restaurant/club in a restored old Hoboken Ferry boat, and hotels; Yaohan, a Japanese mall complete with Japanese supermarket, restaurant, and specialty shops, attracts shoppers from throughout the tri-state area. Interspersed helter-skelter between these waterside centers, are the occasional industrial site, golf driving ranges, a tennis club and marinas.

Edgewater is abuilding, with rental and condo projects proliferating as well as additional retail space and a cineplex. Office complexes are being carved out of abandoned industrial sites. And with this critical mass, the megastores—Bed, Bath and Beyond, Barnes & Noble, Staples etc.—have ventured in, Starbucks, too.

Although there is commuter bus service to the Imperial Ferry in Weehawken and to the Port Authority, a car is a necessity here in the relative isolation of Edgewater's narrow, winding River Road. Realtors handling Fort Lee and Edgewater properties are listed in the next chapter, **Finding a Place to Live**.

Web Sites: www.fortleenj.org; www.njtowns.com

Area Code: 201

Post Offices: Main Branch, 229 Main Street, 201-944-1853, and Palisade Station, 1213 Anderson Avenue, Fort Lee, 201-224-8787; Edgewater Station, 33 Hilliard Avenue, Edgewater, 201-945-0310

Zip Codes: Fort Lee, 07024; Edgewater, 07020

Police Stations: 1325 Inwood Terrace, Fort Lee, 201-592-3500; 916 River Road, Edgewater, 201-943-2200

Emergency Hospitals: Englewood Hospital and Medical Center, 350 Engle Street, Englewood 07631, 201-894-3000; Palisades Medical Center, 7600 River Road, North Bergen, 07047, 201-854-5000

Libraries: Fort Lee Free Public Library, 320 Main Street, 201-592-3614; Edgewater Free Public Library, 49 Hudson Avenue, 201-224-6144

Public School Education: Board of Education, 255 Whitman Street, Fort Lee, 201-585-4600; Board of Education, 257 Undercliff Avenue, Edgewater, 201-945-4106

Transportation—Bus: call New Jersey Transit, 973-762-5100 or 212-564-8484, for routes and schedules, or pick up same at the Port Authority Bus Terminal at Eighth Avenue and 41st Street in Manhattan.

Transportation—Ferry: see Weehawken.

WEEHAWKEN

Boundaries and Contiguous Areas: **North**: West New York; **East**: Hudson River; **South**: Union City and Hoboken; **West**: Union City

Compact little Weehawken (.85 square miles) crests the Jersey Palisades three watery miles across the Hudson from midtown Manhattan. Longtime residents of Irish, German, and Italian heritage, the more recent Latino families, and commuter expatriates of the Big Apple prize that distance and the peace and quiet which it guarantees. The Lincoln Tunnel at the foot of the rocky heights provides Weehawken an enviable half-hour access to Manhattan by car or mini-bus. Little wonder, then, that the modest mansions shoulder to shoulder along cliff-top Boulevard East fetch prices in the neighborhood of $1.5 million for the magnificent skyline view which they command.

The Dutch bought this site in the 17th century from the Leni Lenape Indians and modified its Indian name to suit Dutch tongues. Little had changed in 1804, when Aaron Burr killed Alexander Hamilton in a duel on a grassy plot near the shore here. Shipyards and industry along the shoreline came later, and with them, the mansions on the Heights. Frame, brick, and brownstone row houses were built along the side streets heading west from the cliffs and remain the chief source of prime housing in Weehawken. Most prized are houses in the tiny Bluffs section just south of Hamilton Park.

The housing stock in Weehawken was increased a few years ago by the conversion of a factory complex to 177 condos with Manhattan views, now Gregory Commons. Further expansion will be along the waterfront. Hartz Mountain's 95-acre, mixed-use **Lincoln Harbor** development has transformed Weehawken's southern shore with two 10-story blue glass office buildings, restaurants, a hotel and marina. The residential component, pricey beige-and-pastel Riva Pointe wrapped around a courtyard on a 1,000-foot pier has attracted an affluent young clientele with its amenities and adjacent commuter ferry, not to mention the view. Just to the north at Port Imperial, developer Arthur Imperatore operates NY Waterway, continuous five-minute ferry service to Manhattan with connecting van service to midtown and the Wall Street area. His grander plan for a "Venice-on-the-Hudson" comprised of a convention center, commercial and residential complex has been limited so far to a marina, golf driving range, and waterfront restaurant. But two rental apartment developments, the Landings with 276 units, and Riverbend with 1,032, completed in 2000, are the first of what are expected to be some 4,200 residences within sight of the ferry. Imperatore will open a new ferry terminal north of the present facility in 2002, as construction of residences advances on that site. In time, a planned 18.5-mile walkway from the George Washington Bridge to Bayonne will pass along Weehawken's shore.

Many Weehawken properties are handled by Hoboken real estate brokers, or by their owners. Check the ads in *The Jersey Journal* (see Jersey City) and in *The Weehawken Reporter,* available locally in stores and apartment building lobbies, as well as the list of real estate brokers in the **Finding a Place to Live** chapter.

Web Site: www.njtowns.com
Area Codes: 201, 973
Post Office: Weehawken Substation, 3504 Park Avenue, 201-867-3085; Park Avenue Branch, 4708 Park Avenue, 201-867-0081

Zip Code: 07087

Police Station: 400 Park Avenue, Weehawken 07087, 201-863-7800

Emergency Hospital (nearest): Palisades Medical Center 7600 River Road, North Bergen 07047, 201-854-5000

Library: Weehawken Free Public Library, 49 Hauxhurst Avenue, Weehawken 07087, 201-863-7823

Public School Education: Board of Education, 53 Liberty Place, Weehawken 07047, 201-867-2243

Transportation—Bus: Mini-buses troll Boulevard East for passengers to the Port Authority Bus Terminal in Manhattan continuously weekdays, less frequently on weekends. Jersey Transit service is also 10 minutes to the terminal; call 973-762-5100 or 212-564-8484 for routes and schedules, or pick up same at the Port Authority Bus Terminal, Eighth Avenue and 41st Street in Manhattan.

Transportation—Ferry: service by NY Waterway between Port Imperial and midtown Manhattan and Whitehall is every 15 minutes daily 6:15 a.m. to midnight, until 1 a.m. Fridays, Saturday 8 a.m. to 1 a.m. and Sunday 9 a.m. to midnight. The five-minute ride costs $4.50 each way to midtown, with monthly commuter tickets costing $150, and $5 each way to Whitehall. Parking at the vast lot in Weehawken is $8 for the day. Call 800-533-3779 for information.

HOBOKEN

Boundaries and Contiguous Areas: North: Weehawken; **East**: Hudson River; **South**: Jersey City; **West**: Jersey City and Union City

At the turn of the millennium, Hoboken is reinventing itself. Most of this tidy, small (population 33,000) "Mile Square City" sandwiched between the Hudson River and Jersey bluffs was built between 1860 and 1910. By 1900 Hoboken was famous as the first American port of call for tens of thousands of immigrants, many of whom stayed close by, finding jobs in the city's numerous light manufacturing plants. Industrious working and middle-class citizens built the simple, unadorned brownstone and brick row houses that comprise most of Hoboken's real estate. These large families pushed Hoboken's population to 70,000 at its peak. The patrician Stevens family, who bought what was to become Hoboken soon after the Revolution, lived in relative isolation and splendor in the Castle Point section of town. This tract is now occupied by the Stevens Institute of Technology, the engineering school founded by the family.

Laid out in a grid that encompasses several pleasant, leafy squares, Hoboken still retains a blue-collar tinge. But, with the closing of Maxwell

House Coffee, the last employer of any size within Hoboken's boundaries, the housing here has increasingly been occupied by refugees from across the Hudson, who now gaze back at a Manhattan skyline visually afloat on the river, gleaming in the afternoon sun and ablaze with lights at night.

In the early 1970s a tide of disaffected New Yorkers, many of them singles, was attracted to this community just ten minutes from Manhattan by subway (PATH). Artists and rock musicians as well as young professionals discovered Hoboken, and the row house renovations, the cafes, interesting shops, and galleries dotting the original downtown and Washington Street neighborhoods show it. Where homesteaders pioneer, serious developers almost always follow. Certainly, the conversion to condos of tenement blocks along Monroe, Adams, and the other "presidential" streets west of Washington, as well as the Curling Club, the Hudson Tea, and Hudson Park complexes, among other luxury rental developments on once-industrial land in the northwest quadrant, bear witness to that fact. To the south new brownstone lofts and luxury single-family brownstones stand occupied in formerly "undesirable" streets. Families have returned to Hoboken, and private and charter schools, tanning parlors, and health clubs proliferate.

Long awaited development of Hoboken's moribund mile-long riverfront began with the construction of the Shipyard, which will ultimately comprise some 1,100 high-end rental and condominium apartments along the southern waterfront. Development of the 24-acre Maxwell House property as a mixed-use, housing/commercial complex on the waterfront will complete the process. Once again, the Hoboken Ferry plies the Hudson from two Hoboken piers to Battery Park. The main terminal, which it shares with PATH and Jersey Transit trains, is gloriously restored to its beaux-arts splendor, with Tiffany glass skylight, buff limestone, and ornamental plaster. And Hoboken will be connected by electric trolleys to Jersey City and Bayonne in the next phase of the Hudson-Bergen Light Rail Transit System. Eventually the system will run 20 miles along the west bank of the Hudson, with links to rail and ferry connections to Manhattan. Finishing touch, now partially completed, will be the walking/biking strip of green roughly parallel to the tracks but along the river's edge from Fort Lee to Bayonne. The west bank of the Hudson will have been transformed.

The Hoboken Reporter, 201-659-1213, www.hobokenreporter.com, available free in shops along Washington Street, is an excellent source of rentals, which tend to run 10% or more below comparable Manhattan dwellings. Condos are about one half the cost of comparable Manhattan apartments. For names of local brokers and a shares agency, refer to **Finding a Place to Live**.

Web Sites: www.hobokeni.com; www.njtowns.com
Area Codes: 201, 973 (North and Central New Jersey)

Post Offices: Main Office, 89 River Street, Hoboken, 07030, 201-659-3220. All branches have the same telephone number and zip: Castle Point Station, Stevens Institute of Technology; Uptown Station, 57 West 14th Street; Washington Street Station, 734 Washington Street; West Side Station, 502 Grand Street.

Zip Code: 07030

Police Station: #1 Police Plaza, 108 Newark Street, Hoboken, 07030, 201-420-2100

Emergency Hospital: St. Mary's Hospital, 308 Willow Avenue, Hoboken, 07030, 201-418-1000

Library: Hoboken Public Library, 500 Park Avenue, Hoboken, 07030, 201-420-2346

Public School Education: Hoboken Board of Education, 1115 Clinton Street, 201-420-2162

Community Resources: The Hoboken Chamber Orchestra gives concerts at the Demarest Grammar School. Membership in the Hoboken-North Hudson YMCA, with its tiled pool, workout rooms, and movement classes, is an inexpensive alternative to the health and fitness centers proliferating here. New rock reigns at a number of clubs on Washington Street, The Elysian Cafe, #1001, 201-659-9344, and Maxwell's, #1039, 201-656-9632, to name but two.

Transportation—Subway: PATH trains, 800-234-7284, shuttle between the Hoboken Station next to the Conrail (old Erie and Lackawanna Railroad) Terminal and Manhattan every 10 minutes from about 6:30 a.m. to 8:30 p.m., every 15 minutes between 8:30 and 11:45 and from then on every 30 minutes until 6:30 a.m. A direct line ran between Hoboken and the World Trade Center, and another between Hoboken and West 33rd Street and Sixth Avenue, making stops at Christopher near Hudson Street, then at 9th, 14th and 23rd streets, all on Sixth Avenue. The fare is $1.

Transportation—Bus: frequent commuter bus service on the #126 line operated by New Jersey Transit, 212-564-8484 (and be prepared to wait) for schedules, and on buses operated by Red Apple Transit, 201-440-2636, connect Hoboken Terminal and Manhattan's Port Authority Bus Terminal at Eighth Avenue and 40th Street (the South wing).

Transportation—Ferry: service between both Hoboken Station and the 14th Street Pier and Manhattan at Battery Park. Ferries run every six to eight minutes, 6:50 a.m. to 9 a.m. and 4 p.m. to 8 p.m., every 15 minutes in between and till 11 p.m., every half hour weekends 10 to 10. Tickets are $2 each way, $20 for 10 trips, $75 for a monthly pass. Call 800-533-3779 for information.

JERSEY CITY

Boundaries and Contiguous Areas: **North**: Hoboken; **East**: Hudson River; **South**: Bayonne; **West**: Brunswick Street

Directly across the Hudson River from lower Manhattan, New York's "sixth borough" is a small city with big-city amenities. And they're all new, from the glossy financial centers to the trim apartment towers rimming the Hudson, to the high-tech trolleys gliding between them. A resurgent economy in the late 1990s accelerated the expansion of relatively inexpensive commercial office space and rapidly proliferating housing to add to the city's stock of 19th century brick and brownstone townhouses. All this within five minutes of Manhattan.

New Jersey's first city—"settled in 1630" says the historical marker erected in **Paulus Hook**, the oldest section of town—was for the better part of three and a half centuries largely a working-class community. Today it has a heterogeneous population of 250,000 and an enviable position five minutes by PATH train under the Hudson from Lower Manhattan, ten minutes by ferry.

The arrival of brownstoners presaged the current Jersey City revival. Thirty years ago expatriate New Yorkers began buying and reclaiming townhouses in the historic districts bordering **Hamilton** and **Van Vorst Parks**. Co-ops and condominium conversions sprung up in these neighborhoods and in the adjoining Paulus Hook historic district. And once Banker's Trust leased space at the vast Harborside Financial Center (as the rehabilitated Pennsylvania Railroad warehouse is now called), it became clear that back-office operations of large Manhattan corporations would prove a boon to the local economy.

Now, gleaming skyscrapers soar along wide boulevards that connect Harborside with **Newport**, the enormous, $10-billion apartment, mall, business center and townhouse-marina complex across the Hudson River from Manhattan's Battery Park City. The most recent building phase at Newport has added a hotel and nearly 2,000 apartment units, mostly rentals, to the original 1,500 that opened in 1986. Sears, J.C. Penney, and Macy's anchor the suburban-style shopping mall there. When the bumptious Lefrak Organization has completed their planned 600-acre development around 2010, they expect to have 9,000 apartments on site, truly a city within a city. The size and energy of this project has driven development elsewhere in Jersey City. In fact, Lefrak broke ground in 2001 for a new development of less expensive rentals inland near Hamilton Park, to accommodate some 3,000 apartments ultimately.

South of Newport the expanding **Avalon Cove** development offers one- to four-bedroom rentals with tennis and racquetball courts, a swimming pool and a riverfront walkway. A sugar factory has been transformed into luxury condominiums. And Jersey City has acquired its own acronymic artists' enclave, the **WALDO** (**W**ork **A**nd **L**ive **D**istrict **O**verlay), composed of warehouse conversions to loft-studios. In the historic district at the foot of **Washington Street**, Portside's luxury rentals feature mostly balconied studios to three-bedroom spreads, many with panoramic views of lower Manhattan, the harbor, the Statue of Liberty and Ellis Island. Additional luxury condos at Port Liberté to the south have increased the range of waterfront choices.

West of the harbor developments and 35 minutes from Manhattan by PATH, a 1,176-unit condominium community, **Society Hill**, offers mid-priced town houses and apartments with marina, tennis courts, and two pools. With other projects already in the works, this K. Hovnanian project has spurred the revitalization of this up-and-coming area.

Electric-powered trolleys (fare: $1.50) connect these various communities with one another, with Bayonne to the south and with links to the PATH tubes and ferry connections. The next phase of the Hudson-Bergen Light Rail Transit System will extend north to Hoboken and ultimately north to Ridgefield in Bergen County. These 90-foot cars, winding among the city's mix of glass towers and historic brownstones, are expected to spur further growth in this rapidly changing city.

The Jersey Journal published everyday but Sunday is the best source for Hoboken or Jersey City classified rental ads. In Manhattan, buy *The Journal* at newsstands at the 14th Street Downtown PATH station and outside the 33rd Street PATH station. See **Finding a Place to Live** chapter for names of brokers.

Web Sites: www.cityofjerseycity.com; www.njtowns.com

Area Codes: 201, 973

Post Office: The main Post Office, 69 Montgomery Street, 201-915-7000, is located in downtown

Zip Code: 07302 covers the downtown area; Port Liberte, 07305; Newport, 07310

Police Station: East District, 207 Seventh Street, 201-547-5408

Emergency Hospital: St. Francis Hospital, 25 McWilliams Place, 201-714-8900 or 201-418-1000

Library: The main branch of the Jersey City Public Library, 472 Jersey Avenue, 201-547-4500, is located in downtown.

Public School Education: Jersey City Board of Education, 241 Erie Street, 201-915-6000

Adult Education: St. Peter's College, 2641 Kennedy Boulevard, 201-333-4400; New Jersey City University, 2039 Kennedy Boulevard, 201-

200-2000; and the Jersey City branches of Hudson County Community Colleges, headquartered at 168 Sip Avenue, 201-656-2020.

Community Resources: The Jersey City Museum, fourth floor, Jersey City Public Library, 472 Jersey Avenue, 201-547-4514; Liberty Science Center, 25 Phillip Street, Jersey City, 07305

Transportation—Subway: on PATH, 800-234-7284, the trip between the four stops in Jersey City (Journal Square, Grove Street, Exchange Place and Pavonia-Newport) and the World Trade Center took 10 minutes at most and trains ran at four to six minute intervals during rush hours, every 10 to 15 and 30 minutes at other times. It takes 20 minutes at most from Journal Square or Grove Street to 33rd Street in Manhattan (with stops at Sixth Avenue and Christopher, 9th, 14th and 23rd Streets in between). Service is almost as frequent on the 33rd Street line as on the World Trade Center line. PATH trains also run to Hoboken and Newark from all four Jersey City stations.

Transportation—Bus: the Red & Tan Bus Co., 201-876-9000 or 212-564-8484, operates frequent service between Jersey City and Wall Street or the Port Authority Bus Terminal in Manhattan.

Transportation—Ferry: New York Waterway, 800-533-3779, www.nywaterway.com, operates passenger ferries stopping at the Liberty Harbor Marina, Harborside and Colgate and the World Financial Center in Lower Manhattan, and between Port Liberté and Wall Street.

NEW JERSEY SUBURBS

Check www.njtowns.com for more about New Jersey communities.

- **Bayonne**; a working class city of 62,000 south of Jersey City on Upper New York Bay, affordable and now just 20 minutes from Jersey City and the PATH tubes to Manhattan by the new Hudson-Bergen Light Rail system. www.bayonnenj.org
- **Cliffside Park**, on the Palisades just south of Fort Lee, is an affordable family neighborhood with an ethnically mixed population. Borough Clerk, 201-945-3456; Chamber of Commerce, www.cliffsideparkchamberofcommerce.com
- **Englewood**, cosmopolitan with its multi-racial population and housing that ranges from low-income to turn-of-the-century estates. Traditionally home to affluent business executives, it boasts good shopping and restaurants and a 30-minute bus commute to Manhattan. Chamber of Commerce, 201-567-2381
- **Leonia**, west of Fort Lee but less glitzy and not as high rise—middle-class with a village-like feel. Proximity to the George Washington Bridge makes it a quick commute, by bus, to the city. Borough Clerk, 201-592-5752
- **Montclair**, cosmopolitan and affluent, enjoys a hilly perch from which

Manhattan is visible at a distance to the east. Single-family housing is shaded by towering oaks. The bus commute takes about 30 minutes. Borough Clerk, 973-744-7660

- **Ridgewood**, a 60-minute commute northwest of the city, houses a homogeneous white-collar population along manicured, tree-shaded streets. Schools are excellent, taxes high, and the downtown shopping district seems not to have changed in 50 years. The Paramus malls nearby make up for that. Chamber of Commerce, 201-445-2600; also on the web at www.webridgewood.com

- **Summit** is an affluent community of handsome homes along winding, hilly streets now just 50 minutes from Manhattan on the Midtown Direct train to Penn Station. On the web at www.cityofsummit.com

- **Teaneck**, just west of Englewood and without the estates, is similarly hilly and tree-shaded, more middle-class and proud of its ethnic diversity; a 30-40-minute commute. Chamber of Commerce, 201-801-0012; homepage, www.ziva.com/teaneck

- **Tenefly**, north of Englewood and more homogeneous a suburb, boasts a nice village center clustered around the railroad station and an excellent high school; also an easy commute. Borough Clerk, 201-568-6100

- **South Orange**, with its downtown railroad station, is convenient, small towny. Housing is varied, from modest to upscale up the hill, and 60 acres of parkland with three town pools add to the comfort level. Chamber of Commerce, 973-762-4333, and www.southorange.com

- **Westfield** nestles among the rolling Watchung hills of Union County, about an hour by bus or 35 minutes by train and PATH tubes from midtown. A strong sense of community, excellent schools, extensive sports and recreation activities in three county-run parks make this culturally rich old town attractive to commuters. Chamber of Commerce, 908-233-3021; also on the web at www.westfieldnj.ataclick.com

LONG ISLAND SUBURBS

- **Rockville Centre**, 30 minutes from Manhattan by the Long Island Railroad (which is not the island's finest feature), has easy access to Long Island beaches, an arts guild, eight parks, a thriving shopping center and a variety of housing. But it is best known for its municipal power plant, which gives its residents the cheapest electricity on the island. Village administrator's office, 516-678-9212; Rockville Centre web site, www.ci.rockville-centre.ny.us

- **Garden City** was once a summer resort for Morgans and Vanderbilts, and it's still expensive, tidy and manicured. Squarely in the middle of the island, it's an easy 30-40 minutes to Penn Station. Chamber of Commerce, 516-746-7724

- **Manhasset** residents live in single-family homes and condos, the former most attractively and expensively set around Manhasset Bay in Plandome to the north. Because of the department stores along Miracle Mile, real estate taxes are low here, just about 35 minutes from Manhattan on the LIRR. Call North Hempstead Town Hall, public affairs office, 516-627-0590, for more details about the area. www.manhasset.org
- **Port Washington**, formerly a glamorous summer resort on a peninsula in the Long Island Sound, is still attractive to boaters. The 40-minute train commute is a relatively easy one. Chamber of Commerce, 516-883-6566; web site, www.portwashington.org
- **Old Westbury** once housed the North Shore estates of high society and still has 25 miles of horse trails and a polo club. Besides its rolling hills, the high cost of living here gets you good schools, three colleges and Old Westbury Gardens. Village clerk, 516-626-0800
- **Cold Spring Harbor**, with its cedar shake colonials on a natural inlet on the Sound one-hour from the city by train, has the feel of old Long Island. It also has good schools. A village within greater Huntington, this is Talbots country. Huntington Chamber of Commerce, 516-423-6100, and on the web at www.huntingtonchamber.com

WESTCHESTER COUNTY (NY) SUBURBS

- **Bronxville**, also on the city's northern border and hilly, feels rather English and looks rather Tudor. There are also co-ops and condos, quite elegant ones near the railroad station. Known for its good schools. Chamber of Commerce, 914-337-6040
- **Dobbs Ferry** on the Hudson just to the north, and about 40 minutes by Metro North's Hudson line from the city, also offers a variety of housing possibilities and a heterogeneous population, which makes it appealing to academics and people in the arts. Town Clerk, 914-693-6161
- **Edgemont**, a hamlet within the town of Greenburgh, is adjacent to Scarsdale, but less known and more affordable. Its good schools have attracted a growing foreign-born population, especially Japanese. Houses are traditional in style, co-ops and condos relatively plentiful and reasonable. Greenburgh town clerk, 914-993-1500, and on the web at www.greenburgh.ny.us
- **Hastings-on-Hudson** is diverse in its housing, its population and its terrain, albeit hilly and with river views. Besides one-family houses behind stone walls, apartments are available. The arts are strong here, shopping very small-town. Nature trails and bike paths are an added feature. Village Clerk, 914-478-3400
- **Mamaroneck**, which includes Larchmont, houses a heterogeneous population just west of toney Rye on a neck of land in Long Island

Sound. You'll find co-ops, condos, single-family homes, with few rentals. Waterfront is what it's about, with good recreational facilities including boating and beaches on Harbor Island Park; a 35-minute commute. Town administrative offices, 914-381-7810

- **New Rochelle**, just 32 minutes from midtown on Metro North, is a suburban city of 67,000, with an exceptional variety of housing choices, nine miles of shoreline and 35 parks. On the web at www.newrochelleny.com
- **Pelham**, just over the Bronx County line and a 20-minute train ride north from the city, is cosmopolitan and relatively unknown. Fine old trees line its winding roads, and you can walk to everything, which includes beaches, a golf course and woodland hiking and fishing. Taxes are high. Town Clerk, 914-738-0777
- **Scarsdale**, rocky, wooded and upscale, has few rentals or co-ops, but it does have beautiful homes along winding, wooded roads and about a quarter of the town's area in open land. Its highly competitive public schools have attracted a diverse population, many of them Asian, altering the town's once-waspy image. The commute to Manhattan is about 45 minutes. Chamber of Commerce, 914-722-1110, and on the web at www.village.scarsdale.ny.us
- **White Plains**, 35 minutes from the city, is a city, offering a quick commute by train or express bus, good shopping, ethnic restaurants, a variety of housing choices, and relatively low taxes. Recreational facilities include a golf course, outdoor pools, tennis and an ice skating rink. Town planning department, 914-422-1252, Chamber of Commerce, 914-948-2110; and on the web at www.cityofwhiteplains.com

CONNECTICUT SUBURBS

- **Greenwich** (pronounced Gren-itch), a 45-minute train commute from the city, offers genteel seclusion for the wealthy, the bustle of corporate headquarters as well as upscale shopping and eateries, excellent schools, beaches and recreational facilities. Less expensive than Greenwich "backcountry" is the livelier downtown area. Nearby **Cos Cob**, **Byram** and **Old Greenwich** are also somewhat more affordable. www.greenwichct.org
- **Norwalk** is diverse and less expensive than the surrounding towns, on the whole. Partially rehabilitated, south Norwalk, with its condos, galleries and restaurants, appeals to a young crowd, many of whom work in nearby corporate offices. Boating, fishing, beaches, tennis and paddle tennis are also a draw. **Silvermine** to the west and **Rowaton** on the southwestern tip are more upscale. www.norwalkct.org
- **Stamford**, 40 minutes from Grand Central on Metro North, is at once a city of 111,000 with its bustling downtown on the banks of the Mill

River and the Long Island Sound, a major home of corporate headquarters, and a suburb with sprawling estates to the north. Housing is varied, parks and beaches plentiful. www.ci.stamford.ct.us

- **Westport** on Long Island Sound became a colony of artists and writers in the 1930s and 1940s, and it is still more sophisticated, more like New York City than the rest of Connecticut. There is a summer theater, and the arts are still a presence, as are pricey boutiques and good shopping in nearby Stamford. Water and woods, a variety of single-family homes, a few rentals and condos characterize the town. The train to New York takes about an hour. www.ci.westport.ct.us

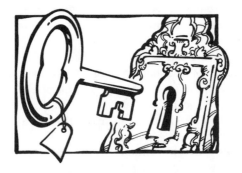

R ENTING AN APARTMENT IN NEW YORK CITY IS ONCE AGAIN A
daunting task. The market has tightened considerably, even at the
high end, with rents rising about 10% a year recently. Less expensive apartments (the affordable one- or two-bedroom, hold the Jacuzzi) are
even harder to find. Though the market eased off late in 2000, sticker shock
among newcomers is still nearly universal.

In Manhattan's established neighborhoods, location doesn't influence
price much. One rental expert estimates that in Greenwich Village and the
neighborhoods between 15th Street and 96th Street (Chelsea, the Upper
East and West sides, Murray Hill, Gramercy Park), the price difference
between comparable apartments is negligible. If cost is a serious concern, it
is best to search in the developing Manhattan neighborhoods, in the outer
boroughs or the suburbs.

Another option, especially attractive at the studio and one-bedroom
level, is to purchase a condo or a co-op. Mortgage rates remain reasonably
low, and with the income tax deduction for mortgage interest factored in,
these apartments may be less expensive than renting an equivalent space.
To see what's involved in buying an apartment or a house, turn to **Buying**
at the end of this chapter.

APARTMENT HUNTING

First, renting—with pluck, imagination, and fortitude you can find an adequate place in an appropriate neighborhood. Various strategies for doing
so are listed below in order of conventionality and practicality. But to start,
some golden generalities:

- **Don't panic**. Don't be immobilized by what you may have heard.
  Negativism will get you nowhere—to live. Start your search a month or
  more before you expect to move, if possible.
- **Be prepared for high rents**. Newcomers, especially, are subject to

shock at New York rents. In the long run it may just be possible to find that charming, sun-drenched apartment in the neighborhood of your dreams for a reasonable sum, but such gems take time and contacts, so brace yourself.

- **Be adventuresome but prudent**. The housing squeeze has intensified gentrification of neighborhoods throughout the city. Yesterday's marginal areas are meccas for today's trendsetters. Behind dusty facades from the Bowery to upper Broadway lurk attractive apartments, but before getting too carried away, realize that not all areas are suitable, especially not for single women.

- **Inquire about a neighborhood**. Local police precincts (see listings under **Neighborhoods**) can supply valuable safety information about a particular neighborhood, street or block within their boundaries. Stop by the precinct for candid and well-founded opinions about the characteristics and police problems of a particular area.

- **Consider subletting or sharing to start**. If you are in desperate need of a roof and have not discovered a feasible rental, seriously consider these alternatives. Subletting or sharing buys time to find the optimum situation in the most suitable neighborhood.

Generalities out of the way, on to ways of finding space.

NEWSPAPER CLASSIFIED ADVERTISEMENTS

Start here, on paper or online, to get a sense of what's available, where and at what price. In fact, it's a good idea to begin in advance of your move by scanning the online classifieds to get some idea of what's possible and where. Because individual landlords, as well as brokers, place ads, classifieds sometimes are a means of avoiding brokerage commissions. Chances are, however, you will end up using a broker. The classifieds provide a good way of finding one and of discovering which brokers are active in a particular neighborhood.

- **The Sunday *New York Times*' Real Estate section**, printed Friday night and delivered to dealers sometime on Saturday, contains the best rental listings in the city. *The Times* actively discourages sale of the Sunday edition before the multi-sectioned paper is completed Saturday evening. However, many outlets sell the sections they have on hand (for full newspaper price) Saturday morning. While far fewer in number, daily ads in *The Times* are also worth checking. Since the race is to the swift, the cyber-connected will do well to check *The Times'* web site, www.nytoday.com, where the Sunday ads appear before 5 a.m. Saturday morning, with daily updates. This site automatically searches the databases of the city's largest brokers.

- **The Village Voice** is a good source of rental listings for Manhattan as well as other boroughs. Newsstand deliveries are made around 5 a.m. Wednesday morning; the newsstand on the island beside the Seventh Avenue IRT Uptown Christopher Street subway entrance at Sheridan Square is one of the first places to receive delivery. Also, you can get early copies Tuesday night at the Village newsstand on Astor/Lafayette; get there between 5 and 6 p.m. to beat the line. Easier yet, the *Voice* listings are online, www.villagevoice.com; updated at 1 p.m. Tuesday, 12:01 a.m. Wednesday-Saturday.
- The **Wall Street Journal's** Friday edition lists apartments for rent in "The Mart" classified section.
- **The New York Post's** rental classifieds are best consulted on Friday. The Friday edition is printed Thursday night and delivered to all-night newsstands in the mid-Manhattan area (try stands at Grand Central or Pennsylvania stations Thursday night around midnight). The *Post* is a particularly good source for apartments in Queens, Brooklyn, and The Bronx. The *Post's* web site, www.nypost.com, is updated daily.
- **The Daily News'** Brooklyn and Queens editions carry numerous rental classifieds for those boroughs. Listings in the Manhattan edition are negligible. On the web at www.nydailynews.com.
- **Newsday**, published daily in Garden City, Long Island, and available in Manhattan, is the best source of listings in Queens and Long Island. On the web at www.newsday.com.
- **New York Press** is a free weekly distributed each Wednesday. Look for it in restaurants, stores, and street boxes all over town. A good source for sublets and shares. Press listings are online, www.adone.com/nypress, at 10 a.m. Tuesday.
- **The Jersey Journal**, published in Jersey City Monday-Saturday, is the paper to consult for rentals in Hoboken and Jersey City. The *Journal* can be purchased at newsstands adjoining the 14th Street and 33rd Street PATH stations in Manhattan.
- New York City neighborhood newspapers—**The Villager, Chelsea-Clinton News, The Spirit** (West Side), **Our Town** (East Side), **The Flatiron News, Tribeca Trib**, and others—occasionally carry a rental ad or two but are not prime sources. In Brooklyn, however, two weeklies, the **Brooklyn Heights Press**, 129 Montague Street, second floor, and **The Phoenix**, 33 Flatbush Avenue, carry sublet and rental advertisements. First copies of the *Press* are delivered to the office around 2 p.m. Thursday afternoon, and *The Phoenix* reaches Brooklyn newsstands early Friday morning.

ONLINE LISTINGS

Increasingly renters and buyers are going online to find an apartment, house or broker to suit their needs before venturing forth streetward. We've mentioned newspaper classifieds above. Oddly, unlike other major US cities, New York City has no multiple-listing service giving buyers and renters access to available properties citywide in one composite listing. A recent attempt to launch such a listing online collapsed, and while multiple listing is probably inevitable here, the search is still piecemeal. And there are other online resources to aid in the search.

New York City Real Estate Exchange, www.cityrealty.com, for example, offers detailed listings, photos and floor plans of houses, co-ops, condos, and apartments for rent or sale in the city. They're updated hourly. You can search by location, price-range, and size, with e-mail notification as properties in your categories come online. The site includes excellent, detailed neighborhood descriptions, and application forms. The computer-challenged can call 212-734-9191 for information.

It may also be worth your while to visit the web sites of some of the major rental agencies, such as Citi Habitats, www.citi-habitats.com, and Feathered Nest, www.featherednest.com, and large owner/management firms such as Rockrose, www.rockrosenyc.com, all to be found in the *Times* real estate ads. These sites are virtual data banks of each firm's entire listings. For a collection of online apartment hunting resources, including a list of local publications and apartment finding services, check Columbia University's housing page, www.hr.columbia.edu/hr/html/housing_resources.

See also **No Fee Apartments Online**, below, and for national relocation services refer to **Online Resources—Relocation** at the end of the **Moving and Storage** chapter.

REAL ESTATE BROKERS

Generally New York City's real estate brokers focus on sales rather than rentals. However, some agencies specialize in rentals, and many have brokers who handle nothing else. Below, we've listed the names of real estate brokers as a service. Their presence in this book indicates no endorsement. Rather, firms and the neighborhoods they cover are given as possible starting points for your search.

Real estate agencies tend to concentrate their efforts on one or a series of contiguous neighborhoods, for example: the Upper East Side; Chelsea, the Village and SoHo; Gramercy Park and Murray Hill. If your heart is set on one location, it is important to discover the most savvy brokers in that area. If almost any neighborhood will do, make sure you list with several knowledgeable firms in order to get the coverage you need.

Count on spending some time and effort discovering a broker sympathetic to your needs and capable of showing you suitable places. In the long run, a broker may well be the best lead to a decent apartment, and she (the majority seem to be women) can save you hours of calling and traipsing on your own. Broker commissions for unfurnished apartments currently run 15% of one year's rent, paid up front by the tenant; in New Jersey, where rentals are more generally available, the commission generally equals one month's rent or, in rare cases, no commission at all.

Recommendations for finding a real estate broker:

- Ask friends, colleagues, your firm, and family for recommendations of brokers who are particularly helpful. As previously mentioned, not all capable agents with good lists advertise widely.
- Gather names from appealing classified listings.
- If your heart is set on one locale, try some of the smaller firms whose storefronts you'll notice when pounding the pavement. These firms seldom advertise but are often good sources for listings in the immediate vicinity.

As a start, we've compiled a list of brokers who handle rentals in Manhattan, parts of The Bronx, Brooklyn, Queens, Staten Island and New Jersey:

MANHATTAN REAL ESTATE BROKERS (AREA CODE 212)

- **Ambrose-Marelia Co.**, 137 Waverly Place, NYC 10011, 675-6980: Upper East and West sides
- **Brocor Realty**, 654 Madison Avenue, NYC 10028, 223-7554: East Side from 96th Street to Gramercy Park
- **Citi Habitats**, 30 East 33rd Street, NYC 10019, 685-7777, and on the web at www.citihabitats.com: all Manhattan
- **City Apartments**, 44 East 29th Street, NYC 10016, 376-4143/4142: all Manhattan
- **Corcoran Group**, 200 West 72nd Street, NYC 10023, 877-2711, www.corcoran.com: city-wide
- **Douglas Elliman**, 103 Fifth Avenue, NYC 10021, 645-4040: Upper East and West sides
- **Dwelling Quest Corp.**, 360 Lexington Avenue, Suite 1601, NYC 10022, 681-9200: Upper East and West sides
- **Eychner Associates Inc.**, 44 Greenwich Avenue, NYC 10012, 807-0700: Greenwich Village and downtown
- **The Feathered Nest**, 770 Lexington Avenue, NYC 10022, 317-7800, www.featherednest.com: all Manhattan
- **Frederick Lee Real Estate**, 306 Fifth Avenue, NYC 10022, 736-6200: Upper East Side

- **Green Realty**, 4310 Broadway, NYC 10033, 795-0144: Washington Heights and Inwood
- **Gumley-Haft Inc.**, 110 East 59th Street, NYC 10022, 371-2525: luxury rentals, Upper East Side
- **Hudson View Associates, Inc.**, 159-00 Riverside Drive West, Suite 1M-70, NYC 10032, 928-0508: Washington Heights
- **Kain Realty**, 37 West 84th Street, NYC 10024, 877-5100: Upper East and West Side and Midtown
- **Macklowe**, 515 East 72nd Street, NYC 10019, 988-5551: all Manhattan
- **M. Woods and Associates**, 645-7158, by appointment only: brownstones primarily, Chelsea, Greenwich Village and downtown
- **Alice F. Mason, Ltd.**, 635 Madison Avenue, NYC 10022, 832-8870: luxury rentals, primarily on the Upper East Side
- **Manhattan Apartments, Inc.**, 225 West 57th Street, NYC 10019, 347-423-7339, www.manhattanapts.com; primarily rentals, mostly lofts and studios, some sales. Will provide corporate relocation services.
- **New Heights Realty**, 632 West 207th Street, NYC 10034, 567-7200: primarily Inwood, some Washington Heights
- **Prolific Realty**, 202 Waverly Place, NYC 10014, 989-3012: Greenwich Village
- **Salon Realty Co.**, 338 East 92nd Street, NYC 10128, 534-3131: Upper East Side
- **Sandra Greer Real Estate**, 201 East 77th Street, NYC 10021, 472-1878: mostly East Side, Upper and Lower
- **Selena Godeau**, 88 University Place, NYC 10013, 645-1800: SoHo, Chelsea, East and West Village
- **Simone Song Properties**, 241 Cabrini Boulevard, NYC 10033, 928-5100: Washington Heights, especially Hudson Heights
- **Spencer Realty**, 353 Lexington Avenue, NYC 10016, 661-9440: all Manhattan
- **Stein-Perry**, 740 West 181st Street, NYC 10033, 928-3805: Washington Heights
- **Stribling & Associates**, 924 Madison Avenue, NYC 10021, 570-2440: uptown
- **Stribling Wells & Gay**, 340 West 23rd Street, NYC 10011, 243-4000: downtown
- **Wendy Walters & Associates**, 201 West 77th Street, NYC 10024, 874-4396: Upper West Side
- **Webb & Brooker Realty Inc.**, 2534 Seventh Avenue, NYC 10039, 926-7100: Harlem

BRONX REAL ESTATE BROKERS (AREA CODE 718)

- **Aztec Realty**, 2006 Williamsbridge Road, Bronx 10461, 822-9100, all Bronx
- **E.R.A. Susan Goldy & Co.**, 6114 Riverdale Avenue, Bronx 10471, 549-4116: Riverdale, Spuyten Duyvil
- **ReMax Deal-Finders**, 2366 Westchester Avenue, Bronx 10462, 829-3325, all Bronx
- **Robert Hill, Inc.**, 279 West 231st Street, Bronx, 10463, 884-2200: Riverdale and Kingsbridge
- **Spero Real Estate**, 33 South Broadway, Yonkers, 10701, 914-968-7862: Riverdale and lower Westchester County
- **Trebach Realty**, 3801 Greystone, Bronx 10463, 543-7174: Riverdale, Spuyten Duyvil

BROOKLYN REAL ESTATE BROKERS (AREA CODE 718)

- **Apollo Real Estate**, 480 76th Steeet, Brooklyn 11209, 238-1354: Bay Ridge, Park Slope, Windsor Terrace
- **Brooklyn Landmark Realty**, 174 Court Street, Brooklyn 11201, 935-9800: Brooklyn Heights, Cobble Hill and vicinity
- **Coldwell Banker**, **Hunt Kennedy & Cranford Agency**, 144 Montague Street, Brooklyn 11201, 624-7000: Brooklyn Heights, Cobble Hill, Boerum Hill, Park Slope
- **David Perlman**, 32 Court Street, Brooklyn 11201, 855-8708: Brooklyn Heights, Park Slope, Cobble Hill, Boerum Hill, Carroll Gardens
- **Flood Company**, 7403 Fifth Avenue, Brooklyn 11209, 238-9800: Bay Ridge and Fort Hamilton
- **Frank Manzione Real Estate**, 223 Columbia Street, Brooklyn 11231, 834-1440, www.fpmre.com: South Brooklyn
- **Kazeroid and Aberman Realty**, 196 Seventh Avenue, Brooklyn 11215, 499-8200: Park Slope
- **Kenn Firpo Realty Corp.**, 158 Bedford Avenue, Brooklyn 11211, 384-4949: Greenpoint and Williamsburg
- **Kline Realty**, 599 Lorimer Street, Brooklyn 11211, 361-1776: Greenpoint and Williamsburg
- **William B. May Co.**, 150 Montague Street, Brooklyn 11201, 875-1289: Brooklyn Heights, Cobble Hill, Carroll Gardens; 397 Flatbush Avenue, Brooklyn 11238, 230-5500, Park Slope, Prospect Park
- **Maguire Real Estate**, 7901 5th Avenue, Brooklyn 11209, 836-4330, and on the web at www.johnmaguirerealestate.com: Bay Ridge

- **Naida McSherry**, 275 Clinton Avenue, Brooklyn 11205, 230-0030: Fort Greene and Clinton Hill
- **Renaissance Properties**, 102 Hoyt Street, Brooklyn 11217, 875-5650: Fort Greene and Clinton Hill

QUEENS REAL ESTATE BROKERS (AREA CODE 718)

- **Bay Benjamin**, 212-89 26th Avenue, Bay Terrace Shopping Center, Bayside 11360, 225-0800, www.baybenjamin.com: Bayside
- **Castle Realty, Inc.**, 28-17 Astoria Boulevard, Astoria 11102, 545-7669: Astoria
- **Century 21 Alexiou Realty**, 31-23 23rd Avenue, Astoria 11105, 204-0101: Astoria
- **Coldwell Banker/Owner's Club Realty**, 31-15 Ditmars Boulevard, LIC 11105, 956-5757: Astoria, Long Island City, Sunnyside
- **First Choice Real Estate**, 61-43 186th Street, Fresh Meadows 11365, 800-875-4111: Flushing, Forest Hills, Kew Gardens, Rego Park, Bayside; ask for Helen Keit.
- **G/M Dynasty Realty**, 34-16 30th Avenue, Queens 11103, 204-4800: Astoria, Woodside, Long Island City
- **Golden Choice Realty**, 37-11A Prince Street, Flushing 11354, 359-1700: Queens, especially Flushing
- **Green-Ways Realty**, 2 Tennis Place, Forest Hills 11375, 544-1952: Forest Hills, Kew Gardens, Rego Park
- **Karan Realty**, 115-19 Liberty Avenue, Queens 11419, 848-8900: Richmond Hill
- **Lane Realty**, 107-40 Queens Boulevard, Forest Hills 11375, 268-3500: Forest Hills, Kew Gardens, Rego Park
- **Nu Place Realty**, 120-10 Queens Boulevard, Kew Gardens 11415, 793-9500: Forest Hills, Kew Gardens, Rego Park, Briarwood
- **Re/Max Today**, 32-75 Steinway Street, LIC 11103, 274-2400: Astoria, Long Island City, Sunnyside
- **SPEC International Realty**, 171-04 Northern Boulevard, Queens 11358, 539-2233: Flushing, Bayside, Douglaston
- **Terrace Realty**, 16 Station Square, Forest Hills Gardens, Forest Hills 11375, 268-1045: Greater Forest Hills, Rego Park, Kew Gardens
- **Welcome Home Real Estate**, 46-15 Skillman Avenue, Sunnyside 11104, 706-0957: Sunnyside, Woodside

STATEN ISLAND REAL ESTATE BROKERS (AREA CODE 718)

- **Gateway Real Estate**, 285 St. Marks Place, St. George 10301, 273-3800: St. George, Snug Harbor, no fee

- **Prudential Appleseed Realty**, 2043 Richmond Avenue, New Springville 10314, 698-9797: North Shore
- **Rachel Gannon Realty, Inc.**, 963 Post Avenue, SI 10302, 273-9200: all Staten Island, specializing in Port Richmond.
- **Rainbow Realty**, 364 Decker Avenue, Port Richmond 10302, 720-2002: Victorian properties in St. George, Stapleton, Snug Harbor, and Port Richmond
- **Vitale-Sunshine Realty**, 1444 Richmond Road, SI 10304, 979-3333: all Staten Island

NEW JERSEY REAL ESTATE BROKERS (AREA CODE 201)

- **Action Agency**, 4301 Bergenline Avenue, Union City 07087, 348-8741: Fort Lee, Edgewater, Weehawken
- **Apartments & Homes of NJ**, Fort Lee Inc., 214 Main Street, Fort Lee 07024, 947-6464: Fort Lee, Edgewater, Weehawken
- **Boyne Real Estate**, 303 Grove Street, Jersey City 07302, 451-0950: Jersey City
- **Crown Properties**, 1500 Summit Avenue, Union City 07089, 319-1500: Weehawken
- **Hoboken Brownstone Co.**, 92 Hudson Street, Hoboken 07030, 792-0100, www.hbrownstone.com, Hoboken, Weehawken, Jersey City
- **McAlear Cavalier Realtors, Better Homes & Gardens**, 327 Broad Avenue, Leonia 07105, 944-4660: Leonia
- **Oppler-Ketive Realtors,** 1372 Palisade Avenue, Fort Lee 07024, 585-8080: All Bergen County
- **Severino Realty**, 920 Washington Street, Hoboken 07030, 653-1800: Hoboken
- **Singleton and Galman**, 1106 Washington Street, Hoboken 07030, 656-5400: Hoboken
- **Sky-Line Realty, Inc.**, 3506 Park Avenue, Weehawken 07087, 863-6090: Weehawken
- **Weichert Realtors**, 310 Main Street, Fort Lee 07024, 592-6888: Fort Lee, Edgewater, Weehawken
- **West Bank Realty, Inc.**, 514 First Street, Hoboken 07030, 792-0100: Hoboken

NO-FEE APARTMENTS ONLINE

You may have noticed among the newspaper listings ads for no-fee services, and if you're determined to avoid a stiff broker's fee one of these may help, at a fraction of the cost. Here's how they work: pay a flat fee, up to $200, detail your specifications online, by phone or fax, and receive a list of no-fee apartments being offered by management companies and private owners. Updates are daily or weekly, and you do the rest of the work. However, listings can be off-base or out-of-date, and some have been found to be fraudulent. We mention four that may be useful.

- **Apartment Source**, apartmentsource.com, online only, lets you search their database for apartments according to price, size, location and amenities, in addition to which you receive daily e-mail updates with new vacancies to meet your specifications. The $39 gives you one month's service, which also occasionally includes sublets and short-term rentals, and gives access to roommateclick.com, a roommate matching service. The site also offers a credit check.

- **Apartment Store**, 212-386-2982, www.nyaptstore.com, charges $80 for a mandatory credit report, which a prospective landlord will require in any case, and gives the client one month's access to their list of no-fee apartments in some 3,000 properties throughout Manhattan, Queens, and Brooklyn. The client specifies what neighborhoods, how many rooms, what features and a price range and receives updates daily by fax or e-mail.

- **Metro List Xpress**, 212-220-4663, extension 224, www.mlx.com, is a Manhattan-wide data base with no-fee and fee listings as well as sponsors offering a variety of products and services at a discount to members. For $169 the subscriber receives an account number and a personal ID number (PIN) which covers specifics such as desired location, apartment size, whether pets are allowed, maximum rent, etc. By fax or e-mail he/she receives a list of all the apartments in the data base fitting these specifications, with updates on request for as long as necessary. You can change specifications to receive listings in other categories: different neighborhoods or rent limits, for example. A free membership gives one access to more limited services. Included among the listings, which are updated daily, are properties handled by some 200 brokerage companies; these would involve fees. Also included: co-ops, condos and houses for sale by owners as well as brokers, photos and layouts included.

- **Rent-Direct**, 166 Fifth Avenue, 4th floor, NYC 10010, 212-645-9797, www.rent-direct.com, has perhaps the deepest list of apartments in the city and New Jersey, and a useful site, as well as seven-day customer support and a walk-in office with computers for customer use. You pay $169 to access the service until you find a suitable apartment. This gives you access to their database of some 1,500 buildings, with floor plans, interior and exterior photos and street panoramas. Updates of apartments fitting your profile are provided as they enter the market, online or by fax. They'll do a credit check for a fee.

A final word about no-fee apartment guides sold in book form at bookstores and some newsstands. They tend to be unreliable and not up-to-date.

NEW BUILDINGS

Renovated factories, warehouses and other commercial buildings occasionally add new rental units to the city's supply. Apartments in reconstructed or totally new buildings command top dollar. However, it is often possible to avoid brokers' commissions in these buildings when landlords and managers pay on-site rental agents to fill the buildings as quickly as possible. The agents, as employees of the landlord, charge no commission.

DIRECT ACTION

In a town where single-minded apartment hunters have been known to read the obituary columns with as much intensity as the real estate classifieds, no one need feel self-conscious about tackling landlords, managing agents, superintendents, or local merchants in order to locate a place in a particular neighborhood or building.

Consider trying some of these alternatives:
- **Call the managing agent of a likely building**. The firm's or agent's name is usually posted near a building's entrance. If no telephone number is given, check the phone book.
- **Speak with the superintendent directly**. To find him, check the building directory, buzzer listings or, in the case of the smaller brownstones with shared part-time supers, your man could be the person sweeping the steps or putting garbage cans out on the sidewalk. If an apartment is available, the super or manager will sometimes send you to a broker to gain access. If a vacant apartment is found through independent efforts, you are not liable for the broker's fee. However, since reasonable apartments are in short supply, need usually overrides the fine points of the legal situation; most people prefer to pay the commission rather than go without the apartment. Once secure in your nest, if you want redress, file a complaint with the Division of Licenses, New York Department of State, 123 Williams Street, 19th floor, NYC 10007, 212-417-5747. This may eventually result in a settlement.
- **Pavement pounding** accompanied by incessant querying of merchants, stoop sitters, dog walkers, postmen—indeed anyone who looks like a resident of the neighborhood—can yield results as well as blisters.
- For the record, some but not all apartment buildings are listed in each borough's **Yellow Pages** by street and number under the alphabetical heading "Apartments and Apartment Houses." Others are listed alphabetically by name.

WORD OF MOUTH

The grapevine approach—broadcasting your need through a network of local friends—is often an effective means to a desired apartment. However, when you're new to town the chances of having such a network are probably slim. But do use any contacts available. Parents can call old college chums; who knows, their children may be leaving a desirable place. Your college friends may have a lead; their in-laws may, too. In any case, personal contacts are often a shot at the type of place that never makes it as far as *The Times* or a broker's office.

BULLETIN BOARDS

Certain neighborhoods, particularly the more homogeneous communities such as SoHo and Tribeca, as well as some large buildings, have bulletin boards where an occasional apartment turns up among the sheets offering children's skis, a ride to California, and opportunities for self-improvement. Inquire locally to find out which bar, supermarket, or grocery store serves this neighborhood function. Bulletin boards in university areas also include valuable information, notably New York University, Columbia, and Hunter College.

HOUSE ORGANS

Many corporations and organizations publish newsletters or magazines for their personnel that print employee advertisements (AOL-Time-Warner's *F.Y.I.* comes to mind). Sublets and the occasional rental turn up in these columns, and it is worth asking friends working for likely concerns to check their in-house publication for leads.

COLLEGE RELATED ASSOCIATIONS

Various New York alumni associations are trying to address the difficulty graduates have settling or relocating in the city. Contact your alumni office or local group to see if they can help. Some university clubs also offer advice and an occasional lead. Alumni magazines and newsletters may also offer sublet opportunities.

EMPLOYERS AND RELOCATION FIRMS

Frequently large companies pay for the services of relocation firms to find suitable long- and short-term apartment rentals for their mid- and upper-level hires and to help solve the various problems associated with moving and settling in. The fortunate employee is saved money and headaches in the bargain. Presumably you'll be informed by the company for which you are working if it is prepared to offer help with your search for living quarters.

A variety of relocation services are also available to individuals through real estate firms, which are part of nationwide franchise networks such as Re/Max, Century 21, Prudential, and Coldwell Banker or networks of independent brokers such as Genesis, First Choice Real Estate, and Relo. Also, there are independent services such as Relocation Consulting Services, located in Bedford, NY. While they exist primarily to service relocating homeowners, or potential homeowners, these services are also sometimes available to renters. Contact a broker near you affiliated with one of these networks before you move. They will help you sell your home, if you own one, and put you in touch with a realtor here who will take you in hand, provide you with information and show you communities which interest you, find you a place, get you pre-qualified for a mortgage, help you with insurance, get you a mover at a discount, help your spouse find a job, find a veterinarian for your cat, a painter for your bathroom, a school for your children. And it's free.

SUBLETS AND SHORT-TERM FURNISHED RENTALS

Lacking the services of a relocation firm, you nevertheless have access to the same resources they use, but you're on your own there. Most brokers offer long-term sublets, furnished and unfurnished, and advertise them, together with regular rentals, in local newspapers and online; expect to pay a broker's fee. You may also find an un-brokered sublet offered among the classifieds by the owner or lessee. In recent years ads have proliferated for short-term furnished rentals without broker's fee but at higher rental rates; these are not sublets, but are specifically marketed as short-term furnished rentals, sometimes with maid service included, a great convenience for those who can afford it. Consider either of these useful interim measures, providing the time needed to discover the optimum rental apartment. **Note**: leaseholders of rent stabilized or exceptionally reasonable apartments have been known to ask for fixture fees or key money in a sublet situation. While some people do pour money and energy into rehabilitating an inexpensive rental apartment and may deserve compensation for their efforts when they move, fixture fees that reflect no real value are tantamount to key money, which is illegal.

Prime sources for sublets and short-term furnished rentals include:

- *The Village Voice* with its special "Sublets" classified section, www.villagevoice.com.

- *The New York Times*, which lists sublets under "Apartments—Furnished" and "Apartments—Unfurnished," www.nytoday.com.
- *New York Press* is a free weekly distributed each Wednesday. Look for it in restaurants, stores and street boxes all over town. Good source for sublets.
- **Brokers** A number of sublet specialists advertise in the *Voice* and *New York Times*. Typically, commissions on furnished rentals run between one-half and one whole month's rent for periods of less than nine months. Most agencies charge 15% for longer sublets. Six brokers and one service currently specializing in sublets:
  - **Apartment Placement Services**, 575 Lexington Avenue, 4th floor, NYC 10022, 212-572-9609, specializes in short-term furnished sublets and unfurnished prime lease rentals for a $950 fee; also places young professionals in shared apartments throughout the city for $750. Call for appointment.
  - **The Feathered Nest**, 310 Madison Avenue, NYC 10017, 212-867-8500, www.feathernest.com, also handles furnished apartments with and without fees, call for appointment.
  - **Gamut Realty Group, Inc.**, 301 East 78th Street, NYC 10021, 212-879-4229, on the web at www.gamutnyc.com.
  - **New York Habitat**, 307 Seventh Avenue, Suite 306, New York 1000l, 212-255-8018, on the web at www.nyhabitat.com; specializes in sublets, short-term and long-term rentals, a no fee service.
  - **Senter Sublet**, 510 Madison Avenue, NYC 10022, 212-935-8730, www.sentersublets.com, call for appointment.
  - **Short Term Housing**, 251 West 81st Street, NYC 10024, 917-441-7922, call for appointment.
  - **Urban Ventures**, 38 West 32nd Street, NYC 10001, 212-594-5650, call for appointment.
- **Bulletin boards** in large buildings, bars or other neighborhood locations. Large apartment complexes have waiting lists for rental apartments the proverbial block long. However, leaseholders arrange sublets directly and occasionally post notices on community bulletin boards. Check with the management of these big units to see if they have a central sublet source.
- **In-house publications** tend to be a better source of sublets than of rentals.

SHARING

One of the best solutions to high housing costs, particularly for young, single people, is an apartment share. But if you are just arriving in the city and don't know anyone, you may not have anyone to share with. If networking with old college buddies fails to turn up anything, your best bet is probably the newspapers or a roommate-finding service.

To find a room or bed in someone else's apartment check *The Times* ads under "Apartments to Share," #1696, and the *Voice's* "Shares." Some leaseholders prefer to have roommates pre-screened and list with agencies that arrange apartment shares for a flat fee up front. Reputations ebb and flow; we can't guarantee satisfaction. But if you want to investigate this option, three of the firms in Manhattan are:

- **Roommate Finders**, 250 West 57th Street, The Fisk Building, Suite 1629, NYC 10019, 212-489-6862, www.roommatefinders.com, open Monday-Friday noon to 7:30, Saturday and Sunday noon to 6 p.m. For the $200 fee the client, after filling out a registration sheet covering personal habits and preferences and discussing specifications in a half-hour interview, is given information sheets on prospective apartments and/or roommates. You can call daily for new listings for up to one year, and if you find your own roommate or apartment, you are entitled to a 50% refund. Listing is free.

- **New York Habitat**, 307 Seventh Avenue, Suite 306, NYC 10001, 212-255-8018, open 9 a.m. to 6 p.m., and on the web at www.nyhabitat.com. This firm, which also handles sublets and rentals, charges the renter only when they agree to rent an apartment share. The fee, a minimum of 30% of one month's rent, maximum of 15% of one year's rent, is based on length of stay.

- **April's List**, www.aprilslist.com, no phone, no fee to access this online list of apartment shares, short sublets and swaps (your apartment here for one in San Francisco, for example, or Barcelona, who knows?). There's also a bulletin board with postings from those who wish to sell or to buy a car, a wedding dress, a kitchen table. Serves a largely youthful clientele.

CHECKING IT OUT

You've found what appears to be the perfect, sunny apartment in a pleasant neighborhood and, best of all, you're the first person to see it! You want to shout, "I'll take it," but you should restrain yourself and spend a few minutes checking it out first. We suggest you bring a checklist of your musts and must-nots. In addition, you should make a quick inspection to make sure the apartment's beauty is not just skin deep. A little time and a few questions asked now can save you a lot of time, money, and headache later on. Specifically, you may want to look for the following:

- Are the kitchen appliances clean and in working order? Do the stove's burners work? How about the oven? Is there enough counter and shelf space? Does it smell funny in the kitchen space—or anywhere else?

- Do the windows open, close, and lock? Do the windows open onto a noisy or potentially dangerous area?

- Are there enough closets and is there enough storage space?
- Are there enough electrical outlets for all your needs? Do the outlets work?
- What about laundry facilities, are they in the building or nearby?
- Outside do you feel comfortable? Will you feel safe here at night? What about public transportation and shopping?

Ed Sacks' *Savvy Renter's Kit* contains a thorough renter's checklist for those interested in augmenting theirs.

If it all passes muster, be prepared to stake your claim without delay.

STAKING A CLAIM

It may seem to newcomers that securing an apartment, after having found one suitable, can be as difficult as gaining membership in an exclusive club. In this tight market, that's not far off the mark. You have to be found acceptable. For starters, arrive on time and presentably dressed for appointments. Even in this city of "attitude," a little politeness goes a long way. Also be sure to come armed with as many of the following as possible when checking out an apartment:

- A certified check, bank check, or money order to cover a deposit equivalent to one to two months' rent. Without this, none of the rest will matter.
- Most recent W-2 form
- Letter from current employer verifying that you are employed and, if possible, will continue to be; lacking that, your employer's business telephone number.
- Pay stubs showing a yearly income(s) equivalent to 40 to 50 times the monthly rent.
- A credit report or money to cover the fee for having a credit-check done.
- Reference letters, business and personal, and one from your current landlord stating you have never been late with a rent check.
- Recent statements from checking, savings, and investment accounts.
- A guarantor, parents for example in the case of youthful renters, with documents showing an income 80 to 100 times the monthly rent, if you do not have an income adequate to satisfy the landlord.

Having successfully navigated these shoals and been accepted, you are ready to sign a lease. First, a **word of caution**: there are fraudulent real estate and rental agents who take advantage of eager and unwary apartment seekers. To avoid them, meet real estate and rental agents only in an office, not on the street. Ask for a Department of State identification card and a photo ID. Give a deposit only to the landlord, and be wary of agents who can only be reached by beepers.

LEASES AND SECURITY DEPOSITS

Whether you're renting or subletting, before you sign a lease you might want to digest the useful information and advice in the 90-page booklet, *What Every Landlord and Tenant Should Know*, published by the **Citizens Housing and Planning Council**; available for $5 from the council at 50 East 42nd Street, Suite 407, NYC 10017-5405. For information call 212-286-9211.

Also helpful regarding landlord/tenant law in New York, is Cornell University's site, www.law.cornell.edu/topics/landlord_tenant. Among other items is a section on knowing your rental rights and links to the Fair Housing Institute, the City of New York Housing Court Information System.

DEPOSITS

The first written check undoubtedly will be a deposit held by the broker or landlord while credit references are being researched. Some landlords require certified check or bank check rather than personal check, so it pays to inquire in advance. The first person to put down a deposit (customarily one month's rent) stands the best chance of signing the lease. The credit investigation should take no more than a couple of days if you have supplied the documentation outlined above. Once you are pronounced credit-worthy, the deposit check should be accepted as your first month's rent, two months in advance in some cases. The interest-earning security deposit, generally one month's rent payable now, will be refunded at the end of your lease, providing the apartment is left in the same condition in which it was found. (Now is the time to walk through with the landlord to record any existing damage.) If a real estate broker is involved, your third payment will be the broker's fee, which currently averages about 15%, of the first year's rent. In some cases, the owner will pay all or part of the fee.

LEASES

Read the lease carefully before signing it and all those checks. Married couples should have both names on the lease; unmarried couples should try to get both names on the lease, though the landlord is not legally obliged to do so. A standard form is customary. Be familiar with the content of the entire lease, but pay special attention to the end of the form where the qualifying clauses are printed. The document should specify any special arrangements made with the landlord about alterations, repairs, painting, and new appliances. If you have a dog, be sure the lease states that dogs are allowed to inhabit the apartment.

Determine how the building is heated and who pays the bills. If the landlord is responsible, there must be a clause in the lease to this effect. Traditionally, landlords pay for steam heat and gas heat. Tenants customarily pay for exceedingly costly electrical heat. In some buildings gas and electricity charges for stoves and ovens are included in the rent, but, in general, count on being billed directly by Con Edison for all utilities in the apartment proper.

Since 1982 smoke detectors, essentially one per sleeping area, have been mandatory in New York apartments. Tenants are responsible for the repair and maintenance of these alarms.

The landlord is legally responsible for ridding apartments of cockroaches. Some provide routine exterminator services; others simply take care of the matter as it crops up. Obviously, the ounce of prevention method is preferable and you should know in advance if regular service is included in your lease.

Check for a sublet clause. Subletting is allowed "with the landlord's permission." This means he can say no. To avoid permission being withheld capriciously, the clause should mention that the apartment can be sublet with written permission from the landlord "which permission shall not be unreasonably withheld."

Conversely, if you are subletting an apartment from the original lessee, determine whether or not you have a legal right to be there. To address this and other questions, the **New York State Tenant and Neighborhood Coalition** (NYSTNC) has a useful 22-page booklet, *A Tenant's Guide to Subletting and Apartment Sharing*, costing $9. Write the NYSTNC, 198 Broadway, Room 1000, NYC 10038, 212-695-8922 (or join the Coalition for $25 and get a tenants' rights newsletter as well as the pamphlet free). The guide details the practical and legal ramifications of apartment sharing and the ins and outs of subletting to, as well as from, another individual. Or, if you have questions about the propriety of a sub-tenancy and the apartment falls under city or state-enforced guidelines, try calling one of the organizations listed below (the Rent Stabilization Association, DHCR office, or the New York Loft Tenants) with your concerns.

Subletting a cooperative apartment can be daunting. Not only is it necessary to prove yourself to the landlord but you must pass the scrutiny of the building's board of directors, too. However, the traditionally restrictive subletting practices of many cooperative buildings are slowly being liberalized. Though unlikely, if you sublet a co-op without the board's approval, be aware that you could be evicted. Free from boards of directors, individually owned condominium apartments can be sublet at the owner's discretion.

Finally, for a comprehensive guide to the ins and outs of renting in the city, including housing law, a list of agencies and resources for tenants, recent articles, and links to related sites, go to **TenantNet**, www.tenantnet.net.

"The Online Resource for Residential Tenants" is partisan and occasionally radical, but practical.

RENT STABILIZATION AND RENT CONTROL

Although municipal rent controls have been eliminated in most of the country, they survive in New York City. Approximately one million apartments on the market today are rent stabilized. Few if any of the estimated 70,500 rent controlled apartments ever reach the market; they either are passed among qualifying members of one family like heirlooms or, once vacant, automatically become rent stabilized (apartments in large buildings) or decontrolled (apartments in buildings with five units or less). Rents for apartments built after January 1, 1974, are not regulated, except for those special few where real estate tax abatements, rehabilitation laws or other forms of housing subsidy apply. Buildings with less than six apartments are free from any rent restrictions unless they contain rent-controlled units. Rents in condominiums and cooperative apartments are left to market forces.

Stabilized rents are negotiated each June under the aegis of the New York Rent Guidelines Board and go into effect the following October 1. A rent stabilized landlord in New York City is not obligated to sign a lease for more than one year the first time around. However, when it comes time to renew, he or she must offer tenants the right to sign a one-or two-year lease. A three-year lease may be requested but the landlord is not required to provide one. The **Board's Housing NYC web site**, www.housingnyc.com, provides a trove of information concerning rent control and stabilization, subleasing, lease renewal, subsidized housing, small claims court, housing court, and more.

The **Rent Stabilization Association** (the landlord group), 1500 Broadway, NYC 10036, will answer questions about tenants' rights under rent stabilization. Call 212-214-9200. If your apartment is rent controlled or rent stabilized, call the **Office of Rent Administration**, State Division of Housing and Community Renewal (DHCR) in your borough with any questions or problems: Upper Manhattan, above 110th Street, 163 West 125th Street, 212-961-8930; Lower Manhattan, below 110th Street, 25 Beaver Street, 212-480-6700; The Bronx, 1 Fordham Plaza, 718-563-5678; Brooklyn, 91 Lawrence Street, 718-722-4778; Queens, 92-31 Union Hall Street, Jamaica 11433, 718-739-6400; Staten Island, 350 St. Mark's Place, 718-816-0277.

Tenants of any stripe can call 212-960-4800, the Central Complaint Bureau of the **New York City Department of Housing and Preservation**, 215 West 125th Street, NYC 10027, 24-hours a day, seven days a week. Bureau operators answer questions and pass along housing complaints to the appropriate New York City agency.

LOFTS

During the 1960s the trickle of hardy artists working and living illegally in industrial lofts located in zoned-for-manufacturing districts became a stream. Living in a vast, often high-ceilinged space with few if any partitions, *à la bohême*, became a desirable alternative life style. Add a few partitions, a restaurant gas stove, some antiques—instant chic. Illegal loft tenancies proliferated.

An amendment to the state's Multiple Dwelling Law legalized loft living in manufacturing buildings (buildings with no residential Certificates of Occupancy) containing three or more rental units. Some areas of the city were exempted, but in Chelsea and lower Manhattan, in the Fulton Ferry area of Brooklyn and Long Island City in Queens, loft dwellers breathed a legal sigh of relief.

The loft law did not, however, create complete order out of chaos, and the legality of some loft-living situations is still in doubt. Anyone considering renting or subletting a loft is well advised to check with the **New York City Loft Board**, 49-51 Chambers Street, 212-788-7610, before signing the lease. This is the city agency charged with overseeing the legalization of residential lofts.

RENTER'S/HOMEOWNER'S INSURANCE

Your neighbor upstairs has a grease fire in his kitchen, which gets out of hand. There is no fire damage to your apartment, but smoke and water damage from extinguishing the fire have rendered your furniture unusable, your walls in need of new paint; and your television and computer are out of commission. The cost of replacing all this stuff is covered by the owner's building insurance, right? Wrong. You're out of pocket, unless you have apartment renter's insurance.

While events such as this are relatively rare, when they occur they can be financially devastating. If your possessions are few, it may be worth the gamble to skip the insurance. However, your possessions can be insured against fire, water damage, and theft. Rates vary from company to company; be sure to shop around. It's a good idea to pay the additional cost for replacement coverage, and be sure your premiums provide personal liability coverage, protecting you and your family against lawsuits resulting from injuries to others, on or off the premises. If you own a dog, be sure the personal liability covers dog bites as well. Insurance is even more important for apartment owners, who will also need to be covered for improvements or alterations after a fire, as well as coverage for loss assessments when their insufficiently insured building needs repairs after some disaster. Such coverage is required by some co-ops and condo buildings.

When seeking insurance from an insurance agent (Yellow Pages under "Insurance"), it's a good idea to get quotes from at least three providers. Expect to pay $150 to $300 a year for a rental policy, more depending on what is covered. One company will be more competitive than another in a specific neighborhood, or in rentals, say, than in condos. Some companies which sell renter's/homeowner's insurance in the metropolitan area:

- **Aetna Inc**
- **Allstate**
- **Chubb**
- **CNA**
- **Firemen's Fund**
- **The Hartford**
- **Liberty Mutual Group**
- **MetLife**
- **Progressive**
- **Prudential**
- **Travelers**

For more information or if you have a problem with your insurer, contact the State Department of Insurance, 212-480-6400.

BUYING

In a city of renters, why buy? Real estate values have risen sharply since the late 1990s, and so have rents. Factoring in the income tax exemption for mortgage interest, which is highest in the early years of the mortgage, the cost of renting now can approach, or even exceed the cost of buying, especially in the studio and one-bedroom apartment category. For some, the idea of building equity, which is portable, as opposed to paying rent to someone else, has a strong appeal. For others, it's the satisfaction and security of home ownership.

That said, nevertheless, the newcomer to New York City would be well advised to rent or sublet for a year at least before buying: become comfortable in the city, familiar with some of its neighborhoods, and develop a sense of how you use the city. Furthermore, the case can be made that, given the expenses incidental to buying (described below) and the fact that real estate values tend to rise and fall in roughly ten-year cycles, it makes sense to buy only if you expect to spend at least ten years in the city.

As with renting, the search for a condo, a co-op, or a house generally begins online or in the classified ads in *The New York Times*, *The Wall Street Journal*, or *The New York Observer*, a weekly newspaper distinctively pink in color and available at most newsstands. The ads lead the seeker to realtor web sites where one can window shop the 3-D virtual house tours. Web sites on the internet offering national real estate listings proliferate, many with virtual tours. Below, a few that may be useful:

- **HomeAdvisor.com**, www.homeadvisor.com, a Microsoft site with a vast list and related services such as assistance in finding home insurance and advice on financing, remodeling, etc.
- **Homes&Land Magazine**, www.homes.com
- **Netprop**, www.netprop.com, especially strong in the New York-New Jersey area.
- **Owners.com**, www.owners.com, a "For Sale by Owners" site, excluding brokers, with area listings in New Jersey and Connecticut
- **Realtor.Com** and **Homestore.Com**, www.realtor.com and www.homestore.com, respectively, are affiliated sites controlled by the National Association of Realtors, a huge listing nationwide.
- **RealtyGuide**, www.xmission.com/~realtor1, with links to broker web sites, lenders, for-sale-by-owner directories and home-for-sale magazines.
- **YahooRealestate**, http://realestate.yahoo.com/realestate, national real estate and rentals listings; relocation advice
- **ZipRealty.com** is a national site that combines internet service with the personal attention of an agent. No cost to register to view listings.

But those looking online to buy a co-op, condo, or house in the city will probably be more successful at city-specific sites, most of which provide neighborhood profiles, comparative prices and mortgage information:

- **MLX**, www.mlx.com, co-ops and condos by neighborhood in Manhattan only
- **Manhattan MLS Joint Industry Task Force**, www.nymls.com, listings in all boroughs from two major realty groups representing 120 realtors
- **New York City Real Estate Exchange**, www.cityrealty.com, with condos, co-ops and houses in all boroughs
- **New York Today**, www.nytoday.com, *The New York Times'* site with extensive real estate listings, which automatically searches the data bases of the city's major brokers

For those who are contemplating buying, a few considerations now, which apply whether you are looking for a house, a co-op or a condo. First, what can you afford to pay? The rule of thumb, and one which lenders use: it is safe to pay three or four times the buyer's yearly income, depending on a variety of factors. The required down payment will generally be 20% of the purchase price; it may go as low as 10%, in which case origination fees (points) to the bank will probably be higher. Be prepared for a thorough examination of your finances, your credit record, and your employment status. This, of course, assumes the buyer is not paying cash but obtains a mortgage from a bank.

Know that the transaction you are about to make is going to cost more than the agreed upon price. How much more? Generally, in New York, closing costs run five- to eight-percent of the purchase price. This includes points, attorney's fees, title insurance, a title search, inspection and survey, recording tax, various fees, and the deposit of some real estate tax payments and homeowners insurance premiums in escrow. The lender (bank or mortgage company) is required to give a good-faith estimate of closing costs. In New York, the seller pays the broker's fee.

Whatever and wherever you are looking to buy, you'll need a good broker who listens to you, knows what is out there and takes you to it, knows the neighborhood, potential lenders and perhaps mortgage brokers, and who can work equitably for you as well as for the seller. (See **Recommendations for Finding a Real Estate Broker**, above.) Buyer's brokers, who represent only the buyer, are becoming commonplace in the suburbs but not in the city to date. You are well advised to get pre-approved for a mortgage before looking; in today's market it can make the difference in your bid winning out against competing bids for a property. You must also have a good real estate lawyer, who you can find through the recommendations of friends, your own lawyer or your broker. If you have no idea where to find an attorney who handles real estate transactions, call legal referral, 212-382-6600, at the Association of the Bar of the City of New York, 42 West 44th Street. If you are buying a **house**, you will do well to hire a building engineer to check the structure of the house, the heating and plumbing systems, fireplaces, etc.; a thorough inspection may save you thousands of dollars or prevent your making a disastrous purchase.

When you buy a **co-op (cooperative apartment)** you are buying shares in the ownership of a building, the other shareholders of which must approve your purchase through their board. And, should you choose to sell or rent your apartment later, the same approval process must be repeated, which can be a problem. In the most desirable buildings approval may prove more difficult than getting a mortgage, as shareholders seek to guarantee the financial reliability and the social acceptability of their new partners. Your finances will be scrutinized, and your life-style may be considered. A good broker will help by running interference for you. Get a prospectus, minutes of the last meeting of the board, and a financial statement from the cooperative, and go over them with your broker and your lawyer. If your purchase is rejected, expect no explanation. Be aware that co-op size may affect your ability to get a mortgage; in co-ops with less than 12 units, lenders may be more likely to reject a mortgage application because the relatively small number of shareholders in such buildings raises the collective risk of default. Also, keep in mind that co-op maintenance fees (the cost of upkeep for everything outside the walls of your apartment) can be more than your mortgage, depending on the building, and only some of the maintenance fee (the portion of the fee that is allocated for property tax payments) is tax deductible. Forty to fifty percent is a ballpark figure.

The purchase of a **condo** involves fewer hurdles, though some condo management organizations are requesting letters of recommendation from prospective buyers. Here you are buying an apartment, a piece of a building, outright, with the right to rent or re-sell when and as you choose. Of course, this means neither you nor the other residents have any control over who your neighbors are. In making this purchase you will also want your lawyer to examine a prospectus and financial statement on the building to avoid buying into a financially unstable property.

Finally, a word about **mortgage brokers**. In the competition to win new mortgage clients banks offer a confusing array of loans. Mortgage broker to the rescue! Think of a mortgage broker as a financial advisor who helps her client get a suitable mortgage. At no charge to you, she will examine your financial situation (age, income, assets, debt load etc.) and the type of property you want to buy and recommend the most likely lender and the best type of mortgage for your needs. Given her relationship with various banks, she can ease your way through the process, especially on co-op loans. If you're the ruggedly independent sort, keep in mind that in New York City your chances of getting a good mortgage are much higher with a qualified mortgage broker than without.

ADDITIONAL RESOURCES

Although useful for anyone in the housing market, but an especially prudent step for the first-time homebuyer would be the purchase of a how-to guide. One we like is *100 Questions Every First-Time Home Buyer Should Ask* by Ilyce R. Glink.

First-time homebuyers will find even more comprehensive help and one-on-one advice from a nation-wide nonprofit established for that purpose, **Neighbors Helping Neighbors, Inc.**, 718-492-3450. In addition to free bi-weekly seminars they offer information and individual counseling through the shoals of home buying. Similarly, the quasi-governmental agency **Fanny Mae**, 800-FANNIE, and on the web at www.homepath.com, is especially helpful in credit counseling, helping to find low-cost mortgages and advice for low-income and first-time buyers.

H AVING FOUND AND SECURED A PLACE TO LIVE, YOU HAVE NOW the task of getting your stuff there, perhaps storing some of it because a New York apartment is smaller than you had expected, and insuring your possessions against fire, theft and the unlikely flood. Let us help you.

MOVING

Disagreeable moving experiences aren't obligatory but they do happen. One option, of course, is **self-moving** by rented mini-van or truck. If you're planning to rent a truck, especially during the busy May-June, August-September moving months, be sure to reserve the vehicle a good month before your moving date.

Once you're on the road, keep in mind that your rental truck may be a tempting target for thieves. If you must park it overnight or for an extended period (more than a couple of hours), try to find a safe place, preferably somewhere well-lit and easily observable by you, and do your best not to leave anything of particular value in the cab.

Four national self-moving companies to consider:

- **Budget**, 800-428-7825, www.budget.com
- **Penske**, 800-222-0277, www.penske.com
- **Ryder**, 800-467-9337, www.ryder.com
- **Uhaul**, 800-468-4285, www.uhaul.com

When **hiring a mover** the busy months are the same as for self-moving—May-June and August-September—so try to plan well in advance of your moving date. Most people use the Yellow Pages to find a mover, and chances are you'll engage a mover from where you are moving. Probably the best way to find a mover is through the recommendation of a friend or relative. For long distance moves the **American Moving and Storage**

Association's web site, www.moving.org, is useful for identifying member movers and for helpful suggestions and packing tips. Check out a recent *Consumer Reports* (www.consumerreports.org) index for articles or surveys they may have published to aid your search. You can consult *The Village Voice* classified ads for short hauls. Whoever you use, make sure they are licensed:

- **Interstate movers** are licensed by the Licensing and Insurance System of the Federal Highway Administration's (FHWA) Office of Motor Carriers, 202-358-7028; in New York, 212-264-1070, or check www.fmcsa.dot.gov. When you're shopping for an interstate mover, it may help to know that federally licensed movers ("Motor Carriers") receive a three to six digit "MC" number that should be displayed on all advertising and promotional literature.
- **Intrastate movers** must be insured to be licensed by the New York State Department of Transportation, www.dot.state.ny.us. To verify certification of your chosen mover, call 800-786-5368 and punch in the state license number listed on the mover's literature.

Once you've narrowed it down to two or three companies, ask a mover for **references**, particularly from customers who did similar moves. Check with the Better Business Bureau, www.bbb.org, as well as with the state's consumer protection board, (in New York call 518-474-1471 or go to www.consumer.state.ny.us), to see if there are any complaints against a prospective mover. Get a free written estimate based on an on-site viewing by the mover. Before a move takes place, federal regulations require inter-state movers to furnish customers with a copy of *Your Rights and Responsibilities When You Move*. If they don't give you a copy, ask for one.

If you're making a long-distance move, keep in mind that your belong-ings may be in transit for a week or more. Plan accordingly. Also, if you have any irreplaceable items such as jewelry, photographs or key work doc-uments, you may want to transport these yourself rather than entrust them to a stranger. Though the movers will put numbered labels on your posses-sions, you should make a numbered list of every box and item. Detail box contents and photograph anything of particular value. In case of claims, this list can be invaluable and useful even after the move.

One alternative to hired movers is **you-pack-they-move**, which costs about half what full-service movers charge and usually takes less time. It's less stressful than moving yourself by van or truck. A useful web site for details and a list of these movers as well as conventional movers and art and antique movers is www.moving.com. Alternatively, call a you-pack mover for details, for example: ABF U-Pack Moving, 800-355-1696, www.upack.com; Moveamerica, 888-701-0123; Consolidated Freightways, www.cfmovesu.com.

The industry-standard 60 cents per-pound **insurance coverage** is insufficient. If you have homeowner or renter's insurance, check to see if it will cover your belongings in transit. If not, consider purchasing "full replacement" or "full value" coverage from the carrier for the estimated value of your shipment. Though it's the most expensive type of coverage offered, it's probably worth it. Trucks get into accidents, they catch fire, they get stolen—if such insurance seems pricey to you, ask about a $250 or $500 deductible. This can reduce your cost substantially while still giving you much better protection in the event of a catastrophic loss.

Be prepared to pay the full moving bill upon delivery. Cash or bank/cashier's check may be required. Some carriers will take a credit card, but it's a good idea to get that in writing.

Members of the American Automobile Association have a valuable resource at hand in **AAA's Consumer Relocation Services**, which will assign the member a personal consultant to handle every detail of the move free of charge and which offers savings from discounts arranged with premier moving companies. Call 800-839-MOVE.

If your move is work-related, some or all of your moving expenses may be **tax-deductible**. Keep your receipts, and consult a tax expert for guidance. Confident do-it-yourselfers can get a copy of IRS Form 3903 (www.irs.gov) and try figuring it out.

If a **move goes badly** and you blame the moving company, you should first file a written claim with the mover for loss or damage. If this doesn't work, and it is an intrastate move, you should write to the New York DOT, Carrier Certification Unit, 47-40 21st Street, Long Island City, 11101, 718-482-4810, as well as the state attorney general's office. You can also turn to the New York State Consumer Protection Board, 5 Empire State Plaza #2101, Albany, NY 12223-1556, 518-474-1471, www.con-sumer.state.ny.us, and the Governor's new consumer hotline, 800-697-1220. You may also want to lodge your complaint with the New York City Department of Consumer Affairs, 212-487-4444.

If your grievance is with an interstate carrier, your choices are limited. FMCSA's role in the regulation of interstate carriers has to do with safety issues, not consumer issues. Your best bet is to file a complaint against a mover with the Better Business Bureau, www.bbb.org, in the state where the moving company is licensed, as well as with that state's attorney general or consumer protection office. You might also seek redress with your congressional representative's office, before you try your last step: talking to a lawyer.

Remember, in the state of New York the Department of Transportation can provide assistance only when you use a certified mover. Hire an unlicensed firm and you're on your own in case of damage or loss.

STORAGE WAREHOUSES

Storage facilities may be required when you have to ship your furniture without an apartment to receive it or if your apartment is too small for all your belongings. If your mover maintains storage warehouse facilities in the city, as many do, you'll probably want to store with them. Some even offer one month's free storage. Most of these warehouses are in Queens, Brooklyn or New Jersey. Look in the Yellow Pages under "Storage Warehouses" and shop around for the best and most convenient deal among many. Below, a few of the major moving/storage companies:

- **Approved Moving and Storage**, 718-622-2660, has a fireproof warehouse in Brooklyn. Charges are 25¢ a cubic foot per month, plus a one-shot warehouse handling charge that amounts to one month's storage. Estimates are based on the number of rooms of furniture and household goods you'll be storing.
- **Brothers Mini Storage**, 718-230-6400, maintains their warehouse in Brooklyn for goods hauled by their trucks and those of other companies.
- **Moishe's**, 800-536-6564, has warehousing in Brooklyn and in Long Island City, for goods hauled by their trucks and those of others. They also own self-storage facilities in Manhattan and Queens.
- **The Seven Santini Bros.**, 201-340-8210, has a warehouse for the storage of household goods at 80 Greenwood Avenue, Midland Park, NJ 07026. The Manhattan warehouse is for fine arts storage only.

The New York City Department of Consumer Affairs licenses storage— but not self-storage—warehouses. Dissatisfied? Call the city's all-purpose complaint number, 212-487-4444.

SELF STORAGE COMPANIES

The ability to rent anything from 3' x 3' lockers to small storage rooms is a great boon to urban dwellers. Collectors, people with old clothes they can't bear to give to thrift shops, and those with possessions that won't fit in a sublet or shared apartment all find mini-warehouses a solution to too-small living spaces.

Rates for space in Manhattan self-storage facilities are competitive: expect to pay about $66 a month for a locker 4' x 4' x 7', $175 a month for an 8' x 8' x 8' space, and so on. Some offer free pick-up, otherwise you or your mover delivers the goods. If you're looking for lower rates, check the prices for storage units located in the suburbs and boroughs other than Manhattan. As you shop around, you may want to check the facility for cleanliness and security. Does the building have sprinklers in case of fire?

Do they have carts and hand trucks for moving in and out? Do they bill monthly, or will they automatically charge the bill to your credit card? Access should be 24-hour or nearly so, and some are air conditioned, an asset if you plan to visit your locker in the summer.

- **Keepers Self Storage Center**, 212-924-8484, has locations at 444 East 10th Street between avenues C and D, and at 2577 Forest Avenue on Staten Island. Prices at the East Side location are slightly less than those on Staten Island.
- **Manhattan Mini Storage**, 212-786-7243 and 212-255-0482, with locations at 520 West 17th Street corner of Tenth Avenue, 524 West 23rd Street, 600 West 58th Street corner of Eleventh Avenue and 570 Riverside Drive, corner of 134th Street, among others, offers private storage rooms from 5' x 5' to 10' x 25' (the size of some NYC studio apartments).
- **U-Haul Moving and Storage** has a mini-warehouse located at 562 West 23rd Street, 212-620-4177, with rooms 4' x 8' for $65 and 8' x 12' for $175, as well as facilities in Brooklyn, The Bronx and Queens, among others.

For other names and addresses in the burgeoning self-storage field, check the Yellow Pages under "Self Storage."

CHILDREN

Studies show that moving, especially frequent moving, can be hard on children. According to an American Medical Association study, children who move often are more likely to suffer from such problems as depression, worthlessness and aggression. Often their academic performance suffers as well. Aside from not moving more than is necessary, there are a few things you can do to help your children through this stressful time:

- Talk about the move with your kids. Be honest but positive. Listen to their concerns. To the extent possible, involve them in the process.
- Make sure the child has his or her favorite possessions with them on the trip; *don't* pack "blankey" in the moving van.
- Make sure you have some social life planned on the other end. Your child may feel lonely in your new home and such activities can ease the transition.
- Keep in touch with family and loved ones as much as possible. Photos and phone calls are important ways of maintaining links to the important people you have left behind.
- If your child is of school age, take the time to involve yourself in their new school and in their academic life. Don't let them fall through the cracks.

For younger children, there are dozens of good books on the topic. Just a few include, *Alexander, Who's Not (Do You Hear Me? I Mean It!) Going to Move* by Judith Viorst; *The Moving Book: A Kid's Survival Guide* by Gabriel Davis; *Goodbye/Hello* by Barbara Hazen, *The Leaving Morning* by Angela Johnson; and the *Little Monster's Moving Day* by Mercer Mayer.

For older children, try: *Amber Brown is Not a Crayon* by Paula Danziger; the *Kid in the Red Jacket* by Barbara Park; *Hold Fast to Dreams* by Andrea Davis Pinkney; *Flip Flop Girl* by Katherine Paterson and *My Fabulous New Life* by Sheila Greenwald.

For general guidance, read *Smart Moves: Your Guide through the Emotional Maze of Relocation* by Nadia Jensen, Audrey McCollum and Stuart Copans (Smith & Krauss)

Visit firstbooks.com to order any of the above resources.

ONLINE RESOURCES—RELOCATION

- **www.apartmentguide.com**, is an online national apartment search service of paid for listings
- **www.erc.org**, the Employee Relocation Council, a professional organization, offers members specialized reports on the relocation and moving industries
- **www.firstbooks.com**, relocation resources and information on moving to Atlanta, Boston, Chicago, Los Angeles, Minneapolis-St. Paul, New Jersey, New York City, Philadelphia, Seattle, Washington, DC, as well as London, England
- **www.homefair.com**, realty listings, moving tips, and more
- **www.moverquotes.com**, comparison shop for mover quotes
- **www.moving.com**, a moving services site: packing tips, mover estimates, etc.
- **www.moving-guide.com**, movers and moving services
- **www.moving.org**, American Moving and Storage Association site
- **http://realestate.yahoo.com/realestate**, national real estate and rentals listings; relocation advice
- **www.rent.net**, apartment rentals, movers, relocation advice and more
- **www.movedoc.com**, visit this site to order a copy of *Steiners Complete How to Move Handbook* by Clyde and Shari Steiner; $14.95.
- **www.usps.com**, relocation information from the United States Postal Service

A FTER FINDING YOUR NEW PLACE OF RESIDENCE, THE NEWCOMER'S first order of business probably will be opening a bank account and establishing credit. The following information about personal savings and checking accounts, online banking, credit unions, credit and debit cards should make the task less daunting. And, finally, for your edification come April 15, federal, state and city income tax procedures.

BANK ACCOUNTS AND SERVICES

While most people tend to choose their bank for its location, offered services, interest rates and minimum balance requirements can be important determinants as well. If the range and quality of services a bank offers is more important to you than location, particularly now that ATMs provide access to cash and account information outside the branch, be sure to shop around for the best deal to serve your banking needs. The city's two largest retail banks, Citibank and JP Morgan Chase & Co., operate more than 100 branches in Manhattan alone, more in the outer boroughs. However, with fees at such interstate banks being significantly higher than smaller banks, as stated in a recent report by the Federal Reserve, it makes sense for the small-wallet customer to investigate local institutions. The Yellow Pages contain some five pages of banks. Below, we list nine banks with multiple branches, starting with the two giants:

- **Citibank**, 212-627-3999, www.citibank.com
- **JP Morgan Chase & Co.**, 800-CHASE-24
- **Fleet**, 800-841-4000, www.fleet.com
- **Apple Bank**, 800-722-6888
- **EAB**, 888-557-3700, www.eab.com
- **Dime Savings**, 212-234-9992
- **Amalgamated Bank**, 212-255-6200

- **HSBC**, formerly Marine Midland, 800-975-4722
- **Republic National**, 718-488-4050

Beyond the telephone, technology has transformed banking and continues to do so daily. What's more, traditional distinctions between commercial banks, savings banks and brokerage houses have become blurred. And financial software has crossed all these lines. In this fluid situation, "It's a consumer's market," says one bank officer. "Our bank's strategy is to establish a relationship with each customer." That's why special windows for affluent customers and business clients are commonplace.

- **Checking accounts**; take a completed application—two references are required, usually the name of your current bank and that of your employer—to the branch where you intend to bank, together with two signed pieces of identification: driver's license, credit card, student ID with photo. Some banks require a minimum start-up deposit. Your account can be opened immediately, but checks and deposit slips won't be issued until your signature is verified. "Regular" non-interest-bearing personal checking accounts carry no charges as long as a minimum daily balance is maintained. A certificate of deposit, money market or savings account linked to your regular checking account may also get you free checking. Institutions offering interest-earning NOW checking accounts charge a fee if the accounts fall below required minimum balances. Generally **debit cards** are issued automatically to new customers. Most can be used to make withdrawals through the nationwide network of CIRRUS and NYCE ATMs and they can be used at retail outlets to pay for goods and services, debiting your checking account directly.
- **Savings accounts**; follow the procedures detailed above for checking accounts to apply for a "statement" savings account, which provides monthly statements of all transactions and can be linked to your checking account. Most banks require an average minimum balance of $1,500 to avoid maintenance charges.
- **Online banking**; with a PC, a modem, and an account in one of the major banks (increasingly the smaller banks, also) you can do most, if not all, of your banking at home electronically. Using software provided by the bank you can review your accounts, transfer funds from one account to another, check the latest stock market figures, assess the current worth of your portfolio, buy and sell stock, and pay your bills without leaving the apartment or touching paper. Services vary from bank to bank and some charge depending on the number and range of services used, and in some cases on the level of combined balance. Online banking also offers the ability to bank at an institution located far from home. Four **internet banks** worth checking out are:
  - **NetBank**, www.netbank.com

- **E*Trade/Bank**, www.etradebank.com
- **VirtualBank**, www.virtualbank.com
- **WingspanBank**, www.wingspanbank.com; the four previous advertise significantly higher interest rates than their so-called "brick and mortar" competitors. Change in this area is occurring at a dizzying pace, leaving the customer to investigate and shop around for the banking services which best fit his/her needs.
- **Banking by phone**; a touch-tone telephone gives access to all the banking services performed by an ATM, except deposits and cash withdrawals: you can check account balances and make transfers between accounts. For a small monthly charge (or free with a minimum combined balance of, say, $10,000) the bank will make scheduled bill payments such as rent, mortgage or car payments, as well as payments on request to designated payees such as stores, credit card companies, and utilities. A year-end annual statement may be provided on request. Again, inquire about the latest refinements and the fees involved.

CREDIT UNIONS

As an alternative to commercial banks, credit unions offer most of the same services, including free checking, online banking, banking by phone, loans, mortgages, car loans and often credit cards, at lower cost. The required balance may be as low as $5. Normally, you must belong to a union, an employee group or certain churches to have access to one of these consumer-friendly non-profits. A few, such as the Lower East Side Peoples' Federal Credit Union, 37 Avenue B, NYC 10009, 212-529-8197, have community charters enabling them to serve anyone who works or lives in that community. And some, such as the Progressive Credit Union at 370 Seventh Avenue, NYC 10021, 212-695-8900, might contact your employer with an offer of free credit union services for his employees, which would qualify you. Credit unions lack the convenience of multiple branches in exchange for considerable financial benefit.

CREDIT CARDS

On the off chance that your mailbox hasn't been filled with credit card applications, you can call to request one. An important twist to consider: frequent-flyer miles earned as you use your card. Shop around for the one best suited to your needs.

- **American Express**, 800-528-4800, all cards except the free Optima Card for students have a minimum income requirement. A Green Card costs $55 per year. The Optima True Grace card, $25 per year with no fee if used three times a year, gives the user 25 interest-free days for all purchases. The Gold Card costs $75 annually. For $300 per year you can possess a Platinum Card; but for this card don't call American Express, they'll call you.

- **Diner's Club Card**, 800-234-6377, costs $80 per year, $25,000 minimum annual income.
- **Discover Cards**, 800-347-2683, are issued by Morgan Stanley with no annual fee for the basic card; minimum income is judged on a case-by-case basis. The Private Issue Card carries a $40 annual fee and requires higher income. With both cards you may get cash back at the end of each anniversary year.
- **VISA and MasterCard** can be obtained from a variety of financial service organizations, usually banks. Interest rates vary, annual fees may even be waived, and many cards offer frequent flyer miles. It pays to shop around, especially if you don't pay off your balance every month.
- **Department stores, store charge accounts** can offer advantages over other forms of payment: advance notice of sales, mail or phone orders, no annual fee. Accounts are approved within three to eight weeks after application. Macy's and Brooks Brothers offer instant store charge account privileges to credit card holders who apply in person with two pieces of identification.

If you don't like wasting hours dialing 800 numbers after a credit card loss, register your cards with an agency that will cancel them for you. Credit Card Protection Service, for example, 800-327-1284, charges a yearly fee to guarantee card replacement. Major banks offer a similar service to their VISA or MasterCard customers for an annual fee.

Note: It pays to read the fine print when you sign up for a major credit card, that is if you can see to read it and you understand it. For example, if you charge that expensive dinner in Paris to your VISA card, you might be charged an extra one percent for conversion of foreign currency. And finance charges on unpaid balances are calculated now on a daily compounding basis, raising the cost of that balance, in addition to which late payment fees have been raised and the grace periods for payment have been shortened from 25 days to as little as 20. Credit card cash advances have also become more expensive.

ADDITIONAL CREDIT CARD RESOURCES

A list of low-rate card issuers can be found on the internet at CardWeb, www.cardweb.com, 800-344-7714, the Consumer Action site, www.consumer-action.org, BankRate.com, www.bankrate.com, and iMoneynet.com, www.imoneynet.com.

CREDIT REPORTS

Those interested in seeing their personal credit report can go to www.icreditreport.com. At this site you can receive a copy (for $8) of your credit report from the three main credit bureaus. Just don't do it more than once a year, otherwise it could adversely affect your credit rating. Or contact each credit bureau directly:

- **Equifax**, 800-685-1111, www.equifax.com
- **Experian**, 888-397-3742, www.experian.com
- **Trans Union Corporation**, 800-916-8800, www.transunion.com

INCOME TAXES

Heralded by freshly painted H&R Block signs and black-bordered boxes in the newspapers warning "Only 10 more days to file your income tax returns," April 15 arrives every 365 days. In New York City, the Internal Revenue Service and New York Department of Taxation and Finance provide literature and telephone taxpayer information services designed to answer your tax questions year round. In case you did not know it before moving here, the bad news is that New York City takes a yearly income tax bite out of you along with state and Federal governments.

- **Federal income tax** forms can be obtained by calling 800-829-3676; they are also generally available in most Post Offices and libraries at income tax time. Call 800-829-1040 to obtain explanatory literature as well as answers to specific questions, such as which of the three tax forms—1040EZ, 1040A or 1040—you should use. If you're comfortable on the internet, visit the IRS's well-regarded URL (www.irs.ustreas.gov), where you can find answers to tax questions as well as downloadable tax forms. The staff at the Internal Revenue Service office, open weekdays 7:30 a.m. to 4:30 p.m. downtown at 120 Church Street, provides instruction in the fine art of calculating your Federal income tax but won't do it for you.
- **New York State and New York City** use a combined income tax form. If you have not received forms in the mail, call 800-462-8100 to order. If you use either IRS 1040EZ or 1040A, choose the IT 100, which you fill in and let the State tax people calculate for you, or the IT 200, which you calculate yourself. For those filing the Federal 1040 long form, you'll need the IT 201. The number for taxpayer assistance is 800-CALL-TAX.

Your Federal Adjusted Gross Income is the tax base for state and city taxes. New York State Taxable Income is calculated by adding and subtracting various New York State "modifications." The New York City

Resident's Income Tax is based on New York State taxable income. Residents pay a percentage of the State category into which their income falls. Software such as Turbotax, available in software specialty shops and departments, for use in compiling your tax returns, walks and prompts you through the process.

PC devotees have been filing their **income tax returns electronically** for several years now. It's getting easier as a result of the IRS e-file program, and ultimately it will be possible to file directly from home to the IRS without an intermediary. For now, Taxpayer completes his federal, state and city income tax return using tax-preparation software such as Web Turbotax, Macintax or TaxCut, which can be downloaded through links on the IRS web site, www.irs.ustreas.gov. Taxpayer transmits the return via modem to the service bureau used by the software's publisher. For a fee, the service bureau checks the return, puts it in an IRS-acceptable format and transmits it to the IRS and state Department of Taxation and Finance. Ideally, the returns are correct and the acknowledgment rapid, but a typing error can cause frustrating delays. Following acknowledgement, Taxpayer will be required to send a signature document form 8453-OL (US Individual Income Tax Declaration for Online Filing) along with W-2 forms and supporting documents to the appropriate service center. Alternatively, there are hundreds of practitioners—CPA's and tax preparation firms, generally—registered to file electronically, and they will file your state, city and federal returns, long or short form, for a fee, approximately $50 per return. If they prepare the return as well, the fee is greater. You will need two forms of identification, including a driver's license or a passport. Your refund, if you have one, should come in two to three weeks instead of six and by direct deposit if you wish. By the same token, payment of taxes due can be made by ACH (for Automated Clearing House) debit, which is simply direct withdrawal from your checking or savings account, as well as by check or credit card. Within 48 hours your filer will receive acknowledgment of receipt and acceptance of the returns. See the Yellow Pages under "Tax Returns" if you do not have a tax preparation firm recommendation from an acquaintance.

Taxpayer-assistance in filing on paper or electronically is available for simple returns at no cost at Manhattan IRS offices: 290 Broadway, 110 West 44th Street and 55 West 125th Street; Bronx IRS: 3000 White Plains Boulevard; Brooklyn IRS: 625 Fulton Street; Queens office: 1 Lefrak City at 59-17 Junction Boulevard in Corona, Queens. No appointment is necessary at these sites, which are open Monday-Friday, 8 a.m. to 4:30 p.m., but don't wait until April, unless you like standing in long lines. Assistance in preparing and filing returns, electronically at some sites, is provided by volunteers under the VITA (Volunteer Income Tax Assistance) program throughout the city and in New Jersey. To find the site nearest you call 212-436-1021 in Manhattan, 718-488-3655 for the other boroughs and 973-

645-6690 for New Jersey. Call the IRS Help Line, 800-829-1040, for information on electronic filing or its Tele-Tax number 800-829-4477 for recorded tax information 24-hours a day. For questions concerning New York State income tax call the New York State Department of Taxation and Finance, 800-225-5829.

STARTING OR MOVING A BUSINESS

Recently, *Business Week* reported that a Deloitte and Touche survey found that New York ranked as the second most expensive (in terms of taxes) city in the country in which to operate a small business. But if proximity to power, money and a diverse and deep talent pool is important to you, then New York City can't be beat as a place to locate a business.

You may choose to hire an attorney who is familiar with the process but if you want to begin your research on your own, the following resources should help you get the ball rolling:

- **Association of the Bar of the City of New York**, Legal Referral Service, 212-382-6600
- **Better Business Bureau**, www.newyork.bbb.org
- **Internal Revenue Service**, 800-829-1040, who you need to talk to get an employer tax ID number.
- **New York City Department of Finance Home Page**, www.ci.nyc.ny.us/finance
- **New York Department of State, Division of Corporations**, 41 State Street, Albany, NY 12231, 518-473-2492; in order to incorporate in New York, you must first reserve a name here. Also, if you're incorporating in New York, they are the folks who you send your incorporation form #A234 and your $135 (at this writing) application payment to.
- **US Small Business Administration** home page, www.sba.gov

L ET'S SEE. YOU'VE SIGNED A LEASE OR MORTGAGE PAPERS AND opened a bank account. So now, keys in hand, it's time to have utilities connected and the telephone installed. You can make yourself at home once you can cook and call, and really settle in once you possess a library card and can vote. The how-to's follow.

UTILITIES

CONSOLIDATED EDISON

Call **Consolidated Edison's** Customer Service to have gas and electricity turned on: in Manhattan, 212-338-3100; The Bronx, 718-409-7100; Brooklyn, 718-802-6000; Queens, 718-830-7400; Staten Island, 718-390-6400. In New Jersey call **PSE&G (Public Service Electric and Gas)**, 800-436-7734, for service. A personal visit from either is not necessary unless the prior tenant's service was cut off for non-payment. Expect to wait at least one business day before service commences; note that PSE&G is open for new accounts Monday-Friday only. Deposits are no longer required for residential accounts unless a credit check indicates the need.

TELEPHONE

So rapidly are communications technologies advancing, barriers crashing and regulations churning to keep up that, however you describe telephone service today, it will be out of date next year. At this writing, local telephone service is provided by Verizon (formerly Bell Atlantic) as well as AT&T, MCI WorldCom, and RCN Communications (Manhattan and Queens on a building by building basis), all of which now offer internet service as well. Cable television giants are poised to offer telephone service over their fiber optic cables, first to businesses then to homes. For their part, regional telephone companies are aiming at the cable market. Today cellular phone service is provided by six major operators (see below), offering a dizzying array of plans, including digital PCS (personal communications services), which may be superior to digital and may be cheaper. Confusing? Stay tuned. Meanwhile, you want a telephone in your apartment now.

To institute new **local service** contact: Verizon, 212-890-2550, www.verizon.com; AT&T, 800-222-0300, www.att.com; for MCI's local service call 800-MCI-LOCAL, www.wcom.com; to check for RCN availability in your building call 800-891-7770, www.rcn.com. Verizon no longer requires a deposit from most customers; where required, the deposit accumulates interest and is refunded in a year's time. MCI and RCN require a credit check but no deposit. The set-up charge at Verizon is $55, more for additional wiring or extra jacks; MCI and RCN have similar charges. Basic monthly line fee will run approximately $6.60, plus $3.50 regulatory fee, after which local calls are charged at about 10.6 cents.

As modems, fax machines and wireless devices proliferate, so do **area codes**. Until recently all Manhattan was in area code 212, while the other boroughs were in area code 718. Now new phones in Manhattan are given area code 646. For the most part, area code 917 in Manhattan and the boroughs serves wireless phones and beepers. Boroughs previously reached at 718 now include 347, and 631 has been added to 516 on Long Island. In New Jersey, part of the 201 area, South Orange for example, has become 973. *To reach a number with another area code, even in the same borough, you must first dial "1" plus the area code.*

Whichever local phone service you choose, you will be offered a bouquet of extra features, each carrying an extra monthly fee, among them: Call Waiting (the most popular), Call Forwarding, Call Answering, Voice Dialing, Call Return, 3-Way Calling, and Caller ID. For any of these services, call the number above.

Chances are you will receive, at no cost, a calling card for local or long distance use. When using the card, however, you will pay a surcharge for this non-regulated service; if another carrier is involved it could be a stunner on your next bill. To avoid this shock, use the toll-free connection number on the card before dialing. Call the same number for current rates. For long distance calls from a pay phone a pre-paid phone card may be the best deal.

In the New York City area, widely used **long distance service** providers include:

- **AT&T**, 800-222-0300, www.att.com
- **MCI**, 800-8950-5555, www.mci.com
- **RCN**, 800-891-7770, www.rcn.com
- **Sprint**, 800-877-4646, www.sprint.com
- **Verizon**, 212-890-2550, www.verizon.com

Bundling is the current buzzword in communications: i.e., charging one rate on one bill for two or more different services, for example for long distance calls made from home phones and internet service. Other variables include volume discounts, monthly minimums, and overseas service. Check around. Currently, the lowest per minute rates are offered to those who agree to pay a flat monthly service fee in return for long distance rates as low as 5 cents per minute. In any case, if you think you could be getting a better deal elsewhere but really don't want to switch companies, call your long distance provider and ask if they'll match a competitor's rates. Internet users looking for good deals on long-distance service must be willing to be billed online and pay using a credit card. For help comparing long distance calling plans see below.

A word about **slamming**, being switched to a different long distance carrier without your knowledge or consent. A customer who notices such a change on his monthly bill, should call his previous provider to report the offense and ask to be switched back. Then call the pirate company, whose name and number will appear on the bill, complain about the change, and ask them to recalculate their charges according to rates of the previous company. Then contact your local provider to request that they install a "freeze" on your account, making it more difficult to slam, and that any switching charges be dropped. Pay your bill on time and check your next bill to be sure you have been switched back and that there are no switching charges. To report the offense to the FCC, should you wish to do so, call 888-225-5322 or their consumer assistance number at 202-418-0200. To inform the NY Public Service Commission, call 800-342-3377. To avoid being slammed, never sign anything without reading it carefully; examine your telephone bill and ask about any names you can't identify. If you think you might have been slammed, dial "00" to get a recorded voice or an operator identifying the current long distance provider on your phone.

Cramming refers to charges billed to you for calls you did not make. If after examining your monthly telephone bill you find such charges, call your local company or the company rendering the bill and inform them of the contested charges. Pay the remainder of the bill on time. If you have any difficulty in disputing the deceptive charge, you may wish to inform the Federal Trade Commission. For information on filing a complaint call their Consumer Response Center at 202-382-4357. Call the New York State Consumer Protection Board at 800-NYS-1220 or better yet, consult their extensive web site, www.consumer.state.ny.us, an encyclopedically useful resource covering every conceivable consumer problem, including slamming and cramming under "consumer law/frames/telephone." Web sites for the FTC, www.ftc.gov, and for the Federal Communications Commission, www.fcc.gov, have tips on combating cramming. See **Rip-off Recourse** below for more on consumer protection.

Most New Yorkers aren't aware of how much good information can be found in the city's telephone books. The **White Pages** includes an extensive listing of community service numbers as well as government listings and an emergency care guide. The **Yellow Pages** is almost in itself a guide to New York City. Seek it as a reference for historical sites and landmarks, public transportation maps, a yearly calendar of events, and sports stadiums and concert hall seating charts! The **Business to Business Yellow Pages**, which lists all wholesalers and manufacturers, is free of charge and can be obtained by calling your local telephone office. Call 800-426-8686 to order consumer and business-to-business 800 directories.

For those whose business requires their constant telephone accessibility, as well as those who suffer telephone separation anxiety, the **cellular phone** provides an umbilical cord, albeit somewhat expensive. Here, too, technology is rapidly changing, and costs are falling, to the point, in fact, where some users have dispensed with their wired phones altogether. Currently, cellular service is provided in the metropolitan area by six major companies:

- **AT&T Wireless**, 800-IMAGINE, www.attws.com
- **MCIWorldcom**, 800-967-5100, www.wcom.com
- **Nextel**, 800-639-8359, www.nextel.com
- **Sprint PCS**, 800-480-4PCS, www.sprintpcs.com
- **Verizon**, 888-466-4646, www.verizonwireless.com
- **VoiceStream** (formerly Omipoint), 800-STREAMS, www.voicestream.com

The equipment, ranging in price from free to about $1,000, is available from a host of manufacturers through local vendors and service providers, whose ads and occasional promotions are to be found in newspapers and in the Yellow Pages. The cost of operation, varying according to carrier and plan, contains a monthly access charge including a specified number of free air-time minutes, air time charges beyond the specified minutes, perhaps landline charges and roaming area charges for use beyond the home area. Airtime includes receiving as well as making calls. Your cell phone, whether analog, digital or PCS, will cost less if you purchase it from your chosen provider, who is subsidizing the cost. New users would do well to try out a plan that does not require a long-term contract and has no early termination penalty. Service will probably cost more than you expect, and special features such as voice mail and caller ID cost extra. Some plans include paging. Service plans are varied and competition fierce, so watch the newspaper ads for the best deals. For **help comparing long distance and wireless calling plans**, visit the Telecommunications and Research and Action Center (TRAC) (not affiliated with the communications industry), www.trac.org or call them at 202-263-2950. Online try:

www.decide.com, www.getconnected.com, www.point.com, or www.telebright.com.

At this writing flat rate plans, providing a set number of minutes of local and long distance service per month, are popular. Of course, if you buy more than you use, the cost per minute goes up. If you exceed your monthly allotment, the additional air time costs about 25 to 35 cents a minute. The appeal of these plans is similar to that of pre-paid cellular, described below. Plans vary and competition is fierce; watch the ads for the best deal.

Pre-paid cellular service is available from the major service providers (except Nextel), usually by phone, online, and in communications equipment stores. Simply purchase a phone that comes with a card representing a specific financial value, say $50. Activate the card, talk, and when the time is running low you'll be warned so you can replenish the time with a payment. No contract, no credit check, no bills. Downside? You'll probably pay more for your handset, more per minute on air and for roaming, long distance, and directory assistance. But rates are coming down, and it is one way to control your (and your children's) mobile phone spending.

Now you can send and receive e-mail, check the weather, your favorite stocks or sports scores using your wireless phone or Palm wireless device— that is, if you have the patience and tapered fingers to work the diminutive keypad. Ordering online may save you money. Check the web sites above for **wireless internet**.

Members of AAA may want to purchase a AAA analog cellular phone, which has no activation fee and is pre-programmed with the AAA emergency road service number. Cellular phones can also be rented from them for short-term use, such as a trip.

CITY WATER

Considering the quantity of commercially bottled water consumed by its residents, you might think that New York City water is either unpalatable or unsafe. In fact, city water, which flows from vast supply systems north of the city in Westchester, the Catskills, and the Delaware River watershed, is both safe and exceptionally tasty when compared to water in other cities. Except in the infrequent years of extreme drought, the supply is ample and unrationed. Water metering was established citywide in the late 1990s, with fees paid by building owners based on consumption. Tenants are not charged for water but are encouraged to avoid water waste, especially in the summer months.

A slight rust-colored tint appears occasionally in water drawn from the Croton system (10% of the total water supply), caused by a bloom of microorganisms, which are tasteless and harmless, if unappealing. Filtration of this water system, soon to be completed, should prevent discoloration.

Questions about water quality or about the water system should be addressed to the NYC Department of Environmental Protection, Bureau of Public and Intergovernmental Affairs, 59-17 Junction Boulevard, Corona, NY 11368. Or contact the department's 24-hour Communications Center at 718-DEP-HELP, where you can also address concerns about air quality, noise, hazardous materials, or sewers. Visit the DEP's web site at www.nyc.gov/dep.

GARBAGE AND RECYCLING

Recycling has become a part of life in New York City, and, as with garbage collection, the service is provided by the city at no charge. One day each week residents place, on the curb, their newspapers, magazines, and corrugated cardboard, neatly tied with string or placed with other mixed paper in a clear plastic bag or in a rigid plastic container, preferably green, labeled "RECYCLING—MIXED PAPER." (Service is once every two weeks in some parts of the outer boroughs.) Washed cans, plastic, and glass bottles, and aluminum foil go out on the same day in the blue drums provided by the Sanitation Department, or in blue plastic bags. Garbage is collected curbside in covered garbage cans or secured black plastic bags three times a week in Manhattan, two to three times elsewhere. Bulk trash, such as furniture and appliances, is picked up on the last day of regular garbage collection weekly. (To find out the pickup days for your neighborhood call the **Department of Sanitation Action Center** at 212-219-8090, 8 a.m. to 4 p.m., leave a message after 4.) Returnable bottles and cans should be redeemed; in many neighborhoods they can be left neatly outside for the homeless to collect: it's their living. For drivers with a New York driver's license and registration the Sanitation Department operates self-help bulk sites (for large items) in four boroughs; call the Action Center for locations and hours. The department's "Digest of Codes," available at the same number, outlines what residents are responsible for, regulations, penalties and procedures; or visit the department's web site, www.nyc.gov/sanitation. Fines for improper trash disposal range from $25 to $250 for the first offense, depending on the seriousness of the offense, and go up with each succeeding violation.

In the New Jersey communities profiled above (see **Neighborhoods**) garbage collection and recycling is provided municipally. The department to call for these services and the telephone number are listed below.

- **Edgewater**: Department of Public Works/Recycling, 201-943-2626
- **Fort Lee**: Department of Public Works, 201-592-3634
- **Hoboken**: Hoboken Environmental Services, 201-420-2385
- **Jersey City**: Waste Management, 201-435-1345
- **Weehawken**: Department of Recycling, 201-319-6070

INTERNET SERVICE PROVIDERS

Your phone is connected, and now you want to connect online. Choices in internet service providers (ISPs) in the metro area are numerous, varied, and rapidly changing as technology advances. Newspaper ads occasionally offer deals on internet service. These and coverage of the rapidly changing cyber-world are to be found in the "Circuits" section of the Thursday *New York Times*—also a good place to look for deals in computer hardware and software.

National internet services currently available in the metropolitan area are:
- **America Online**, 800-827-6364, www.aol.com
- **AT&T WorldNet**, 800-967-5363, www.att.com/net
- **Compuserve**, 800-848-8199, www.compuserve.com
- **Earthlink**, 800-359-3900, www.earthlink.net
- **Microsoft Network**, 800-386-5550, www.msn.com
- **MindSpring**, 800-719-4332, www.mindspring.com
- **Prodigy**, 800-776-3449, www.prodigy.com

Countless regionally operated service providers include **Verizon**, 888-638-6100, www.bellatlantic.net, and **RCN**, 800-RING-RCN, www.rcn.com, and others. See the Verizon Yellow Pages. Most ISPs charge about $20 per month for unlimited internet access. You *can* get it for free, nominally at least, from one of a dozen national and more regional ISPs, but you'll pay for the software and often a hefty set-up fee. Most are not Macintosh-compatible. Customer service is sparse, on-screen commercials thick, and user privacy transparent. Of the following "free" providers, only the first is Macintosh-compatible:
- **AltaVista**, www.altavista.com
- **BlueLight**, www.bluelight.com
- **Excite@Home**, www.excite.com
- **Freei**, www.freei.net
- **Juno**, www.juno,com
- **NetZero**, www.netzero.net

And now, **broadband**, high-speed, (almost) always-on internet connection via cable, telephone or satellite. **Cable TV** subscribers can access this speedy connection for about $40 monthly, plus the cost of installing the cable modem; non-TV subscribers will pay more, that is if the cable is installed in your building. Call TimeWarner, 212-674-9100, or go to www.twcnyc.com; in Brooklyn and The Bronx call Cablevision, 718-252-3700, Jersey City, 201-217-0800, www.optimumonline; or RCN, 800-891-7770, www.rcn.com. **DSL (digital subscriber line)** delivers high-speed internet connection over regular phone lines without disrupting simultaneous phone service. Where available, it costs $40-$50 per month plus a one-time installation charge usually, but there may be a bundling advantage if you buy the service from your phone service provider. To evaluate the various DSL providers for your needs in the metropolitan area, go to www.get-speed.com and/or www.dslreports.com. In either case, cable or DSL, getting connected can be an exercise in frustration. Where neither is available **satellite** service *may* be the answer. You will need a special dish antenna and receiver, installation of which should run about $300, and in some cases dial-up internet service for up-stream (outgoing) communication. Two-way satellite service recently inaugurated by StarBand ("if you can see the southern sky, you can get StarBand"), 800-421-3466, www.starband.com, may require purchase of a PC. The other metropolitan area provider at this writing is DirecPC at 800-347-3272, www.direcPC.com.

Finally, **wireless modem**, e-mail, and internet access for your handheld device, means you can shop and trade stocks or gossip anywhere without a cellular phone or laptop. Rebate deals from OmniSky generally cut the cost of the device to about $100; the service costs about $40 per month. Call OmniSky, 800-668-5228, or go to www.omnisky.com. Watch the ads for more deals.

TELEVISION & RADIO

TELEVISION STATIONS

So that you may tune in your favorite show immediately upon arrival, we list national television networks (and local independents) and their New York channels: **Channel 2**—WCBS; **Channel 4**—WNBC; **Channel 5**—WNYW (Fox); **Channel 7**—WABC; **Channel 9**—WOR (an independent New Jersey-based station); **Channel 11**—WPIX (independent community station serving the tri-state area); **Channel 13**—WNET (Public Broadcasting System). Note that an Ultra High Frequency station, **Channel 21**—WLIW (Long Island's public network channel), broadcasts many of the public network TV series ("Masterpiece Theater" and the like) carried on Channel 13 but at different times. When you miss an episode on Channel 13, you can usually catch it a night or two later on Channel 21.

You'll find weekly programs for the broadcast channels as well as cable channels (including HBO, Showtime and the like) printed in *TV Guide* and the Sunday *New York Times'* "Television" section. This supplement also carries a complete "Station Guide" detailing the ownership and/or focus of broadcast and cable stations.

CABLE TELEVISION AND THE DISH

Expanded programming and famous skyscrapers make cable an attractive and often necessary option in New York City. Like the telecommunications industry, the cable industry is in the throes of change. Currently, service in Manhattan is quasi-monopolistic: Time Warner and RCN serve Manhattan and Queens; Brooklyn is split between Time Warner and Cablevision, which also serves Queens; Staten Island Cable is the sole server in Staten Island.

If your building isn't already wired, the owner or manager must request hookup, which has been known to take anywhere from several months to a year. In Manhattan call Time Warner, 212-674-9100, and do not "press 1 for English" but stay persistently on the phone if you are not already a customer, or go to www.twcnyc.com; for RCN service, call 212-378-8000 in Manhattan or 800-891-7770, or go to www.rcn.com. Queens and Brooklyn call Time Warner at 718-358-0900; The Bronx and Brooklyn call Cablevision at 718-617-7700, www.cablevision.com; Staten Island Cable is at 718-816-8686, www.statenislandcable.com.

The latest alternative to lousy reception via the rabbit ears and the tyranny of the cable companies is **direct broadcast satellite (DBS)**, more commonly known as "the dish." DBS provides the clearest reception available and hundreds of channels, now including the local channels, though only if you are in position suitable for mounting an 18- to 36-inch dish outside your home, a difficult proposition for most Manhattanites. Basically, you'll need to own your building so you can use the roof or have a southwest-facing balcony on which to mount the thing, and there can be no taller building to block the signal from the southwest. Clearly, TV junkies in the outer boroughs and the suburbs, where buildings are lower and spread out, have the advantage here. Currently two DBS signal providers compete in the metropolitan area: DirecTV, 800-347-3288, www.directv.com, and Dish Network, 800-333-3474, www.dishnetwork.com. You buy the receiver and dish, pay a one-time installation fee and a monthly programming fee. Watch for occasional ads in *The Times* offering free installation with a one-year programming contract.

RADIO STATIONS

Music lovers are best served by their FM dials; news and talk shows dominate the AM band. However, on either broadcast frequency most stations specialize further still, emphasizing one format or one sound. Check below to find your station. For program particulars, consult *Time Out New York's* "Radio" page, which is particularly good; *The New York Times'* daily "Radio Highlights" and "Radio Highlights" in *New York* magazine's "Cue" entertainment guide.

- **AM News**: CBS 880—"Newsradio" WINS 1010—"Give Us 22 Minutes and We'll Give You the World"
- **AM Talk**: WABC 770; WMCA 570—"The Voice of New York;" WNYC 830—features cultural and consumer-oriented broadcasts and National Public Radio's "All Things Considered;" WOR 710—insomniac radio (talk around the clock).
- **AM Nostalgia**: WLUX 540; WVOX 1460
- **AM Sports**: WFAN 660; WJWR 640
- **FM Classical**: WKCR 89.9—classical when it isn't jazz, country or talk; WNYC 93.9—classical, swing and jazz interspersed with PBS programs including "All Things Considered" and "Prairie Home Companion;" WQXR 96.3—*The New York Times'* mostly-music but some-news-too station.
- **FM Jazz**: WBGO 88.3—contemporary jazz from Newark; WKCR 89.9— about half the time Columbia University's station plays and talks about jazz; WFUV 90.7—Fordham University's station, playing classic rock to contemporary jazz.
- **FM Listener Sponsored Radio**: WBAI 99.5—just like the populace that supports it, this talk and music station is invigorating, maddening and appealing all at the same time; also WNYC, above under classical.
- **FM Country**: WYNY 103.5, WMJC 94.3, WWXY 107.l, and WFMU 91.1—Saturday 1 to 3 p.m.
- **FM World Music**: WNYE 91.5, 1 a.m. to 6:30 a.m., musical map-hopping for insomniacs.

In hot pursuit of the all-important 20- to 35-year old market, many New York FM stations feature "Top 40 Radio" and are fiercely competitive. New York's contemporary FM music stations currently fall into the following trade categories:

- **Urban Contemporary** (dance music with a driving beat): WBLS 107.5 and WRKS (KISS) 98.7
- **Alternative/Active Rock**: WXRK 92.3
- **Current Hit Radio**: WPLJ (Power 95) 95.5
- **Hot Hits** (slightly wilder than Current Hit Radio; more novelties): WHTZ (Z100) 100.3; WGHT 97.1—hip-hop, R&B
- **Adult Contemporary** (soft sounds aimed at 24-to 54-year-olds): WLTW 106.7
- **Golden Oldies** (rock and roll from the 1950s and 1960s): WCBS 101.1
- **Salsa**, **Merengue**: WSKQ ("Mega") 97.9; WCCA ("Latino Mix") 105.9

OWNING A CAR IN NEW YORK

DRIVER'S LICENSES, AUTOMOBILE REGISTRATION (AND STATE IDs)

New residents with valid foreign or out-of-state licenses have 30 days to apply for a New York State driver's license and to register their cars and motorcycles. Licenses and vehicle registrations are issued by the **District Office of the New York State Department of Motor Vehicles**, 141-155 Worth Street, corner Centre Street, NYC 10013, open Monday-Friday 8:30 a.m. to 4 p.m. Pick up a license application (which will have a convenient voter registration form attached), driver's manual and, if necessary, an automobile registration form at the District Office or have them sent by calling 212-645-5550. A valid out-of-state license exempts you from the road test, but you must pass the vision, road sign and written tests.

Unless you get lucky, happening by when the examiner has a time slot open, you must make an appointment in advance to take the written test. Write to the Preliminary Test Office of the Department of Motor Vehicles in whichever borough you live, or stop by in person. If you don't mind making automated arrangements, you can schedule your test appointment by calling the New York State Road Test Scheduling System at 800-801-3614. The written tests, based on the driver's manual, are given between 9 a.m. and 3 p.m.

Tests are scored there and, if you pass, you are issued a temporary license allowing you to drive immediately. Your official license, the one with the photograph, is mailed to you. On testing day, you must have the completed application form, your current license and $32.25, which includes the written test fee, license validation fee and picture, taken at the time your license is issued. New York State licenses are valid for four years.

If your license has lapsed or this is your first, pick up the materials and take the vision, road sign, and written tests noted above. You'll then be eligible for a learner's permit. With this in hand, after a three-hour course at a licensed driving school, it is possible to take the road test, the ultimate qualification for the New York Driver's License. Examiners can be finicky, but the most frustrating aspect of the road test is getting an appointment to take it. If you can arrange to take the test out of town, or at least out of Manhattan, do so.

If you do not have a driver's license and wish to have a **New York State Identification** card, visit any DMV office with at least two original identification documents, a combination of passport and Social Security card, for example, at least one of which must show date of birth and one with your signature. You can have your picture taken on site, pay for your ID: $7.50 for five years, $12.50 for ten years, seniors $4.50 for ten years, and receive a temporary ID without a photo. The permanent ID will arrive by mail in four to six weeks.

You need the following documents to **register** your car or motorcycle: registration application or title, completely filled out, proof of ownership, proof of insurance, proof of vehicle inspection, sales tax clearance, and proof of your identity and birth. Read the back of the registration application to determine what "proofs" are acceptable. The registration fee depends on vehicle weight. New York State requires liability insurance on all automobiles, upon the purchase of which, from a licensed insurance company, you will be provided with an FS-20 card, which is your **proof of insurance**. New York is a no-fault insurance state. Auto **emission tests** are part of the annual inspection procedure necessary to operating a registered vehicle.

You may find it easier to do your DMV business in one of the other offices listed below:

- 2110 Adam Clayton Powell Boulevard, at 126th Street, NYC 10027, 212-645-5550, Monday-Friday, 8:30 a.m. to 4:40 p.m., Thursday, 10 a.m. to 6 p.m.
- 481 Hudson Avenue, Brooklyn 11201, 718-966-6155, Monday-Friday, 8:30 a.m. to 4 p.m., Thursday, 10 a.m. to 6 p.m.
- 2875 West 8th Street, Brooklyn 11224, 718-966-6155, open same as above
- 2265 East Tremont Avenue, Bronx 10462, 718-966-6155, open same as above
- 168-46 91st Avenue, Jamaica 11432, 718-966-6155, Monday-Friday, 8:30 a.m. to 4 p.m.
- 168-35 Rockaway Boulevard, Jamaica 11434, 718-966-6155, Monday-Friday, 8:30 a.m. to 4 p.m., Thursday, 10 a.m. to 6 p.m.
- 30-56 Whitestone Expressway, Flushing 11354, 718-966-6155, Monday-Friday, 8:30 a.m. to 4:15 p.m., Thursday, 8:30 a.m. to 7:15 p.m.
- Showplace Bowling Center, 141 East Service Road, Staten Island 10314, 718-966-6155, Monday-Friday, 8:30 a.m. to 4 p.m., Thursday, 10 a.m. to 6 p.m.

Long lines are a Department of Motor Vehicles tradition. Best time to go is early in the week. Fridays are particularly busy. The last workday of any month can find the line spilling out onto Worth Street's sidewalk and is to be avoided, period. **Note**: for a quickie (10-minute) renewal of your NY State driver's license or car registration, go to the DMV office at 300 West 34th Street between Eighth and Ninth avenues, Monday-Wednesday, 8 to 5:30, Thursday to 7 p.m. The fee is $27.25.

For up-to-date information from the state Department of Motor Vehicles visit their web site at www.nydmv.state.ny.us; in New Jersey go to www.state.nj.us/mvs.

PARKING

You *can* park legally on city streets if you are prepared to spend several hours a week switching parking spots to conform to the city's alternate side of the street parking laws. Call 212-225-5368 to find out what regulations are in effect on any given day or, better yet, get a free copy of the Department of Transportation's calendar showing the days your car doesn't have to be moved. Send a stamped, self-addressed envelope to Calendar, NYC Department of Transportation, 40 Worth Street, NYC 10013.

Most people working full time must find private parking for their cars. Monthly garage rates keep rising. In any of Manhattan's prime areas, count on paying between $240 and $400 a month. There are alternatives, however, to be found in garages around the fringe of town, on the Lower East Side, south of Greenwich Village along the West Side Highway, and north of Morningside Heights. A favorite for the budget-conscious below 14th Street is Mayor Parking, Pier 40, West and Houston streets, 800-494-7007. More Than Parking has relatively inexpensive indoor parking at 540 West 59th Street, 212-307-7886, and at 627 West 125th Street, 212-280-7487. Open lots are cheaper and some are better guarded than others. Again, however, the more reasonably priced lots tend to be on the periphery of town.

Note: city residents are exempt from 8% of the 18.25% parking tax. To apply for the exemption call or write the NYC Department of Finance, 25 Elm Place, 3rd Floor, Brooklyn 11201, 718-935-6000. You must send the name and license number of the lot or garage you use and proof of residence, which can be a copy of your car registration and driver's license. The process must be repeated yearly, but the savings make it worth the trouble.

If you use a car only occasionally, consider a private garage in a nearby community that is easily accessible by public transportation. See **Transportation** section for information about car rentals.

AUTO SERVICES AND REPAIR

Keeping a car in New York City is a luxury and a headache. You've stood on line (New Yorkers don't stand *in* line) for registration and license, what you're paying the garage would rent a studio apartment somewhere else, now who can you trust to repair your car without ripping you off? There are hundreds of auto repair shops throughout the city, and many of them are competent and honest. Which ones? Alas, there is no consumer rating system for auto repair shops. Talk to friends and colleagues for their recommendations before you have a problem; you may find a gem of a repairman. Membership in AAA (American Automobile Association) for $55 the first year, $45 thereafter, is probably the best investment you can make in your car in the city. The emergency road service alone, with free battery charge and free towing within a three-mile radius to an AAA-affiliated service station is worth the price of admission. Their list of affiliated stations is a valuable starting point. Members also receive free maps, trip-planning services, trip interruption insurance, the service of AAA travel agents, travel discounts and a host of products and services highlighted in their monthly magazine, *Car and Travel*. Drop in to their Manhattan branch at 1881 Broadway at 62nd Street or call 212-586-1166 or 718-224-2222. In Brooklyn AAA has an office at 2334 Ralph Avenue between Avenues M and N, 718-279-7272; in Queens, 186-06 Hillside Avenue, Jamaica, 718-279-7272. They're on the Web at www.aaany.com.

TRAFFIC TICKETS AND TOWING

What's the price if you get caught? To help you decide whether to take that parking chance or not, here is what tickets currently cost below 96th Street in Manhattan (tickets in the boroughs are sometimes cheaper): $40 if the meter has expired; $55 if you're parked on the wrong side of the street in an alternate-side-parking zone; $55 for double parking or parking within 15 feet of a fire hydrant, or in a No Parking or No Standing zone. No ticket costs more than $55, though fines increase by $10 per day after 30 days and by $20 per day after 45 days. If you want to find out all there is to know about the latest on traffic tickets in Gotham go to the **New York City Department of Finance Parking Violations Operations'** web page at www.ci.nyc.ny.us/finance and scroll down until you see "Parking in New York City." If you have to pay your fines, do it immediately. Pay by mail for the cost of a postage stamp; or by phone for $3, by dialing 877-NYC-PAY or 718-422-7800 and punching in the numbers requested by the automated system, including credit card data for VISA, MasterCard, Discover or American Express accounts; or online at www.nyc.gov for $1.50 service charge.

But tickets are only a part of the penalty. The real deterrent to joining the ranks of New York's parking scofflaws is the threat of having your automobile towed. It costs $150 to retrieve your car from the pound on Pier 76 (Twelfth Avenue and 38th Street) in Manhattan, plus $15 a day (not including the day your car was towed) for storage. You must produce the car's registration and your driver's license to get the automobile back. If your name is on the registration papers, you can pay by check—that is, if your name is printed on the check. Otherwise, or if you have accumulated unpaid traffic tickets, you must produce cash, certified check or traveler's check for payment. The pound is open 7 a.m. to 6 p.m., seven days a week. Call 212-TOW-AWAY to determine whether your car has been towed; if it isn't in the pound (and you haven't misplaced it), your car has been stolen or the Marshall has towed it away for nonpayment of tickets.

To find out if you have an accumulation of tickets (they often blow off the windshield; then, too, other drivers swipe them to put under their windshield wipers in order to fool the cops) call the **Parking Violations Bureau's Help Hot Line**, 212-422-7800. All five boroughs have Help Centers where you can get a free computer printout of your tickets: 150 Nassau Street, Manhattan; 1400 Williamsbridge Road, 1st floor, and 1932 Arthur Avenue, The Bronx; 144-06 94th Avenue, Jamaica, Queens; 210 Joralemon Street, 9th floor Brooklyn; 350 St. Mark's Place, 3rd floor, Staten Island. Or go online to www.ci.nyc.ny.us.

Don't Even Think of Parking Here! by Paul Trapido and Barbara Ensor covers just about every topic a car owner in New York needs to know (published by Simon & Schuster).

KEEPING PETS

Can you bring your Portuguese Water Dog and your Burmese cat to New York? Will that pose a problem? Yes and maybe. The biggest hurdle to clear will be the first: finding a place to live that will accept pets (fish don't count). Increasingly, landlords and co-ops are prohibiting pets in their buildings, which means you may have to choose between the perfect apartment and the perfect pet. Be sure to inquire as you search for a pet-friendly home, and don't plan to sneak one in where they are prohibited. One web site, www.nycdoglife.com, is worth checking for its listing of pet-friendly rentals, condos and co-ops, as well as other pet-related information. Dogs and cats being the most common city pets, we'll address their needs here. If yours is an exotic pet, say a miniature pig, you're on your own.

You will want to have a vet lined up before you need one. Start by calling the **Veterinary Medical Association of New York City**, 212-246-0057, for a list of accredited vets in your neighborhood. Visit the dog run, park or vacant lot in your neighborhood where dog owners hang out with their dogs to glean information on local vets and the whole range of dog-owner concerns. Choosing a vet, like choosing a doctor, is largely a subjective thing. Beyond the cleanliness and user-friendliness of the establishment, you and your pet will want to be comfortable with this vet. You may want to inquire to be sure your vet is available or covered after hours by answering service. In case of a serious emergency after hours, the Manhattan Veterinary Group, a private animal hospital at 240 East 80th Street between Second and Third avenues, 212-988-1000, is open until 1 a.m. daily; the Animal Medical Center at 510 East 62nd Street at York Avenue, 212-838-8100, is open 24-hours a day.

Dogs must be licensed by the city's Department of Health, 212-676-2120, for which you will need proof of rabies vaccination. Dogs must be leashed, except inside fenced dog runs and in city parks between 9 p.m.

and 9 a.m.; they may not enter playgrounds. **Note**: Besides keeping your dog leashed outside of fenced dog runs, you must clean up after your dog. This last ordinance has made it possible to look up when walking in the city.

Dogs need to be walked at least three times a day, not a problem if you work at home. Being social animals they suffer more than cats from being left alone for long periods. Consider the proposition that two dogs is not much more bother than one, and both are happier together than one alone. In any case, if you are away for more than eight hours a day, you will probably need a **dog walker**, a person who has your keys and who will come in and take your dog out for 15 to 60 minutes. Expensive? Yes. To find a reliable walker check with other dog owners and your vet for recommendations. Some of the better pet care establishments keep a list of walkers whose credentials they can vouch for. Some dog walkers will also pet-sit when your are away, either staying in your home to care for your pets and plants or visiting three times a day to feed, water, play with, and walk your pet. The price? Currently a minimum of $22 a day for cats, $25-$30 a day for dogs, more in some neighborhoods. There are kennels in the city, at least one without pens; those out of town, most of which will pick up and deliver your dog, tend to be roomier and less expensive.

Dog runs, fenced in enclosures in which dogs can play off-leash, have proliferated in the city in recent years. At this writing there are 33 in the five boroughs, with more planned. Most, such as those in Riverside Park, are open to all non-aggressive dogs, which are not in heat. Others, such as the run at West Houston and Mercer Streets in the Village, are by membership only and often have a waiting list to get in. To find a dog run in your neighborhood go to www.urbanhound.com/houndplay, which also has useful information on dog-friendly getaways, transportation with dogs and links to other canine sites.

If you're looking to **acquire a dog or cat** you might consult the classified ads in the Sunday Sports Section of *The New York Times*. There are purebred rescue groups in the city for most breeds; they find homes for animals of a particular breed that need to be placed, usually at less cost than from a breeder. And finally, if you adopt a pet from the **Center for Animal Care and Control**, the largest animal adoption organization in the city, you are saving it from almost certain euthanasia. For $60 you can adopt a mixed breed dog ($100 for purebreds) or a cat, complete with vaccinations, spaying/neutering, and an implanted ID microchip, at any of the CAC adoption centers in the five boroughs. In Manhattan the shelter is at 326 East 110th Street, 212-722-3620, open for adoptions daily, 11 a.m. to 6 p.m. Call 212-442-2076 for the location and hours of the other four shelters or visit their web site at www.nycacc.org; with links to petfinder.org it allows you to search other shelters in the metropolitan area. The ASPCA Shelter and Adoption Center, 424 East 92nd Street at First Avenue, 212-

876-7700 ext. 4120, also offers animals for adoption. The Bide-A-Wee Manhattan Shelter at 410 East 38th Street east of First Avenue, 212-532-4455, does not destroy animals but offers dogs and cats for adoption at minimal cost.

A recent, probably inevitable, entry into the field of animal medicine is the pet HMO, Pet Assure, which offers members 25% off all medical care and supplies for pets using participating veterinarians and 10% to 50% off of cost of pet foods, supplies, training, grooming and boarding at participating establishments in the five boroughs, Manhattan especially. Call 888-789-PETS, www.petassure.com. Or, for straight medical coverage try Veterinary Pet Insurance, 800-872-7387.

Dog owners may find useful information, training advice and links to other dog-related web sites at www.canine.org. Equally helpful to New York dog owners is www.urbanhound.com, where you'll find critical reviews of dog runs and pet supply stores, and a directory of veterinarians, groomers, and trainers.

Two books that offer useful information for New York City dog owners:
- *The Great New York Dog Book* by Deborah Loven, HarperCollins
- *The Dog's Guide to New York City, With Jack, the City Dog* by Jan Rohman, Richmond Press

FINDING A PHYSICIAN

"What about how to find a doctor?" a plaintive reader inquires, adding, "it's been tough." Indeed. They're out there, more than 13,000 of them in Manhattan alone, but choosing a personal physician is more like choosing a mate than buying a car. You're looking for a doctor who has graduated from an excellent medical school, done residency in a good teaching hospital, is board-certified, has practiced long enough to know what he/she is doing but not so long as to be out of touch with the latest research and technology, and has just the right professional manner—concerned, straightforward, a listener with, perhaps, a good sense of humor. If you put it off until you need one, you're apt to wind up sitting miserably in the nearest Emergency Room, followed by a big bill. Maybe worse.

If you are enrolled in an HMO (Health Maintenance Organization) through your employer or independently, you are probably limited in your choice of physicians to those listed by that HMO. This makes choosing somewhat easier, but the criteria for choosing remain the same as they are at-large. More about HMO's below.

You may choose a physician as many do, on the basis of the recommendation of friends, and there is something to be said for that. Do, at least, question your friend closely as to what exactly he/she does and does not like about this physician. If you had a physician you liked before moving here, he may be able to recommend a colleague here who will suit you.

Conventional wisdom says that one should have a doctor who is on staff or is an attending physician at one of the **teaching hospitals**. These physicians have been carefully screened and their credentials certified, the reasoning goes, and the teaching hospitals tend to offer a wider range of services and sophisticated procedures than do the smaller community hospitals. Bear in mind also, that as a patient in a teaching hospital, you may expect to be poked and probed by students and residents, and some care may be provided by residents without additional supervision. In such cases, insist on seeing your own doctor. In any case, these hospitals have referral services, which is one place to start your search. Referrals are based on medical specialty and location and often come up by computer rotation. The major academic hospitals in Manhattan, with their physician referral lines, are:

- **Beth Israel-St. Luke's-Roosevelt**, First Avenue at 16th Street, NYC 10003, 888-445-0338
- **Columbia-Presbyterian Medical Center**, 622 West 168th Street, NYC 10032, 800-227-CPMC
- **Mount Sinai Medical Center**, Fifth Avenue at 100th Street, NYC 10029, 800-MD-SINAI
- **NY Hospital-Cornell Medical Center**, 525 East 68th Street, NYC 1002l, 800-822-2NYH
- **NYU Medical Center**, 550 First Avenue, NYC 10016, 888-7-NYU-MED
- **St. Luke's-Roosevelt Hospital Center**, 1000 Tenth Avenue, NYC 10019, 888-445-0338
- **St. Vincent's Hospital and Medical Center**, 153 West 11th Street, NYC 10011, 888-478-4362

Some of these hospitals also have treatment centers elsewhere, and their doctors practice throughout the metropolitan area. See the Yellow Pages for more hospitals in Manhattan and in the other boroughs.

Another source of referrals is the **county medical society**, which in Manhattan (NY County Medical Society, 12 East 41st Street, NYC 10016, 212-684-4670) has some 6,000 members. The caller can specify the area of choice, hospital of choice, specialty, sex, and be given three names. **Note**: you can also check on the credentials, training, and board specialties of a physician recommended to you elsewhere.

Referral(s) in hand, call the specific doctor's office to ask about an introductory visit. Inquire about office hours and their procedure for an introductory interview, which may be by phone or in person, and what the charge will be. Is the office staff helpful? Before talking with the physician have your questions written down: what hospitals does he/she practice in, who covers for him/her when he/she is unavailable, can he/she be

reached by phone after hours if need be, what are his/her billing procedures, etc. You may also want to discuss such sensitive issues as his/her
views on abortion and life support. If you are satisfied so far, you'll probably make an appointment for a physical exam and some tests to establish
a baseline profile. Ask about that and what it will cost. If you are not satisfied, go elsewhere.

A word about **HMOs**; if you are not covered by some form of health
insurance and are not in an HMO connected with your place of employment, you can join one directly yourself on a "direct pay" basis. That means
you pay, and it isn't cheap, at least until you consider the alternative,
should you or a family member become ill or injured. Competition among
HMO's is intense, and the field is rapidly changing. It's a good idea to
request information from a number of organizations in order to determine
what is available and what best suits your situation and your pocketbook.

To assist in this and/or in the choice of a physician or hospital, one
book, known as "Best Doctors," is especially useful. Based on extensive surveys of health care professionals, statistics and other data, *How to Find the
Best Doctors, New York Metropolitan Area* by John Castle and John Connolly
is available in bookstores and in area library reference rooms.

Should you have a **serious complaint**, which you cannot resolve
with your physician, contact the NY State Board for Professional Medical
Conduct, NY State Department of Health, Office of Professional Medical
Conduct, 433 River Street, Suite 303, Troy, NY 12180, 518-402-0855,
www.health.state.ny.us. In New Jersey, contact the NJ State Board of
Medical Examiners, 140 East Front Street, Second Floor, Trenton, NJ
08608, 609-826-7100.

VOTER REGISTRATION

Registering to vote is as simple as calling the **Manhattan Board of
Elections**, 212-868-3292 and requesting an Application for Registration
and Enrollment by Mail, completing the form and returning it to the
board. If you live in another borough, the Manhattan Board will pass the
completed application along to the appropriate borough board: Bronx,
718-299-9017; Brooklyn, 718-330-2250; Manhattan, 212-886-3800;
Queens, 718-392-8989; and Staten Island, 718-876-0079. Under the
1995 "Motor Voter" law, the pre-stamped applications are also available
now in post offices, libraries and some public agencies. If you enroll in a
political party, the form must be received by the Board of Elections 25
days before the primary or general election. You can also register in person
during specific central registration periods at Election Board headquarters,
32 Broadway, NYC 10013.

LIBRARY CARDS

The New York Public Library, with four research libraries, numerous special divisions for various disciplines, famous reference collections and over 80 branches in Manhattan, The Bronx and Staten Island, is one of the city's great treasures. Residents of Brooklyn and Queens, however, aren't book-less: the Brooklyn Public Library has 59 branches, the Queens Borough Public Library, 60. Neighborhood branch libraries are listed at the end of each neighborhood profile in **Neighborhoods**.

Library cards are free and entitle you to borrow or request circulating books from any branch in the system. To obtain a card, give your name, address and proof of residence to the staffer at the return desk of the near-est branch library. Call 212-661-7220 for library hours—which vary widely from branch to branch.

A wonderful resource is the library's Telephone Reference Service, 212-340-0849. Library researchers try to answer all viable questions and, if they cannot, will refer you to the department most likely to have the required data. If the Manhattan number is too busy, try the Brooklyn, 718-780-7700, or Queens, 718-990-0714, Telephone Reference Service numbers.

Before there were public libraries, there were private membership libraries, three of which survive in New York, a clubby step back in time and a haven for the book lover. Membership in The New York Society Library at 53 East 79th Street, 212-288-6900, founded in 1754, costs $135 per year. The Mercantile Library at 17 East 47th Street, 212-755-6710, formed in 1820, is all-fiction and noted for its lively panel discussions and renting space to writers, membership $75 yearly. The General Society Library, 20 West 44th Street, 212-921-1767, also founded in 1820, is a bargain at $35 per year.

PASSPORTS

Whether you are applying for a passport for the first time or renewing, do not wait until just before your summer or Christmas vacation to do so. Apply early and relax. First, call the **Passport Agency** at 212-206-3500 to obtain recorded factual information. With luck, the recording will answer all your questions. For more detailed information and to download the proper mail-in forms, you can visit the Bureau of Consular Affairs' home page at www.travel.state.gov. Or call the National Passport Information Center (NPIC) at 900-225-5674 for detailed recorded information (35 cents a minute) 24-hours a day or to speak with a live operator ($1.05 a minute) from 8 a.m. to 8 p.m.

If you are applying for a passport for the first time, you must have 1) proof of citizenship: an original, or copy, of your birth certificate with a raised seal, or naturalization papers, and 2) proof of your identity: a driver's license or other ID with a photograph and signature. (If you don't have these papers, call the number above for alternatives.) You will need two passport photos (which can be made while you wait in most neighborhood photo shops) and $60 if you are over age 18, $40 for minors. You will find the necessary forms (DSP-II) at all of the addresses listed below, and you must appear in person to get your first passport. But don't go to the Passport Agency unless you have an appointment for a priority passport, covered below. These centers can process your application:

- **Clerks of the State Supreme Court**: (Manhattan) Court House, 60 Centre Street, 10007; (Brooklyn) New Supreme Court, 60 Adams Street, 11201; (Bronx) County Building, 851 Grand Concourse, 10451; (Queens) County Court House, 88-11 Sutpin Boulevard, 11435
- **Post Offices**: (Manhattan) General Post Office, 8th Avenue and 33rd Street; Ansonia Station, 40 West 66th Street; Church Street Station, 90 Church Street; Cooper Station, 90 Fourth Avenue; Franklin D. Roosevelt Station, 909 Third Avenue at 54th Street; and Manhattanville Station, 365 West 125th Street; call the General Post Office for stations with passport windows in the other boroughs.

To renew a passport, pick up form DSP-82 (or, if you were under 18 when you obtained your previous passport, form DSP-11) at any of the addresses listed above and mail it as directed with two passport pictures, $40 and your expired passport. Allow four to six weeks, more if you're applying in high summer season, or mention the date of your departure on the form; passports are processed on the basis of departure date. A passport is good for ten years and can be renewed within two years after expiration.

If you must leave the country in a hurry, it is possible to obtain or renew a passport in three days by calling 212-206-3500 from a touch-tone phone to make an appointment at the Passport Agency, 376 Hudson Street at West Houston Street, open 7:30 a.m. to 3 p.m. You will punch in your Social Security number, the date of your travel ticket, and other information and be given a choice of three appointments. To your appointment, bring your ticket and other necessary papers and cash or check for the fee, plus an extra $35 for priority handling, and be prepared to wait and to return for your passport. In high season (April through June, just before Christmas, Easter and other school holidays) an applicant with an appointment made by phone is likely to need two hours to get to the head of the line.

Suppose you've got to go to Botswana on short notice, you don't even know what documents and shots you need, and you're too busy to get it together. What to do? For a fee (up to $150 for a same-day passport renewal) a knowledgeable staff at Passport Plus, 20 East 49th Street, 212-759-5540, will handle it for you. So will: It's Easy, 30 Rockefeller Plaza, concourse level, 212-586-8880; Red Tape Cutters, 1 Beekman Street, Suite 401, 212-406-9898; and Travco Services, 1265 Broadway, 212-684-2433.

SOCIAL SECURITY

It is the rare American citizen who does not have a Social Security number, a virtual necessity for most. Non-citizens who are working or studying here will also need a number. This can be done by mail by first calling 800-772-1213 and answering five automated questions, then mailing a completed application form with the necessary documents or by going online to www.ssa.gov. Or visit the nearest Social Security office (see the telephone book or get the address from the 800 number above), no appointment necessary.

Bring with you a birth certificate, an original with raised stamp, not a copy, and two other pieces of identification: passport, driver's license, school or government ID, health insurance card, military records, an insurance policy. A Social Security employee will complete the application, and you should receive a card with your number within several weeks.

Non-citizens need a birth certificate and/or a passport and a green card or student documentation, as well as whatever immigration documents you have. It may take a month or more to receive a card.

If you already have a number but have lost your card, call the number above to apply for a new card.

BUILDING STAFF

New Yorkers rely on the staff of their buildings in ways that are unique to the city—and they reward their staff in an equally unique manner.

Most multi-unit residences have a superintendent (the "super") who is responsible for the maintenance and day-to-day operation of the building. Many superintendents may be assisted by porters and hallmen. There are also doormen (and today, doorwomen) in many buildings, and in luxury buildings, perhaps a concierge.

Because many New Yorkers do not rely on their cars to accomplish their daily tasks, goods and services are delivered by businesses to the consumer's home even when they are not there, hence the importance of the building staff. Other staff duties may include hailing cabs, supplying important building information, directing repair people, door holding and—in some buildings—even mail delivery. Most of all, your staff (particularly the doorman) is the first line of security in your building, making certain that anyone who desires entrance truly belongs there.

In addition to the generally higher rents found in staffed buildings, there is an unspoken cost associated with the extra service. It is widely expected that a building's residents tip the staff at Christmas-time for general services rendered throughout the year. (Anything beyond a general service, such as pet-walking or heavy lifting, is best attended to at the time the service is performed.) The tip is by no means mandatory but individual service has been known to decline precipitously for those tight-fisted residents. The custom varies widely from building to building both in terms of cost and how the money is dispersed. It is a good idea to find out what is customary in your building and budget for the holiday season accordingly.

CONSUMER PROTECTION—RIP-OFF RECOURSE

It goes without saying that the best defense against fraud and consumer victimization is to avoid it. You read all contracts down to the smallest print, save all receipts and canceled checks, get the name of telephone sales and service people with whom you deal, check a contractor's license number with the Department of Consumer Affairs for complaints. But you've been stung. A dry cleaner returns your blue suit, but now it's purple and he shrugs. A shop refuses to refund as promised on the expensive gift that didn't suit your mother. Your landlord fails to return your security deposit when you move. After $458 in repairs to your automobile's engine, the car now vibrates wildly, and the mechanic claims innocence. Negotiations, documents in hand, fail. You're angry, and embarrassed because you've been had. There is something you can do.

- **Call the NYC Department of Consumer Affairs, Complaints Department**, 212-487-4444, for information on filing a complaint; have all your information organized before calling, and be prepared to spend some time on the phone. Better yet, file a complaint online at www.ci.nyc.ny.us, go to "agencies—consumer."
- File a complaint with the **New York State Consumer Protection Board**, 800-NYS-1220, www.consumer.state.ny.us, or the **NY State Consumer Frauds and Protection Bureau, Office of the Attorney General**, 120 Broadway, NYC 10271. You may want to call the bureau's complaint line, 212-416-8000, first for advice or a complaint form. Or go in to the office in person, third floor, open Monday-Friday 9:30 to 4:30. Again, have all your documentation organized and in hand.
- File suit for relief, up to $3,000, in **Small Claims Court**. You do not need a lawyer, and some 60,000 New Yorkers use this resource annually. There are six Small Claims locations in the city, two of them in Manhattan, all open one evening until 10. For details call 212-791-6000; ask for two excellent booklets, *A Guide to Small Claims Court* and *Preparing for the Collection of a Small Claims Judgment*. Be advised that winning in court is easier than collecting on a judgment.

Before doing any of the above, inform your adversary of your intentions, politely but firmly. You may force a settlement, thereby saving yourself the trouble of following through.

SAFETY IN NEW YORK CITY

During the 1990s the incidence of violent crime in New York City declined significantly and although many American urban areas have higher crime rates, an important part of getting settled in New York is learning to live safely. What follows are some basic guidelines:

- Always remain alert to what is around you (in front and in back); if you don't pay attention to your surroundings—for example, by walking while listening to a Walkman—you make yourself a target for crime.
- Trust your instincts; they are usually right.
- Stay clear of deserted areas such as empty streets, uninhabited subway cars or platforms and lonely automatic teller machines.
- If you must take the subway late at night, always get in the car that houses the brakeman (generally one of the middle cars). Typically, there is a black and white "zebra" sign marking the spot where the brakeman's car stops—ask the station attendant where it is. Alone in the station, wait near the attendant's booth.
- Look for children playing outside or women walking on their own as signs that an area is safe.
- If you do find yourself on an ominous-looking block, avoid the sidewalk and walk directly in the street to be in view of traffic.
- If you feel you are being followed, walk into the nearest restaurant or store.
- Conceal your valuables, and if you wear a diamond ring turn it around so only the band is showing. Cover watches and necklaces.
- Hold your handbag close to you, wearing the strap across your chest. Don't hang a purse on a restaurant chair or restroom hook.
- Do not count your money in public or use big bills.
- Resist the temptation to play three-card monte on the street; *you won't win!*
- Beware of operators working as a team: someone who tells you she just dropped her contact lens might well have a friend who is reaching in your handbag.
- *Remember:* you do not owe a response to anyone who asks for one. This may seem callous but it is better to err on the side of bad manners rather than bad judgment.

The New York City Police Department publishes free brochures on safety. These booklets include safety precautions addressed to men, women, children, and the elderly—even to runners. Brochure topics also include how to safeguard your apartment, car and small business. See the final section of this book for emergency phone numbers.

If your security desires can only be satisfied by hi-tech gadgetry, you may want to pay a visit to the Counter Spy Shop at 444 Madison Avenue or in the lobby of the Waldorf-Astoria.

Finally, become involved in your neighborhood. All over town, people organize block associations to monitor crime. To find out if a block association exists in your neighborhood, or to set one up, call **Citizen's Committee for New York City** at 212-989-0909.

I T SHOULD COME AS NO SURPRISE THAT THE INTERNATIONAL SERVICE capital is as energetic in supplying the needs of New Yorkers as it is of those the world over. Multitudinous talents and supremely innovative minds combine to provide a mind-boggling array of services, for individuals as well as for industry. Shelter magazines and newspapers seldom let a month or week go by without feature articles about umbrella repair specialists, third-generation tapestry re-weavers, or the pair of clever Upper East Side women available to organize your closets and living space. We'll leave these summaries of the city's more récherché services to the press and provide instead the names of a few representative firms and organizations which supply basics such as cleaning men and women, mail and shipping service, and computer technicians, or which address the concerns of the lesbian and gay communities and the needs of senior citizens and people with disabilities.

HOUSE CLEANING

Word of mouth is your best bet for finding a cleaning person (women have no monopoly on the profession here). Ask friends and neighbors if they know of someone with a few hours available. If this doesn't work, you might try one of the services listed below. The hourly rates quoted include dusting, changing linens, mopping, vacuuming, laundry, cleaning bathrooms, and washing dishes. The same firms provide specialists to handle floor waxing, washing walls, and other heavy-duty jobs at higher fees. For more help with **domestic services** refer to the listings under **Nanny** and **Babysitting Agencies** in **Childcare and Schools**. The *Irish Echo's* classifieds, published in the city and available at newsstands throughout the city, are a good place to look for house-cleaning personnel.

- **Lend-A-Hand, Inc.**, 627 East 11th Street, 212-614-9118; housecleaning is one of the many services provided by this agency's actors, musicians, and dancers. The rate is $18 per hour, four-hour minimum, plus a $25 finder's fee, for one person, whose references are checked before going out on a job.

- **Maid in NY**, 200 Park Avenue South, 212-777-6000; homes as well as industrial sites and business offices are serviced by some 100 employees who currently work for $14 an hour (four-hour minimum) plus $2.50 for transportation. Times and schedules are arranged to suit the client: weekly, bi-weekly or just once for a thorough spring cleaning.
- **Maids Unlimited**, Flatiron Services, 230 East 93rd Street, 212-369-9100, $17 an hour for a four-hour minimum, $13.50 each additional hour in Manhattan. For regular service, the same person would be sent if possible. One or two days' notice required. Help is bonded. Maid uses your supplies.

MAIL AND SHIPPING SERVICES, TELEPHONE ANSWERING, AND BEEPERS

You haven't found an apartment yet, or are out of town frequently and want to keep in touch. Telephone answering services either answer your own phone or assign you a number from which you can retrieve voice mail. Mail receiving agencies or "mail centers" hold or forward mail, receive and ship packages. Shipping services, a way of life now, will pick up and ship just about anything just about anywhere, fast—for a fee. Beepers keep you in touch with the telephone away from a telephone; they are also more affordable than cellular service.

Setting up call forwarding with your telephone service will allow you to use your own phone number with an **answering service**. You connect your phone to the answering service by dialing 72 plus the service number; to disconnect when you return, dial 73. The one-shot installation charge is $16; the carrying charge is $4.15 a month for residential use. Using an answering service you can begin receiving messages the day you sign up and the phone is answered and the message conveyed to you by a human being. Elect service 24-hours a day, seven-days a week or during business hours only (9 a.m. to 5 p.m. or 8 a.m. to 6 p.m., Monday-Friday). Monthly fees include a specified number of messages; additional messages cost about 50¢ each. Expect to pay the answering company about $70 a month for 24-hour service or $50 for service during business hours only, in addition to which there may be a one-time set-up charge of about $10. Another, less expensive voice message option is to sign up for **voice mail** through your local telephone service provider. See **Getting Settled**.

Some telephone answering services also offer **mail service** but you may prefer to use a mail service closer to your home. Mail boxes rent from about $82 (including tax and $10 key deposit) for a standard size box for four months to $288 total for a large box for 12 months. Mail services will also forward mail and typically offer fax and copy service. They've been known to accept dry cleaning and flowers for their customers. Mail Boxes Etc. is the most prolific chain in the city. Check the Yellow Pages under "Mail Receiving Services" and "Telephone Answering Services" for more comprehensive lists. Less expensive are the neighborhood businesses that take in mail and offer no services beyond renting boxes and notifying their occupants of package arrival, at about $10 per month. Cheaper yet, the **Post Office** rents boxes for less than $5 a month ($27.50 for six months), when they have unoccupied boxes; to snag a box at a high-occupancy station line up early on the 15th of the month, when leases expire.

You want to send a set of golf clubs to your mother in Kansas. You need a **shipping service**. The Yellow Pages under "Delivery Service" lists a host of them, from local to national and overseas shipping services moving a letter or a carload. National package delivery services are listed below:

- **Airborne Express**, 800-247-2676, www.airborne.com
- **DHL Worldwide Express**, 800-225-5345, www.dhl.co.id
- **FedEx**, 800-238-5355, www.fedex.com
- **FedEx Ground** (formerly **RPS**), 800-238-5355, www.fedex.com
- **United Parcel Service** (**UPS**), 800-742-5877, www.ups.com
- **US Postal Service Express Mail**, 800-222-1811, www.usps.com

Beeper service, indispensable to doctors, photographers, drug dealers, and those on the go who need to be in touch, can be arranged in several ways. First, you buy a beeper/pager at an electronics store (see the Tuesday *Times*, the Yellow Pages or walk down the street); it will cost from $20 to $200, depending on its range and whether it is numeric, giving you simply the number of your caller or, as with the case with alpha/numeric, giving you a message. At some stores the beeper will be activated on the spot for a one-time fee, generally about $20; you will be assigned a beeper number and you will pay for the first four months to two years. Numeric service costs from $6.50 to $12 a month, depending on length of payment in advance; an 800 number, giving access to long-distance callers, if available, will cost extra. Alpha/numeric service allows for an 800 number at no extra cost, and runs from $20 to $25 a month. Other stores, such as The Wiz chain, sell you the beeper, and you call the service that handles their equipment for activation and billing. Some telephone answering services also offer beeper service, but it is likely to cost more. Most beeper services cover the better part of the tri-state area.

COMPUTER REPAIRS

Of course, you always back up your files. So when the crash comes...well, you know. But that won't save you from unscrupulous computer repair shops. Stories abound, but in fact there are reliable repair shops out there. We list a few that *New York* magazine rated highly. First, a few guidelines: if you have a problem with your computer, call the repair shop and describe the problem; a good shop may be able to talk you through a diagnosis and a self-repair. Before taking the computer in, ask if there is a diagnostic fee, and if that fee will be deducted from the work done. Some shops do not charge a diagnostic fee. Ask if the shop stocks spare parts, what the cost of repairs is likely to be and get an assurance they will do no work until it is authorized. If the technician seems vague or intimidating, call someone else.

- **Ampex Service Center**, 229 East 53rd Street, 212-593-2425
- **CompUSA**, 420 Fifth Avenue, 212-764-6224
- **Crocodile Computers**, 360 Amsterdam Avenue near 78th Street, 212-769-3400, PCs
- **Machattan**, 381 Park Avenue South, 212-242-9393, Macintosh only
- **Macvision**, 210 East 6th Street, 212-586-8445, Macintosh only
- **Tekserve**, 155 West 23rd Street, 212-929-3645, fourth floor, www.tek-serve.com, Macintosh only

LESBIAN AND GAY CONCERNS

In a city with large and established lesbian and gay communities, there are many organizations, businesses, and publications which address their various needs and interests—too many to detail here. We mention one important umbrella organization and six other resources as starting points.

- **The Lesbian & Gay Community Services Center**, 208 West 13th Street, NYC 10011, 212-620-7310, is just that, and the services it offers in a newly-renovated, 150-year-old former schoolhouse in Greenwich Village seven-days a week are myriad. Besides social, cultural, and recreational offerings and events galore there is alcohol and substance abuse counseling; adoption and parenting support; a gender identity project; a variety of HIV/AIDS-related services, counseling and bereavement support; couples mediation; and public policy programs, among others. Center orientation provides newcomers to the city "a map of New York's organized lesbian and gay community"; offers a monthly open house known as the "Orientation Welcome Wagon"; and a "Welcome Packet" for gay, lesbian, bi-sexual, and transgender tourists, which includes entertainment guides listing gay bars, clubs, and restaurants, fliers on cultural programs, and a monthly calendar of events. The Center maintains a web site, www.gaycenter.org, updated daily and hyper-linked with most New York City and national gay organizations, which contains a daily calendar of events and a bi-monthly newsletter.

- **Callen-Lorde Community Health Center**, 356 West 18th Street, NYC 10011, 212-271-7200, is the largest primary health care center in the country devoted to lesbians, bisexuals, gay men, and transgenders. Patients pay on a sliding scale, according to their income.
- **A Different Light**, 151 West 19th Street, 212-989-4850, www.adlbooks. com, is a bookstore and more, including CDs, occasional films and book readings/signings, a busy coffee shop and open mike Saturday nights in the basement; all this in the heart of the gay community in Chelsea.
- **Gay Roommates Information Notebook** (**GRIN**), 57 West 16th Street, second floor, NYC 10011, 212-627-4242, is a roommate exchange.
- **Gay Women's Focus** at Beth Israel Medical Center, 10 Union Square East, Suite 2B, NYC 10003, 212-844-8500, is a full service internal medical practice with links to OB-GYN, psychiatric, and social work specialists.
- **Oscar Wilde Memorial Bookshop**, 15 Christopher Street, 212-255-8097, said to be the world's first gay and lesbian bookshop.
- **Rainbow Roommates**, 268 West 22nd Street, NYC 10011, 212-627-8612, www.rainbowroomate.com, is an apartment share referral service for the gay and lesbian community throughout the city and in New Jersey. Membership costs $150 for four months of updates.
- **Senior Action in a Gay Environment** (**SAGE**), 212-741-2247, is a non-profit community support agency, which offers workshops, discussion groups, and day trips for gay seniors, many of them for free. With a $35 annual membership one receives a monthly newsletter and discounts on those activities for which there are fees.

RESOURCES AND SERVICES FOR PEOPLE WITH DISABILITIES

Living in New York City with a disability has never been easy, but after passage of the federal Americans with Disabilities Act (ADA) in 1990 it became easier as the city began to address the needs of the disabled more seriously. Increasingly, street curbs and public buildings were modified to become wheelchair accessible. Following are some of the services, organizations and resources that make life safer, easier and more pleasant for people with disabilities.

GETTING AROUND

- **Buses**: all buses operated by the Metropolitan Transit Authority (MTA) are wheelchair-accessible, with lifts at the rear door. Reduced fare for seniors and customers with disabilities means a bus ride costs 75 cents one way, using tokens or the pre-paid plastic MetroCard. To get the reduced fare card and for more information, call 718-243-4999, or for the deaf or hearing impaired, TTY, 718-596-8273.

- **Subway**: *Accessible Transfer Points* within the New York City Subway, a pamphlet of the MTA, lists all the subway stations and transfer points in the system which are wheelchair-accessible by elevator, with a map of the system. Reduced fare by token or MetroCard as described above applies to the city's subway system as well, and to the Long Island and Metro-North Railroads, except at morning peak hours. The pamphlet, also in large type and on audiotape, is available from Customer Assistance, MTA NYC Transit, 370 Jay Street, 8th Floor, Brooklyn, NY 11201, or by calling 718-330-3322.

- **ACCESS-A-RIDE**, administered by the MTA through contracts with private carriers, provides rides for customers who are unable to use city bus or subway service for some or all of their trips. Customers call in advance, or subscribe for transportation on a regular basis, to ride Monday-Friday, 6 a.m. to 6 p.m., Saturdays and Sundays, 10 a.m. to 6 p.m. The one-way fare is the same as is charged for buses and subways, and accompanying personal care attendants ride free. For more information or to obtain an application contact ACCESS-A-RIDE, Paratransit Division, New York City Transit, 10 Columbus Circle, 17th Floor, NYC 10019, 718-403-1234 or TTY, 718-722-4403.

- **Parking Permits for People with Disabilities (PPPD)**: the city Department of Transportation issues two types of permits for citizens with disabilities: the New York State permit, which allows the driver to park in spaces marked by the International Symbol of Access, which in the city are all off-street in parking lots; and the NYC permit, which allows the driver to park on city streets in all No Parking and restricted parking zones. For more information and to request an application for either or both permits write: Parking Permits for People with Disabilities (PPPD), NYC Department of Transportation, 28-11 Queens Plaza North, 7th Floor, Long Island City, NY 11101-4008, or call 718-433-3100 and on pickup push the # key, then 11. For the deaf or hearing impaired, call TTY, 718-433-3111.

COMMUNICATION

The Verizon Communications Center for People with Disabilities, 204 Second Avenue at 13th Street, NYC 10009, offers information, services and a variety of adaptive communications equipment necessary or useful to people with various disabilities. Some of these devices, such as enlarged number rings, are free; others, such as Weak Speech Handsets, may be rented, leased, or purchased. The Teletypewriter Device for the Deaf, alternately referred to as TTY or TDD and available at cost through Verizon, sends typed words over the phone lines to the New York Relay Center, from which special operators relay conversations verbally 24-hours a day. The service is confidential and free of charge, except for the cost of the call, and users get a 50% discount on the cost of Bell Atlantic regional calls. Hearing callers to TTY users reverse the process, calling a number (below) from which a special relay operator types the message to the TTY recipient, etc. To qualify for this and other services you must be certified at the Center after providing an approved application and a letter from a doctor or an authorized social service agency.

- **Verizon Communication Center for People with Disabilities**, 800-974-6006; TTY users call 888-663-0363
- **New York Relay Center**, TTY 800-835-5515; others 800-421-1220

OTHER RESOURCES

- **Andrew Heiskell Library for the Blind and Physically Handicapped**, 40 West 20th Street, 212-206-5400, TTY, 212-206-5458, wheelchair accessible, offers books in Braille and recorded books, an extensive collection of large-print books, print and non-print materials on disabilities. Also here, a Community Information Service collection on resources for people with disabilities, as well as recreational, cultural and service-oriented programming for and about people with disabilities. Materials are for use on site or by postage-free mail to those who are homebound, 212-621-0564, TTY, 212-621-0553.
- **Associated Blind**, 135 West 23rd Street, NYC 10011, 212-255-1122, operates 205 apartments for the blind and wheelchair bound at this address, but there is a long waiting list. Non-resident blind also have access to social workers, recreation, and the fitness center here.
- **Con Edison Concern Program** for the hearing-impaired and sight-impaired, 800-872-8846, TTY, 800-642-2308.
- ***Exceptional Parent Magazine***, a guide for parents of children and young adults with disabilities or health problems, publishes an annual *Resource Guide* available in bookstores or through the magazine, 800-372-7368. Their web site, www.eparent.com, is also useful.
- **Goodwill Industries International**, 4-21 27th Avenue, Astoria, Queens 11102, 718-728-5400, www.goodwill.org, offers a host of job training and computer classes for people with physical and mental disabilities.
- **Hospital Audiences Inc. (HAI)**, 220 West 42nd Street, 13th floor, NYC 10036, 212-575-7660, publishes the indispensable *Access for All: A Guide to New York City Cultural Institutions for People with Disabilities,* which lists 300 cultural venues accessible to the handicapped, including major gal-

leries and historical monuments ($5). Their hotline, 888-HAI-HOTLINE, provides similar information, with hotels and restaurants as well.

- **International Center for the Disabled (ICD)**, 340 East 24th Street, NYC 10010, 212-585-6250, TTY, 212-585-6060, provides primary medical care, vocational evaluation, job training and placement for learning and physically disabled.
- **League for the Hard of Hearing**, 71 West 23rd Street, NYC 10010, 917-305-7700, services and provides hearing aids. Call for their resource manual, $5.
- **Learning Disabilities Helpline**, 212-645-6730, operated by the Learning Disabilities Association of New York, 27 West 20th Street, Suite 303, NYC 10011, provides information and referrals in English and Spanish from their database of resources for the learning disabled.
- **The Lighthouse, Inc.**, 111 East 59th Street, NYC 10022, 212-821-9200, ext. 251, or 800-829-0500, www.lighthouse.org, provides vision rehabilitation and other services to the visually impaired. Services include readers, mobility training, computer training, career services, a child development center and adaptive skills classes.
- **Mayor's Office for People with Disabilities**, 52 Chambers Street, Room 206, NYC 10007, 212-788-2830 or TTY, 212-788-2838, for information and referrals.
- **Metropolitan Museum of Art**, 1000 Fifth Avenue at 81st Street, NYC 10028-0198, 212-879-5500 or TTY, 212-570-3828, is wheelchair accessible and has programs with sign language interpretation for the hearing impaired; guides by appointment only for the visually impaired; tours and programs for the developmentally disabled.
- **National Center For Learning Disabilities**, 381 Park Avenue South, Suite 1401, NYC 10016, 212-545-7510, www.ncld.org, provides information and referrals concerning learning disabilities in children and adults on their toll-free line at 888-575-7373, and on their web site, which has links to related organizations and resources, publications, and recent events. Their concerns include dyslexia and adult literacy.
- *New York Able*, a monthly newspaper *Positively For, By & About the Disabled*, with news, commentary, a calendar of events and ads of interest to people with disabilities. Write P.O. Box 395, Old Bethpage, NY 11804, or call 516-939-2253 or 718-792-3533.
- **New York Public Library Branches** (see also Andrew Heiskell Library above) that are wheelchair accessible include: Donnell Library Center, 20 West 53rd Street, 212-621-0618; the Library for the Performing Arts, 40 Lincoln Center Plaza at 65th Street, 212-870-1630; Mid-Manhattan Library, 455 Fifth Avenue at 40th Street, 212-340-0863; Science, Industry, and Business Library, 188 Madison Avenue at 34th Street, 212-

592-7000; the Fordham Library Center, 2556 Bainbridge Avenue, The Bronx, 718-579-4200; and St. George Library Center, 5 Central Avenue, St. George, S.I., 718-442-8561, among others. Project ACCESS, by appointment at the Mid Manhattan, St. George and Fordham branches, uses Kurzweil Personal Readers to give sight-impaired readers access to the full range of the library services and materials. Other assistive technology, such as Braille writers, is available here and at some other branches. For information about these and other services call 212-340-0843, TTY, 212-340-0931.

- **New York Society for the Deaf**, 817 Broadway at 11th Street, 7th Floor, NYC 10003, 212-777-3900, provides multiple services for the deaf.
- **Resources for Children With Special Needs**, 200 Park Avenue, NYC 10003, 212-677-4650
- **Rusk Institute of Rehabilitation Medicine's** driver training program, 400 East 34th Street, Room RR312, 212-263-6028, offers technicians to evaluate the particular needs of prospective drivers with physical handicaps, adapting each car with special devices, and train the driver to operate the adapted car.
- **Technology Resource Center**, operated by United Cerebral Palsy of New York City, at 120 East 23rd Street, NYC 10010, 212-979-9700. You can come in to the demonstration center here to view, learn about and try a range of adaptive products and get information about others through a resource specialist and catalogues. Products range from adapted toys to augmentative communication devices, computers, home products and accessibility modifications.
- **TAP, Theater Access Project of the Theatre Development Fund**, 1501 Broadway, 21st floor, NYC 10036, 212-221-1103, TTY, 212-719-4537, e-mail tap@tdf.org, offers signed performances of selected shows and discounted tickets for people with physical disabilities. Call 212-221-0016 to hear a list of currently signed shows. To arrange wheelchair seating in the theater, call the Tele-Charge wheelchair hotline, 212-947-8844.
- **Visions Services for the Blind and Visually Impaired**, 500 Greenwich Street, 16th Floor, NYC 10005, 212-625-1616, offers free and low-cost rehabilitation and social services to the blind and multi-handicapped, including those who are non-English speaking. Self-help audio guides at cost teach life skills, and there are peer support groups and recreation year-round at Vacation Camp for the Blind in Rockland County, transportation provided.
- **Walter Reade Theater**, 70 Lincoln Center Plaza at 67th Street, 212-875-5600, shows first-run features with open captions for the deaf once a month. Call after 3 p.m. for details.

RESOURCES AND SERVICES FOR SENIORS

If you're a senior, or expecting to be a senior, living in New York City get yourself a copy of *Take Charge! A complete Guide to Senior Living in New York City* by John Vinton (1999, New York University Press), a comprehensive reference to services, resources, and some practical advice you didn't know you'd need. The latter includes guidance on avoiding rip-offs in home repair and other areas in which seniors are targeted, where to get help with financial/estate planning, resources for long-term care, end-of-life concerns such as hospice, assisted death and burial.

The prime source of services and assistance for seniors here is the city's **Department for the Aging (DFTA)**, whose web site, www.ci.nyc.ny.us/aging, is useful in discovering and accessing these services. Write or call the department at 2 Lafayette, Street, NYC 10007, 212-442-1000. DFTA operates 335 senior centers throughout the boroughs, where meals are served, cultural trips originate, and outreach gives access to other services. The department offers guidance on government benefits and referral to community services; transportation for health care, social services and necessities; arranges home care for the qualified; helps victims of elder abuse; offers job training for the employable unemployed; subsidizes part-time employment; offers computer training and customer service skills and placement in jobs in private industry; arranges legal assistance to those in need; and more. Some useful numbers:

- **Alzeimers and Long Term Care Services**, 212-442-3086, offers counseling and referrals for families of seniors with Alzeimers disease.
- **Elder Pharmaceutical Insurance Coverage** (**EPIC**) offers savings on the cost of drugs for qualified individuals, 800-332-3742.
- **Health insurance information and counseling**, 212-333-5511
- **Housing** for the department's *Alternatives in Senior Housing: A Comprehensive Guide for New York City*, call 212-442-1384. In recent years complexes for senior "assisted living" at market prices have sprung up throughout the city and in the greater metropolitan area; see ads in the *New York Times*.
- **Legal assistance**: in Manhattan, 212-426-3000 and 718-488-7448; The Bronx, 718-220-0030; Brooklyn, 718-645-3111; Queens, 718-897-2515; Staten Island, 718-273-6677
- **Reduced fare for seniors**: people with disabilities and those 65 and older can purchase a MetroCard at half-price. Write MTA, Reduced Fare, P.O. Box 023158, Brooklyn 11202-0064, or call 718-243-4999, TTY (for hard of hearing) 718-596-8273.
- **Senior Citizen Rent Increase Exemption** (**SCRIE**) is for those over 62 whose income falls below $20,000; this is a city subsidy. Call 212-442-1000 for more information.

- **State School Tax Relief (STAR)** offers reduced school property taxes for homeowners (condos and co-ops included) whose income does not exceed a maximum. Write STAR Program, NYC Department of Finance, 50 Lafayette Street, Rm. B2, NYC 10013, or call 212-442-0320.

Under state law **new rental housing** in the city is frequently classified **80/20**, which means that 20% of the apartments are reserved for seniors at below-market rents. Applicants are chosen by lottery, and the waiting list is long. Get on the list before you need the apartment. To find out if you are eligible and to get on line, call the New York State Housing Finance Agency (HFA), 212-688-4000, *and* the New York City Housing Development Corp., 212-344-8080. There are developments under both authorities.

The city abounds in culture at a discount for seniors. Most notably the **Senior Cultural Discount Program**, administered by Hospital Audiences, Inc., (HAI) provides $10 tickets to events on Broadway, at Lincoln Center, BAM and elsewhere. Call HAI to register for this benefit, 888-424-4605. Museums, movie theaters, and some theaters discount admission for seniors as well. State parks and historic sites are free to seniors who present a photo ID, which includes date of birth.

Exercise programs for seniors, free or at low cost, are widely available. Exercise classes, stress management, and walking clubs are located in many of the senior centers. Call Health Promotion Services (HPS), 212-442-0954, to find out more. The Parks and Recreation Department operates 25 recreation centers in the city (membership, $25 annually), some of which offer senior aerobics and activities. For details, call 212-360-8131 in Manhattan; in The Bronx, 718-430-1838; in Brooklyn, 718-965-8995; in Queens, 718-263-4121; in Staten Island, 718-390-8023. And, finally, there are exercise programs for seniors at many YMCAs and YMHAs (see **Health Clubs, YMCAS and YMHAS** in the **Sports and Recreation** chapter).

Access to **college courses** on a "space available" basis is offered to seniors at a discount by most of the major universities and colleges in the city. To name some:
- **Brooklyn College**, "Institute for Retired Professionals and Executives," 718-951-5647
- **City University of New York**, "Quest" Program, 212-925-6625, offering free course auditing to those 60 and older in the four-year colleges, enrollment courses (for credit) in the community colleges.
- **College of Staten Island**, "Options for Older Adults," 718-982-3772
- **Columbia University**, "Life Long Learners," 212-854-2820
- **Fordham University**, "College at 60," 212-636-6740
- **New School**, "Institute for Retired Professionals," 212-229-5682
- **NYU** School of Continuing Education, 212-998-7080

- **Pace University**, "Adult Resource Center," 212-346-1288
- **Queens College**, "Center for Unlimited Enrichment," 718-997-3635
- **St. John's University**, Queens, 718-990-6161

A host of volunteer opportunities are available to seniors (See **Volunteering** chapter), and some of the resources detailed above (**Resources and Services for People with Disabilities**) are valuable for seniors as well. A few other resources are worth noting:

- **Alzeimers Association**, 212-983-0700, www.alz.org, is a useful resource for those who are diagnosed with the disease and for their families.
- **Con Edison**, 800-872-8846, in their "Concern" program for seniors age 62 and older provides a newsletter and advice on bill payments, financial assistance, a Home Energy Assistance Program (HEAP), and turn-off protection for seniors who are blind or disabled. **Brooklyn Union Gas (BUG)**, 718-330-0600, also provides a variety of free services for seniors under their "Star Program."
- **New York Foundation for Senior Citizens**, 212-962-7559/7653, offers a free Home Safety Audit to homeowners (condos and co-ops included) 60 and older. They also have a home repair program, providing minor electrical, plumbing, masonry, and carpentry repairs.
- **SAGE**, Senior Action in a Gay Environment, is a non-profit community support agency described above under **Lesbian and Gay Concerns**.
- **Verizon**, 800-779-6874, under their "Life Line" program provides reduced rate phone service to low-income seniors, disabled veterans and those on surviving spouse veterans pensions.

I F YOU'RE PLANNING TO RAISE CHILDREN IN NEW YORK CITY, FRIENDS and relatives (from out of town) will look at you with concern, pity, disbelief, perhaps. And it *is* a challenge to raise children here. But it is also richly rewarding, for child and parent alike. In fact, it isn't so much difficult as it is just different here. This chapter attempts to make it a little easier by describing the available options in childcare, nursery schools, primary and high schools—public, private, and parochial—with information to help parents choose between them. We begin with baby sitters and infant care and wind up with high schools.

CHILDCARE

Quality day care, generally called childcare now, is hard to find and more expensive in New York than anywhere else in the country, thanks to the tremendous cost of real estate and the need for stringent standards governing the operation of day care centers. Asked what is required to open a day care center here, Frances Alston, former program director of the not-for-profit Day Care Council, says, "First thing is, rob a bank. You can't start a day care center in New York for less than a quarter million dollars."

Non-profit agencies which act as go-betweens for parents and day care providers are proliferating. We list some below under **Information Sources**. Some corporations have begun to distribute day care information to their employees, while others have gone so far as to add on-premises facilities. Nursery schools that used to start with three-year-olds now have toddlers' groups for twos.

Listed below you'll find thumbnail descriptions of the kinds of pre-school care (and education) available in New York City. Arranged chronologically by ages covered—from birth through six years—these categories are followed by the names of organizations that provide specific day care recommendations.

New York State establishes the eligibility requirements for publicly funded day care, be it family day care in a private home or group care at a center. To be eligible, a family must meet established maximum income requirements. Almost all those entitled to assistance still pay something; currently fees range from a low of $1 per week, per child, up to $99 per week.

Note: The US Department of Education provides a useful source of parenting information covering such topics as children's television viewing habits, sleep problems, behavioral issues, child care and the like, with a library of articles and book abstracts and links to special interest organizations; see them at www.ed.gov, or call, 800-USA-LEARN. The National Parent Information Network is on the web at www.npin.org, or dial 800-583-4135. Also useful, especially in researching day care facilities, is www.kidcare.net, which lists 180,000 facilities, 1,805 of them in New York City, including address, phone number, ages of children served and some descriptive material. Call the Consumer Product Safety Commission, 800-638-2772 or check their site, www.cpsc.gov, for a day care safety-hazard checklist and safety recalls.

Available free in school lobbies, pediatricians' offices and laundromats, a variety of monthly parents' magazines, the most ubiquitous of which is *BigAppleParent* (as well as *QueensParent* and *WestchesterParent*), offer useful advice and information on everything from nutrition to single parenting, to day care, schools and child health and recreation. *BigApple's* web site, www.parentsknow.com, has links to current and past articles, an extensive monthly calendar of events for parents and children and a bulletin board worth checking—baby sitters, nannies, playgroups, Spanish classes for children, "Any Danish mothers around NYC/NJ?"

AU PAIRS AND NANNIES

When it comes to sitters, New York's no different than the suburbs. Neighborhoods are stocked with reliable teenagers looking for jobs. But it takes time to meet them and, occasionally, they aren't available on short notice or for New Year's Eve. As with many services, the best source for good baby sitters or nannies is often friends, relatives, or colleagues who can recommend one. That failing, we've listed a number of alternatives. Some of the agencies also provide full-time, sleep-in or live-out help.

Au pairs are young women (between 18 and 25), usually European, who provide a year of in-home childcare and light housekeeping in exchange for airfare, room and board, and a small stipend ($110 to $120 per week). Less expensive than nannies, they are also less experienced, may be less mature, and are gone in a year. The program is certainly valuable for the cultural exchange it offers the host family and the au pair. The US Information Agency oversees and approves the organizations that place au pairs. Any of the national agencies listed below will connect you with a local coordinator who will match up your family with a suitable au pair:

- **Au Pair International**, 800-654-2051
- **Au Pair in America**, 800-928-7247
- **EF Au Pair**, 800-333-6056
- **Interexchange**, 800-479-0907

Good fortune is having a friend who passes on to you her excellent **nanny**, her children having outgrown the need, just when you need one. That failing, you have want ads, the internet, and nanny agencies to fall back on. An invaluable source of full- and part-time nannies, both live-in and out, as well as house-cleaning personnel is the classified ad section in the *Irish Echo*, published in the city and available at newsstands throughout the city. Those seeking positions are not necessarily Irish, and some of the ads under "situations wanted" are placed by the satisfied employers of nannies whose services they no longer need. On the internet one site, www.4nannies.com, carries classified nanny listings allowing you to avoid agency fees, which can run $800 to $3,000. You simply pay the $189 application fee. The site has links to firms that do background checks and some that provide nanny tax advice and/or service.

An agency, on the other hand, will have checked the nanny's background, perhaps by detective, her Social Security record, her driving record, her credit record and so far as possible, any chance of criminal record. Note that there are no national criminal records available to investigators. But the agency will also have interviewed the nanny, in person or by phone, and will have checked her references. The agency can inform you about necessary nanny tax procedures and insurance and should provide a detailed contract. The International Nanny Association maintains a useful web site, www.nanny.org, which coaches you through the agency and nanny selection process. Another site, which is advertiser supported, www.nannynetwork.com, contains a database of nanny placement agencies and referral services, nanny insurance services, and background verification services as well as a library of articles.

However you find your nanny, be sure to check at least two of the prospective nanny's references, questioning them carefully, and repeatedly, if necessary. You will also want to interview the nanny in your home if possible in order to insure a good fit.

NANNY AGENCIES

- **Best Domestic**, a national agency at 2 West 45th Street, Suite 1000, 212-685-0351, www.bestdomestic.com, handles nannies, live-in or out, as well as housekeepers and other domestic help. Weekly wage for a nanny runs $400 to $500, with a two-month guarantee and an agency fee of 10% of one year's salary, paid one week after the nanny starts work.

- **Elite Nannies**, 49 Park Avenue, 212-246-0600, and 70-09 Austin Street, Suite 203, Forest Hills, 718-544-9800, www.elitenanny.com, provides full- or part-time nannies, as well as housekeepers, baby nurses, baby sitters and companions. They also provide nannies on a short-term basis to visiting families and baby sitters for hotel guests. Their nannies work a minimum of five days a week for $400 or more, part-time for $19 per hour or $100 per day. For full-time nannies there is a 60-day guarantee and a five-percent fee, paid up front.
- **Fox Agency**, 30 East 60th Street, NYC 10022, 212-753-2686, providing baby nurses and nannies since 1936. Rates are hourly, daily or weekly. Nannies, screened by the agency, run $350 to $550 living out weekly, $400 to $650 living in (the rate may or may not include the legally mandated Social Security taxes and unemployment insurance). The fee for temporary baby nurses is 10% of the salary, for nannies it is six weeks' salary.
- **In Home Help**, 800-626-6948, www.inhomehelp.com. This Connecticut-based agency supplies full-time nannies and babysitters to the metropolitan area and beyond, Europe included. Salaries range from $350 to $850 per week on a one-year contract, though many stay longer, and the agency fee is 20% of the first year's gross up front, nine months' guarantee with free replacement.
- **Irish Agency**, 10 East 39th Street, 212-473-5263 (IRE-LAND), and 43 Center Drive, Old Greenwich, CT, 800-462-6697, provides full-time nannies, live-in or out, throughout the metropolitan area for $400 to $500 a week, with an agency fee of four weeks' salary, a minimum of $1,800, up front. As their nannies, not necessarily Irish, have been with them for some time, they do not do a background check unless it is requested, however they do check references. There is a guarantee with the contract.
- **NY Nanny Center**, **Inc.**, 31 South Bayles Avenue, Port Washington, NY 11058, 516-767-5136, www.nynanny.com, specializes in live-in nannies in the tri-state area. The nannies are evaluated by the director, a former social worker. Nannies in this program attend a monthly support meeting. Weekly wages range from $400 to $500, with an agency fee of $2,500 and a 60-day guarantee.
- **Pavillion Agency**, **Inc.**, 15 East 40th Street, NYC 10016, 212-889-6609, www.pavillionagency.com, specializes in nannies (as well as butlers, domestics and chauffeurs), who negotiate their rates depending on the needs of their clients. Currently nannies, living in or out, cost $450 to $1,200 weekly, plus Social Security taxes and unemployment insurance. The agency fee is 15% of the annual salary, with a 60-day guarantee.

BABYSITTERS

AGENCIES

- **Avalon Nurses Registry**, 162 West 56th Street, 212-245-0250, $15 per hour for one to two children, four-hour minimum. Travel is $3 during the day, $8 after 8 p.m., and $15 after midnight. Each additional child is $2.50 per hour. You can call them 24-hours a day, seven-days a week. Fees include the agency commission.
- **Baby Sitter's Guild**, 60 East 42nd Street, 212-682-0227, hourly fee for one or two children is $17, $2 per hour extra for each additional sibling and $5/hour extra for a visiting friend. With enough advance notice a sitter with a nursing background is provided for children under one year. There is a four-hour minimum plus $4.50 to $7.00 for travel, depending on time of day. For an extra $2 per hour the Guild can provide a baby-sitter fluent in one of 16 languages. Fee includes the agency's commission. Call between 9 a.m. and 9 p.m. seven-days a week. While requests made during the day for that evening can usually be filled, it is better to call a day ahead. The Guild was established in 1940.
- **Elite Nannies**, 49 Park Avenue, 212-246-0600, and 70-09 Austin Street, Suite 203, Forest Hills, 718-544-9800, www.elitenanny.com, provides full- or part-time nannies, as well as housekeepers, baby nurses, baby sitters, and companions (see listing above under **Nanny Agencies**).
- **In Home Help**, 800-626-6948, www.inhomehelp.com (see listing above under **Nanny Agencies**).
- **Pinch Sitters**, 799 Broadway, NYC 10003, 212-260-6005, baby sitters, on short notice if necessary, at $14 per hour, plus transportation at night, four-hour minimum. Call Monday-Friday, 7 a.m. to 5 p.m.
- **Town & Country Domestic Agency**, 250 West 57th Street, #303, 212-245-8400, $13 per hour for children under six months ($12 over six months) with a four-hour minimum; add $1/hour per sibling; $2/hour per visiting child. Daytime carfare is $4, nighttime car fare is $8. Call Monday-Friday 9 to 5. Same-day service is possible but plan a few days ahead for weekends.

NON-PROFIT

- **Parents League**, 115 East 82nd Street, 212-737-7385; the League's baby-sitting service is just one of several benefits included in the $50 annual membership fee. Sitters are students, ages 13 to 18, who attend League member schools or who are the children of members. Riffle through the sitter files, arranged by neighborhood, in the League's office between 9 a.m. and 4 p.m., Monday-Wednesday, 9 a.m. to 7 p.m. on Thursday, until noon on Friday.

SCHOOLS

- **Barnard College Baby-sitting Service**, 606 West 120th Street, 212-854-2035, to pre-register, call in your name, address, phone number and name of your pediatrician. Once you are in their file, call Monday-Friday between 10 a.m. and 5 p.m., two days in advance of your needs. A student will call you back. Minimum rates are $6.50 per hour, though most parents pay more in this competitive market. There is also a $15 annual fee.
- **St. Francis College**, 180 Remsen Street, Brooklyn, 718-522-2300, ext. 260, if you live in the Brooklyn Heights area, phone in your needs; minimal information is posted and the student who wants the job goes to the Student Placement Office for details. Rates are up to the individual sitter.
- **St. Vincent's Hospital School of Nursing**, 27 Christopher Street, don't call; mail or bring a notice to "Re: Tina" to be posted on the school's bulletin board. Negotiate a rate with the student who calls you.

FAMILY DAY CARE

More and more middle-class parents are electing family care for their toddlers. Said to be the most widely used form of day care in the country, here in New York City the Health Department and/or other agencies involved in the field certify and supervise individuals caring for infants and toddlers in their apartments. These "providers," often mothers of young children drawn to childcare as a means of remaining at home with their own youngsters, are allowed to oversee up to six children—no more than two of whom can be infants—in their dwelling at one time. Typically, parents who do not qualify for assistance pay between $30 and $40 per child for a six- to eight-hour day. To access the network of publicly funded providers or those listed with the city's Agency for Child Development for private clients, call the agency at 718-367-5437. The city's Department of Health, Division of Day Care licenses all providers, public and private, and will provide a list on request at 212-676-2444.

GROUP DAY CARE CENTERS

These city-licensed facilities, be they in the private or public sector, offer educational as well as care-taking programs for groups of children primarily, but not exclusively, between the ages of two and six years for an extended (beyond normal nursery school hours) or a full eight-hour day.

- **Publicly funded day care centers** are usually found in, or contiguous to, neighborhoods with the greatest economic need. Even with an income above the maximum allowed by the state (see introduction for specifics), parents proving "social" need—those working full time qualify—can apply to publicly funded day care centers, if they are prepared to pay the full cost for their child's care, currently between $80 and $217 a week, depending on the facility.
- **Private centers** tend to be either nursery schools, which have added all-day care to the regular school curriculum or centers established to supply day care, which also offer education.

Call the city's **Agency for Child Development**, 718-367-5437, or the **Department of Health, Division of Day Care**, 212-676-2444, for a list of publicly funded day care centers. Ads for private centers and for the occasional playgroup will be found in parent magazines such as *Big Apple Parent*, which are distributed free in school lobbies.

INFANT CARE

Formal programs for the two-month-old to two-year-old set are almost all publicly funded and appended to day care centers. Call the New York City Health Department's Division of Day Care, 212-676-2444, for the names of city-licensed facilities. Infants can also be placed in Family Day Care homes.

PLAY GROUPS

Neighborhood parents often band together informally, usually in cooperative fashion, to care for a small group of pre-schoolers for a half-day or so, one, two or three times a week.

INFORMATION SOURCES

New York Parents' Book by Lois Gilman (Penguin) covers everything from having the baby to care to entertainment. Several non-profit organizations as well as the Agency for Child Development, jointly sponsored by the city, state and federal governments, provide accurate information about local facilities. To determine the most suitable day care solution for your family's needs, consult these sources while pursuing the other leads suggested below.

- **Agency for Child Development**, 30 Main Street, Brooklyn 11201, call 718-260-6000, for pre-school information and referrals from the ACD's Vacancy Information Service. Their staff provides names and addresses of private as well as publicly funded and Head Start childcare facilities located in the five boroughs. This information is supplied to ACD by the Department of Health's Bureau of Day Care, 212-676-2444, the group charged with licensing pre-school facilities. Their Directory of Day Care Services in New York City is available by mail free of charge.

- **Child Care Inc./The Pre-School Association**, 275 Seventh Avenue, NYC 10001, 212-989-8360, a knowledgeable, non-profit group, has a corporate program. Member firms receive counseling on childcare in New York City as well as detailed publications on the subject for distribution to employees. The organization, funded also to assist individual parents, offers telephone counseling to all callers. They also provide three packets ($5 each), one each on in-home care, family day care and early childhood programs—which contain an informative booklet, checklist, licensing information sheet and, most helpful of all, names of day care providers appropriate to your needs in your specific neighborhood.
- **Day Care Council of New York, Inc.**, 10 East 34th Street, NYC 10016, 212-213-2423, has 50 years' experience as a non-profit providing free information, counseling and referrals on all types of childcare, including baby sitters, nannies and day care throughout the five boroughs.
- **The New York Public Library's Early Childhood Resource Center** at the Hudson Park Branch on Leroy Street off Seventh Avenue in Greenwich Village, 212-929-0815, devotes one whole floor to resource materials for parents and a playroom for kids.
- *Solving the Childcare Puzzle*, a booklet covering the range of child care options in the city, is available on request from the Office of the Manhattan Borough President, 1 Centre Street, 19th Floor South, NYC 10007, 212-669-8300.

OTHER LEADS

Check out some of the following resources for referrals in your particular neighborhood:

- **Churches**, large and small; old-fashioned, wall-mounted **bulletin boards**, most often, but not exclusively, found in the larger supermarkets; private schools, ask the admissions director for the names of feeder schools, day care centers or playgroups; **pediatricians**; **hospitals**, talk with the administrative officer in charge of residents and interns; and, last but perhaps most accessible and knowledgeable of all, **playground and park bench parents**.

SCHOOLS

NURSERY SCHOOLS

It is at this point, typically, that parental anxiety sets in. And it needn't. In Manhattan alone there are more than 175 privately run pre-school programs, generally geared to three-, four- and five-year-olds, often including toddlers' groups and sometimes all-day care as well. They vary widely in educational philosophy and style, and admission to none of them is essential to a child's later success at Harvard. *The Manhattan Directory of Private Nursery Schools* by Linda Faulhaber (SoHo Press) is a detailed listing of more than 150 nursery and all-day programs plus other useful information. It's a good place to start. Meanwhile, talk with mothers in the parks you frequent and with parents of children in neighborhood nursery schools. The search process typically begins just after Labor Day preceding application, and many schools will have open houses; this is also the time to request information from the schools you might wish to consider. And finally, in helping you decide what might be the best school for your child (and for you), the two sources below should be helpful:

- **The Independent Schools Admissions Association of Greater New York (ISAAGNY)** publishes the New York Independent Schools Directory containing page-long descriptions of more than 120 private member schools enrolling pre-schoolers through high-schoolers. Nursery schools and toddler groups, as well as numerous elementary and secondary schools, along with pre-school groups, are listed, and a useful geographical index is included in the appendix. This directory provides an excellent overview of New York's varied private schools. Copies cost $10 and can be picked up at the office of the Parents League of New York, 212-737-7385, or ordered from them by mail ($11.50).

- **Parents League of New York, Inc.**, 115 East 82nd Street, NYC 10028, 212-737-7385, with 106 member schools, mainly in Manhattan, is an excellent source of private school information. One counseling session with a specialist from their School Advisory Service— for example, their expert on toddlers' groups and nursery schools—is well worth the League's annual $30 membership fee. A panoply of other child-related services, not the least of which is their reliable Baby Sitter-Young Helper listing, a great boon to any newcomer with kids, also comes with League membership, as does their 80-page Toddler Activities directory.

GRADE SCHOOLS

Here, decision-making becomes more difficult because there are so many options. To begin with, the choice between public, private, and parochial school; for some it is a choice easily made; they know they want one or the other, or they can't afford private school. A word to the undecided: know that there are some excellent public schools in the city, just as there are some dreadful ones.

If your child is in a nursery school in the city, you can expect some guidance in choosing a primary school, both in general and specific to your child's temperament and style of learning. Beyond that, you want a school that reflects your values. Those opting for **private school** will find the resources above under **Nursery Schools** helpful. *The Manhattan Family Guide to Private Schools* by Catherine Hausman and Victoria Goldman (SoHo Press, 1999) offers an independent evaluation of the specific schools; however the focus is distinctly uptown, giving scant attention to some excellent downtown schools. They do provide useful information and advice on navigating the admissions process.

Catholic **parochial schools**, which cost considerably less than the city's private schools, have found favor in recent years with non-Catholics as well as Catholics as an attractive alternative to public schools. The Archdiocese of New York operates 144 elementary and 39 high schools in Manhattan, The Bronx and Staten Island. For information about schools in your neighborhood or beyond, call 800-SCHOOL4 or 212-371-1000. The Roman Catholic Diocese of Brooklyn and Queens operates 156 elementary schools and 22 high schools. Call the Superintendent's office, 718-965-7300, for more information. There is no source of comparative evaluation of the parochial schools, which are independently run, so interested parents are left to make their own evaluation on a school by school basis.

Visit the schools that seem to suit your child's needs, and yours. Read the school literature carefully. Examine the physical plant. Observe the relationships between children, staff and administration. Consider the program, in theory and in practice. Finally, what is your gut reaction? Remember, you and your child may spend the next eight to twelve years here, and no decision is irrevocable. Just hard.

Parents considering **public school** should begin by contacting the community school board in their district (see **Neighborhoods**) for a list of schools in the district and to find out what school they are zoned for. Many of the boards have brochures describing the various schools in the district, from which it is possible to get a sense both of the character of this school district and of the particular schools. In most districts there is a variance procedure allowing a child to go out of his zone within the district, space permitting. Plan to start such a procedure in January for the following year.

Register at your school and arrange to visit for a good look at the physical plant, teacher-student interaction, student engagement and attentiveness, the feel of the school. Ask questions.

It is often possible to send a child to a school out of district, space permitting, if the process is begun early enough. A child may be enrolled in a school in another district if a parent's workplace is in that district; inquire in that district about the required variance procedure.

In recent years several grade groupings have evolved among the city's schools, making choice more complicated. And within these groupings are schools with varying focus. The most common configurations below the high school level are:

- **Early childhood schools**, pre-kindergarten to second or third grade, popular for their focus on the needs of young children.
- **Elementary schools**, K-fifth or -sixth grade, are the most common configuration. Many districts are now shifting sixth grade to middle schools to avoid crowding.
- **Grammar schools**, K-8, making a comeback and popular with parents as an alternative to middle school.
- **Middle schools** or **intermediate schools**, containing sixth through eighth grades or seventh and eighth. Many of these are theme schools, focusing on a particular subject area, such as the performing arts or technology. Junior high schools, seventh through ninth grades, once common, are in decline.

For further guidance and encouragement in choosing a public school for your child, turn to *The Parents' Guide to the Best Public Elementary Schools In New York City* by Clara Hemphill, researcher at the Public Education Association, published in 1997 by SoHo Press. She profiles the top 100 (out of 676) elementary schools in the city. Now you can find much of this information on the web site of Advocates for Children at www.advocatesforchildren.org, which includes digests on more than 50 schools and a complete list of programs for gifted children and their admissions criteria. More recently Ms. Hemphill published *Public Middle Schools: New York City's Best*, which provides excellent descriptions and ratings of middle schools, district by district.

HIGH SCHOOLS

Decisions at this level, however fraught, are made somewhat easier by the guidance procedures at whatever school the child is already enrolled in and (or more difficult) by the fact that the child will participate in the decision. Again, public or private? Information sources for the private schools are as noted above.

Admission to many of the public high schools is citywide, a trend which is increasing as theme schools proliferate at this level. The various categories of high school include the following major groupings:

- **Audition schools**, such as Fiorello LaGuardia High School of Music and Art and the Performing Arts and High School of Art and Design, to which the student must be recommended and must audition or present a portfolio for admission.
- **Competitive schools** to which admission is by competitive exam; Bronx High School of Science, Brooklyn Tech, Hunter High School and Stuyvesant are the most well known and desirable schools in this group.
- **District schools**, which range from abysmal to excellent.
- **Special Interest schools** include the School of Fashion Industries and the New York School of Printing, among others.

INFORMATION SOURCES

The annual public school options fair, with workshops and guides to schools in several Manhattan districts, at the 92nd Street YMHA, 212-996-1100, is worth a visit. The Parenting Center there has a variety of seminars on public and private schools, and one need not be a member to attend. Call the Center for particulars.

- **The Board of Education**, in conjunction with the Fund for New York City Public Education publishes "The Directory of Public High Schools" annually. Call or write Office of Access and Compliance, Division of High Schools, Board of Education, 110 Livingston Street, Brooklyn 11201, 718-935-3415.
- **The Division of Assessment and Accountability of the Board of Education**, 110 Livingston Street, Brooklyn 11201, 718-935-3767, publishes an annual report, commonly known as the "Report Card," which describes each of the public schools statistically for the previous year. It's a source of information on enrollment, ethnic composition, reading scores etc.
- **The Manhattan Borough President's Office**, 1 Centre Street, 19th Floor South, NYC 10007, 212-669-8300, will send *Parent's Guide to Choosing a Public Elementary School in New York City*, on request, free.
- **The Public Education Association**, 28 West 44th Street, NYC 10036, 212-868-1640, offers seminars for parents and publishes a free *Consumers Guide to High Schools*, and a *Consumer's Guide to Middle Schools* for the cost of the postage, and *Lend a Hand to NY City Public Schools*, which is a guide to the system and to organizations that help the schools. Judith Baum at PEA is an understanding source of particular information and advice.
- **The Toussaint Institute**, 212-422-5338, offers an annual Spring

seminar on New York City public schools for African-American and Hispanic parents. Call for details.

- **School Match**, 5027 Pine Creek Drive, Westerville, OH 43081, 800-992-5323, www.schoolmatch.com, is a private organization which, for $97.50, will send a ranked list with descriptions of 15 schools, public or private, in a specific area, which best suit your requirements as determined by questionnaire.

BIG CITY LIVING ENCOURAGES IDIOSYNCRATIC LIFE STYLES. AND New Yorkers pursue their interests and goals singularly unencumbered by considerations as to "what the neighbors might think." Home decoration is a striking case in point. Anything (within the terms of the lease) goes, and when it comes to providing all the goods and services necessary for us to feather our wildly divergent, albeit mainly minuscule, nests, the city really comes through for its residents. Generally speaking, there are at least three approaches to shopping in Manhattan: 1) largish, fairly priced, standard sources; 2) famous signature shops and upscale boutiques; and 3) discounters, warehouse-style superstores and/or alternative resources such as wholesale districts and sample sales.

Note from the shopping strategies department: unless you are literally sitting and sleeping on the floor of your new apartment, it pays to wait until winter for the annual, city-wide furniture and housewares sales to make those major purchases. In both department stores and specialty shops the savings in January and February are considerable, 20% to 50% off. Watch for the ads in *The Times*. And it's worth noting, especially if you anticipate making a major purchase, that the **sales tax** in New York City is 8.25%, in some New York suburbs 8.5%, but the tax bite in Connecticut and New Jersey is 6%.

Finally, even if you're addicted to take-out and fast food, you've got to shop for groceries. The choices in this city of immigrants are mind-boggling. You'll find your favorite providers, but until then look below for where to find just about anything to eat.

FULL SERVICE DEPARTMENT STORES

As designer boutiques fragment row upon heretofore sensibly labeled row of merchandise into seemingly hundreds of glass cubicles, one-stop shopping at the full-service store has lost cohesiveness. Still, it beats 15 stops in a 20-block neighborhood. Although more difficult than it once was, it's comforting to take a 15-item list—silk pins through box springs—and pass the afternoon under one roof. So, we lead off with the royalty of New York's merchandise scene, along with a few lesser lights listed alphabetically, before splintering into our own smaller sections.

- **Bloomingdale's**, Third Avenue at 59th Street, 212-705-2000, www.bloomingdales.com, open 10 a.m. to 6:30 p.m., to 9 p.m. Thursday, 11 a.m. to 6 p.m. Sunday. For all the zap and glitter, Bloomie's has a sturdy core: you can leave your watch for repair, order Christmas cards, shop the best white sales in town—January and August—buy a TV, a mattress, and sweat socks, as well as try out glittery shoes to a funky beat, or nosh the food of the moment at one of five chic cafes. Services include Beatrice Dale personal shoppers, 212-705-2380, and translators, a bridal registry, decorators, and 24-hour telephone order service.
- **K-Mart**, 770 Broadway at 8th Street, 212-673-1540, www.bluelight.com, open Monday-Friday 9 a.m. to 10 p.m., Saturday 10 a.m. to 9 p.m., Sunday 11 a.m. to 8 p.m.; okay, it's not a department store like Bloomingdale's is a department store, but it is fairly comprehensive, including even a houseplants department as well as clothing, furniture, housewares, and appliances, not to mention Martha Stewart linens, paints and furniture—all at downtown prices. Another K-Mart at 1 Penn Plaza, 34th Street between 7th and 8th avenues, 212-760-1188, open Monday-Friday 7 a.m. to 9 p.m., Saturday and Sunday 9 a.m. to 9 p.m., is much smaller, not really a department store.
- **Macy's**, Broadway at 34th Street, 212-695-4400, open 10 a.m. to 8:30 p.m., Monday, Thursday and Friday, to 7 p.m. Tuesday, Wednesday and Saturday, 11 a.m. to 6 p.m. Sunday, www.macys.com. Enormous! Complete! And can it be overwhelming! First-timers take advantage of the multilingual information booths and descriptive giveaway location maps at first floor information booths. Others use Macy's By Appointment, the personal shopping service, and the 24-hour telephone ordering service, 212-494-3800. A total revamp of the beloved behemoth began at the basement level with the creation of the superb Cellar, a bazaar-like warren of individual food and housewares shops, and moved skyward as each floor was completely redone with pizzazz and flair. A merchandising tour de force and, equally miraculous, the sales help's attitude and quality of service has improved beyond belief.
- **Macy's** (formerly A & S), 420 Fulton Street, Brooklyn, 718-875-7200, open 9:45 a.m. to 6 p.m., to 7 p.m. Monday, to 9 p.m. Thursday, noon to 5 p.m. Sunday, www.macys.com. Talk about full service! Lucky Brooklyn residents need travel no further than the Hoyt Street stop on the #2 or #3 train for practically any nicety or necessity. Macy's has both

an optometrist and a podiatrist on duty and a fur storage and restyling service. From TVs, furniture and electronics on the lower level to fabric on Six, this rather reserved, no-nonsense institution also heeds the latest fashions with up-to-the-minute styles from leading designers on Three.

- **Macy's**, 90-01 Queens Boulevard, Elmhurst, 718-271-7200, open Monday through Saturday 10 a.m. to 9 p.m., Sunday 11 a.m. to 7 p.m. Not as vast as Herald Square, but it's full service and convenient to all Queens. All Macy's online at www.macys.com.

- **Saks Fifth Avenue**, 611 Fifth Avenue at Rockefeller Center, 212-753-4000, www.saksfifthavenue.com, open 10 a.m. to 6:30 p.m., to 8 p.m. Thursday, noon to 6 p.m. Sunday. Carefully coifed customers, self-assured and tan, and elaborate bouquets spraying nonchalantly into the glowing, wood-paneled aisles characterize Saks Fifth Avenue. So do the most refined escalators in New York. They float you silently past eight well-lit shopping floors against a backdrop of perfectly placed plants, mirrors and pinky-beige marble. Luxurious Saks exudes well-being from every tasteful counter. Faced with the largest selection of Vuitton luggage in town, a Revillon fur boutique and the stylish men's department on Six, you may forget that Saks harbors a useful set of shops along 49th and 50th streets. Housewares, luggage, bathing suits and sportswear, the bath and linen shop, and the art gallery all have private entrances. Recently, the store has made a fetish of personalized service. The Fifth Avenue Club, 212-753-4000, ext. 4200, on three shelters five personal shopping services, among them the Executive Service for women executives.

- **Sears**, Cross County Parkway and Route 87, Yonkers 10704, 914-377-2100, www.sears.com, open Monday-Friday 10 a.m. to 9:30 p.m., Saturday 9:30 a.m. to 9:30 p.m., Sunday 10 a.m. to 7 p.m.; 50 Mall Drive West in the Newport Mall, Jersey City, NJ 07310, open Monday-Friday 10 a.m. to 9:30 p.m., Saturday 9:30 a.m. to 9:30 p.m., Sunday 11 a.m. to 7 p.m. Other Sears stores at 2307 Beverly Road, Brooklyn, 718-826-5800; 96-05 Queens Boulevard, Rego Park, Queens, 718-830-5900; 137-61 Northern Boulevard, Flushing, 718-460-7000; 5200 Kings Plaza, Brooklyn, 718-677-2100, call for hours. For those with wheels this reliable old standby still represents a convenience and good value. Parking is free, and in the New Jersey store just outside the Holland Tunnel the sales tax bite is less painful.

- **Target**, 135-05 20th Avenue, College Point, Queens, 718-661-4346, and 543 River Road, Edgewater, NJ, 201-402-0253, www.target.com, open 8 a.m. to 10 p.m. every day. New to the metropolitan area in 1998, this popular department store, nestled in a shopping center among other national chain giants, lacks only a full furniture department. Everything else, from clothes to appliances and their exclusive line of household products for the garden, the kitchen, and the living room, designed by architect Michael Graves is here; check their cryptic newspaper ads.

DISCOUNT DEPARTMENT STORES

- **Century 21**, 22 Cortlandt Street, 212-227-9092 and 472 86th Street, Bay Ridge, Brooklyn, 718-748-3266, open 7:45 a.m. to 7:30 p.m., Monday-Friday, 10 a.m. to 7:30 p.m., Saturday. Not the nationwide real estate broker but something that is unique to New York City—a full service department store where everything is discounted. There are many real bargains here and the service is pleasant and no-nonsense. Beware: the Manhattan store can be a zoo, especially around Christmas-time.
- **T.J. Maxx**, 620 Avenue of the Americas (Sixth Avenue) at 19th Street, 212-229-0875, open Monday-Saturday 9:30 a.m. to 9 p.m., Sunday 11 a.m. to 8 p.m. Again, not one of the grand old department store dames, but it's more than just off-price clothing. You'll find housewares and some small furniture items. The location upstairs over Filene's Basement (clothing only) doesn't hurt.

APPLIANCES, ELECTRONICS, CAMERAS

These three categories have been lumped together because many of the stores listed below cross merchandise lines.
- **Macy's**, see **Full Service Department Stores**, above.
- **Sears**, see **Full Service Department Stores**, above.
- **Willoughby's Camera Store**, 136 West 32nd Street, 212-564-1600, open Monday-Thursday 8:30 a.m. to 7:30 p.m., Friday to 4 p.m., Sunday 10 a.m. to 7 p.m.; 385 Fifth Avenue at 36th Street, 212-213-1515; and 50 East 42nd Street between Park and Madison avenues, 212-681-7844, open Monday-Friday 8:30 a.m. to 7:30 p.m., Saturday and Sunday 10 a.m. to 7 p.m. Offers phone quotes. Complete rental and service departments complement the most extensive new and used photographic stock in the city. Willoughby's also has a computer department.

SPECIALTY SHOPS

- **Alkit Image Express**, 820 Third Avenue at 50th Street, 212-832-2101; 222 Park Avenue South at 18th Street, 212-674-1515; 830 Seventh Avenue near 53rd Street, 212-262-2424; and 466 Lexington Avenue at 46th Street, 212-286-8700, open 7:30 a.m. to 6:30 p.m., Saturday 9 a.m. to 5 p.m. "Generally" gives phone quotes. Full video and stereo line but fame rests on the quality and quantity of the professional and amateur cameras and other photographic equipment offered, as well as Alkit's custom order department and rental and repair services.

- **Harvey Electronic**, 2 West 45th Street, 212- 575-5000, and Broadway at East 19th Street inside ABC Carpet & Home, 212-228-5354, open Monday-Friday 9:30 a.m. to 6 p.m., Thursday to 8 p.m., Saturday 10 a.m. to 6 p.m., Sunday noon to 5 p.m.. "The best of the best for everybody," they say. High end audio equipment, including free at-home consultation. On the internet at www.harveyonline.com.

- **Innovative Audio**, 150 East 58th Street between Lexington and Third avenues, 212-634-4444; and 76 Montague Street, Brooklyn Heights, 718-596-0888, www.innovativeaudiovideo.com, open 10:30 a.m. to 7 p.m., Thursday to 9 p.m., Saturday to 6 p.m., Sunday noon to 5 p.m. The Manhattan store is perhaps a bit higher-end, though both stores offer the full range of quality equipment. The home theater demo setup for projectors and surround sound at the new site is especially advanced. Noted for their helpful sales staff.

- **Lyric High Fidelity**, 1221 Lexington Avenue at 83rd Street, 212-439-1900, open 10 a.m. to 6 p.m., noon to 5 p.m. Sunday. "Only the finest stereo components." A strong selection of speakers.

- **Sound by Singer**, 18 East 16th Street, 212-924-8600, open 10 a.m. to 6 p.m., to 8 p.m. Tuesday and Thursday, noon to 5 p.m. Sunday. Full range of audio equipment, quiet listening rooms and an extremely knowledgeable sales staff. Specializes in American brands.

- **Stereo Exchange**, 627 Broadway at Houston Street, 212-505-1111, open Monday-Friday 11 a.m. to 7:30 p.m., Saturday 10:30 a.m. to 7 p.m., Sunday noon to 7 p.m. This established sound emporium specializes in home theater, audiophile stereo and new components. Used high-end components, expertly repaired in-house and sold at 60% to 70% off what they might cost new, are a real draw.

DISCOUNT STORES

The Lower East Side doesn't have a monopoly on good buys. Appliances and electronics are sold all over the city at less than retail. A few of the many discounters in Manhattan:

- **ABC Trading Co.**, 31 Canal Street near Essex, 212-228-5080, open 10 a.m. to 6 p.m., to 1 p.m. Friday, closed Saturday. No credit cards. No phone quotes. Photographic equipment, small as well as major appliances, audio equipment and supplies, TVs and VCRs. ABC's special department for merchandise adapted to cycles and broadcast standards found throughout the world is a favorite of UN personnel and others living overseas.

- **Adorama**, 42 West 18th Street near Sixth Avenue, 212-741-0052 and 800-648-5710, www.adoramacamera.com, open Monday-Thursday 9 a.m. to 6:45 p.m., Friday 9 a.m. to 2 p.m., Sunday 9:30 a.m. to 4 p.m. A favorite of professional photographers and filmmakers, this store carries a truly staggering array of cameras, accessories, video equipment, lighting, lenses, VCRs and more. Call for their specialty catalog or drop by for one.
- **B&H Photo-Video-Pro Audio**, 420 Ninth Avenue at 34th Street, 212-444-6670, www.bhphotovideo.com, open 9 a.m. to 6 p.m. Monday-Thursday, to 2 p.m. Friday, 10 a.m. to 5 p.m. Sunday, closed Saturday. Whether you need an English-made Billingham photographer's vest, a point-and-shoot or a Hasselblad, professional lighting and movie equipment, a wireless mike or camcorder, you'll find it in this sprawling audio-video bazaar with knowledgeable sales staff, a large professional clientele, and an encyclopedic catalog. Biggest price breaks are on professional equipment.
- **Cambridge Camera Exchange**, 119 West 17th Street, 212-675-8600, open 9 a.m. to 6 p.m., Thursday to 7 p.m., 10 a.m. to 5 p.m. Sunday, closed Saturday. No phone quotes. Complete photographic line, mostly mail order (free catalog) but good buys available to the walk-in trade.
- **Circuit City**, 52 East 14th Street at Union Square, 212-387-730; 232 East 86th Street, 212-734-1694; 625 Atlantic Avenue, Brooklyn, 718-399-2990, www.circuitcity.com, open Monday-Saturday 10 a.m. to 9 p.m., Sunday 11 a.m. to 6 p.m. One-stop shopping for computers, telephones, hope appliances, CD players, TV specials, VCRs, car stereo and video games. Cruise the store on their web site, www.circuitcity.com.
- **J&R** Music World, 31 Park Row across from City Hall for audio-video hardware and 27 Park Row for kitchen and small personal appliances and fitness equipment, 212-238-9000, www.jandr.com, open 9 a.m. to 6:30 p.m., Monday-Saturday, Sunday 11 a.m. to 6 p.m. It's definitely not all music, though their stereo selection is perhaps the best among the discounters. This string of outlets along Park Row also draws shoppers from all over for CDs, cameras, camcorders, cellular phones, television and video equipment, home office equipment, computer hardware and software (see **Computers**).
- **P.C. Richard & Son**, 120 East 14th Street between Third and Fourth avenues, 212-979-2600, and 205 East 86th Street between Second and Third avenues, 212-289-1700, and at more than 40 other locations in Brooklyn, Queens, Westchester, Long Island and New Jersey, all open Monday-Friday 9 a.m. to 9:30 p.m., Saturday to 9 p.m., Sunday 10 a.m. to 7 p.m. Home appliances, digital cameras, VCRs, Play Stations. The uptown store is "slightly more upscale" than is typical.

- **Vendome Trading Corp.**, 345 Seventh Avenue at 29th Street, 212-279-3333, open 8:30 a.m. to 5:30 p.m., 11 a.m. to 3 p.m. Saturday, closed Sunday. Offers phone quotes. A member of a cooperative buying group that has its own warehouse, Vendome sells air conditioners, washing machines and other major, as well as small, appliances, computers, TVs and stereos. Major credit cards on small appliances but not on electronic equipment.
- **The Wiz**, 726 Broadway, 212-677-4111, www.thewiz.com; and 17 Union Square West, 212-741-9500; 555 Fifth Avenue, 212-557-7770; and 170 East 87th Street, 212-876-4400 are among the many city locations. Open 10 to 10, to 8 Saturday, 11 to 5 Sunday. No phone quotes. Their claim: "no one goes lower" on stereo, small electronics and TV prices.

ALTERNATIVE SOURCES

Head to lower First Avenue for discounts on brand name appliances. Try both Gringer & Sons at 29 First Avenue at Second Street, 212-475-0600, and Bloom & Krup, 504 East 14th Street between avenues A and B (for years at First and 12th Street), 212-673-2760, for bargain prices on dishwashers, freezers, refrigerators and stoves. Garland, SubZero, Traulsen, GE, KitchenAid and European manufacturers such as Gaggenau and Miele, among others, are in stock or can be ordered.

BEDS, BEDDING AND BATH

Department stores can take care of all your bedding needs under one roof. Lay in supplies during January and August, traditional White Sale months. Bloomingdale's becomes particularly generous at these times, stocking irregular Martex towels and name brand sheets at great savings.

SPECIALTY SHOPS

- **Ad Hoc Softwares**, 410 West Broadway at Spring Street, 212-925-2652, open daily 11:30 a.m. to 7 p.m., to 6 p.m. Sunday. The high tech bed and bathroom furnishings displayed in this light struck corner store are softened by the inclusion of a few more traditional, even old-fashioned, lines. Pale blue and rose French Jacquard hand towels, napkins and place mats and Carpe Diem lace curtains and lampshades add a little romance to Ad Hoc's own somber, rather austere collection of all-cotton sheets and to bed linens by international manufacturers including Wamsutta, Palais Royale, and Castelini.
- **Bed**, **Bath & Beyond**, 620 Sixth Avenue at 18th Street, 212-255-

3550; 410 East 61st Street at First Avenue, 646-215-4702; 96-05 Queens Boulevard, Rego Park, Queens, 718-459-0868; and 489 River Road, Edgewater, NJ, 201-840-8808; www.bedbathandbeyond.com, open Monday through Sunday 9 a.m. to 9 p.m.. As the name declares, this popular (and affordable) chain store has almost everything for your household needs.

- **Dixie Foam**, 104 West 17th Street, 212-645-8999, open 10 a.m. to 6 p.m., closed Sunday. In this factory/showroom, 4" and 5 1/2" thick foam mattresses are the forte. Choose standard sizes or have irregular sizes cut and covered to order.

- **Futon Warehouse**, 113 University Place at 13th Street, 212-473-4400, open Monday-Friday 10 a.m. to 8 p.m., Saturday 10 a.m. to 6 p.m., Sunday noon to 6 p.m. Mecca for students and first apartment furnishers and conveniently located near NYU, this is probably the largest futon merchant among many. The cotton and foam futons come in all sizes, in stock and custom-covered, with a selection of frames as well as shelving, loft beds and occasional tables

- **Gracious Home**, 1220 Third Avenue between 69th and 70th streets, 212-517-6300, open 8 a.m. to 7 p.m., Saturday 9 a.m. to 7 p.m., Sunday 10 a.m. to 6 p.m.; and at 1992 Broadway at 67th Street, 212-231-7800, www.gracioushome.com, open Monday-Thursday 9 a.m. to 8 p.m., Friday and Saturday to 9 p.m., Sunday 10 a.m. to 7 p.m. Imported linens for the Upper East Side, bath ware, fabrics, stationery and giftware. Free gift-wrapping and delivery in Manhattan, not to mention phone orders.

- **Kleinsleep**, 962 Third Avenue at 58th Street, 212-755-8210; 874 Broadway at East 18th Street, 212-995-0044; 2330 Broadway, Second Floor, 212-501-8077, and in Westchester, New Jersey and Connecticut, call 800-KLEINSLEEP for locations; open Monday-Friday l0 a.m. to 9 p.m., Saturday 10 a.m. to 8 p.m., Sunday 11 a.m. to 6 p.m. Beds, beds, beds of all kinds, frames and headboards, mattresses as well.

- **Laytner's Linen & Home**, 2270 Broadway at 81st Street, 212-724-0180; 237 East 86th Street, 212-996-4439, www.laytners.com, open Monday-Friday 10 a.m. to 7:30 p.m., Saturday 10 a.m. to 7 p.m. (to 6:30 p.m. at East 86th Street, to 6 p.m. at 2270 Broadway), Sunday noon to 6 p.m. Outfit your bedroom and bath here, and then some. Besides a limited selection of handsome cotton drapes, you'll find bedding, feather beds, duvets, spreads, towels and bathroom and closet supplies, tablecloths, chenille throws and scatter pillows, but none of it in overwhelming quantities. Scattered among these soft good are items of Mission-style furniture, also for sale.

- **Sleepy's**, 157 East 57th Street, 212-421-3090; 25 West 34th Street, 212-736-9287; 2080 Broadway, Second Floor, 212-769-3635; 337 East

86th Street, 212-534-7836; 611 Sixth Avenue at 18th Street, 212-414-9791; 201 East 34th Street, 212-725-9842; 2581 Broadway, Second Floor, 212-749-3802; 44 Park Avenue South, 212-725-1492; 810 Lexington Avenue at 62nd Street, 212-317-8494, plus stores in Brooklyn, Queens, Staten Island, New Jersey, Westchester and Connecticut. Call 800-SLEEPYS for locations. Open Monday-Friday 10 a.m. to 9 p.m., Saturday l0 a.m. to 8 p.m., and Sunday 11 a.m. to 8 p.m. Perhaps the best deal in name-brand mattresses, especially during their sales. And you live near one.

ALTERNATIVE SOURCES

Household linens on the **Lower East Side** are squooshed into two blocks on Grand Street between Allen and Forsyth. An uptown look has intruded on the cram-jammed bargain basement fustiness always considered de riguer in the city's most raffish bazaar area. The uninitiated will find comparatively sleek **Harris Levy**, 278 Grand, 212-226-3102, easier to take, but the same Laura Ashley, Marimekko, Martex, Wamsutta, Cannon and Stevens lines are handled by **Ezra Cohen**, 275 Grand, 212-431-9025, and other unreconstructed firms along Grand. All closed Saturday, open Sunday. Department store White Sale prices match those you're likely to find on the Lower East Side but, if you avoid the Sunday crush, you'll discover sales personnel often more knowledgeable and helpful than their uptown counterparts.

- **ABC Carpet & Home**, 888 Broadway at East 19th Street, 212-473-3000, www.abccarpet.com, open 10 a.m. to 7 p.m., to 8 p.m. Monday and Thursday, to 6 p.m. Saturday, 11 a.m. to 6 p.m. Sunday. It's certainly not just carpets anymore, but "the ultimate in home furnishings adventure": uptown imported and domestic designer lines, spreads and towels at downtown prices, along with a fetching array of country furniture, folk art objects, decorative pieces and scatter pillows. Now there's crystal, earthenware, Limoges, bone china and flatware as well. Sink into the Pipa Restaurant and refuel when energy flags, or book a reservation at Chicama, also on the main floor.

- **Dial-A-Mattress**, showroom at 31-10 48th Avenue, Long Island City, 11101, 718-628-8737, dialamattress.com. But you don't go there, unless you want to try out a mattress, or look at their bedding, sofa beds, frames or accessories. Simply dial, 24-hours a day, and a bedding consultant will help you choose among discounted Sealy, Simmons, Certa or Spring Air mattresses according to size, firmness and price range. Delivery ($19 to $39) is within 24 hours, on approval, with a 36-day comfort exchange (softer or firmer). It's hard to beat for the busy.

- **Kleinsleep**, 962 Third Avenue at 58th Street, 212-755-8210, www.kleinsleep.com, open 10 a.m. to 7 p.m., 11 a.m. to 6 p.m. Sunday.

Remainders from the six-store chain's extensive line of innerspring and foam mattresses and beds of all shapes and sizes are sold in the clearance center downstairs.

- **J. Schacter Corp.**, 5 Cook Street, Williamsburg, Brooklyn, 718-384-2732, open 10 a.m. to 5 p.m. Monday-Thursday, 10 a.m. to 1 p.m. Friday, Sunday by appointment only, closed Saturday. New York's leading feather merchants, famous for standard and custom-made pillows and comforters in various mixes of feathers and down and for reprocessing and cleaning already fabricated down bedding and garments.

CARPETS AND RUGS

For an overview, check the department stores, in particular **Macy's**, for broadlooms and **Bloomingdale's** for imports.

- **Einstein Moomjy Inc.**, 141 East 56th Street between Third and Lexington avenues, 212-758-0900, open 9:30 a.m. to 6:30 p.m., to 8 p.m. Thursday, to 6 p.m. Saturday, noon to 5 p.m. Sunday. At this self-described "Rug Department Store" located in the Architects and Designers Building, the very best broadlooms share floor space with luminous Orientals as well as domestic and imported carpets of all kinds. Don't worry about missing an Einstein Moomjy sale: newspapers and TV are flooded with ads.
- **Safavieh**, 902 Broadway at 20th Street, 212-477-1234, www.safavieh.com, open Monday-Saturday 10 a.m. to 7 p.m., Sunday 11 a.m. to 6 p.m., selling a variety of hand-made Oriental rugs new and antique, silk and wool, and an assortment of Aubusson weaves. Watch for their sales. See their web site for stores in Connecticut, Long Island and New Jersey, which also sell antique reproduction furniture.

SPECIALTY SHOPS

Oriental rug dealers are concentrated on, but by no means limited to, **Madison Avenue** from 57th Street up past the Carlyle Hotel as far as 86th Street and in the 30s. **A. Beshar & Co. Inc.**, 1513 First Avenue at 79th Street, 212-288-1998, not only sells Orientals but is a cleaning specialist of top repute. In Brooklyn, **D. Kalfaian & Son**, 475 Atlantic Avenue between Third Avenue and Nevins Street, cleans and repairs Orientals as well as sells them; watch for their annual unclaimed Orientals sale.

DISCOUNT STORES

- **ABC Carpet & Home**, carpets at 881 Broadway at East 19th Street, rugs across the street at 888 Broadway, 212-253-7039, www.abccarpet.com, open 10 a.m. to 7 p.m., to 8 p.m. Monday and Thursday, to 6 p.m. Saturday, 11 a.m. to 6 p.m. Sunday. ABC Warehouse Outlet in The Bronx at 1055 Bronx Avenue, 718-842-8770. Call for hours. Offers an overwhelming selection of broadlooms from all the mills. The rug store carries new imports and, down in the basement, an in-depth stock of carpet remnants at bargain prices. As noted above under Beds and Bedding, you can furnish your home at ABC after you carpet it.

- **Central Carpet**, 81 Eighth Avenue at 14th Street, 888-414-7847, www.centralcarpet.com, open 10 a.m. to 7 p.m., Thursday to 8 p.m., 10 a.m. to 6 p.m. Saturday, 11 a.m. to 6 p.m. Sunday. For over 50 years, Central has been supplying New Yorkers with antique and semi-antique Oriental rugs—from earthy Kilims to elegant Kashans. Go upstairs for more mundane mill ends and discounted broadlooms. The downtown store, resplendent in a landmarked former bank building, has a larger selection of machine-made rugs and wall-to wall carpeting, and all but the smallest rugs are hanging, not stacked.

ALTERNATIVE SOURCES

Carpets and rugs also turn up at thrift shops, auctions and flea markets. See **Furniture** for details.

COMPUTERS AND SOFTWARE

Personal computers can be bought in a variety of places, from comparatively cozy neighborhood centers to barn-like discount warehouses. Many outlets offer courses as well as literature on the subject. For an overview of current prices and trends, check the "Circuits" section of the Thursday *New York Times*, where the weekly computer columns are flanked by ads for hardware, software and allied services.

- **Circuit City**: see **Appliances, Electronics and Cameras** above.
- **CompUSA**, 420 Fifth Avenue at 37th Street, 212-764-6224, and 1775 Broadway at 57th Street, 212-262-9711, www.compusa.com, open 8:30 a.m. to 8 p.m. Monday-Friday, 10 a.m. to 7 p.m. Saturday, and 11 a.m. to 6 p.m. Sunday. Astonishing, this hardware/software supermarket, 26,000 square feet of PCs, printers, modems, "scuzzys" and "gooeys," joysticks and trackballs, and, yes, the latest games. The enthusiastic help can talk techie, but the computer-challenged may feel more comfortable at a smaller, more personal computer shop. CompUSA also offers many courses, from PC fundamentals to advanced graphics.
- **J&R Computer World**, 15 Park Row across from City Hall, 212-238-9100, www.jandr.com, open 9 a.m. to 6:30 p.m. Monday-Saturday, 11 a.m. to 6 p.m. Sunday. A knowledgeable sales staff and a showroom

with all the major computer hardware lines available to try out, in stock and discounted, have made this the largest single (non-chain, that is) computer store in the country. They'll install your upgrades for you or repair your old PC. Call for a catalogue, and if you know what you want, phone order, 800-221-8180.

- **Personal Computer Power Center**, 1650 Broadway at 51st Street, 212-315-0809, by appointment. Writers and other professional computer users who need occasional hand-holding, or at least guidance, with their systems swear by this former SoHo outfit, which went from retail to selling and consulting. For $75 to $100 a consultation they'll advise you on what you need, help you build a system and, if you like, sell you what you need. They also offer a consumers' guide course and a bookkeeping conversion course.
- **RCS Computer Experience**, 1230 Avenue of the Americas (Sixth Avenue) at 48th Street; 575 Madison Avenue at 56th Street; 575 Fifth Avenue at 47th Street, and 425 Lexington Avenue at 44th Street, 212-949-6935 for all stores; out of town 888-251-5236, www.rcseshop.com. Open Monday-Saturday 9 a.m. to 7 p.m., Sunday 10 a.m. to 6 p.m. An experienced sales staff at these service-oriented stores handle the major computer lines, Apple included, desktop and laptop as well as accessories, peripherals, software and digital cameras at competitive prices. The bonus is a service staff prepared to make home and office calls and telephone help technicians to talk you out of digital blind alleys. The 7,000 square foot showroom on two levels on Sixth Avenue is the flagship.
- **Staples**, 489 Broadway at Broome, 212-219-1299; 5 Union Square at 14th Street, 212-929-6323; 699 Avenue of the Americas at 23rd Street, 212-675-5698; 425 Park Avenue at 56th Street, 212-753-9640; 1280 Lexington Avenue at 86th Street, 212-426-6190; 2248 Broadway at 81st Street, 212-712-9617, www.staples.com; and at other locations. Open Monday-Friday 7 a.m. to 8 p.m., Saturday 9 a.m. to 6 p.m., Sunday 11 a.m. to 6 p.m. Everything for the (home) office, including computers, peripherals and software. There's probably one near you.

Of course, you can **rent** a computer, PC or laptop, by the day, week or month; the Yellow Pages list scores of sources under "Computers—Renting and Leasing." Some of these concerns may resell their **used computers**, though the term used may be "refurbished," "reconditioned" or "pre-owned." For example: **USPC** Rentals, 360 West 31st Street between 8th and 9th avenues, NYC 10001, 212-594-2222, www.uspcrental.com, open Monday-Friday 8 a.m. to 6 p.m. cleans and reconditions major brand PCs and laptops after they've been rented out for 18 months and sells them with a six-month guarantee at about a third of the original purchase price.

When buying a second-hand computer be sure you are dealing with a licensed business which offers a warranty. With a little more daring, one can purchase a used "remanufactured" or reconditioned computer with a warrantee, online. One firm specializing in **online sales** is **Datatech Remarketing**, 800-281-3661, www.datatech-rmkt.com, specializes in reconditioned Macs and other Apple products, which it sells with a six-month guarantee.

With even more daring, and preferably some expertise, you can buy used computer equipment at online auction sites. You're on your own out there.

FABRIC—DECORATING

Ringed around the **Decoration & Design Building**, 979 Third Avenue between 59th and 60th streets, wholesale fabric showrooms marked "To The Trade Only" usually require shoppers to be accompanied by a decorator or to possess a decorator's card. No entrée? Try the department stores or the retail fabric importers or discount merchants listed below, all of whom stock dress goods as well as slipcover, curtain and upholstery fabrics.

SPECIALTY SHOPS

Retail Imports; fabrics identified with a specific nation form the basis for some of Manhattan's most enchanting retail outlets. You can buy yardage as well as decorative accents, clothes and accessories made from the goods featured at the following shops: **China Seas**, 152 Madison Avenue, 212-752-5555, has few direct imports but a wide array of Orient-inspired patterns; **April Cornell**, 487 Columbus Avenue between 83rd and 84th streets, 212-799-4342, and 860 Lexington Avenue between 64th and 65th streets, 212-570-1816, with hand-stamped and hand-woven Indian cottons and an outstanding Dhurrie rug selection; **Laura Ashley**, 714 Madison Avenue at 63rd Street, 212-735-5000, and at 79th Street and Columbus Avenue, 212-496-5110, displays three floors of furnishings, accessories and yardage in sprigged Victorian-style cottons.

DISCOUNT STORES

- **Martin Albert Interiors**, 9 East 19th Street, 212-673-8000, open Monday-Thursday 10 a.m. to 6 p.m., Friday to 5 p.m., Saturday 10 a.m. to 5 p.m., Sunday noon to 5 p.m. Formerly located on Grand Street, this discounter still sells uptown fabric at downtown prices.
- **K Trimming & Zippers**, 519 Broadway at Spring, 212-431-8929, open 9:30 a.m. to 6 p.m. Dig through boxes stuffed with grommets, braids and hundreds of buttons for low, low prices on all the trimmings.

- **Beckenstein Home Fabrics**, 150 Fifth Avenue, entrance at 4 West 20th Street, 212-366-5142, open daily 10 a.m. to 6 p.m., Thursday to 8 p.m., Sunday noon to 5 p.m. For 80 years the place to go on Orchard Street, this Lower East Side bastion of discount fabric has moved uptown and somewhat upscale. With fabric on racks now and some furniture as well, the selection in decorating fabric remains broad and the prices still represent a saving over the uptown boutiques.
- **Long Island Fabric**, 406 Broadway at Canal Street, 212-925-4488, open 9 a.m. to 6 p.m., to 7:30 p.m. Thursday, 10 a.m. to 5 p.m. Saturday and Sunday. Right in the heart of the fabric wholesale district between SoHo and City Hall, this ramshackle three-story outlet houses notable bargains.
- **Paterson Silks**, 151 West 72nd Street, 212-874-9510; 152-154 East 86th Street, 212-722-4098, open Mondays and Thursdays 9 a.m. to 8 p.m., Tuesday, Wednesday, Friday and Saturday to 7 p.m., Sundays 10 a.m. to 5 p.m. Besides a wide selection of fabrics, this old standby specializes in custom draperies, slipcovers and re-upholstery. Shops in Flushing and Astoria as well. Call 800-522-5671 for shop-at-home decorating.
- **Baranzelli/Silk Surplus**, 1127 Second Avenue between 59th and 60th streets, 212-753-6511, open 10 a.m. to 5:30 p.m., 11 a.m. to 4 p.m. Saturday, closed Sunday. While noted for Scalamandre seconds, heavy embroideries and other elegant coverings, including silks, are stocked here, along with some traditional furniture.

ALTERNATIVE SOURCES

Long a mecca to home decorators and seamstresses, the Lower East Side fabric shops clustered on **Grand Stree**t at the Eldridge Street intersection (between Forsyth and Allen), like the household linen outlets adjacent, are open Sunday-Friday, closed on Saturday. But just as uptown shops are moving downtown, so Lower East Side is moving uptown. Three of the major fabric discounters have decamped for uptown locations and two appear above now. The remaining grand old man, **Harry Zarin Company**, 318 Grand Street, 212-925-6112, holds the fabric fort. Prices for the curtain, upholstery and slipcover fabrics in stock are almost always a better bargain than materials you select from the sample books. But these too are discounted. You'll find stellar names printed on the selvages of velvets, embroideries, cottons and tapestries: Brunschwig & Fils, Givenchy, Schumacher, and Stroheim & Roman among them.

FURNITURE

Antique furniture dealers (at least in their shops) tend to cluster. Rare pieces from the 17th, 18th, and 19th centuries, the quality found at the Winter Antiques Show held late each January at the Seventh Regiment Armory, are most likely to be found in elegant shops along Madison Avenue north of 63rd Street. Increasingly, retail outlets for less prestigious pieces are infiltrating the wholesale "To The Trade Only" antique district located in the quadrant formed by University Place, Broadway, East 9th and East 11th streets in the Village. Art Deco dealers and those specializing in the Depression era, in retro furniture and the now-fashionable Fifties clump together in SoHo and NoHo. A handful of good sources can also be found in Greenwich Village. The more upscale antique stores, dealing mostly in Early American and French country furniture, line Bleecker west of Seventh Avenue. A bit downscale, the Chelsea Antiques Building, 110 West 25th Street or Sixth Avenue, 212-929-0909, open Monday-Friday, 10 a.m. to 6 p.m., Saturday and Sunday 8:30 a.m. to 6 p.m., houses scores of antiques and collectibles dealers on 12 chock-full floors.

Look for furniture sales post-Christmas. Those held by New York department stores at their warehouses in the boroughs and suburbs offer especially large savings for anyone with a car and enough stamina to brave the stampede.

- **Carlyle Custom Convertibles**, main store 1056 Third Avenue near 62nd Street, 212-838-1525; Studio Collection at 1375 Third Avenue near 79th Street, 212-570-2236; and Chelsea/clearance at 122 West 18th Street between Sixth and Seventh avenues, 212-675-3212, www.carlyle-sofa.com; open 10 a.m. to 7 p.m. Monday-Friday, Saturday to 6 p.m., Sunday noon to 5 p.m. Offers quality custom-made sofas in a variety of fairly conservative styles and fabrics. Allow four to six weeks for delivery.
- **Castro Convertibles**, main store, 43 West 23rd Street, 212-255-7000, www.castroconvertibles.com, open 10 a.m. to 7 p.m., Monday and Thursday to 9 p.m., Saturday to 7 p.m., Sunday 11 a.m. to 6 p.m. and 51 East 34th Street, 212-679-6099, open 10 a.m. to 6 p.m., seven days a week. First major distributor of the time-honored (since WW II anyhow) sofa bed solution for a one-room apartment.
- **Crate & Barrel**, 650 Madison Avenue, 212-308-0011, www.crateand-barrel.com, open 10 a.m. to 8 p.m., Saturday to 7 p.m., Sunday noon to 6 p.m. Somewhat incongruously located at the base of a sleek office tower, this emporium of handsome, countryish furniture, dish and cookware, decorative items and linens is theme-decorated in natural pine. The earth tones are muted, and reasonably priced glassware is extensive. It's affordable and stylish one-stop home furnishing.

- **The Door Store**, 1 Park Avenue at 33rd Street, 212-679-9700; other stores: 1201 Third Avenue at 70th Street, 212-772-1110; 123 West 17th Street west of Sixth Avenue, 212-627-1515, all open 9:30 or 10 a.m. to 5:45 or 6 p.m., later Monday and Thursday, noon to 4:45 or 5 p.m. Sunday. An excellent source of reasonably priced contemporary furniture, especially desks, wall units, chairs and tables in oak, teak and pine—but no doors. Their sales are well worth watching for.
- **Ethan Allen**, 192 Lexington Avenue at 32nd Street, 212-212-0600, www.ethanallen.com, open Monday and Thursday 10 a.m. to 8 p.m., Tuesday, Wednesday and Friday 10 a.m. to 6:30 p.m., Saturday 10 a.m. to 6 p.m., Sunday noon to 5 p.m.; 1107 Third Avenue at 65th Street, 212-308-7703, open Monday-Saturday 10 a.m. to 6 p.m., Thursday to 8 p.m., Sunday noon to 5 p.m.; 2275 Richmond Avenue, Staten Island, 718-983-0100, open 10 a.m. to 6 p.m., Monday and Thursday to 8 p.m., Sunday noon to 5 p.m. Handsome, well-made traditional furniture for the whole house. Watch *The Times* for their sales.
- **IKEA**, 1000 Center Street, Elizabeth, NJ, 908-289-4488, www.ikea.com, open 10 a.m. to 9 p.m. Monday-Saturday, 10 a.m. to 6 p.m. Sunday; Broadway Mall, Hicksville, Long Island, 516-681-4532, same hours as NJ, except on Sundays when it is open 11 a.m. to 7 p.m. Those without wheels can take the LIRR from Penn Station to the Hicksville station; or call 800-287-4532 for details about the bus service from Mid-town to the Elizabeth location. Borrow a car, if you can, to stock up on inexpensive pine dressers, kitchen tables, beds, living room furniture, all designed Swedish-style with clean lines and natural materials. Pick up sheets, glasses, wallpaper, lamps and more—for less. At the Jersey store have a Swedish meatball lunch for less than $5 in the spacious, clean (if slightly antiseptic) cafeteria, also open for breakfast and dinner. IKEA does not accept American Express but they do accept VISA, MasterCard, Discover as well as personal checks. Delivery is available.
- **Jennifer Convertibles**, largest store, 1430 Third Avenue at 79th Street, 212-535-1242, www.jenniferfurniture.com; other stores: 1014 Second Avenue at 54th Street, 212-751-1720; 153 East 57th Street, 212-752-2078; 902 Broadway, 212-677-6862; 1770 Broadway at 57th Street, 212-581-1559; 2424 Broadway at 89th Street, 212-787-8507; and 206 Eighth Avenue at 20th Street, 212-924-8828; also in Brooklyn at 142 Montague Street, 718-852-3400, 280 Livingston Street at Bond Street, 718-643-8581, and 498 Fifth Avenue at 12th Street, 718-788-8119; and in Jersey City, Hudson Mall at Route 440, 201-451-2211; open 10 a.m. to 9 p.m., to 6 p.m. Saturday, noon to 5 p.m. Sunday. No question, stores in this chain, which bills itself "America's largest sofa bed specialist," have the city's widest selection of relatively inexpensive convertible sofas, including Sealy and Simmons models.

- **Jensen-Lewis**, 89 Seventh Avenue at 15th Street, 212-929-4880, open 10 to 7, to 8 Thursday, noon to 5:30 p.m. Sunday. Famous for deck chairs, satchels, backpacks and other canvas products in lots of zippy colors. In big, bright quarters puffy sofas and easy chairs, beds and an expanding house-wares department fill the showroom as canvas seems to recede as Jensen-Lewis' bag.
- **Maurice Villency**, 200 East 57th Street at Third Avenue, 212-725-4840, www.mauricevillency.com, open 10 a.m. to 6 p.m., to 9 p.m. Monday and Thursday, noon to 5 p.m. Sunday. If sleek and modern, embellished with glass and brass, is the look you favor, then head for this sparkling showroom, where furniture lines exclusive to Maurice Villency are displayed.
- **Pottery Barn**, 600 Broadway at West Houston Street, 212-219-2420, www.potterybarn.com: 1965 Broadway at 67th Street, 212-579-8477, open Monday-Saturday 10 a.m. to 9 p.m., Sunday 11 a.m. to 6 p.m. Where's the pottery? Mostly gone now. This former emporium of table-ware has evolved into a design studio and catalogue operation focusing on home furnishings in a fairly country mode. Reasonably priced sofas and chairs often covered in tough cotton, rugs, dining and occasional furniture, drapes and decorative items fill their catalogs and the stores. There's also a selection of inexpensive to moderately-priced imported glassware, china and table settings, augmented by quality cookware, sometimes below list price, and occasional gourmet items. Their periodic sales of specific merchandise are worth catching.
- **Restoration Hardware**, 935 Broadway at 22nd Street, 212-260-9479, and 103 Prince Street at Greene Street in SoHo, 212-431-3518, www.restorationhardware.com, open Monday-Saturday 10 a.m. to 9 p.m., Sunday 11 a.m. to 8 p.m. Hardware? In fact, there are some drawer pulls, some bathroom hardware, fireplace and cleaning supplies, but these spacious showrooms, part of a nation-wide chain, are furniture and house-wares emporiums. You can buy sturdy garden furniture and the garden clogs and tin floral buckets to go with it, rugs, picture frames and the like, but the draw here is the mission-style furniture with its clean lines and sturdy oak construction so popular now for city apartments.
- **George Smith**, 73 Spring Street in SoHo, 212-226-4747, www.georgesmith.com, open Monday-Friday 9 a.m. to 5 p.m., Saturday 11 a.m. to 6 p.m. It's quiet here in two vast rooms just steps from the bustle of lower Broadway, perhaps because all the large sofas, chairs and stools are down/feather filled, muffling sound. Then again, this is high-end, meticulously English-made furniture in the classic style and requiring space most city apartments haven't got. Upholstered to order in your fabric or theirs, in cotton brocades, florals, checks, antique kilim or leather, they'd all look good in a paneled home library.

Custom orders take 10 to 12 weeks, or you can buy off the floor.

- **Workbench**, main store, 470 Park Avenue South at 32nd Street, 212-481-5454, www.workbenchfurniture.com; other stores: 176 Avenue of the Americas at Spring Street, 212-675-7775; 336 East 86th Street between First and Second avenues, 212-794-4418; 2091 Broadway off 72nd Street, 212-724-3670; 130 Clinton Street, Brooklyn Heights, 718-625-1616; all open 10 a.m. to 6:30 p.m., to 8 p.m. Thursday, to 6 p.m., Saturday, noon to 5 p.m. Sunday. Excellent resource for clean-lined wood and tubular steel furniture, platform beds, lamps and all sorts of desks.
- **Zona**, 97 Greene Street between Spring and Prince Streets, 212-925-6750, open 11:30 a.m. to 6 p.m., to 7 p.m. Thursday, noon to 5 p.m. Sunday. Oh-so-tasteful, hand crafted Southwestern furniture, antique and contemporary, plus Navajo rugs, wood and clay artifacts. It's Santa Fe in SoHo.

ALTERNATIVE SOURCES

- **Salvation Army**, main store: 536 West 46th Street between Tenth and Eleventh avenues, 212-757-2311, www.thesalvationarmy.org, and seven other outlets, open 9 a.m. to 4:45 p.m., closed Sunday. Credit cards accepted for purchases over $50. With great pride, the Army explains that the two huge warehouse floors on 46th Street contain everything a homemaker needs to set up housekeeping. Some fine bargains, and clothes too.
- **Thrift shops**: charities and hospital research programs benefit from the proceeds of these stores, just as donors benefit from the tax deductions and buyers benefit from the bargains in designer clothes to silver pitchers to down sofas. Head to Third Avenue between 80th and 86th streets and east to Second Avenue for new and gently used goods. **Spence-Chapin Corner Shop**, 1473 Third Avenue, 212-426-7643, and 1850 Second Avenue at 96th Street, 212-737-8448; **Irvington House Thrift Shop**, 1534 Second Avenue, 212-879-4555; **and Memorial Sloan-Kettering Cancer Center Thrift Shop**, 1440 Third Avenue at 82nd Street, 212-535-1250 are just four among many thrift stores concentrated in this neighborhood.
- **Housing Works Thrift Shops**: 143 West 17th Street at 7th Avenue, 212-366-0820, and 202 East 77th Street between Second and Third avenues, 212-772-8461, open Monday-Saturday 10 a.m. to 6 p.m., Sunday noon to 5 p.m.; 306 Columbus Avenue between 74th and 75th streets, 212-579-7566, open Monday-Saturday 10 a.m. to 6 p.m., Sunday 1 p.m. to 5 p.m.; and in SoHo at the Used Book Café, 126 Crosby Street, 212-334-3324, open Monday-Wednesday 10 a.m. to 8 p.m., Thursday and Friday 10 a.m. to 9 p.m., Saturday noon to 9 p.m., Sunday noon to 7

p.m.. Selling clothes, books, records, bicycles and whatever, but furniture is the best buy here, where proceeds go to house and service homeless people living with AIDS/HIV. Come at 10 a.m. for best buys.

- **Atlantic Avenue**, Brooklyn: *The Village Voice* describes this as the best strip in the five boroughs for vintage furniture above the junk category. Beware of pricey delivery costs, the *Voice* warns, and think about renting a van. Atlantic Avenue between Nevins and Bond streets.

- **Auction houses**: diverting, and occasionally rewarding, auctions are another way of obtaining basic necessities such as mattresses, as well as moth-eaten moose heads, which, in fact, make poor hat-racks. Check the auction pages at the back of the Arts and Leisure section of the Sunday *Times* for sale descriptions and viewing hours. The big three, **Christie's**, 20 Rockefeller Plaza, 212-636-2000, www.christies.com; **Phillips**, 3 West 57th Street Street, 212-570-4830, www.phillips-auctions.com; and **Sotheby's**, 1334 York Avenue, 212-606-7000, www.sothebys.com, hold specialty auctions of interest to collectors and connoisseurs (and voyeurs) once or twice a week in season. The second tier, including Christie's East, 219 East 67th Street, 212-606-0400 (weekly); **William Doyle Galleries**, 175 East 87th Street, 212-427-2730, www.doylenewyork.com, (every other Wednesday); and **Sotheby's Arcade Auctions**, 1334 York Avenue, 212-606-7000, usually auction off a varied selection of household goods in a single session. Note: Interior designers prowl the tag sale operation where Doyle's disposes of high-class flotsam from the adjacent gallery 8:30 to 4:30 Monday-Friday, 10 to 5 Saturday; you can too. For erratic quality, more fun and lower prices try **Swan Galleries**, 104 East 25th Street, 212-254-4710, www.swanngalleries.com, and **Tepper Galleries**, 110 East 25th Street, 212-677-5300, www.teppergalleries.com.

- **Flea markets**—this raffish country custom adapts well to New York's jostling sidewalks. Check the "Art & Antiques" classified column near the back of the Weekend Fine Arts and Leisure section in the Friday *Times* for flea market listings. All but the hardiest markets (and those held indoors) shut down from late fall until spring. The **Annex Antiques Fair**, Avenue of the Americas at 26th Street, 212-243-5343, 9 a.m. to 5 p.m. Saturday and Sunday, levies a $1 admission charge, but 80 to 100 dealers make it the largest and best of the lot. The same management runs the **Annex Flea Market** two blocks south at 24th Street, where new and used clothing and house-wares are sold. Condos rising here on Sixth Avenue threaten to displace these markets, which are shifting northward. They've been joined by The Garage on 112 West 25th Street, Manhattan's largest indoor flea market. All three markets are run by Alan Boss, and they are the closest thing in New York to a European flea market *à la* London's Portobello Road or Paris' *Marché aux Puces*.

- **Public school PTAs** sometimes sponsor flea markets on school grounds in order to raise funds. These are rain-or-shine affairs; sometimes they take place on Saturdays and Sundays and sometimes they don't. The most consistent markets include the one in the Greenwich Avenue school yard of P.S. 41 between Seventh Avenue and 10th Street and in the Columbus Avenue yard of I.S. 44 between 76th and 77th streets.

- **The street**: a *New York Times* Home section featured the apartment of a dedicated young middle-class scrounger who furnished his two rooms with street finds. The comfortable living room looked just like home in the heartlands, traditional with overstuffed chairs, a coffee table and standing lamp. Resourcefulness, a strong back and willing cabbies are all that's required for street shopping—well, that and a knowledge of the Sanitation Department's collection days for whatever area you're combing. It's legal to put large items on the sidewalk after dark the evening before any regular collection day. Upper East Side tends to be fertile territory for found furniture, so if that's your game, Sunday, Tuesday, and Thursday evenings after 8 p.m. are the time to canvas. For other neighborhood collection days, call the 24-hour Sanitation Department line, 212-219-8090, and navigate the menus.

- ***New York City's Antique News***: a free monthly distributed in sidewalk boxes and in antique shops, keeps the antique maven up-to-date on auctions, flea markets, special shows and dealers' ads, interlarded with special interest articles and suggestions for out-of-town antiquing. For $25 a year you can have it mailed to your home; write the newspaper at P.O. Box 2054, NY, NY 10159-2054, online at www.nycan.com.

HARDWARE, PAINTS AND WALLPAPER

On Saturdays, slow-moving lines make local hardware stores as good a way of meeting people as local bars later that night. But once you've made new friends along with those seemingly endless purchases, you may require more than the good old, all-purpose neighborhood reliable to fill decorating needs. Some specialty resources, then.

- **Gracious Home**, www.gracioushome.com, 1220 Third Avenue at 70th Street, 212-517-6300, and 1217 Third Avenue, 212-988-8990; open 8 a.m. to 7 p.m., Saturday 9 a.m. to 7 p.m., Sunday 10 a.m. to 6 p.m.; and at 1992 Broadway at 67th Street, 212-579-9957, open Monday-Thursday 9 a.m. to 8 p.m., Friday and Saturday to 9 p.m., Sunday 10 a.m. to 7 p.m. Sprawling along one full block of Third Avenue, this hardware/houseware/home-furnishings center for the Upper East Side is exceedingly well organized and staffed. From screws to decorative bathroom fixtures, paints and electrical fixtures and power tools to glassware and hard-to find-vacuum cleaners. The newer West Side store is nearly as large and stocked with the same quality wares.

- **Kraft Hardware**, 306 East 61st Street between First and Second avenues, 212-838-2214, open Monday-Friday 9 a.m. to 5 p.m. Just the place to find those special pewter or bronze drawer pulls, mahogany switch plates and elegant hinges and door knobs, fluted porcelain sinks and the like.
- **Janovic Plaza**, main store, 1150 Third Avenue at 67th Street, 212-772-1400, open 9:30 a.m. to 6 p.m., 9:30 a.m. to 5:30 p.m. Saturday, 11 a.m. to 4:30 p.m. Sunday. Other stores: 2475 Broadway at 92nd Street, 212-769-1440, open 7:30 a.m. to 6:30 p.m., Saturdays 9 a.m. to 6 p.m., and Sunday 11 a.m. to 5 p.m.; 159 West 72nd Street between Broadway and Columbus Avenue, 212-595-2500, open 7:30 a.m. to 6 p.m., to 8 p.m. Thursday, 9 a.m. to 6 p.m. Saturday, 11 a.m. to 5 p.m. Sunday; 771 9th Avenue at 52nd Street, 212-245-3241; 215 Seventh Avenue between 22nd and 23rd streets, 212-645-5454; 161 Avenue of the Americas at Spring Street, 212-627-1100; 125 4th Avenue at 13th Street, 212-477-6930; 292 Third Avenue at 22nd Street, 212-777-3030; and 1555 Third Avenue at 87th Street, 212-289-6300, open 7:30 a.m. to 6:30 p.m., 9 a.m. to 6 p.m. Saturday, 11 a.m. to 5 p.m. Sunday. The Bloomingdale's of the paint-and-wallpaper scene, Janovic's image is as glossy as its enamels and printed foil papers. At the Third Avenue store, they can computer-match any color you bring in. For the latest colors and trends, as well as an overall view of what's available, Janovic can't be beat.
- **Simon Hardware and Bath**, 421 Third Avenue near 30th Street, 212-532-9220, open 8 a.m. to 5:30 p.m., 10 a.m. to 5 p.m. Saturday. Join the inevitable throng of contractors and decorators shopping Simon's first-rate stock of brass, bronze, pewter, plastic, wood, steel—whatever!—decorative hardware. They've recently expanded to include tile, bath fixtures and lighting as well.

ALTERNATIVE SOURCES

Hardware and plastics—nuts and bolts made dingy by neighboring bright, bouncing baubles—overflow rows of cut down cardboard boxes that alternate with the racks of surplus and flea market clothing lining Canal Street between West Broadway and Broadway. Most of this sidewalk hardware and pretty plastic bric-a-brac is useful only to the professional, handyman or collage artist, but inside, generalists revel in complete selections of quality merchandise at exceptionally fair prices. Try any of the stores sitting side by gray dilapidated side on Canal west of Broadway.

- **Pearl Paint Co.**, 308 Canal Street, 212-431-7932, www.pearlpaint.com, open 9 a.m. to 5:30 p.m., Thursday to 7 p.m., 10 a.m. to 5:30 p.m. Sunday. Listed here because of the discounted house paints, including Benjamin Moore, sold on One, Pearl Paint is in fact renowned for art-related materials and accessories and its four upper floors are usually swamped with an international array of fine artists.

HOUSEWARES

- **Bazaar Stores** are a three-store chain easily identified by bright yellow plastic signs with bold blue letters: Third Avenue Bazaar at 1145 Third at 67th, 212-988-7600, and 1362 Third at 77th, 212-861-5999; and the Third Street Bazaar, 125 West Third off Sixth Avenue, 212-673-4138, open 10 a.m. to 6:30 p.m., 11 a.m. to 5:30 p.m. Sunday. All-purpose emporiums with adequately tasteful, moderately priced rattan chairs, painted glasses, curly plastic cords, greeting cards, black pressboard stacking tables, aluminum and enamel pots, etc., etc., etc.
- **Lechter's Housewares**, 15 locations, home store at 60 East 42nd Street, 212-682-8476, www.lechtersonline.com, open 8 a.m. to 8 p.m., Saturday 9 a.m. to 5:30 p.m., Sunday 11 a.m. to 5 p.m. With outlets from 111th Street and Broadway south to Manhattan, you're never far from a Lechter's, and a good thing too. They've filled the void left by disappearing Woolworth's, nicely organized and well stocked with all the basic kitchen cookware and gadgetry, bathroom and closet essentials, plus frames, gift items, gizmos and much more. Hours vary from store to store.
- **Macy's Cellar**, Broadway at 34th Street, 212-494-2283 (see Macy's, above, for hours). A vast emporium in its own right, The Cellar stocks everything from traditional Pyrex bakeware to imported kitchen cutlery, dinnerware and the like, all at highly competitive prices.
- **Zabar's**, 2245 Broadway at 80th Street, 212-787-2000; housewares department on the mezzanine, open 8 a.m. to 6 p.m. daily. Food shops downstairs open 8 a.m. to 7:30 p.m., to midnight on Saturday and 6 p.m. on Sunday. Expansive Zabar's, mecca to millions for unequaled edibles, houses an equally esteemed and often bargain-priced selection of supplies for the home and kitchen in four rooms on the mezzanine. Try to avoid weekend forays there.

SPECIALTY SHOPS

- **Bridge Kitchenware**, 214 East 52nd Street off Third Avenue, 212-688-4220, 9 a.m. to 5:30 p.m., 10 a.m. to 4:30 p.m. Saturday, closed Sunday. Purveyors of durable, professional-quality kitchen equipment—for example, chrome-topped glass shakers found on every luncheonette counter worth its salt, an enviable selection of French tin-lined copper pots, huge Hobart dough mixers—to the city's food establishment and serious cooks the world over.

- **Broadway Panhandler**, 477 Broome at Wooster Street, 212-966-3434, open 10:30 a.m. to 7 p.m., 11 a.m. to 7 p.m. Saturday, 11 a.m. to 6 p.m. Sunday. $20 minimum on credit card sales. Discounted cookware (Calphalon, All Clad, Le Creuset) and quality kitchen tools for the serious cook. Hit the Gourmet Garage at 453 Broome for your ingredients.
- **S. Feldman Housewares, Inc.**, 1304 Madison Avenue near 93rd Street, 212-289-7367, open Monday-Saturday 9 a.m. to 6 p.m. Upscale cookware, including Calphalon, LeCreuset and All-Clad, as well as the popular Miele vacuum cleaners. Watch for their sales.
- **Fishs Eddy**, 889 Broadway at 19th Street, 212-420-9020, and 2176 Broadway at 77th Street, 212-873-8819, www.fishseddy.com, open 10 a.m. to 8 p.m. Monday-Saturday and 11 a.m. to 7 p.m. on Sunday. Offers surplus restaurant china where you can buy just one piece. Everything guaranteed chip and crack-free.
- **Hammacher Schlemmer**, 147 East 57th Street, 212-421-9000, open 10 a.m. to 6 p.m., closed Sunday. Accordion-like, the size of this establishment stalwart seems to expand and contract. Like its growing catalog business, Hammacher's features a collection of premier quality kitchen and barware, electronic products and gadgets galore.
- **Hold Everything**, 2109 Broadway at 73rd Street, 212-595-5639; 1309 Second Avenue at 69th Street, 212-535-9446; 104 Seventh Avenue at 15th Street, 212-633-1674, www.holdeverything.com, open Monday-Saturday 10 a.m. to 8 p.m., Sunday 11 a.m. to 6 p.m., hours varying slightly from store to store. Organize your closets, your kitchen, your drawers, your desk, your life! This Williams-Sonoma subsidiary is the last word in containers: garment bags, shelving, shoe holders, drawer dividers, wicker boxes, closet accessories, you name it. They'll satisfy your inner neatness freak.
- **Tiffany and Co.**, 727 Fifth Avenue at 57th Street, 212-755-8000, open 10 a.m. to 5:30 p.m., closed Sunday. Something a bit more upscale than rainbow plastic dinnerware from the Third Avenue Bazaar? Head past the world famous array of jewels and jewelry on Tiffany's high-ceilinged hallowed first floor and up to three, where, against shimmering ivory walls, plates by Picasso nudge Royal Crown Derby place settings. Tired of jelly glasses? Crystal's to your right.
- **Williams-Sonoma**, 20 East 60th Street, 212-980-5155; 110 Seventh Avenue, 212-633-2203; 611 Broadway, 212-677-9203; 1175 Madison Avenue, 212-289-6832, www.williams-sonoma.com, open 10 a.m. to 7 p.m., Sunday 11 a.m. to 6 p.m. Known through their appealing catalogue to serious cooks nationwide, this California-based firm specializes in quality cookware, handsome glassware, and mostly imported, country-style tableware. The familiar pieces, and then some, are available here, along with gourmet food items and cookbooks. For lovers of blue

and color-coordinated kitchens it's a treasure trove. Where else would you find a blue Kitchen Aid mixer?

ALTERNATIVE SOURCES

- **The Restaurant Supply District**: as the use of professional kitchen-ware in the home increases, the wholesale restaurant strip along the seedy Bowery between West Houston and Broome streets has become an accepted destination for retail shoppers in spite of its derelict state. Pots, pans, butcher block, Robot Coupes, Garland ranges, bar ware and thick, nigh on to unbreakable dishes are available from most stores at less than uptown retail. Outlets include **Bari Restaurant Equipment Corp.**, 240 Bowery, 212-925-3786 for a grand assortment of pots, pans, strainers, stirrers and such must-haves as pizza ovens and gigantic wooden pizza spatulas; and **Chef Restaurant Supply**, 294 Bowery, 212-254-6644, "unbelievably cheap" and favored by uptown chefs.
- **Secaucus Outlet Center**, Secaucus, NJ and Flemington, NJ; don't visit during the Christmas rush without armor plate. At other times, values obtained in these two discount meccas may well be worth the schlep. To get to Secaucus, located about 15 minutes from the Lincoln Tunnel, fol-low signs to Route 3 West continuing about 6 miles to the "Meadowlands Parking" exit, take the down ramp to the light, then a left and continue past two more sets of lights to American Way, take another left and you will be confronted by a number of warehouses. Bring boxes for your gleanings and a companion to watch them as you gather. Get a booklet containing a map and brand names by merchan-dise category from the first warehouse. Mikasa and Copco both have large outlets here. While you're at it, if you've the stamina, load up on discount Gucci shoes, Liz Claiborne goodies, Oleg Cassini and the like. It takes an hour or so to reach Flemington and Dansk, Mikasa and an inter-minable number of other house-wares outlets, but if quality doesn't give you the vapors, the quaint Victorian houses (filled with discount opera-tions) lining the main street make shopping here less onerous. Fastest route is via NJ Turnpike South to Exit 10 "Methuen," picking up I 287 North to Exit 10 (again), marked "22 West," and "202/206" continuing 2 1/2 miles to a circle exiting on Route 202, to "Flemington/Princeton."

LAMPS AND LIGHT FIXTURES

You can't beat the department stores for variety and choice; wait for the winter sales if you can. But if you want better prices, or the newest imports, shop some of the sources below.

SPECIALTY SHOPS

- **Cho Lite & Shade**, 1264 Second Avenue at 66th Street, 212-737-8512, open 10 a.m. to 7 p.m., Saturday to 6 p.m. Repair a lamp, buy one or get a new shade in this tiny shop among the apartment megaliths. There's a surprising selection of contemporary and traditional light fixtures and lamps, some of them fashioned from antique objects.
- **Gracious Home**, 1220 Third Avenue at 70th Street, 212-517-6300, and 1992 Broadway at 67th Street, 212-231-7800, www.gracioushome.com, along with just about everything else for the home, stocks a profusion of lampshades in every style and material.
- **Just Bulbs Ltd**., 936 Broadway between 21st and 22nd streets, 212-228-7820, www.justbulbs.com. An eclectic and funky mix of bulbs (and more bulbs!). The sister store next door at 934, Superior Lamp, 212-228-1308, specializes in residential lighting, including track lights and low-vision lights.
- **The Lighting Center**, 1111 Second Avenue between 57th and 58th streets, 212-888-8383, open 10 a.m. to 6 p.m., 11 a.m. to 5:30 p.m. Saturday, closed Sunday. Although a large selection of mainly American contemporary lighting fixtures crams the center's small, gray-walled retail shop, the specialty is track lighting. Have a system custom designed or choose from the Halo, Lightolier, Lighting Services or Altalite lines already on hand.
- **Lightforms**, 168 Eighth Avenue, 212-255-4664; 509 Amsterdam Avenue, 212-875-0407, interesting, moderate to expensive contemporary light fixtures; at the downtown location customer service may seem a forgotten art.
- **Oriental Lampshade Company**, 223 West 79th Street, 212-873-0812, and 816 Lexington Avenue near 62nd Street, 212-832-8190, www.orientallampshade.com, hand-made shades to order and less expensive ready-mades in a great variety of colors, shapes and styles. Lamp repair too.
- **Rosetta Lighting & Supply Co**., 21 West 46th Street, 212-719-4381, open 9 a.m. to 6 p.m., Thursday to 7:30 p.m., Saturday to 5 p.m., a wide variety of lighting fixtures, more traditional than chic or high tech, at reasonable prices makes this a source worth investigating, especially if you live or work in midtown.

ALTERNATIVE SOURCES

The Lamp and Light Fixture District concentrated on The Bowery between Broome and Canal Streets abuts wholesale restaurant supply stores that begin at Broome and end a few blocks north at Houston. If you know what you want, don't be daunted by lurid window displays of fantasy fixtures. Push on past high kitsch, find a salesman and describe your product. Chances are the fixture can be ordered or will be in stock at less than retail. But don't count on tender loving care. That's reserved for large wholesale buyers. Try **Bowery Lighting Corp.**, 148 Bowery, 212-941-8244, one of the largest stores in the district. **Just Shades**, 21 Spring Street, 212-966-2757, covers the gamut from burlaps to fine pleated ivory silks in all sizes; and **Grand Brass Lamp Parts**, 221 Grand Street, 212-226-2567, just around the corner from the lamp stores, is the place to go for fittings.

SUPERSTORES

Well established in the suburbs and rural areas across the country, big box stores such as Home Depot arrived in the outer boroughs in the late 1990s and at this writing were poised to invade Manhattan, where the cost of space and community resistance pose the ultimate challenge to these warehouse-style behemoths. For those who have the stamina to roam their vast aisles and the storage space at home for, say, 32 rolls of toilet paper, they represent real savings, though some require yearly membership fees. **Note**: a car is a definite asset, if not a necessity, when shopping these outlets.

- **BJ's Wholesale Club**, 13-705 20th Avenue, College Point, Queens, 718-359-9703, www.bjs.com, open Monday-Saturday, 9 a.m. to 10 p.m., Sunday to 6 p.m.; 396-420 Marin Boulevard, Jersey City, 201-798-0500, open Monday-Saturday 9 a.m. to 9:30 p.m., Sunday 10 a.m. to 7 p.m. Selling baloney to tires to diamonds. Members pay $40 annually for access.
- **Costco**, "Your one-stop shop," 32-50 Vernon Boulevard, Long Island City, Queens, 718-267-5500, www.costco.com, open Monday-Friday, 10 to 8:30, Saturday and Sunday to 6; 2975 Richmond Avenue, Staten Island, 718-982-9000: and 976 Third Avenue, Brooklyn, 718-965-7600. Vast and comprehensive; membership $45 per year.
- **Home Depot**, 50-10 Northern Boulevard, Long Island City, 718-278-9031, www.homedepot.com, open 24 hours; 550 Hamilton Avenue, Brooklyn, 718-832-8553, open 24 hours; 131-35 Avery Avenue, Flushing, Queens, 718-358-9600, open 24 hours; 112-20 Rockaway Boulevard, Jamaica, Queens, 718-641-5500, open Monday-Saturday 5 a.m. to midnight, Sunday 8 a.m. to midnight; 1806 East Gunhill Road, Bronx, 718-862-9800, open Monday-Saturday 5 a.m. to midnight, Sunday 8 a.m. to midnight; 2501 Forest Avenue, Staten Island, 718-273-5069, open 24 hours; 75-09 Woodhaven Boulevard, Glendale, 718-830-3323, open 24 hours; 440 Route 440, Jersey City, 201-521-9437, open Monday-Saturday 6 a.m. to 10 p.m., Sunday 8 a.m. to 7 p.m. This mecca

for do-it-yourselfers offers clinics on how to build it, paper it, paint it, wire or plumb it, and plant it; and they stock everything you'll need to do it.

SAMPLE SALES

These are special sales of a designer's leftover inventory (from jewelry to furniture to upscale bathroom fixtures), and they offer considerable savings for the determined shopper. Typically, designers do not advertise their sample sales, but predominant sale months are November, December, April and May. Scan *New York* magazine's "Sales & Bargains" section for some sale times and locations. Better yet, subscribe to the *S&B Report*, 212-683-7612, a monthly publication stating every major designer showroom sale in the city. A one-year subscription is $50. The "preferred" subscription, at $104, includes weekly updates throughout the year, listing 5 to 15 additional sales (by fax or mail).

FOOD

New York eats, but in ways that take some getting used to. To the newcomer it may seem to have the best and the worst of choices. The city is host to some of the finest, and some of the most expensive, restaurants in the world, as well as hundreds of excellent eateries of every ethnic and national persuasion, large and small throughout the city. For this you're on your own to explore the city's restaurant riches as far as your pocketbook permits, and with perhaps a *Zagat's Restaurant Guide* in hand. You're also on your own to explore the possibilities of take-out, which has become a ubiquitous part of the food-life of the city. It seems you're never more than a block away from a source of take-out; many New Yorkers live on it. And the host of corner deli's throughout the city providing late night sandwiches, coffee, milk, beer and snack food, needs no chronicling. You have one in your immediate neighborhood. Chances are, you also have an open-air fruit and vegetable stand operated nearly round-the-clock and stocked with beautifully displayed, fresh but somewhat pricey produce. These islands of color, almost invariably operated by Korean-Americans, brighten the city streets while they offer convenience and a sense of neighborhood.

Sooner or later, though, you'll need that jar of spaghetti sauce, a steak, a box of rice, salt, not to mention some toilet paper. Thanks to the high cost of space here, the city is not supermarket proud. They're scarce in some neighborhoods, lackluster in others. The best of them are clean but crowded, with narrow aisles. Beginning with **D'Agostino's**, that perhaps is the best in terms of cleanliness, quality of selection and consumer friendliness, we list the main chains that operate multiple supermarkets in the city. Within chains, some outlets are better than others:

- **Associated Food Stores and Supermarkets**
- **Food Emporium**
- **Gristede's/Sloan's**
- **Met Food**
- **Pioneer**

You want some good French or Italian bread, a decent paté, smoked salmon and some frisé for Sunday brunch. Manhattan especially is well served by excellent bread bakers in just about every neighborhood, and by gourmet shops, which carry good breads and every other imaginable edible, at a price. Listed in the Yellow Pages under "Gourmet Shops," these are some of the best:

- **Agata & Valentina**, 1505 First Avenue at 79th Street, 212-452-0690
- **Balducci's**, 424 Sixth Avenue at 9th Street, 212-673-2600, 155 West 66th Street, 212-653-8320, www.balducci.com
- **Citarella**, 2135 Broadway at 75th Street and 1313 Third Avenue at 75th Street, 212-874-0383
- **Dean & Deluca**, 560 Broadway at Prince Street, 212-226-6800
- **E A T Gourmet Foods**, 1064 Madison Avenue between 80th and 81st streets, 212-772-0022
- **Fairway**, 2127 Broadway at 74th Street, 595-1888; and 2328 12th Avenue at 132nd Street, 212-234-3883
- **Garden of Eden Farmers Market**, 162 West 23rd Street, 212-675-6300, and 314 Third Avenue at 23rd Street, 212-228-4681
- **Gourmet Garage**, 117 Seventh Avenue South at Christopher, 212-414-5910; 453 Broome Street at Mercer, 212-941-5850; 301 East 64th Street between First and Second Avenues, 212-535-6271; and 2567 Broadway at 96th Street, 212-663-0656
- **Grace's Marketplace**, 1237 Third Avenue at 71st Street, 212-737-0600; and 528 East 119th Street, 212-427-9100
- **Jefferson Market**, 450 Sixth Avenue between Tenth and Eleventh streets, 212-533-3377
- **The Vinegar Factory**, 431 East 91st Street, 212-987-0885
- **Todaro Bros.**, 555 Second Avenue at 30th Street, 212-532-0633
- **Zabar's**, 2245 Broadway at 80th Street, 212-787-2000

Vegetarians and those in search of organic foods find the farmers' markets a good source, and the better gourmet stores have organic sections as well as some of the soy and grain products favored by vegetarians. But there are also stores catering to this market. They can be found in the Yellow Pages under "Health and Diet Food Products—Retail." Some of the better-known are listed here:

- **Commodities East**, 165 First Avenue between 10th and 11th streets, 212-260-2600
- **Healthy Pleasures**, 93 University Place, 212-353-3663
- **Integral Yoga**, 229 West 13th Street between 8th and 9th avenues, 212-243-2642
- **LifeThyme**, 410 Sixth Avenue at 8th Street, 212-420-9099
- **Whole Foods**, 117 Prince Street between Greene and Wooster, 982-1000; and 2421 Broadway at 89th Street, 212-874-4000
- **Whole Foods Market Chelsea**, 250 Seventh Avenue at 24th Street, 212-924-5969

Foodies know it is not for nothing that they live in a sprawling city of immigrants. The ongoing immigration history of the city is displayed in the sidewalk stalls and food markets of its ethnic neighborhoods. New Yorkers go to Chinatown, on either side of Canal Street downtown, or to Flushing on either side of Main Street or to Sunset Park in Brooklyn for every conceivable item of **Chinese** vegetable, ingredient and condiment, not to mention fish and **Korean, Japanese, Thai and Malaysian** food items, all very reasonably priced. For the ultimate in **Japanese** food shopping, Yaohan on River Road in Edgewater, NJ, is the place to go. Little Italy just north of Chinatown isn't the only place to buy **Italian** food items; it just feels more authentic. In fact there are pockets of Italian specialty stores in the Village, on Ninth Avenue in the Thirties, and along legendary Arthur Avenue in the Bronx. Pungent **Indian** spices scent the air along Lexington Avenue between 23rd and 28th streets. Polish and **Ukrainian** foods hold their ground among other ethnic outlets along First and Second Avenue between 14th and Houston streets, but Greenpoint, Brooklyn, is the **Polish** food capital of the city. **Latino** food specialties are to be found throughout the city, especially in East Harlem along 116th Street, along Broadway in Washington Heights and in Jackson Heights, Queens. No city outside Israel has more to offer in the way of **Jewish** foods than New York, in parts of the Bronx, Brooklyn and Queens. In Manhattan aficionados go to Broadway on the upper West Side, East Houston Street near Orchard and elsewhere in the Lower East Side especially for "the best" bagels, lox, pastrami, smoked whitefish, stuffed derma etc. It's Brighton Beach, Brooklyn, no question about it, for **Russian food** (and some more Jewish, as well), sold in Russian.

GREEN MARKETS/FARMERS' MARKETS

One of the surprises and joys of New York shopping has been the great success of the many green markets that now take place throughout the city. The Council of the Environment of New York City sponsors these affairs by arranging for farmers and bakers from the tri-state area to sell their produce and goods at various outdoor locations within Manhattan, Brooklyn, The Bronx and Staten Island. In addition to fruit and vegetable growers, the Council invites suppliers of beef, pork, lamb, poultry, eggs, honey, dairy, breads, wine, flowers, maple syrup and other delectable items. Prices are competitive and the offerings are fresher than anything else except home-grown. All this and a general air of festivity is the reason why so many urbane New Yorkers—as well as some of the city's top chefs—have made green markets a regular part of their shopping routine, especially at Union Square, the Mother of all green markets. Keep in mind that because the produce does come from the tri-state area, the warmer months are the most bountiful time to shop the markets. *Unless otherwise noted, market hours are from 8 a.m. to 6 p.m.*

MANHATTAN

- **Bowling Green** . . . . Thursday . . . . Year round
- **City Hall** . . . . Tuesday, Friday . . . . Year round
- **Church & Fulton Street** . . Thursday . . . . Year round
- **Federal Plaza** . . . . Friday . . . . Year round
- **Washington Market Park** Saturday . . . . Year round
  (Greenwich and Reade streets)
- **St. Mark's Church** . . . . Tuesday . . . . June-December
  (10th Street and 2nd Avenue)
- **West Village** . . . . Saturday 8 to 3 . . . . May-December
  (Abington Square and Hudson)
- **Union Square** . . . . Mon., Wed., Fri., Sat. . . . . . . Year round
  (17th & B'way)
- **Sheffield Plaza** . . . . Wed., Sat. . . . . Year round
  (57th Street and 9th Avenue)
- **West 70th Street** . . . . Saturday . . . . June-November
  (Amsterdam-West End)
- **I.S. 44** . . . . Sunday 10 to 5 . . . . Year round
  (77th and Columbus)
- **West 97th Street** . . . . Friday . . . . June-December
  (at Amsterdam Avenue)
- **Minisink Townhouse** . . . . Tuesday . . . . July-October
  (Lenox Avenue and West 143rd Street)
- **West 175th Street** . . . . . . Thursday . . . . June-December
  (at Broadway)

THE BRONX

- **Lincoln Hospital** . . . . Tuesday, Friday . . . . July-October
  (149th Street and Park Avenue)
- **Poe Park** . . . . Tuesday. . . . . June-November
  (Grand Concourse and East 192nd)

BROOKLYN

- **Borough Hall** . . . . Tuesday and Saturday. . . . . . Year round
  (Court and Remsen)
- **Grand Army Plaza** . . . . . . Saturday . . . . Year round
  (Prospect Park entrance)
- **Albee Square** . . . . Wednesday. . . . . July-November
  (Fulton St. & DeKalb Avenue)
- **Windsor Terrace** . . . . Wednesday . . . . May-November
  (15th Street and Prospect Park)
- **Williamsburg** . . . . Thursday . . . . May-November
  (Havemeyer & B'way)

STATEN ISLAND

- **Municipal Lot**. . . . . Saturday 8 to 2 . . . . July-November
  (Hyatt and St. Marks)

Personal tours may be arranged of the **Union Square** green market, the acknowledged granddaddy of them all. These tours take place on Wednesdays, Fridays and Saturdays and take about 90 minutes. Call the Council on the Environment of New York City at 212-477-3220 for more information.

THE INCREDIBLE DIVERSITY AND DEPTH OF THE CITY'S CULTURAL, intellectual, and artistic life is a magnet for many. Nowhere else can such an enormous range of interests and avocations be accommodated on so many levels. While it is impossible to cover all the opportunities New York offers, we can help the newcomer, young and old alike, access this cultural smorgasbord by providing a compilation of ticket, subscription, and membership information for leading opera companies, symphony orchestras, dance companies, theatrical repertory groups and museums. And we've added at the end a selective list of bookstores as well as the major colleges and universities in the city, with the emphasis on Manhattan. In addition to graduate degrees and an inviting array of evening courses, these schools also offer lectures and workshops of interest, not to mention musical and theatrical performances.

First, what is showing, where, and when? Two particularly useful sites for tracking down event details are *The New York Times'* www.nytoday.com, and the extensive web site of the Alliance for the Arts, **NYC Arts On Line**, at www.allianceforarts.org. The latter comprehensive compendium lists and maps concert halls, galleries, museums, theaters, historical structures, monuments and parks throughout the five boroughs, with links to their web sites, information about hours and admissions, timely articles, performance calendars, and a culture guide for children. Area publications offering event information include:

- **"Weekend,"** *New York Times'* Friday Edition, in two sections, features reviews, articles, and tips on the endless arts and entertainment possibilities for Friday, Saturday, and Sunday. The "Performing Arts" section also contains an up-to-the-minute Movie Clock, useful in a town where movie schedules are notoriously unreliable.
- **"Arts and Leisure,"** *New York Times'* Sunday Edition, besides reviews and critical articles on current trends and upcoming events in the arts, includes listings for the arts with thumbnail reviews.

241

- **The New Yorker**, on the stands Wednesday, includes not just plays, opera, and museums in its comprehensive "Goings on About Town," but also poetry readings, sporting events, and nightlife. Most listings include abbreviated reviews.
- **New York** magazine, on the stands Monday, incorporates Cue, "A Complete Guide to Entertainment, the Arts, and Dining for the Week." Included are brief movie and theater reviews. Comprehensive. www.newyorkmag.com
- **Time Out New York**, on the stands Wednesday, offers comprehensive listings in all aspects of entertainment and the arts, as well as gay and lesbian features and listings, reviews and articles on who's doing it this week, all for a somewhat younger audience than the above. www.time-outny.com
- **The Village Voice**, free on the street Wednesday, is filled with entertainment ads and carries a "Listings" column of weekly free events. Particularly good for alternative events. www.villagevoice.com
- **New York Press** is distributed free in restaurants, stores and in street boxes below 28th Street; sparsely uptown. A favorite with downtowners as a reference for what's going on in the arts and music, the weekly also includes restaurant reviews and feature stories. Attitude at no extra cost.
- **Free Time**, a monthly sold at a dozen Manhattan newsstands and by subscription, is indispensable for the culturally active but financially challenged New Yorker, listing as it does a host of free and cut-rate lectures, dance and theater performances, concerts, walking tours, film screenings, poetry readings, street festivals and the like, mostly in Manhattan. Just goes to prove you can pig out culturally in the city for free. To find the *Free Time* outlet nearest you or to subscribe call 212-545-8900 or write them at 20 Waterside Plaza, Suite 6F, NYC 10010.

For performance information by telephone try **New York City/On Stage**. Dial 212-768-1818 for up-to-the-minute information and ticket availability. Once connected with this 24-hour recorded service, you are asked to choose a category: Press 1 for Theater and Performance, 2 for Dance and Music, 4 for Family Entertainment, 5 for Events accepting TDF vouchers, 8 for Information on TKTS booths, and so on. Recorded information is also available in Spanish.

Suppose you don't know what you want to see, or your bowling league wants to buy a block of seats to a musical. Call the **Broadway Show Line**, operated by the League of American Theatres and Producers, 888-292-9669, for descriptions of Broadway and off-Broadway shows, performance schedules, seat locations and group sales information. You can also order tickets here, with service charges the same as from Tele-charge.

TICKETS

How can you buy tickets to New York's plays, concerts, ballets, operas and special mega-events? Let us describe the ways.

BOX OFFICE

To get the best seats for the day you want, go to the appropriate box office in person well in advance of the performance desired, cash or charge card in hand. Not only can you check the theater's seating diagram (usually posted near the ticket window) but you won't pay a handling fee. When ordering by telephone or mail, you have no control over the exact row or seat issued because orders are filled automatically on a "best available" basis. Box offices are usually open from 10 or 11 a.m. until the evening performance. Note: Sometimes producers, directors or actors release their personal tickets and these go back to the box office for sale at the last minute, making it possible for the persistent to see a hot show which has officially sold out. Line up.

TELEPHONE ORDERS

Most theaters list a special number to call for reservations. Billed to credit cards, tickets are mailed if time allows; otherwise pick them up at the theater the day of the performance. Tele-charge, 212-239-6200, represents some 20 Schubert Theaters in New York City and adds $4.50 per off-Broadway ticket and $5.50 per Broadway ticket to your bill. Ticketmaster, 212-307-7171, now handles theater productions as well, collecting $3 to $5 per ticket plus a handling fee of $2.50. It all adds up; the theater box office is less convenient but much cheaper if you're buying more than one ticket to an event.

ONLINE ORDERS

Individual tickets and subscriptions to most major concert series, operas, dance programs and the like can be ordered online from their web sites using a major credit card. Likewise, tickets to plays, sporting events, and popular entertainment can be ordered, generally through www.telecharge.com or www.ticketmaster.com.

TICKETMASTER

Promoters determine how tickets to their events will be sold: at Ticketmaster outlets, by calling Ticketmaster, or both. First call 212-307-7171 to find out what performances they are offering and whether tickets can be ordered by phone and charged to a credit card (fees range, depending on the venue and type of ticket) or whether they must be picked up in person and paid for in cash at one of Ticketmaster's 2,200 outlets in the US and Canada. There are 160 outlets in the tri-state area; prime locations in Manhattan include Tower Records, 692 Broadway corner of East 4th Street and Broadway at 66th Street; Tower Video, 215 East 86th Street, and 42nd Street east of Avenue of the Americas. Call 212-307-7171 for the location nearest you, or check www.ticketmaster.com.

BROKERS

Unless you have a friend with a personal broker or an "in" with a hotel concierge or unless your corporation runs a ticket service, don't expect to walk into a ticket agency and get front row center for the town's hottest musical the day of performance. These seats are held for valued clients. However, for most, events brokers who usually handle only orchestra, mezzanine and box seats, are still probably the easiest way to get into a show or sporting event in a hurry. Expect to pay 10% to 50% over the total price for their service. **Note**: Deal only with licensed brokers in the city; out-of-town brokers operating with 800 numbers are not regulated, and you can get burned. See "Ticket Sales—Entertainment and Sports" in the Yellow Pages for names, among whom American Tickets and Continental Guests Services, operating out of major hotels, are large and well established.

ALTERNATIVE SOURCES

At the **Times Square Visitor's Center**, 1560 Broadway between 46th and 47th streets, 212-869-5667, www.timessquarebid.org, open daily 8 a.m. to 8 p.m., you can buy same-day and advance sale tickets to Broadway and off-Broadway shows at box office prices (subject to availability) plus a $4.50 per ticket service charge. The center, in a winsomely renovated old movie theater, also sells MetroCards and tickets to sightseeing tours, and airport shuttles, and provides free internet access, multilingual tourist counselors, theater seats in which to rest, and clean, handicap-accessible public restrooms.

Tickets to sports events, tours and other entertainment, as well as theater tickets, can be bought at a kiosk at the city's official **Visitor Information Center**, 810 Seventh Avenue at 53rd Street, 212-397-8200, www.nycvisit.com, Monday-Friday, 8:30 a.m. to 6 p.m. and Saturday and Sunday, 9 a.m. to 5 p.m. There is a service charge for these tickets. Also available here is the CityPass, a steeply discounted ticket to six major tourist attractions good for nine days, maps and brochures, and multilingual tourist counselors.

Suppose you've just got to have tickets to that hot show now, and cost is no object. Call the **Actors' Fund of America**, 212-221-7301, extension 133, or **Broadway Cares/Equity Fights AIDS**, 212-840-0770, for best seats at hard-to-get shows. The tariff? You'll pay twice the box office price, but half of that is tax-deductible.

DISCOUNTS

TKTS is one of the city's great bargains. The Theatre Development Fund operates two outlets for half-price and 25%-off day-of-performance tickets to Broadway and off-Broadway shows. Availability information is posted on large boards near ticket sales booths, and a small fee—currently $2.50—is charged for each ticket. Cash or travelers' check only. **Note:** Ticket selection is better and lines shorter early in the week. For a list of discounted tickets available that night go to www.newyork.citysearch.com or www.nytoday.com after 4 p.m.

- **TKTS Times Square**, West 47th Street and Broadway, sells Broadway, off-Broadway, dance, and music event tickets for evening performances from 3 to 8 p.m., Monday-Saturday. Matinee tickets go on sale on Wednesdays and Saturdays 10 a.m. to 2 p.m., Sunday 11 a.m. to 7 p.m. for matinee and evening tickets.
- **TKTS Lower Manhattan**, 2 World Trade Center, mezzanine, open Monday-Friday from 11 a.m. to 5:30 p.m., Saturday 11 a.m. to 3:30 p.m. Seats for Broadway evening performances go on sale here earlier—at 11 a.m.—than those at Times Square, and the lines are a lot shorter at the World Trade Center TKTS. Matinee tickets are sold from 11 a.m. to 5:30 p.m. on the day prior to performance. Sometimes ticket selection is more limited here than uptown, but lines are shorter and indoors.
- **Passport to Off Broadway**, 888-625-5129, is a seasonal discount offering by the Alliance of Resident Theatres during the relatively slow theater season, February-April. Tickets to some 200 off-Broadway productions, including many for children, are discounted up to 50%. Call to receive their booklet, "Hotseats," with coupons with which to purchase discounted tickets. If you purchase your tickets at the theater box office rather than by phone, you'll save further by avoiding excessive service charges. Visit www.newyork.sidewalk.com/offbroadway.
- **Twofers** resemble theater tickets but are, in fact, passes. When exchanged at Broadway (and some off-Broadway) box offices, twofers entitle the bearer to two tickets for little more than the price of one. A convenient way to keep a show open after bad reviews or at the end of a long run, twofers can be found all over town, for example at restaurant cash registers, the city's official Visitor Information Center at 810 Seventh Avenue at 53rd Street, in college dorms and on hotel desks.

- **The Theatre Development Fund**, 1501 Broadway, Attention: Applications, NYC 10036, 212-221-0013, www.tdf.org, offers tickets to a variety of plays, musicals, dance, and jazz performances at about $12.50 to $22 each to its members. If you are retired, a student or teacher, a clergyman, performing professional, union member, or in the armed forces, you can get a membership application by mailing a self-addressed, stamped envelope with your request. Upon acceptance and payment of $15 or more, you'll be on the mailing list to receive their offerings. You will also be eligible to purchase their TDF vouchers for off-off-Broadway shows, music, and dance events. For $15 you get vouchers good for five performances over a six-month period, plus a calendar of events to which they apply.
- **ArtsPassNY**, 250 West 57th Street, Suite 1222, NYC 10107, 212-307-6655, offers its members discounted tickets to the best seats at selected performances of Young Concert Artists, the American Ballet Theatre, the Roundabout Theatre and the New York City Opera. Membership, costing $115 and open to adults under 40, entitles you to choose one of the selected performances from each of the participating companies. The same seats without the discount would run $205. Call 212-307-6655 to inquire or subscribe.
- **Audience Extras**, 109 West 26th Street, NYC 10001, 212-989-9550, www.audienceextras.com, provides free tickets to plays in preview and post opening (whose producers wish to "paper" the house, i.e., fill it with freebies to stimulate word-of-mouth) to its members in the theater industry. For $130 you get a one-year membership card with a reserve fund against which a $3.50 service charge per ticket is charged as well as access to their 24-hour hotline, which lists available shows. There is no limit on free shows, and you can bring up to three guests.
- **Quicktix**, a small allotment of seats for each of the various performances at the New York Shakespeare Festival's Public Theatre on Lafayette Street (see Theater section) go on sale at 5:30 p.m. the day of performance for about half the price of regular tickets. Call 212-260-2400 for information on general availability.

Student tickets at half price or less are often available to those holding bona fide student IDs as follows:
- **New York Philharmonic** at Avery Fisher Hall, Lincoln Center, has two arrangements. They sell $10 tickets for the Thursday morning rehearsals about a month before the actual date. In the Student Rush Program you should line up with ID and $10 at Window 6 about an hour and a half in advance of a Tuesday or Thursday concert. At 7:30 p.m. available tickets go on sale. Call 212-875-5656 to check ticket availability first.
- **New York City Opera**, also at Lincoln Center, sometimes has student

tickets for those who line up at the theater by 10 a.m. on the morning of a performance, 11:30 a.m. on Sunday. Tickets, if available, are $10. Call 212-870-5570 for more information.

- **Carnegie Hall** sells $8 tickets, when available, on a first-come, first-served basis. You can call 212-247-7800 between noon and 1 p.m. on the day of performance to see if tickets will be available.
- **Grace Rainey Rogers Auditorium** at the Metropolitan Museum of Art sells standing room tickets for half price on the day of a concert. Call the box office at 212-570-3949 to check on availability.

High school students have access to the best deal of all on tickets to music, theater, museums, dance, and more through **High 5 Tickets to the Arts**. Students 13 to 18 years old can get $5 tickets to weekend (Friday-Sunday) performances, two for $5 for weekday performances by presenting school ID at any Ticketmaster outlet, including HMV, Tower Records, The Wiz and other stores in the city and in much of New Jersey, at least a day before the performance. Museum admission is two for $5 any day, with ID, at the museum. Free catalogs of High 5 events are available at participating Ticketmaster outlets, public libraries, Barnes & Noble stores and at High 5's office, 1 East 53rd Street. Or visit the web site at www.high5tix.org.

A few of the smaller to mid-size Manhattan theaters (generally off-Broadway and off-off Broadway) will exchange admission for volunteer ushering, a boon to the theater devotee who is light of wallet. Call around for participating theaters.

An indispensable aid for the dedicated theater-goer, sports fan, or classical music enthusiast is *STUBS*, a paperback which publishes the seating plan of every concert hall, opera house, stadium, arena and theater in town. *STUBS* in hand, you can immediately locate the seats being offered by TKTS booths, brokers, Ticketmaster outlets and others who have no seating diagrams available for ticket purchasers.

SUBSCRIPTIONS

Common practice dictates that new subscriptions to any series—symphonic, operatic, dance, theatrical—must wait to be filled until the previous season's subscribers are given an opportunity to renew. Once the renewal deadline is past, new subscriptions are processed on a first-come, first-served basis. The initial announcement of each new season's schedule is sent to everyone on the mailing list anywhere from six weeks to six months before performances are scheduled to begin. To assure a position near the beginning of the line, call whatever institution interests you well in advance of its season and ask to be put on the mailing list. Upon receipt of the announcement schedule, choose your series and return the coupon and a check quickly. Often this can be done online at the appropriate web site. Full-page ads in *The New York Times* Sunday "Arts and Leisure" section herald symphonic, operatic, and dance seasons five to six months before performances begin, but usually a week or two after the first public subscription mailers have been sent out.

Incidentally, certain nights are traditionally more popular than others. If good seats are more important than sitting next to the right people, find out which night or series has the best tickets available.

GRAND OPERA

- **Metropolitan Opera**, Metropolitan Opera House, Lincoln Center, NYC 10023; Subscriptions, 212-362-2080; Met Ticket Service for current sales, 212-362-6000; www.metopera.org; subscriptions range from $200 for an eight-opera series high up in the Family Circle to $2,000 for an eight-opera series in the Center Orchestra. The Met charges $20 per subscription for handling. Renewal notices are mailed to current subscribers, and once these orders are processed in the spring, new subscriptions are filled. The Met's season is broken into three periods for the sale of individual seats: fall, winter and spring. Subscribers are given first crack, then seats for single performances are offered to the public, first through a mailing, then via newspaper ads about a month and a half before each of the three seasons begins. Standing room goes on sale the Sunday before performance.
- **New York City Opera**, New York State Theater, Lincoln Center, NYC 10023; Subscriptions, 212-496-0600; Box Office, 212-870-5570; www.nycopera.com. The New York City Opera offers numerous two- to four-opera series for performances September-April. The cheapest seats for a four-performance series cost $76; the most expensive for four performances, $320. With a top ticket price of $98, City Opera performances are a grand bargain.
- **Opera Orchestra of New York**, 239 West 72nd Street, NYC 10025, 212-799-1982, www.oony.org, under the musical direction of Eve Queler, performs three non-staged (that is, concert style) operas per season at Carnegie Hall. Performed by singers of the first rank but not super-stars, these are usually operas by major composers, which are rarely staged. Subscriptions to the 2001-2002 season are $69 for a seat in the rear balcony and $300 for parquet center and first tier.

CLASSICAL MUSIC

- **New York Philharmonic**, Avery Fisher Hall, Lincoln Center, NYC 10023; subscriptions, 212-875-5656; Center Charge for current sales,

212-721-6500; www.nyphilharmonic.org. Numerous different series are available for a September-June season. Easiest to obtain are subscriptions to the three-concert mini-series. Prices run from $30 in a third tier box with partial view for the three-concert series to a top of $432 for six concerts in the first tier. Fall schedules are announced in late February/early March.

- **Carnegie Hall**, 57th Street and Seventh Avenue, NYC 10019; subscriptions, 212-903-9700; current sales, 212-247-7800; www.carnegiehall.org. One hundred years old and still counting, Carnegie is still the concert hall preferred by many performers, and it continues to host programs by a variety of virtuosos and orchestras (to say nothing of popular superstars) with age-given grace. The Philadelphia, Cleveland and Boston Symphony Orchestras all hold their New York concert series here. Call Carnegie Hall for subscriber information. A series can cost from $45 and $525.

CHAMBER MUSIC

Several halls traditionally host the extraordinarily popular chamber music groups that perform here regularly. The Guarneri Quartet, the Juilliard Quartet and the Beaux Arts Trio might give three or more New York concerts during any given year, each at a different location. Only the Lincoln Center Chamber Music Society has a hall—Alice Tully Hall in Lincoln Center—which it can call home. Good seats go fast once the *Times* advertisements appear, so it's important to get on each group's mailing list. The following spaces are most likely to host chamber music performances. Call them or keep your eyes on the "Arts and Leisure" section of the Sunday *New York Times* in late spring and summer.

- **Abraham Goodman House**, Merkin Concert Hall, 129 West 67th Street between Broadway and Amsterdam Avenue, NYC 10023, 212-362-8719
- **Alice Tully Hall**, Lincoln Center, NYC 10023; subscriptions, 212-875-5050; Center Charge for current sales, 212-721-6500. Concerts by the Lincoln Center Chamber Music Society as well as other groups.
- **Brooklyn Academy of Music (BAM)**, 30 Lafayette Avenue, Brooklyn 11217, 718-636-4100
- **Carnegie Hall**, 57th Street and Seventh Avenue, NYC 10019; subscriptions, 212-903-9700; current sales, 212-247-7800
- **Metropolitan Museum of Art**, Grace Rainey Rogers Auditorium, 83rd Street and Fifth Avenue, NYC 10028, 212-570-3949
- **92nd Street Y (YM-YWHA)**, Kaufmann Concert Hall, 1395 Lexington Avenue, NYC 10028, 212-427-6000

DANCE

It could be argued that New York is the dance capital of the world. Certainly it is possible to see a performance of some form of dance—ballet, modern, jazz, ethnic, avant-garde—just about any night of the week somewhere in the city. Dance enthusiasts watch the publications above to catch visiting troupes and local groups at alternative sites. Among the latter, for example, are **Dance Theatre Workshop** at 219 West 19th Street, 212-924-0077; **Danspace Project at St. Mark's Church**, 131 East 10th Street, 212-674-8112; **Florence Gould Hall** at 55 East 59th Street, 212-335-6160; Performance Space 122, 150 First Avenue at Ninth Street, 212-477-5288; **The Guggenheim Museum's Peter B. Lewis Theater**, 1071 Fifth Avenue at 89th Street, 212-423-3857; **Joyce Soho**, 155 Mercer Street south of Houston Street, 212-334-7479; **Context Theater**, 28 Avenue A at East Third Street, 212-613-8456; and **Theater of the Riverside Church**, 91 Claremont Avenue at 120th Street, 212-496-5497. Below we've listed the established troupes and theaters to which one can subscribe. Get yourself on one mailing list and others are likely to find you.

- **American Ballet Theater**, 890 Broadway, Third Floor, NYC 10003; subscriptions, 212-799-3100; Met Ticket Service for current sales, 212-362-6000; for individual tickets to the two-week fall season at City Center, call 212-581-1212, www.abt.org. Subscription series are offered, for the ABT's spring season at the Metropolitan Opera House April through June. The first announcement, mailed to friends in late December, is followed shortly by a new subscriber mailing, then a week or so later by the traditional January *New York Times* ad. Subscriptions for seats high up in the Family Circle cost $75, while way down in the Orchestra they command $275, with a range in between. Individual tickets at the Box Office and by phone from the Met Ticket Service go on sale in March.

- **New York City Ballet**, New York State Theater, Lincoln Center, NYC 10023; subscriptions and current sale information, 212-870-5570; www.nycballet.com. Two seasons provide balletomanes the opportunity of feasting on dancing by Balanchine's company. Both the Winter Season, November-February, and the Spring Season, April-June, have sixteen four-performance series, and good seats are easiest to come by for weekend matinees. First announcements go out nine weeks before the season begins. A tip for Nutcracker ballet fanciers: first orders for single, non-subscription performances of the Nutcracker are accepted in late October. Call 212-870-5500 for prices and dates, and if certain seats for special performances are important, make your order several weeks before that time.

- **The Joyce Theater**, 175 Eighth Avenue at 19th Street, NYC 10011, 212-242-0800; celebrating dance of all kinds—ballet, modern, flamenco—the Joyce is an elegantly revamped former Art Deco movie house in Chelsea. Your reward for buying tickets to performances by four different dance groups during the fall or spring season is a membership that entitles you to 40% off on all tickets purchased subsequently. Your membership card also entitles you to priority seating and various discounts at fifteen Chelsea restaurants located between 14th and 23rd streets and Sixth and Tenth avenues.
- **The City Center Theater**, 131 West 55th Street, NYC 10019, 212-581-1212, www.citycenter.org; dance companies dominate City Center's performance schedule. The house, open from mid-September through June, is in fact almost totally given over to productions of modern dance and modern ballet. The following are among the major groups performing regularly here:
- **Martha Graham**, 316 East 63rd Street, 212-838-5886
- **Alvin Ailey American Dance Theater**, 211 West 61st Street, 212-767-0590
- **Paul Taylor Dance Company**, 552 Broadway, 212-431-5562
- **Dance Theatre of Harlem**, 466 West 152nd Street, 212-690-2800
- **American Ballet Theater**, 890 Broadway, Third Floor, NYC 10003, 212-581-1212

As with the chamber music ensembles, it is best to get on each particular company's mailing list. Call the company direct or City Center's Subscription Department. Prices vary for each series. Single tickets run between $15 and $45.

THEATER

Broadway, besides designating Manhattan's longest avenue, refers to the midtown theater district on and around "the Great White Way," where famous musicals are born and live on, home of comedy and stage drama on a grand scale. It's the big time and a magnet for theater-lovers everywhere. But a high percentage of the most critically acclaimed plays and musicals produced in any given year originate off-Broadway, more often than not in theaters that offer subscriptions as a means of financing productions. Season tickets not only ensure exposure to new artists, playwrights and directors, but in most cases save money as well. A few of the most established groups are mentioned here, but please don't be limited by this list. Many more experimental but no less rewarding companies exist and should be explored.

- **Circle in the Square**, 1633 Broadway at 50th Street, NYC 10019-6795,

212-581-6371; beginning in the 1950s in the Village, plays by Tennessee Williams and Eugene O'Neill premiered at Circle in the Square with such young actors as Jason Robards and George C. Scott. Uptown now, the theater continues to stage some of the best contemporary drama and comedy with first rate actors and directors. A $40 membership gives the owner a year's access to each production for only $10 each. Non-members pay $45 a seat to any of the three to four yearly presentations.

- **CSC Repertory Theater**, 136 East 13th Street, NYC 10003, 212-677-4210; founded in 1967, CSC has been performing Ibsen, Strindberg, Brecht and other mostly-contemporary classics in this comfortably intimate theater since then. It's not a resident company, but three or four plays are performed in repertory throughout the season, with an occasional lecture bonus. The season is announced in August, but you can subscribe anytime for $45 to $250 (for opening night performances).

- **Joseph Papp Public Theater**, 425 Lafayette Street south of East 8th Street, NYC 10003, 212-260-2400; Joseph Papp was perhaps the single most important figure in the post-WWII American theater. With his death in 1992, and after 40 years of his leadership, it was not surprising that the Public experienced some turmoil as it sought its way through a difficult transition. With the appointment of George Wolfe (acclaimed director of *Angels in America*) as its artistic director, the renamed New York Shakespeare Festival's Public Theater—actually a cluster of theaters and a cabaret, Joe's Pub, in one handsome Romanesque revival building—is once again on firm ground, offering events that are hailed for their diversity as well as their excellence. A membership package plan allows the public inexpensive access to productions and flexibility in choosing which of the season's productions one wishes to see. Packages start at $112 for three productions. Seats are not pre-assigned at The Public, so members simply call the members' hotline to order tickets, which are then mailed or held at the box office. A small allotment of the seats for any performance at The Public are held for same-day sale at a discount. The tickets, called Quicktix (see **Discounts** section), go on sale at 6 p.m. for about half the price of regular tickets.

- **Lincoln Center Theater**, 150 West 65th Street, Attention: Members Department, NYC 10023, 212-239-6277, www.lct.org; members in this innovative theater program have access, at $30 a ticket, to a potpourri of presentations from Shakespeare to Mamet, with an occasional first-rate musical thrown in, be it at Lincoln Center, on Broadway or off-off-Broadway at the experimental LaMama. The $35 membership fee buys one year's access to Lincoln Center Theater plays already in progress around town and first crack at six new productions a year as they come up. Popular productions with outstanding casts have included *Our Town*, *Waiting for Godot* and *Anything Goes*.

- **Manhattan Theatre Club**, 311 West 43rd Street, NYC 10036, 212-399-3030, www.mtc-nyc.org; has been producing critically acclaimed plays since its founding on the Upper East Side in 1972. After some years with one foot at City Center on West 55th Street, MTC has settled in there, at 299-seat Stage I and at 150-seat Stage II. Productions that prove to be especially successful typically move to larger Broadway or off-Broadway venues. In the 2001-2002 season a four-play series cost $185; a five-play series, $230. Subscribers have the benefit of ticket-exchange and can purchase tickets to additional shows at 20% off the box-office price.
- **Pearl Theatre Co.**, 80 St. Marks Place, NYC 10003, 212-598-9802, www.pearltheatre.org, a repertory theater company, mounts regular productions of theater classics such as Ibsen, Chekhov, and Shakespeare for a loyal audience in an intimate East Village theater. Subscriptions to a five-play series running from September-May range from $95 to $115; three plays for $80.
- **Roundabout Theatre Company**, 231 West 39th Street, Suite 1200, NYC 10018, 212-719-13000, www.roundabouttheatre.org; with a sub-scription base of some 20,000, the Roundabout is obviously doing something right. What that involves is presenting revivals such as Pinter's *Betrayal* and O'Neill's *Anna Christie* and musicals such as *Cabaret* with such stars as Natasha Richardson, Nathan Lane, Laura Linney and Alan Cumming in their handsome new home, The American Airlines Theater, 227 West 42nd Street, as well as new plays by established writers off-Broadway. A seven-play series currently averages $330, with shorter series offered as the season progresses, a bargain considering the Roundabout is a Broadway house. The Roundabout has also pioneered special subscriptions for singles (straight and gay), teachers, the early to bed crowd, and such that are a good way for fellow theater lovers to meet.

ALL OF THE ABOVE

- **Brooklyn Academy of Music**, 30 Lafayette Avenue, Brooklyn 11217, 718-636-4100, is a center for all the performing arts. Best known for its Next Wave Festival, which takes place September to December, BAM (as it is popularly known) is a prime showcase for cutting-edge dance, theater, music and opera. From the intimate LeClerq Space to the magnificent Opera House and the rejuvenated Majestic Theater, BAM presents everything from small chamber performances like Eiko and Komo to Peter Brook and Arianne Mnouchkine epics. With several series taking place year-round, it is best to call and get on the mailing list in order to have a shot at getting tickets. Subscriptions represent a real value here, and if you become a Friend of BAM you'll get priority seating.

- **Queens Theatre in the Park**, Flushing Meadow Corona Park, Flushing 11368, 718-760-0064, brings major dance companies, off-Broadway plays and children's theater to its two theaters located in the Philip Johnson-designed New York Pavilion of the 1964-65 World's Fair. Subscriptions range from $60 to $84 for four theater productions or four dance programs. Call for details.

FILM

New York is a movie buff's paradise. **The Museum of Modern Art**, 11 West 53rd Street, 212-708-9480, is famous for its carefully planned retrospectives. Screening of new filmmakers' works are a constant at the **Whitney Museum of American Art**, 945 Madison Avenue, 212-570-3617, as well as at most of those all-encompassing, art-encouraging alternative spaces sprinkled throughout New York. **The New School**, 66 West 12th Street, 212-229-5600, and the Cinema Department of **New York University**, 721 Broadway, 6th floor, 212-998-1600, explore movies in depth through numerous seminars and courses and, almost every semester, sponsor a film series or two as well.

Some of Manhattan's remaining revival and art film showcases include: **Angelika Film Center**, 18 West Houston Street, NYC 10003, 212-995-2000; **Anthology Film Archives**, 32 Second Avenue at Second Street, NYC 10003, 212-505-5181; **Cinema Village**, 12th Street east of Fifth Avenue, NYC 10003, 212-924-3363; **Film Forum**, 209 West Houston, NYC, 212-727-8110; the **Paris Theater** at 4 West 58th Street, 212-371-5782; the **Public Theater**, 425 Lafayette Street, NYC 10003, 212-598-7170; **The Screening Room**, 54 Varick Street, NYC 10013, 212-334-2100; and the **Walter Reade Theater**, 165 West 65th Street at Broadway, NYC 10023, 212-875-5600. Weekly schedules for these theaters, as well as first and rerun houses, are found in the "Arts and Leisure" section of the Sunday *Times* and *The New Yorker*. More comprehensive yet and including films shown in *truly* alternative venues is *Time Out New York's* "Film, Alternatives and Revivals" section.

- **The American Museum of the Moving Image**, 36-01 35th Avenue at 36th Street, Astoria 11106, 718-784-0077, www.ammi.org, is a continuous movie, animation and video art retrospective with exhibits, speaker series, symposia, celebrity appearances and film series throughout the year to quicken the pulse of the true movie maven. Membership, $50 for individual, $60 for family, gives you admission, reservation privileges for screenings, a subscription to the *Quarterly Guide*, a 15% discount at the museum shop, and reduced admission to special programs and celebrity appearances.
- **The Film Society of Lincoln Center**, 140 West 65th Street, NYC

10023, 212-875-5600, presents the New York Film Festival each fall (late September through October) at the Walter Reade Theater as well as the New Directors/New Films series in conjunction with the Museum of Modern Art each spring. Established in 1963, the Film Festival presents some 20 films during its annual run. A $50 membership in the Film Society ($35 for students) provides the following perks: right to buy two twelve-film subscriptions to the New York Film Festival and first crack at certain other Festival tickets, discounts on tickets for New Directors/New Films at the Museum of Modern Art, and a free subscription to the society's bi-monthly magazine, *Film Comment*.

If you're not interested in membership, it's a good idea to get on the society's mailing list before the Film Festival's program is announced the last week in August, in order to obtain the schedule before it appears in the papers. The Box Office for performances at Alice Tully Hall is at 1941 Broadway at 65th Street, NYC 10023, 212-875-5050. It opens the Sunday after Labor Day for single ticket sales to the public.

BROADCASTING

The Museum of Television and Radio, 25 West 52nd Street, 212-621-6800, www.mtr.org, shouldn't be missed as a chance to revisit your childhood and experience American culture in video and audio tape form. "...The Shadow knows," Fred Allen on radio, "All in the Family," "I Love Lucy"—it's all there. Call for schedule listings of special screening events. Annual memberships begin at $35 for students, $50 for the general public, and allow you free admission to the museum's theaters and screening and listening rooms. The museum offers 96 video monitors for individual viewing of any television program in their collection. Membership also gives you a discount on museum seminars and magazines as well as all gift shop items. For more membership information, call 212-621-6600.

MEMBERSHIPS

The benefits to be reaped by joining any of the city's myriad non-profit institutions are really quite amazing. There seem to be museums and societies for every possible interest, so if you're an aficionado of a particular discipline, seek out the institution which best reflects your avocation and join. You'll be inundated with free literature, offered perquisites of many kinds and probably be invited to teas, cocktail parties, and even banquets if your contribution is big enough. For the generalist, membership in one or two of the city's established cultural citadels is a wonderful way of obtaining well-researched information on any number of subjects. For those who want to keep up with the latest in museum happenings, there's a colorful bimonthly magazine, **Museums of New York**, which will inform you of all of the museum news and events in town. Call 800-NYC-MUSE for a subscription. As an indication of the kind of benefits memberships provide, we've noted below details for a few of New York's major institutions:

- **Metropolitan Museum of Art**, Fifth Avenue at 82nd Street, NYC 10028, 212-879-5500; www.metmuseum.org. The sumptuous Bulletin published quarterly by the Met, filled with high-quality color photographs and illuminating texts of catalog caliber, comes free with the museum's $80 Individual Membership ($50 if purchased online, $40 for students). Other bonuses include the bi-monthly *Calendar News*, free admission to the museum and the Cloisters, invitations to previews and private viewings of two exhibitions a year, and copies of the Met's Christmas and spring catalogues illustrating the museum's publications and glamorous reproductions of everything from Chinese scarves to early American pewter pitchers, which, as a member, you can buy at a 10% discount. But probably the biggest bonus you'll receive is the program and exhibition information, which will impel you to get over to the Met more often than you might otherwise.

- **American Museum of Natural History**, Central Park West at 79th Street, NYC 10024, 212-769-5100, www.amnh.org; a $45 Associate Membership here entitles you to as many visits to the dinosaurs as you wish, to say nothing of the new Rose Center for Earth and Space, a subscription to *Natural History* magazine and a 10% discount in the store. A $75 family membership provides as well a monthly newsletter and calendar, 25% discount on Hayden Planetarium tickets and invitations to previews of the exhibitions. You also receive a 10% discount on most educational programs at the museum and a 40% discount at the IMAX Theater with its oversized retractable screen and a dizzying IMAX projector.

- **The Museum of Modern Art**, 11 West 53rd Street, NYC 10019, 212-708-9480, www.moma.org; MoMA embarked in 2001 on its most ambitious expansion ever to substantially increase space for its unparalleled collection of 20th century art. In the spring of 2002 museum operations will move to MoMA QNS, in a former Swingline factory at 45-20 33rd Street, Long Island City, a half-block from the #7 train, where it will remain until the expanded new museum re-opens in late 2004. The first exhibit in its temporary home, *Collection Highlights,* will open during summer, 2002. Meanwhile, those who pay $75 for an entry level membership can lunch in the members' restaurant, receive 25% discounts at the museum store and on catalog merchandise (10% on non-museum merchandise), free admission to the galleries and daily film programs, discounted admission for guests, reduced subscription rates on major art magazines, invitations to exhibition previews and special events as well as free subscriptions to the monthly *Members' Calendar* and to *MoMA*, the quarterly newsletter.

- **Guggenheim Museum**, 1071 Fifth Avenue, NYC 10128, downtown at 575 Broadway at Prince, NYC 10012, 212-423-3500, www.guggenheim.org; even the basic individual membership at $60 confers an architectural bonus, providing free admission to the justifiably famous Frank Lloyd Wright spiral uptown, the handsome brick and cast iron SoHo museum downtown and the Peggy Guggenheim Collection in her palazzo on the Grand Canal in Venice. In addition members get an invitation to one gala preview, to private viewings, subscription to the museum newsletter, 10% off at all museum stores, at the Dean and DeLuca Cafe uptown and discounts on guest admission and on parking uptown. Fellow Associates, at $250 per, also attend special openings, and receive one major show catalogue, a private reception and tour of the permanent collection (mostly Impressionists), and free guest privileges.

- **Whitney Museum of American Art**, 945 Madison Avenue, NYC 10021, 212-570-3676, www.whitney.org; an Individual Membership costs $65 and benefits its holder with free museum admission for two, 20% discount on museum publications, two invitations to exhibition opening receptions and a free museum publication, as well as calendars of events. If American art or experimental film interests you particularly, it is worth belonging to the Whitney to have ready access to its excellent series of large and small exhibitions and also to the works presented by the museum's New American Filmmakers series in some 25 or 30 different programs every year.

- **Frick Collection**, 1 East 70th Street, NYC 10021, 212-288-0700, www.frick.org; a $60 membership in Friends of the Frick entitles you to unlimited free admission to the collection, a subscription to the new Frick Members' Magazine with information on special exhibits, lectures and concerts, and a 10% discount in the museum shop.

- **South Street Seaport Museum**, 207 Front Street, NYC 10038, 212-748-8600, www.southstreetseaport.org; despite the commercial redevelopment of the Seaport's facilities by the Rouse Corporation—in main part the construction of a glimmering glass Pier Pavilion over the East River—Phase 1, encompassing the new Fulton Market with its intriguing stores and jolly restaurants, the restoration of Schermerhorn Row's handsome brick houses, and the Museum Block with old shops and new walkways, continues to attract crowds. For $35, the cost of an Individual Seaport Membership ($25 for students), you become involved with conserving an historically valuable part of downtown and preserving New York's maritime traditions while receiving discounts and free admissions in a vibrant entertainment area. Museum members tend to be a youngish crowd, drawn as much by the ambiance and the idea of the museum as by the perks, which include free admission to the ships and the Seaport Gallery on Water Street, quarterly copies of Seaport magazine and the museum's bulletin, as well as reduced admission to the South Street Venture multimedia show and other special events. Furthermore, you get first shot at seats for the free Summerpier jazz concerts and special member rates on the Pioneer's two-and three-hour sails of New York Harbor.

- **The Bronx Zoo** (its official name: **New York Zoological Society International Wildlife Conservation Park**), Fordham Road and Bronx River Parkway, Bronx, 718-367-1010, www.wcs.org, is the largest zoo in the five boroughs and, stretching over 265 acres, the largest urban zoo in the world. An annual membership costs $45, $75 for a family membership, and gives you free admission to this zoo as well as to the **Central Park Zoo**, Central Park, East 64th Street and Fifth Avenue, 212-861-6030; the **New York Aquarium**, Surf Avenue and West 8th Street, Coney Island, Brooklyn, 718-265-3474; and the **Queens Wildlife Center**, 718-271-1500, and **Children's Farm**, 111th Street at 54th Avenue, Corona Park, Flushing, Queens. Bronx Zoo membership also includes three free parking passes and tickets to seven seasonal attractions. Call 718-271-1500 for membership information.

For the record, the comprehensive *New York City Culture Catalog* and *Kids Culture Catalog*, compiled and published by the Alliance for the Arts, 330 West 42nd Street, #1701, NYC 10036, 212-947-6340, briefly describes and gives directions to scores of local institutions and attractions—from historic houses and botanical gardens to alternative spaces and zoos. Their excellent *New York Culture Calendar* is published four times yearly, $3.95 from the Alliance and free at the city Visitors Center (above). Call for further details, or visit the Alliance's equally useful web site at www.allianceforarts.org.

CULTURE FOR KIDS

Probably the greatest asset in raising children in the city is the astonishing wealth of theater, film, museums, and programs designed for them. It goes without saying that all of the institutions and organizations above are accessible to and appropriate sooner or later for children: the New York City Ballet's exquisite "Nutcracker," "Hansel and Gretel" at the Metropolitan Opera, the popular armor collection at the Metropolitan Museum, so much of the Museum of Natural History, the Bronx Zoo, to name just a few. Many of them design exhibits and programs specifically for children. And there are institutions and groups that exist specifically for the younger population.

How to find it all? You'll pick up a lot about what's going on where from school bulletin boards, from other parents, and from the parent magazines distributed free in school lobbies and libraries, themselves. Neighborhood weeklies such as *The Villager* often include events for children in their weekly listings. Beyond the neighborhood:

- **The New York Times** in Friday's "Weekend" sections carries extensive descriptions of theater, museum and zoo events for children in the "Spare Times for Children" column, further descriptions of special events under "Family Fare," and reviews of new movies from the perspective of their suitability for children.

- **New York magazine** in the Cue section has a "Kids" page that carries listings of children's events and attractions, with free events marked and including times, prices and telephone numbers.

- **The New Ultra Cool Parents' Guide to All of New York** by Alfred and Helen Rogan describes resources and destinations you might not find elsewhere, such as "art you can climb on" at Socrates Sculpture Park in Astoria.

- **Kids Culture Catalog**, published by the Alliance for the Arts, $16.95, and their semi-annual **Kids Culture Calendar**, $3.95 each, are comprehensive. They are free online, below.

- **Online** www.newyork.sidewalk.com/entertainment/cool parents guide is useful; the Alliance for the Arts' web site, www.allianceforarts.org, has links to kids' culture, which is encyclopedic.

THEATER

New Victory Theater, 209 West 42nd Street, 212-382-4000, where bump-and-grind was once the ticket, is the opening act on the "new 42nd Street," gussied up with a grand staircase rising to a jewel-box theater imaginatively designed and programmed for families. If that sounds boring, it is, in fact, consistently engaging. Programming ranges from the pleasingly silly to the avant-garde but remains respectful of the audience's intelligence.

Other venues offering theater for children include the following:

- **Abrons Arts Center**, 466 Grand Street, Lower East Side, 212-598-0400
- **ArtsConnection Center**, 120 West 46th Street, 212-302-7433, ext. 1440
- **Asphalt Green's Mazur Theater**, 555 East 90th Street, Manhattan, 212-369-8890
- **Brooklyn Academy of Music**, 30 Lafayette Avenue, Brooklyn, 718-636-4100

- **Brooklyn YWCA**, The Shadow Box Theatre, 30 Third Avenue at Atlantic Avenue, Brooklyn, 212-724-0600
- **Fairbanks Theatre**, 432 West 42nd Street, 212-947-8840
- **52nd Street Project**, Ensemble Studio Theatre, 549 West 52nd Street, 212-642-5052
- **Gowanus Arts Exchange**, 421 Fifth Avenue at 8th Street in Park Slope, 718-832-0018, also has classes for kids in theater, dance and choreography.
- **Grove Street Playhouse**, 39 Grove Street near Bleecker Street, 212-741-6436
- **Henry Street Settlement**, 466 Grand Street, Lower East Side, 212-598-0400
- **La Mama E.T.C.** (annex theater), 74A East 4th Street, 212-475-7710
- **Lincoln Square Studio Theatre**, 218 West 64th Street, 212-262-4989
- **Theatreworks USA**, 2162 Broadway at 76th Street, 212-627-7373
- **South Street Seaport Museum and Marketplace**, South and Fulton streets, Lower Manhattan, 212-748-8600
- **Staten Island Institute of Arts and Sciences**, 75 Stuyvesant Place, St. George, Staten Island, 718-727-1135
- **Sylvia and Danny Kaye Playhouse**, 68th Street and Park Avenue, 212-772-4448
- **Symphony Space**, 2537 Broadway at 95th Street, 212-864-5400
- **Thirteenth Street Repertory Company**, 50 West 13th Street, 212-675-6677
- **Tribeca Performing Arts Center**, 199 Chambers Street, campus of Borough of Manhattan Community College, 212-346-8510

MUSEUMS AND LIBRARIES

Many of the major museums and libraries host events and exhibitions specifically for children; and there are whole museums designed just for them.
- **American Museum of Natural History**, 79th Street and Central Park West, 212-769-5100, a must, naturally.
- **Brooklyn Children's Museum**, 145 Brooklyn Avenue at St. Mark's Place, Crown Heights, 718-735-4402, wonderfully hands-on and inventive.
- **Brooklyn Museum of Art**, 200 Eastern Parkway at Prospect Park, 718-638-5000, ext. 327
- **Children's Museum of the Arts**, 182 Lafayette Street near Broome Street, 212-274-0986
- **Children's Museum of Manhattan**, 212 West 83rd Street, 212-721-1223, imaginative enough to be fun for adults too.

- **Historic Richmondtown,** Staten Island Historical Society, 441 Clarke Avenue, Richmondtown, Staten Island, 718-351-1611
- **Intrepid Sea Air Space Museum,** Pier 86, West 46th Street at 12th Avenue, 212-245-0072
- **Jewish Museum,** 1109 Fifth Avenue at 92nd Street, 212-423-3200
- **Lower East Side Tenement Museum,** 90 Orchard Street at Broome Street, 212-431-0233
- **Museum for African Art,** 593 Broadway near Prince Street, 212-966-1313
- **Museum of American Folk Art,** Columbus Avenue between 65th and 66th streets, 212-977-7298
- **Museum of Chinese in the Americas,** 70 Mulberry Street, Lower East Side, 212-619-4785
- **Museum of Jewish Heritage,** 18 First Place at West Street and Battery Place in Battery Park City, 212-509-6130
- **Museum of Modern Art,** 11 West 53rd Street, Manhattan, 212-708-9848
- **Museum of Television & Radio,** 25 West 52nd Street, 212-621-6600
- **Museum of the City of New York,** Fifth Avenue at 103rd Street, 212-534-1672
- **New York City Fire Museum,** 278 Spring Street, SoHo, 212-691-1303
- **New York Hall of Science,** 47-01 111th Street, Flushing, Queens, 718-699-0005, highly regarded and recently expanded
- **New York Historical Society,** 2 West 77th Street, 212-873-3400
- **New York Public Library,** various branches, 212-340-0849, www.nypl.org
- **Queens Public Library,** various branches, 718-990-0700, www.queenslibrary.org
- **Staten Island Children's Museum** at Snug Harbor Cultural Center, 1000 Richmond Terrace, Livingston, Staten Island, 718-273-2060

FILM

The **Museum of Modern Art**, above, screens movies for children, some of them about art, some artful, in their Roy and Niuta Titus Theater, 11 West 53rd Street, 212-708-9848.

Children and their parents who attend the annual **New York International Children's Film Festival** at NYU's Cantor Film Center, 36 East 8th Street, 212-998-1212, in February choose the grand prize winners. Www.gkids.com describes the films and gives their showing times.

MUSIC AND DANCE

Many of the major venues for music and dance in the city present special programs for children. Among them are the following:

- **Alice Tully Hall**, Jazz for Young People, Broadway at 65th Street, 212-721-6500
- **Carnegie Hall**, family concerts, 57th Street and 7th Avenue, 212-247-7800
- **Florence Gould Hall**, Little Orchestra Society, 55 East 59th Street, 212-971-9500
- **Brooklyn Arts Exchange**, 421 Fifth Avenue at 8th Street in Park Slope, Brooklyn, 718-832-0018
- **Joyce Theater**, Eliot Feld Kid's Dance, 175 Eighth Avenue at 19th Street, 212-242-0800
- **Symphony Space**, 2537 Broadway at 95th Street, 212-864-5400
- **The Town Hall**, 123 West 43rd Street, 212-840-2824

PARKS

The city's parks and botanical gardens are hopping with children's programs and activities year-round. To name just several:

- **Central Park**, Charles A. Dana Discovery Center, 110th Street near Fifth Avenue, 212-860-1370, has free activities and nature programs for children most weekends. Registration required. The Central Park Zoo East 64th Street at Fifth Avenue, 212-861-6030, and Children's Zoo are perennial favorites and more accessible than the Bronx Zoo, below.
- **New York Botanical Garden**, 200th Street and Kazimiroff Boulevard in The Bronx, 718-817-8700, has a Children's Adventure Garden in addition to occasional programs for children.
- **Prospect Park** on Flatbush Avenue in Brooklyn hosts a small zoo near Empire Avenue with sheep, chickens, rabbits and a friendly snake, as well as activities for children, 718-399-7339. The Lefferts Homestead Children's Museum in the park along Flatbush Avenue near the zoo offers demonstrations and activities, 718-965-6505.

Not to be forgotten, of course, are the **Bronx Zoo**, Fordham Road and Bronx River Parkway, Bronx, 718-367-1010, and the **New York Aquarium**, Surf Avenue and West 8th Street, Coney Island Brooklyn, 718-265-3400, beloved of children and adults alike. In Queens, the **Queens Wildlife Center** and **Children's Farm** at 111th Street at 54th Avenue, Corona Park, Flushing, 718-271-1500, is a draw for Queens kids.

BOOKSTORES

Bibliophiles are amply served in New York City. The Yellow Pages list 16 chain outlets in Manhattan alone: two for **Borders**, one each for **B. Dalton** and **Tower Books**, and 13 for **Barnes & Noble**, most of which will provide a latté at a table while you browse possible purchases (or other browsers, if that's your main mission). But there are times when you don't know just what book you want, perhaps for your mother, or when you want Donald Westlake's latest and don't know what it is, or who was that Polish Nobel-Prize-winning poet you meant to read? At such times a particular bookstore with a knowledgeable staff and the cozy feel of a traditional small bookshop is what you want. Latté later. Such stores abound here. You'll find descriptions of the best *in New York's 50 Best Bookstores for Book Lovers*, a paperback by Eve Claxton. We list a few of Manhattan's more notable ones:

- **Argosy Book Store**, 116 east 59th street, between Lexington and Park avenues, 212-753-4455, rare books, antique maps, photos and documents.
- **Bank Street Bookstore**, corner of 112th Street and Broadway, Bank Street College, 212-678-1654, offers books for and about children.
- **Books of Wonder**, 16 West 18th Street, 212-989-3270, offers a lovely selection of children's books, readings and events.
- **Coliseum Books**, 1771 Broadway, 212-757-8381, a large general bookstore, particularly well stocked in performing arts, music, and travel.
- **Corner Bookstore**, 1313 Madison Avenue, 212-831-3554, an established independent, offers everything from Art and Architecture to children's books. Will do special orders.
- **A Different Light Bookstore**, 151 West 19th Street, 212-989-4850, specializing in gay and lesbian books, readings and the occasional film.
- **Gotham Book Mart**, 41 West 47th Street, 212-719-4448, 20th century literature, film and drama
- **Gryphon Bookshop**, 2246 Broadway at 80th Street, 212-362-0706, used and rare books, records
- **Hacker Art Books Inc**. 45 West 57th Street, 212-688-7600
- **Holland & Holland Limited,** 50 East 57th Street, 212-752-7755, new and rare books on hunting, fishing and travel
- **Housing Works Used Book Cafe**, 126 Crosby Street, 212-334-3324, sip espresso, browse books and pick up a used couch, proceeds going to house the homeless with AIDS.
- **Kitchen Arts & Letters**, 1435 Lexington Avenue at 93rd Street, 212-876-5550, new and hard-to-find books on food and wine
- **Labyrinth Books**, 536 West 112th Street between Broadway and Amsterdam Avenue, 212-865-1588, university press, scholarly books and journals
- **The Military Bookman**, 29 East 93rd Street, 212-348-1280

- **Murder Ink**, 2486 Broadway and West 92nd Street, 212-362-8905, and 1465 Second Avenue, 212-517-3222, where you'll find that Donald Westlake.
- **Posman Books**, 1 University Place, 212-533-2665, frequented by students and faculty alike, offers an eclectic selection of books and frequent author readings.
- **Quest Book Shop**, 240 East 53rd Street, 212-758-5521, theosophy, mysticism, healing, tarot, etc.
- **Rand McNally Map and Travel Store**, 150 East 52nd Street, 212-758-7488; 555 7th Avenue, 212-944-4477, preeminent travel store.
- **Rizzoli Bookstore**, 31 West 57th Street, 212-759-2424, exquisite art books
- **Shakespeare & Co.**, 716 Broadway at Washington Place, 212-529-1330; 939 Lexington Avenue at 68th Street, 212-570-0201; 137 East 23rd Street at Lexington Avenue, 212-505-2021; and 1 Whitehall south of Bowling Green, 212-742-7025
- **Strand Bookstore Inc.**, 828 Broadway at 12th Street, main store, 212-473-1452, and 95 Fulton Street, 212-732-6070, the world's largest used book store, they say ("8 miles of books"), and mind-boggling.
- **Three Lives & Co.**, 154 West 10th Street, 212-741-2069, one of the oldest bookstores in New York City located in the heart of the Village, includes frequent readings by contemporary authors.
- **Urban Center Books**, 457 Madison Avenue, 212-935-3595, urban history and architecture

COLLEGES AND UNIVERSITIES

You can visit some of these institutions on their web sites via links at www.ny.com/academia.

MANHATTAN AND THE BRONX

- **Bank Street College of Education**, 610 West 112th Street, NYC 10025, 212-875-4400
- **Barnard College**, 3009 Broadway, NYC 10027-6598, 212-854-5262
- **Baruch College of Continuing and Professional Studies**, 17 Lexington Avenue, 10010, 212-802-5600
- **City College**, CUNY, 138th Street and Convent Avenue, NYC 10031, 212-650-7000
- **City University of NY Graduate School and University Center**, 365 Fifth Avenue, NYC 10016, 212-817-7000
- **Columbia University**, Broadway at 116th Street, NYC 10027, 212-854-1754
- **Fordham University**, 113 West 60th Street, NYC 10023, 800-FORDHAM

- **Hebrew-Union College-Jewish Institute of Religion**, One West 4th Street, NYC 10012, 212-674-5300
- **Hunter College**, 695 Park Avenue at 68th Street, NYC 10021, 212-772-4000
- **Jewish Theological Seminary**, 3080 Broadway, NYC 10027, 212-678-8000
- **Manhattan College**, Riverdale 10471, 718-862-8000
- **Marymount Manhattan College**, 221 East 71st Street, NYC 10021, 212-517-0400
- **New School University**, 66 West 12th Street, NYC 10011, 212-229-5600
- **New York University**, 50 West 4th Street, NYC 10003, 800-771-4NYU
- **Pace University**, 1 Pace Plaza, NYC 10038-1598, 212-346-1200
- **Parsons School of Design**, 66 Fifth Avenue, NYC 10011, 212-229-8900
- **Pratt Manhattan**, 295 Lafayette Street, NYC 10012, 212-461-6000
- **Union Theological Seminary**, Broadway and 120th Street, NYC 10027, 212-662-7100
- **Yeshiva University**, 500 West 185th Street, NYC 10033, 212-960-5400

BROOKLYN

- **Brooklyn College**, 2900 Bedford Avenue, Brooklyn 11210, 718-951-5000
- **Pratt Institute**, 200 Willoughby Avenue, Brooklyn 11205, 718-636-3600
- **St. Joseph's College**, 245 Clinton Avenue, Brooklyn 11205, 718-636-6800

QUEENS

- **Queen's College**, 65-30 Kissena Blvd., Flushing 11367, 718-997-5000
- **St. John's University**, Grand Central and Utopia Parkways, Jamaica 11439, 718-990-6161

STATEN ISLAND

- **College of Staten Island**, CUNY, 130 Stuyvesant Place, Staten Island 10301, 718-982-2000
- **St. John's University**, 300 Howard Avenue, Staten Island 10301, 718-390-4000
- **Wagner College**, 631 Howard Avenue, Staten Island 10201, 718-390-3100

I N NEW YORK YOU CAN ROOT, ROOT, ROOT FOR THE HOME TEAM, canter along Central Park's cinder track, join a pickup basketball game, swim laps after work, or sit spellbound at the US Open Tennis Championships. The city hosts events for every season and activities for every appetite. As an aid to sorting out the teams you wish to follow and the activities you wish to pursue, ticket information and other details about the area's major teams are listed below followed by a section devoted to **Participant Sports**. For specifics about ticket sales see also **Tickets** in the chapter on **Cultural Life**.

PROFESSIONAL SPORTS

For weekly specifics on leading amateur and professional sporting events check "This Week in Sports," a box in the Sports section of the Sunday *New York Times*, and *Time Out New York's* Sports section.

BASEBALL

The season begins in late March and lasts until early October. General admission costs $6 at Yankee Stadium in The Bronx. Single tickets for Yankee games are $20 to $30 for box seats, $12 and $18 for reserved seats; Mets tickets cost $7, $18 and $19; there is no general admission to Shea Stadium in Queens, the Mets' home base. Reserve seats for Yankee games through Ticketmaster, 212-307-7171, or www.ticketmaster.com; you can charge tickets to a credit card and have them sent or pick them up at one of 20 locations in Manhattan. The Mets use Ticketmaster, 212-307-7171, for phone orders and for direct sales. **Note**: as with theater tickets, there is a service charge (or several) tacked on to the price of each ticket purchased through Ticketmaster, which can be costly.

- **New York Mets** (National League), Shea Stadium, 126th Street and Roosevelt Avenue, Flushing, NY 11368, 718-507-8499, www.mets.com; the Mets have innumerable subscription plans ranging in cost in 2001 from $299 for 13 Saturday games to $2,700 for the full plan of box seats. Call Shea for everything in between. Availability is generally good, and applications for new subscriptions are filled around January.
- **New York Yankees** (American League), Yankee Stadium, 161st Street and River Avenue, Bronx, NY 10451, 718-293-6000, www.yankees.com; season tickets at Yankee Stadium run from $80 for a reserved seat for 15 games to $4,050 for a full season's box seat. For a chance at a desirable location, get on the mailing list by November.

BASKETBALL

Basketball begins when baseball leaves off, around late October, and continues through mid-April. Home games are played in Madison Square Garden and at the Meadowlands, the huge sports complex in New Jersey that each year seems to have attracted yet another New York City team across the Hudson and into the marshlands. Single seats for the Nets and the Knicks range between $20 and $1,000 each and go on sale late October. Call Ticketmaster, 212-307-7171, for mail orders, or visit a Ticketmaster outlet to pick up your tickets.

- **New Jersey Nets** (NBA) play in the multi-million-dollar Byrne Meadowlands Arena, East Rutherford, NJ 07073, six miles west of the Lincoln Tunnel; call 800-7NJ-NETS or go to www.njnets.com for ticket information. Season tickets for the 43-games start at $430 and reach a top of $3,010 for the 10th row; good luck tracking down anything closer than that. They go on sale at the end of the previous season.
- **New York Knickerbockers** (NBA), Madison Square Garden, 33rd Street between Seventh and Eighth avenues, NYC 10001, 212-465-5867, www.nba.com/knicks; individual tickets for all games go on sale in early September and can be purchased through Ticketmaster outlets, 212-307-7171, as well as at the Garden Box Office. There is a three-year waiting list for season tickets.

FOOTBALL

The popularity of Jets and Giants games during the pro football season, September-December, is clearly demonstrated by ticket scarcity. Business contacts or generous friends are about the only ticket sources for Giants games; chances of buying Jets tickets are slightly better.

- **Giants** (NFL), Giants Stadium, Meadowlands, East Rutherford, NJ 07073, 201-935-3900; regular season tickets, $450 to $500 for ten home games, are sold out about thirty years in advance at this point. Individual tickets, $45 and $50 each, are also sold out for next season.

- **New York Jets** (AFL) play at the Giants Stadium in the Meadowlands too. Call 516-560-8200 for ticket information. Renewals for season tickets to the eight home-game season are filled by May 15. New subscriptions ($200 a seat) are then issued from the fairly long waiting list on a first-come, first-served basis in early June.

HOCKEY

The New York Rangers play their home games at Madison Square Garden between late September and early April. An alternative to the Rangers is the Islanders, considered a local team by many New Yorkers. Call the Nassau Coliseum, the Islanders' home rink in Uniondale, Long Island, NY 11553, 516-587-9222, for information and tickets.

- **New York Rangers** (NHL), Madison Square Garden, 33rd Street between Seventh and Eighth avenues, NYC 10001, 212-465-6000; Rangers management must be overjoyed with the team's present "sold out" state. Waiting list requests are accepted only for seats in the 300- and 400-level sections near the Garden's ceiling. Individual tickets, again available only in those sections, go on sale in early September.

RACING: HARNESS AND THOROUGHBRED

All the local tracks are easily reached by public transportation. Call the numbers listed below for directions.

- **Aqueduct**, Jamaica, Queens, 718-641-4700; the track is open from October until May for thoroughbred races starting at 1 p.m. daily.
- **Belmont Park**, Elmont, Long Island, 718-641-4700; thoroughbred races May through July and again, after the Saratoga meet, August through October begin at 1 p.m. every day (1:05 p.m. Sunday) except Tuesday.
- **Meadowlands Racetrack**, East Rutherford, NJ, 201-935-8500, www.thebigm.com; harness racing every day but Monday at 6 p.m., January through mid-August. Thoroughbreds run September through December.
- **Monmouth Park**, Oceanport, NJ, 201-222-5100; thoroughbred races daily except Sunday at 1:30 p.m., June through late August.
- **Yonkers Raceway**, Yonkers, NY, 914-968-4200; the season's dates for the trotting races at Yonkers are determined by the New York State Racing Board. The post time is 8 p.m., and the track is closed Sundays.

TENNIS

The biggest tournament held in the New York area is listed below. The West Side Tennis Club at Forest Hills, once the site of the US Open, now hosts the Tournament of Champions for men in May.

- **United States Open Tennis Championships**, United States Tennis Center, Flushing Park, Queens, NY 11365, 718-592-8000; the US Open consists of 13 days of afternoon and evening matches held in late August and early September. The finals take place the weekend after Labor Day. Individual tickets for the finals and semifinals are sold as soon as the first mailing goes out in late March or early April and cost $15 to $45. Tickets for matches earlier in the tournament aren't so hard to come by and are sold at Ticketmaster outlets, 212-307-7171, as well as the Tennis Center.

PARTICIPANT SPORTS

Swimming pools, tennis, squash and racquetball courts, bowling alleys and billiard parlors as well as roller and ice skating rinks dot the island for your sporting pleasure, and practically any outdoor recreation you want can be found in Central Park. It's not just a super place to ride bikes or listen to classical performances on a summer evening. You can also schedule football and softball games, play tennis or row a boat around The Lake. Flanked by Central Park West and Fifth Avenue to the east, the park covers some 750 acres between 59th and 110th streets and is Manhattan's prime outdoor recreation area. So, before listing information about sports citywide, as well as multipurpose facilities such as health clubs and Ys, we've detailed opportunities to be found in the park, sport by sport. To learn more about the park itself see the chapter on **Greenspace and Beaches**.

CENTRAL PARK

The park's Visitor's Information Center is located at the Dairy, 65th Street between the Zoo and the Carousel. Call 212-360-8146 for event information. The Arsenal, 830 Fifth Avenue at East 64th Street in front of the Zoo, is the park's administrative hub. For parks information call the Central Parks Conservancy, which runs the park under contract from the city, 212-360-3444, or 212-360-3456 for recorded general information about parks citywide.

- **Ball: Baseball, Softball, Football, Rugby**, and **Soccer** fields are located in the North Meadow, at the Great Lawn and Heckscher Playground. Call 212-408-0209 for permits.
- **Bicycling** is encouraged when the park drives (but not the sunken

cross-town transverses) are closed to motorized traffic on weekends from 7 p.m. Friday until 6 a.m. Monday (all day on holidays), and from 10 a.m. to 3 p.m. and 7 p.m. to 10 p.m. weekdays, from April through October. For rentals, see **Bicycles** under **Participant Sports** for names of bicycle shops near the park.

- **Boating**; the Loeb Boathouse, near East 74th Street, 212-517-2233, rents rowboats at $10 per hour for sorties onto The Lake between 9 a.m. and 5 p.m. daily in season. For $30 per half-hour you can glide beneath Bow Bridge in a black Venetian gondola, complete with, though not necessarily Venetian gondolier. Armchair sailors can enjoy the comfort and cuisine of the glass-enclosed Boathouse Cafe March 21 through Thanksgiving. Fast food is available year round.

- **Horseback Riding**; the Claremont Riding Academy, 175 West 89th Street, 212-724-5100, rents mounts to experienced riders for rides along the six miles of bridle paths that circle the park. You must reserve in advance.

- **Ice Skating**; the park boasts two beautiful rinks: Wollman Memorial on the East Side near 62nd Street, 212-396-1010, and Lasker Memorial at Lenox Avenue at 110th Street, 212-534-7639. Wollman is open September through April, 10 a.m. to 4 p.m. Monday, to 9:30 p.m. Tuesday-Thursday, Sunday, and to 11 p.m. Friday and Saturday. Admission is $7 for adults, $3.50 for children under 12, and skate rentals are $3.50. Besides being less crowded, Lasker is a bargain, with admission at $6.50, $5 for children, rentals included. Lasker is open November 15 through March 15, Monday-Thursday 10 a.m. to 3 p.m., Friday to 2 and then 5 to 9 p.m., Saturday 11 a.m. to 10 p.m., Sunday 11 a.m. to 6 p.m. In either case, mornings and weekdays offer the best ice time: i.e., fewer skaters.

- **Ice Hockey**; every Saturday and Sunday morning between 7:30 and 9 a.m., ice hockey games are played at the Lasker Rink. The fee is $4 and anyone can join in the mayhem. Call the rink for more information (see above).

- **Paddleball and Handball**; you can use the ten courts located near the North Meadow at West 97th Street and Transverse Road on a first-come, first-served basis. Watch the all-City and Budweiser Championships on the park courts or join the informal round robin tournaments held during the summer. Call 212-348-4867 for more information.

- **Roller/In-line Skating**; in-line skaters and old-fashioned roller skaters can be found strutting their stuff (or falling down) throughout the park, but the road west of the Sheep Meadow near 69th Street is designated specifically for blading and skating. Skates can be rented for use at Wollman Memorial (see above) April through November. Hours and admission are the same as for ice-skating.

- **Running**; joggers traditionally work out on the 1.58 mile cinder track girdling the Reservoir between East 85th and 96th streets, but running isn't limited to that patch. The New York Road Runners Club, 9 East 89th Street, 212-860-4455, sponsors races and clinics during the season. The 97th Street Field House houses lockers and showers for men and women.
- **Sledding**; the park has hills for all kinds of sledders, from the beginner to the more advanced. For children or timid sledders, a perfect spot is Pilgrim Hill by the 72nd Street and Fifth Avenue entrance closest to the pilgrim statue. For more of a challenge, try Cedar Hill close to the Belvedere Castle at the 77th Street entrance off Central Park West.
- **Tennis**; twenty-six clay and four all-weather courts, open from 7 a.m. to dusk, are located on the west side of the park near 95th Street. In the summer, play necessitates tennis permits, which in turn require a 1½″ x 1½″ photo (there's a photograph machine in the Arsenal), a completed application blank and $50 (no personal checks). Permits can be obtained by mail or in person at the Arsenal Building, Fifth Avenue and 64th Street, NYC 10021, 212-360-3456, between 9 a.m. and 4 p.m., weekdays. Permit holders can reserve a court for $5 by going to the Tennis House adjacent to the 95th Street Courts, 212-280-0206. Single play tennis tickets cost $5 for one hour of court time and are issued at the Arsenal on a first-come, first-served basis.

BASKETBALL

The Department of Parks and Recreation maintains more than 1,000 courts throughout the city in gyms (see **Swimming** below) as well as in city parks, large and small. Call 212-408-0209 for the location nearest you. Some of the health clubs and YMCAs have basketball courts, and the Chelsea Piers Sports and Entertainment complex, 212-366-6600, includes two new courts with electronic scoreboards for league basketball, open to players of all skill levels.

BASEBALL

Most of Manhattan's 26 diamonds, seven of which are located in Central Park, are under the aegis of the DPR. Call 212-408-0209 for information.

BICYCLING

- **Century Road Club Association**, P.O. Box 20412, Greeley Square Station, NYC 10001, www.crca.net, is a racing club, which provides coaching and sponsors competitions for all ages.
- **Five Borough Bicycle Club**, 891 Amsterdam Avenue, 212-932-2300,

extension 115, www.5bbc.org, organizes bicycling events, rides, and courses. Their web site has links to ski and hiking clubs.

- **Fast and Fabulous Cycling Club**, 212-567-7160, www.fastnfab.org, is a gay and lesbian bicycle club affiliated with Front Runners New York (see **Running**, below). They organize training, morning rides in city parks and road trips.

- **Hostelling International New York**, 891 Amsterdam Avenue, 212-932-2300, the city's largest cycling organization, sponsors Bike New York: The Great Five Borough Bicycle Race, which bumps and winds its way through New York each spring. Hostelling International New York also promotes a number of day rides as well as weekend trips for enthusiasts.

- **New York Cycle Club**, P.O. Box 20541, Columbus Circle Station, NYC 10023, 212-828-5711, www.nyrc.org, sponsors rides in and around the city, offers training, and its members receive discounts from a handful of bike shops in the city.

If you don't own a bike, you may well want to rent one on a beamish spring day. At least half of Manhattan's bike dealers rent both three-and ten-speed bicycles. Rates average $4 an hour for a three-speed, $7.50 an hour or $35 per day for a hybrid, an 18-speed cross between a mountain bike and a road bike. You'll have to leave money, or a driver's license or major credit card behind as a rental deposit. A handful of the many bike rental outfits include:

- **Bicycles Plus**, 1690 Second Avenue at 87th Street, 212-722-2201
- **Fourteenth Street Bicycle Discount House**, 332 East 14th Street at First Avenue, 212-228-4344
- **Metro Bicycles**: 1311 Lexington Avenue at 88th Street, 212-427-4450; 360 West 47th Street, 212-581-4500; 231 West 96th Street, 212-663-7531; 332 East 14th Street, 212-228-4344; 417 Canal Street, 212-334-8000; and 546 Avenue of the Americas at 15th Street, 212-255-5100
- **Midtown Bicycles**, 360 West 47th Street at Ninth Avenue, 212-581-4500
- **Pedal Pusher Bike Shop**, 1306 Second Avenue at 69th Street, 212-288-5592

BILLIARDS

There are 29 pool halls in New York City at last count, and no doubt Minnesota Fats would still be comfortable at many of them. Others, with a clubby ambiance rather than the smoke-filled hustler hangouts of yore, have attracted women to the traditionally male pastimes of pocket pool, billiards and snooker and have brightened the sport's image in the process.

- **Amsterdam Billiard Club**, 344 Amsterdam Avenue at 76th Street, 212-496-8180, and 210 East 86th Street, 212-570-4545, open 11 a.m. to 3 a.m., 4 a.m. on weekends. Some 350 enthusiasts participate in league billiards here, where you can also throw a pool party without water—or liquor either, it's illegal in NY pool halls—improve your skills in private or group instruction and take a cappuccino break. The fare ranges from $5 to $15 an hour, depending on the day and time, and there are special rates for groups.
- **The Billiard Club**, 220 West 19th Street between Seventh and Eighth avenues, 212-206-7665, open 10 a.m. to 3 a.m., Friday and Saturday until 5 a.m. It's $5 an hour to shoot pool here, $10 after 7 p.m., on two floors of a converted warehouse with 33 tables beneath brass chandeliers, two private rooms and a snack bar with waitresses. In fact, you can rent the whole place for a party, or rack 'em up with the lunch crowd.
- **Brownstone Billiards**, 308 Flatbush Avenue at Seventh Avenue, Brooklyn, 718-857-5555, open noon to 1 a.m., to 4 a.m. Friday and Saturday. With 32 tables, including one snooker and one billiard, six ping pong tables, air hockey and video games, Brownstone has positioned itself to be a family entertainment center. The rate is a flat $4.50 per hour for pool. There's a concession stand with coffee and snack food and a Wednesday night pool class at 8 p.m., registration required. Is available for children's parties.
- **Chelsea Billiards**, 54 West 21st Street west of Fifth Avenue, 212-989-0096, open 24-hours, is the biggest in the country at this writing, with 44 Brunswick pool tables, four antique snooker tables and two billiard tables on two floors of a converted printing plant. Yet you might have to wait for a table, Friday nights especially. Best times are mornings and Sunday daytime. The tariff is $5 per hour, 9 a.m. to 5 p.m., $7 per hour 5 p.m. to 9 a.m., and $14 on weekends, $2 per hour each additional person. Snooker costs $10 and $12 per hour, $2 for each additional person. There is a private room with two tables for private parties.
- **Corner Billiards**, 11th Street and 4th Avenue, 212-995-1314, open 11 a.m. to 2 a.m., Friday to 3 a.m., Sunday noon to 2 a.m., Saturday to 3 a.m. This is the only pool hall in Manhattan with a license to sell beer, but you can also get cappuccino in the cafe. A fairly collegiate crowd, but serious about their pool, patronizes the 28 tables here at $7 per hour weekdays, $9 after 6 p.m. and daytime weekends, $12 Friday and Saturday after 6 p.m. Each additional player, up to four, costs $2 per hour. Special rates for students and seniors.
- **East Side Billiard Club**, 163 East 86th Street between Lexington and Third avenues, 212-831-7665, open daily from noon to 3:30 or 4 a.m. A little jazz plays in the background, the ambiance is cozy, despite 18 regulation tables in 50,000 square feet, and, well, upscale. You take a

break at the cappuccino bar. Early evening after the high school kids have left it's relaxed before the crowds arrive. There's tournament and league billiards. It costs $4 to $7 a hour to play here, depending on the time. Monday night is ladies' night; they play half-fare.

BIRD WATCHING

"Oh! A winter wren," warbles naturalist Sarah Elliott as she leads a group of bird-watching enthusiasts through the Ramble in **Central Park**. Unlikely as it may seem, Central Park is a mecca for birders because it is a magnet for migrating birds; encircled in concrete, from the sky it appears as an oasis in which to land, rest and refuel. The city's outer parks also offer prime sites for the city's dedicated birders. Below are a few organized groups and walks. For a greater selection, turn to *New York's 50 Best Places to Go Birding in and Around the Big Apple* by John Thaxton and Alan Messer.

- **The American Museum of Natural History**, 212-769-5700; the **Brooklyn Botanical Garden**, 718-622-4433; and the **New York Botanical Garden** (Bronx Park), 718-817-8700, make the guidebooks as good bird-watching areas. Rare Bird Alert, 212-979-3070, provides recorded information on interesting sightings in the New York City area.
- **Brooklyn Bird Club**, www.brooklynbirdclub.org, founded in 1909, hosts lectures, monthly meetings and weekly field trips, open to both non-members and members (membership $15) alike. Their attractive web site includes detailed maps and descriptions of some 15 excellent bird locations in Brooklyn and Queens, directions, some history and lists of the species one is likely to find at each site. There are more than 30 links to other bird-watching organizations and magazines as well.
- **Central Park Conservancy**, 212-310-6600, sponsors a Family Bird Watching Club, which meets every Saturday from 11 a.m. to 1 p.m., April through June and September through December at the Charles A. Dana Discovery Center at 110th Street near Fifth Avenue. Here Urban Park Rangers teach participants to identify birds by their song.
- **Linnaean Society of New York**, 15 West 77 Street, NYC 10024, holds its meetings at the American Museum of Natural History and is open to amateurs and professionals interested in ornithology. The organization does not list a phone number; for more information, write to the address above.
- **New York City Audubon Society** naturalists lead a walk around the Harlem Meer and surrounding woodlands every Saturday from 9 to 11 a.m., April through June and September through December. The walk leaves from the Dana Center. Call 212-691-7483.
- **Sarah Elliott** has become a noted fixture, a movable one, in Central Park, with her Wednesday and Sunday morning walks, spring and fall.

She teaches bird-watching basics and leads her pack on their quest for the indigo bunting, the grackle and the pileated woodpecker. The walks leave at 9 a.m., Wednesdays from Fifth Avenue and 76th Street, Sundays from the Loeb Boat House. Call 212-689-2763 to sign up for five sessions at $35. Drop-ins pay $10. To subscribe to her chatty bimonthly The Elliott Newsletter: Nature Notes from Central Park, send a check for $20 to her at 333 East 34th Street, #4D, NYC 10016.

- **The Urban Park Rangers** sponsor a variety of bird walks, such as the fall hawk watch, in all five boroughs. For times and meeting places call 800-201-PARK.

BOWLING

- **AMF Chelsea Piers Bowling**, Pier 60, West Side Highway at 23rd Street, 212-835-2695, www.chelseapiers.com, 40 lanes, open Sunday-Thursday, 9 a.m. to midnight or 1 a.m., Friday and Saturday 9 a.m. to 4 a.m. There's a bar (smoking allowed) and restaurant on site, a pro shop and arcade with video games to keep the kids occupied. Friday and Saturday nights they offer Xtreme Bowling ("glow-in-the-dark" bowling). League bowling and lessons are also available. Call for lane availability and/or to reserve.
- **Bowlmor Lanes**, 110 University Place, between 12th and 13th streets, 212-255-8188, 42 lanes, open 10 a.m. to 1 a.m. Sunday-Thursday, 10 a.m. to 4 a.m. Friday and Saturday, call for lane availability. Fast food, beer, wine and liquor are available, and Friday, Saturday and Monday are DJ nights from 8 p.m. to 4 a.m.
- **Gil Hodges Lanes**, 6161 Strickland Avenue, Brooklyn 718-763-6800, named after the famed Brooklyn Dodgers first baseman. This 68-lane alley is the biggest in the five boroughs, open 9 a.m. to midnight, Sunday-Tuesday, 9 a.m. to 2:30 a.m. Friday, 9 a.m. to 2 a.m. Saturday.
- **Leisure Time Bowling**, 625 Eighth Avenue (in the Port Authority Building), 212-268-3539, 30 lanes, open 10 a.m. to 11 p.m. Sunday-Thursday, 10 a.m. to 2 a.m. Friday and Saturday. No-frills and a best buy price wise.

BOXING

- **Church Street Boxing Gym**, 25 Park Place off Church Street downtown, 212-571-1333, www.nyboxinggym.com, open Monday-Friday, 7 a.m. to 9 p.m., Saturday, 11 a.m. to 3 p.m., bills itself as "New York's last authentic boxing gym," (translate: Manhattan's). It's not a health club or fitness center; it's about boxing. The 10,000 square foot gym has two full-size rings and co-ed membership classes in boxing, kick boxing, Thai boxing and "lunch box." Membership is by the month, quarter or year. Trainers quote monthly fees. It's probably also the best place in the city to watch boxing; enthusiastic crowds pack the occasional Friday night fights.

- **Gleasons's Gym**, 75 Front Street at the foot of the Brooklyn Bridge in Brooklyn, 718-797-2872, boasts seven world champions among its past or present membership, Riddick Bowe included. Women work out here too in this old-style boxing gym. Get lean and mean working up a sweat on the equipment for $10 an hour or $45 a monthly membership, or work with one of 62 trainers at $15-$20 an hour. Those willing to work with a trainer daily have a shot at winning the monthly "White Collar Sparring." Hours are Monday-Friday, 7 a.m. to 9 p.m., Saturday, 9 a.m. to 5 p.m., closed Sunday.

CHESS

Though it's not a "sport," enthusiasts pursue chess with the intensity of an athletic competition. New York City, with its huge immigrant community, has a large and active chess community. If you're looking for information about where to play or compete, try the following leads:

- **The Chess Forum**, 219 Thompson Street, NCY, 10012, 212-475-2369, www.chessforum.com
- **The Chess Shop**, 230 Thompson Street, NYC 10012, 212-475-9580
- **Manhattan Chess Club**, 353 West 46th Street, 212-333-5888
- **US Chess Federation**, 3054 NYS Route 9W, New Windsor, NY 12553, 914-562-8350; their web site, www.uschess.org, contains a great list of places to play.

FENCING

- **Blade Fencing**, 245 West 29th Street, 212-244-3090, arms and dresses the duelist for competition with a full range of foils, épées and sabers, masks, gloves, knickers, fencing jackets and shoes.
- **Metropolis Fencing School**, 45 West 21st Street, second floor, 212-463-8044, is open Monday-Friday from 3 to 10 p.m., weekends noon to 7 p.m., to help you perfect that thrust and parry. There are private and group classes for children through adults, beginner through Olympian. Private lessons cost $25 per half-hour for members, $30 per half-hour for non-members. Membership costs $250 per year. Group classes in foil cost $20 for three one-hour classes, in épée and saber $25 for three one-hour classes. Children's fencing birthday classes can be booked, and there is a seven-day foil fencing camp for children in August.

- **The New York Fencers Club**, 154 West 71st Street, 212-807-6947 (after 4:30 p.m.), offers duelists a place to parry and thrust, as well as a space for lessons to better foil their opponents. Dues for this member- ship organization cost an average of $550 a year.

FOOTBALL

Most playing fields fall under the Department of Parks and Recreation, call 212-408-0209 for information and permits. Eighteen football fields, some of which are suitable also for soccer, are located in Manhattan.

GAMES

- **The Complete Strategist**, 11 East 33rd Street, 212-685-3880, www.thecompletestrategist.com, selling war games, sci-fi, fantasy and role-playing games, plus the classics and offering games workshops.
- **The Mayfair Club**, 51 East 25th Street, 212-779-1750, is not a casino or a gambling house, says its owner. "It's a place to play games." Poker is the game most played, but there's bridge and backgammon too.
- **Neutral Ground Gaming Room**, 122 West 26th Street, fourth floor, 212-633-1288, www.neutralground.net, offering role-playing games and games workshops daily.

GOLF

Manhattan boasts no 18-hole golf courses (a 17-acre course on Randall's Island has been in planning stages for years), but the American Golf Corporation operates seven city-owned public courses in the outer bor- oughs. Manhattanites seem to favor the two courses at **Pelham/Split Rock**, 870 Shore Road in The Bronx, 718-885-1258, both of which are handsomely located, Split Rock being the more challenging of the two; the **Van Cortlandt Golf Course**, the oldest public course in the country, at Van Cortlandt Avenue South and Bailey Avenue, 718-543-4595, also has its partisans. Fees, uniform for the seven courses, as of the 2001-2002 season are $24 for weekends and holidays before 1 p.m., $20 after 1 p.m.; $21 for weekdays before 1 p.m., $18 after. Reservations, recommended, especially on weekends, are $2 per player with a resident card (costing $6 one time at the course). Call 718-225-GOLF from late March through early November to reserve at any of these American Golf courses, all of which are listed under "Golf" in the Manhattan Yellow Pages. During the winter months, call the individual course directly.

Plenty of slightly tonier public clubs surround the metropolitan area. Higher fees, averaging $25 Monday-Friday and $27.50 on weekends, are the norm at suburban courses. Typical of the county-run golf links is **Mohansic Golf Club**, 914-962-4065, in Yorktown Heights, where it costs non-residents of Westchester $46 to play, weekdays or weekends, $3 to reserve. Carts cost $25 for two players. Westchester residents pay $18 weekdays and $21 on weekends. Rental equipment is available here, just as it is at other clubs found in New Jersey, Long Island and Connecticut, but balls must be purchased.

Tonier yet and with generally finer courses are the private clubs to be found in suburbs surrounding the city. There are none in the city itself.

The city-bound golfer isn't entirely without recourse. **Miniature golf courses** abound, and **driving ranges** from which to tune up that swing. Two of them:

- **The Golf Club at Chelsea Piers**, Hudson River at 17th Street, 212-336-6400, www.chelseapiers.com, open 7 a.m. to 11 p.m., to midnight during summer months. This golf club with its white shingled clubhouse entrance, pro shop, putting green and golf academy has, as its *pièce de résistance*, 52 heated, weather-protected driving stalls with Japanese-designed, computerized automatic ball returns and tee-ups in four tiers fronting on a 200-yard, net-enclosed artificial turf fairway with four target greens. Pay according to the number of balls used. Wet your whistle afterward at the micro-brewery restaurant next door.
- **Golfport**, next door to Tennisport at 51-24 Second Street, Long Island City (opposite Manhattan on the East River near Midtown Tunnel exit), 718-472-4653, is closed until further notice.

HANDBALL

A city sport, in which two or four players hit a rubber ball with their hands against a cement wall, volleying furiously for points, handball is played on outdoor courts all over the city. And at many sites it is also a spectator sport. Among the many handball courts in the city, two stand out as shrines:

- **Surf Avenue** at West Fifth Street, Coney Island, on whose six courts the Nationals are played, attracts a colorful crowd of betting spectators.
- **"The Cage"** at West Fourth Street and Sixth Avenue, the Village, where the action on the adjacent basketball court is equally spectacular.

To learn more about one of the world's oldest games go to www.ushandball.org.

HORSEBACK RIDING

Care to canter Central Park bridle trails, or brush up on your dressage in the ring? Manhattan has one stable. In the outer boroughs and near New

Jersey the trail rides meander woods and seaside, and you can practice your jumping outdoors.

- **Claremont Riding Academy**, 175 West 89th Street corner Amsterdam Avenue, 212-724-5100, for reservations, essential weekends. Open 6:30 a.m. to 10 p.m., 6:30 a.m. to 5 p.m. on weekends. They stable about 100 horses here, some 70 for rental, English saddle only, at $40 an hour either in Central Park or in the ring. Private lessons cost $50 per half-hour; group lessons $40 per hour.
- **Jamaica Bay Riding Academy**, Belt Parkway East between Exits 11 (King's Plaza) and 13 (Rockaway Parkway), Marine Park, Brooklyn, 718-531-8949, open daily 9 a.m. to 5 p.m. You need no appointment for a guided trail ride along Jamaica Bay beach, 45-minutes for $20. Lessons cost $50 an hour, private. Bring your own helmet.
- **Kensington Stables**, 51 Caton Place at Coney Island Avenue, Brooklyn, 718- 972-4588, open daily 10 a.m. to sunset, operates guided trail rides, English or Western, in lovely Prospect Park for $20 an hour. Private lessons, indoors or out, are $40 an hour, $25 a half-hour; $30 an hour in a group. Call ahead. Take the F train to Ft. Hamilton Parkway.
- **Lynne's Riding School**, 88-03 70th Road, Forest Hills, 718-261- 7679, open daily 8 a.m. to 4 p.m. You can take public transportation—the F train and then the Q23 bus—to Queens where Lynne's offers riders a choice between Eastern or Western tack. Private lessons cost $35 a half-hour, $50 an hour, and renting a horse costs $20 an hour English or Western.
- **Overpeck Riding Center**, 40 Fort Lee Road, Leonia, NJ 07605, 201-242-0022; open 9 a.m. to 5 p.m., Saturday and Sunday to 6 p.m., by appointment. By #4 Red and Tan Lines or #166 New Jersey Transit bus from the Port Authority Terminal, have the driver let you off at Overpeck Park. By car, take Route 80 off the George Washington Bridge, off at the first exit ("70—Leonia"). A quarter mile south on the right are the stables, which are run by Claremont, offering private lessons at $34 a half hour, $68 an hour, and group lessons for $34 an hour. There are riding clinics, shows and competitions in the indoor and outdoor rings. Boarding is also available. Bergen County residents are offered discounts.
- **Pelham Bay Riding**, 9 Shore Road, City Island/Orchard Beach, 718-885-0551; open daily 8 a.m. until dusk, but call ahead for a guided trail ride, Western only, through woods by the Split Rock Golf Course and Pelham Bay, $25 for one hour, $50 for a two-hour loop. Lessons, English or Western, are $50 for one hour, $45 for 45 minutes, $35 for a half- hour, private; a group lesson is $25 an hour. Reachable by car from the New England Thruway; or take the #6 train to the last stop and walk east or take the Bx29 City Island bus, which stops across the street from the stable.

- **Riverdale Equestrian Centre**, West 254th Street and Broadway, inside Van Cortlandt Park, 718-548-4848; open 8 a.m. to 8 p.m., Saturday and Sunday 9 a.m. to 5 p.m. Rabbits, raccoons and other wildlife are a bonus on the guided trail rides in this large city park. Tack is English, and the cost, after a one-time half-hour evaluation lesson, is $67 per hour, $36 per half-hour, private; $37-$43 per hour in a group. Pony rides for children are $5 and pony parties can be arranged. All rides by appointment. To get there by public transportation take the #1 train to 242nd Street (last stop) and the #9 bus (262nd Street) from there; ask to get off at the stables. Or take the Liberty Line Bx-M3 bus, which goes up Madison Avenue, stopping every 10 blocks, and drops you at the stable door, 20 minutes from the Upper East Side.

ICE SKATING

Besides the Wollman and Lasker rinks (and the Sailboat Pond at 73rd Street when it freezes) in Central Park, Manhattan boasts six other fine places to skate. In Queens try the Flushing Meadow rink.

- **Riverbank State Park**, 145th Street and Riverside Drive, 212-694-3642; skate outdoors just above the Hudson River Monday-Wednesday 12:30 to 1:30 p.m., Tuesday and Thursday 8:30 to 10 p.m., Friday 5 to 6 p.m. and 8:30 to 10 p.m., Saturday and Sunday noon to 1 and 5:15 to 6:15 p.m. Private and group lessons at other times. Skate rentals available.
- **Rockefeller Center Rink**, 50th Street off Fifth Avenue, 212-332-7654; open daily and evenings in season; skate rentals.
- **Skyrink at Chelsea Piers**, Pier 61 at Hudson River and 22nd Street, 212-336-6100, www.chelseapiers.com, open for general skating Monday and Tuesday, noon to 6:20 p.m. and 8 to 9:20 p.m. Monday; Wednesday-Friday, noon to 9:20 p.m.; Saturday 11:45 a.m. to 4:45 p.m. and 8 to 10:20 p.m.; Sunday 12:30 p.m. to 4:45 p.m. With two indoor rinks in use some 20 hours a day, this facility offers public skating, figure skating and hockey instruction for adults and children, league hockey, a skating club and ice theater. Rentals and a skate shop are on site, as well as audience seating for 1,600, including two sky boxes for special events, and a snack bar.
- **Kate Wollman Rink**, sister to Central Park's Wollman Rink, is located on the east side of Prospect Park, off the Parkside and Ocean Avenue entrance, in Brooklyn, 718-287-6431. Open 8:30 a.m. to 2 p.m. Monday, to 5 p.m. Tuesday, to 4 p.m. Wednesday, 8:30 a.m. to 8 p.m. Thursday, to 9 p.m. Friday, 10 a.m. to 10 p.m. Saturday, and 10 a.m. to 6 p.m. Sunday and holidays.
- **World's Fair Skating Rink**, 111th Street, Corona, Queens, in Flushing Meadow Park, 718-271-1996. You can walk to this large,

indoor rink from the Shea Stadium—111th Street stop on the #7 train. Open Monday, Wednesday, Friday, Saturday and Sunday, call for hours and prices; skate rentals available.

LACROSSE

- **Chelsea Piers Field House**, 23rd Street and the Hudson River, 212-336-6500, www.chelseapiers.com, call for hours. Registration is open to individuals and complete teams, men and women, for indoor adult lacrosse league play on a variety of skill levels. Teams play one night a week for a season of 8 to 12 games and league playoffs. Games consist of two 25-minute halves.
- **New York Lacrosse Club**; this dues-paying amateur group fields both an A and B team and competes against members of an Eastern Seaboard league of lacrosse clubs. New York City is their home base but the home field is on Long Island. Write Dr. Bernard Schoenbaum, 21 Ridge Road, Little Falls, NJ 07424, for information.

RACQUETBALL

Devotees of this popular sport can burn off calories at two of the Ys we mention below—the West Side YMCA at 5 West 63rd Street and the 92nd Street YMHA at Lexington Avenue (three practice courts only)—as well as:
- **Gravity**, 119 West 56th Street at Avenue of the Americas (Hotel Meridien), 212-245-1144; tucked beneath the hotel are four racquetball courts and one squash court, which are open to the public by reservation. A one-day guest fee is $25, plus $10 to $20 per hour of court time, depending on time of day.
- **Manhattan Plaza Racquet Club**, 450 West 43rd Street, 212-594-0554, a tennis club with two regulation courts. Use does not require membership but costs $45 per hour, plus $20 per person guest fee.
- **New York Health and Racquet Club**, 110 West 56th Street, 212-541-7200, www.hrcbest.com, has two courts costing members nothing to $20 per hour weekdays and $10 on weekends, depending on time of day; non-members pay an extra $50 for a day pass, $20 if accompanying a member. The club at 39 Whitehall Street between Pearl and Water Streets downtown, 212-269-9800, has somewhat lower court fees for their two courts.
- **Printing House Fitness and Racquet Club**, 421 Hudson Street in Greenwich Village, 212-243-7600, is a membership club with five racquetball and four squash courts on the first floor. Membership rates depend on how much of the club the member intends to use. Call for specifics.

ROLLER/IN-LINE SKATING

For exhilarating outdoor fun, try **Central Park** blade action. Roller disco, though passé, still has followers here also. Other in-line skating hot-spots: **Union Square**, **Battery Park City**, "the banks" under the Manhattan side of the **Brooklyn Bridge**, and Brooklyn's **Prospect Park**. In fact, now you can skate (walk or bike) along the Hudson River from Gansevoort Street to Battery Park City. If you plan to rent, bring a credit card for a deposit on the equipment.

- **Blades Board and Skate**, 160 East 86th Street, 212-996-1644; 120 West 72nd Street, 212-787-3911; 1414 Second Avenue, 212-249-3178; Pier 61, Chelsea Piers, 212-336-6199; Pier 62, Chelsea Pies, 212-336-6299; 659 Broadway in the Village, 212-477-7350; outlet store at 128 Chambers Street downtown, 212-964-1944, www.blades.com, open 10 a.m. to 8 p.m. weekdays and Saturday, 10 a.m. to 6 p.m. Sunday. With the help of the friendly staffers at either of these locations, you too can join the fun (and risk your neck) by in-line skating. Rollerblades, the best-known brand, can be rented for $20 a day, wrist guards and knee pads included. And if you want to join the growing army of neon-clad bladers permanently, you can also buy skates, equipment, and gear here ($95-$350).
- **Chelsea Piers Roller Rinks**, 23rd Street and Hudson River, 212-336-6200, www.chelseapiers.com; open for general skating Monday-Friday 10 a.m. to 6 p.m., Saturday and Sunday noon to 5 p.m., DJ parties Saturday 8 p.m. to 1 a.m. in summer. Besides general skating in two outdoor, regulation-sized in-line and roller rinks, there are classes at various levels from basic technique to hip-hop to aggressive, and league hockey games for adults and youths. Also two half-pipes with 11- and 6-foot walls respectively. Or you can just watch. BLADES, 212-336-6299, operates a board and skate pro shop and rental outlet, and there's a snack bar. Admission is $8 for adults, $6 for children. DJ parties cost $12, children $7, and classes cost $15, with equipment $3 extra if needed. A credit card is required for security when renting equipment.
- **Lezly Dance and Skate School**, 14 Washington Place in the Village, 212-777-3232, holds classes for every level; skate rentals available for classes only.
- **Skate Key Roller Rink**, 2424 White Plains Road, near Pelham Parkway, Morris Park, The Bronx, 718-401-0700, open for general skating Wednesday and Thursday 8 p.m. to midnight, Friday 4:30 to 7:30 p.m. and 8 p.m. to 1 a.m., Sunday 12:30 p.m. to 12:30 a.m. Parties on Monday and Tuesday are open to the public, with variable hours. Special nights for reggae, women, adults only and house music offered.

RUGBY

- **Gaelic Park**, 718-548-9568, in The Bronx is the center of rugby play in New York City. The park is located at Broadway and West 240th Street.

RUNNING

- **Front Runners**, NY, 212-724-9700, www.frontrunnersnewyork.org, is the hyper-active local branch of Front Runners International, which organizes running, walking, cycling and triathlon events for lesbians, gay men and supportive non-gays. Their weekly Fun Runs are Saturday in Central Park at 10 a.m., leaving from the Daniel Webster statue at West 72nd Street and West Park Drive; Wednesday at 7 p.m. from 72nd Street and Central Park West; and Tuesday evening in Prospect Park in Brooklyn, leaving from the entrance at Third Street and Prospect Park West. Participants gather after the runs for a snack or a meal. The organization also offers coaching and training, events for cyclists and walkers, and competitions for runners and tri-athletes.
- **Hash House Harriers**, 212-427-4692, www.hashhouseharriers.com, a group of not-totally-serious joggers who meet at various locations throughout the city and in Westchester to follow a flour-marked trail looping four to five miles and winding up at a bar for post-run analysis fueled by food and copious quantities of beer. Runners are called "hashers;" trails are set by "hares." You need only running shoes and about $15 in "hash cash" to join in. Some call it "the drinking club with a running problem." Hashing originated in 1938 in Kuala Lumpur and is now international, so you can hash away from home. Information is on the web at www.gthhh.com.
- **The New York Road Runners Club**, with over 25,000 members "the world's largest running club," maintains an "International Running Center" at 9 East 89th Street, NYC 10128, 212-996-6577. Road Runners sponsors the New York Marathon and more than 150 other races a year. Regular annual membership costs $30.

SAILING

If you want to bound over Long Island Sound, City Island in The Bronx is an accessible starting point. Take the #2 (Seventh Avenue) or #6 (Lexington Avenue) train to Pelham Parkway and transfer to the Bronx #12 City Island bus. This and some other watery options, below.

- **Great Hudson Sailing Center**, Chelsea Piers, 23rd Street and Hudson River, www.greathudsonsailing.com, 212-741-SAIL, call for hours. Learn to sail a 22-foot Beneteau sailboat at the beginner, intermediate or coastal cruising level in weekend classes, four 4-hour lessons for $400. Private lessons also available, as are rentals of one of the center's six, 22- to 40-foot Beneteaus, $65-$85 an hour.

- **Manhattan Sailing School**, 393 South End Avenue in Battery Park City, NYC 10280-1003, 212-786-0400, www.sailmanhattan.com; sail out of classy North Cove Yacht Harbor in front of the World Financial Center. Beginners can take a 20-hour basic sailing course and continue on to basic coastal cruising, also 20 hours, in J-24 sailboats, each course for $540. Private lessons as well, and rentals at $240 per day. Affiliated with the Manhattan Yacht Club.

- **New York City Community Sailing Association**, 545 West 111th Street, NYC 10025, 212-222-1405; operating with five 22- to 24-foot keel sloops out of the 79th Street Boat Basin on the Hudson, this non-profit organization was founded in 1996 with the idea that sailing ought to be easy and viable all over the city. Call it "not the yacht club." Lessons cost $35 per hour. high school students learn free. There are no rentals, but a $175 membership entitles qualified sailors to five weekend or summer evening sailing sessions, two-hour minimum; the same sessions on weekdays before 3 p.m. cost $75. Renew for more sessions.

- **The New York Sailing School**, 697 Bridge Street, City Island, The Bronx 10464, 718-885-3103, www.nyss.com, offers a 28-hour sailing course for $545 on board one of its Solings, Sonars, Merit 25s or J-22s. You can also rent boats here for $80 to $200 a day, depending on the size of the boat, day of the week and whether or not you are a Sailing School graduate.

- **North Cove Sailing School and Club**, 393 South End Avenue in Battery Park City, NYC 10280, 800-532-5552, just down the pier from the Manhattan Sailing School, teaches basic keelboat sailing and basic coastal cruising in a J-24 for $395 each. Membership in the club, with access to their boats, is a bit less expensive than at the Manhattan Yacht Club.

- **Offshore Sailing School**, locations in Jersey City, NJ and Stamford, CT, 800-221-4326, has a fleet of 26- to 46-foot boats on which they teach beginning three-day courses for $799 weekdays, $895 weekends. Advanced courses available for slightly more (2001 rates). There is a 50% tuition discount for groups of four or more.

SCUBA

While no one's suggesting dives to the murky depths of the Hudson, you can take certification courses in local pools preparatory to plunging into the Caribbean's turquoise waters.

- **PanAqua Diving**, 460 West 43rd Street between 9th and 10th avenues, 212-736-3483, www.panaquadiving.com, open Monday-Friday noon to 7 p.m., Saturday 10 to 7 and Sunday noon to 5 p.m., is the only dive shop with a compressor on site. In addition to selling and repairing equipment, they organize group and individual diving travel and run certification courses evenings and weekends. Courses, held variously at the West Side Y, Vanderbilt Y, 92nd Street Y and Manhattan Plaza, range from one weekend intensive to five weeks of evenings and vary in price from $215 to $295. The open water dive required for certification is extra.

SEA KAYAKING

That's right—sea kayaking. For those who seek watery adventure in and out of the city, the **Metropolitan Association of Sea Kayakers**, www.seacanoe.org, unites groups of paddlers who plan trips up and down the East Coast as well as to locations as far north as Greenland and Alaska. Two or three trips around the island of Manhattan each summer, light and currents permitting, start and end in Liberty State Park (NJ) and take about 11 hours. B.Y.O. kayak. Membership, $20, includes a published schedule, a quarterly newsletter, and a guide to coastal launch sites along the East Coast. Contact Capt. Al Ysaguirre, 212-260-5185 or 718-783-2306, or write 195 Prince Street, basement, NYC 10012. You can store your kayak at the **Downtown Boathouse** at Pier 26 on the Hudson, near North Moore Street; call 212-966-1852. Membership in the non-profit organization costs $50 a year, and storage is $200 per boat for those who do volunteer work here.

SKIING

You won't schuss downhill in New York City, but cross country skiers take to the gentle slopes of Central Park and, in the boroughs, Van Courtland Park, Split Rock Golf Course in Pelham Bay Park, The Bronx, Prospect Park in Brooklyn and Flushing Meadow Park in Queens.

The **New York-New Jersey Trail Conference**, 232 Madison Avenue, 212-685-9699, can provide ski touring information by phone.

SOCCER

The Cosmopolitan Soccer League, 201-861-6606, represents amateur and semi-pro clubs from New York, New Jersey and Connecticut. The League has one semi-pro and two amateur divisions consisting of about 20 clubs each. You don't have to join a club to play on a team, but club facilities are limited to members. Coaches are available for training; all age groups are welcome.

Indoor league play is available now in the field house at **Chelsea Piers**, 23rd Street at the Hudson River, 212-336-6500, www.chelseapiers.com. Teams accommodating men and women at various skill levels play one night a week on an Astroturf indoor field. A season consists of eight or 12 games, consisting of two 25-minute halves, and league playoffs.

SQUASH

When you consider that a tennis court takes up about ten times as much space as a squash court, it is easy to understand the great attraction squash holds for sports club operators as well as for a population determined to exercise, but at the lowest cost possible. See **Health Clubs** and **Ys** for other locations with courts.

- **Club La Raquette**, 119 West 56th Street at Avenue of the Americas (Hotel Meridien), 212-245-1144, has one squash court, which must be reserved; one-day guest fee costs $26, plus a court fee which depends on the time of day.
- **New York Sports Clubs**, www.nysc.com; 61 West 62nd Street, 212-265-0995, four courts; 151 East 86th Street, 212-860-8630, five courts; 575 Lexington Avenue, 212-317-9400, three courts; and 110 Boerum Place (Cobble Hill), 718-643-4400, two courts.
- **Metropolitan Squash and Raquets Association**, 718-237-2450, organizes leagues, tournaments and clinics, mostly in Manhattan. Members receive a monthly magazine.
- **Park Avenue Athletic Complex**, 3 Park Avenue at 34th Street, 212-686-1085; one squash court
- **Printing House Fitness and Racquet Club**, 421 Hudson Street at Leroy Street in Greenwich Village, 212-243-7600, is a membership club with five international squash courts on the first floor. Membership rates depend on how much of the facility the member wishes to use. Call for specifics.

SWIMMING—POOLS

The Department of Parks and Recreation, www.nycparks.org, maintains a number of indoor and outdoor pools throughout the city with inexpensive admission. In the heat of summer, the outdoor pools are more for play and cooling off than serious lap swimming. The swimming is easier during off-hours in winter. Winter indoor pool hours are generally 3 p.m. to 10 p.m. weekdays, 10 a.m. to 5 p.m. Saturday, closed Sunday. Summer hours for the outdoor pools are 11 a.m. to 7 p.m. daily. The indoor pools are closed in summer. Note that gyms are attached to the city pools listed, which are but some among many. For salt water swimming at city beaches see the chapter on **Greenspace and Beaches**.

- **Asser Levy Pool**, 23rd Street, between First Avenue and FDR Drive, 212-447-2020; built in 1906 as a public bath modeled on the Roman baths, this granite gem with a marble lobby and 20-foot ceilings re-opened in 1990 after extensive renovations. A $25 membership dona-tion ($10 for seniors) gives you a year's entree to the 21' by 65' indoor pool and the popular workout room, which is used from 7:15 a.m. until 10 p.m., including some 60 classes from aerobics to yoga. The 50' by 125' outdoor pool is free.
- **Carmine Street Gymnasium and Pool**, Clarkson Street and Seventh Avenue South (Greenwich Village), 212-242-5228, offers a 20' by 70' indoor pool and a 50' by 100' outdoor pool. Two upstairs gyms and a running track. $25 annual membership.
- **East 54th Street Gymnasium and Pool**, 342 East 54th Street between First and Second avenues, 212-397-3154, offers a 50' by 54' indoor pool (open year round) and an upstairs gym and running track. $25 annual membership donation.
- **Hansborough Recreational Center**, 35 West 134th Street, 212-234-9603, in Harlem has an indoor pool and gym with dance and aer-obic classes. Membership is $25 annually.
- **Metropolitan Pool and Fitness Center**, 261 Bedford Avenue, Greenpoint, Brooklyn, 718-599-5707, recently renovated, is probably the most beautiful of the pools operated by the city's Department of Parks and Recreation. Light pours through a copper-framed skylight into the somewhat Andalusian pool area, which is handicap-accessible. Monday, Wednesday and Friday 10 a.m. to noon is ladies only. Best to avoid early evenings and Saturdays. Mornings from 7 to 9:30 are quiet.
- **West 59th Street Gymnasium and Pool**, West 59th Street and West End Avenue, 212-397-3166 or 3159, offers a 34' by 60' indoor pool and a 75' by 100' outdoor pool. The gym has basketball and pad-dleball courts. $25 annual registration fee.

Health clubs and Ys with pools are described at the end of this chapter. Dedicated swimmers might wish also to check out other swimming situa-tions such as:

- **Coles Sports and Recreation Center**, Mercer and Houston streets, 212-998-2020; New York University's sports facility, with racquet ball and squash courts, a weight room and 25-meter pool with six lanes beneath frosted glass windows, is available to residents from 14th to Canal streets, Fourth to Eleventh avenues. After a three- to six-month wait to register you may purchase a punch card good for 12 weekend admissions between 9 a.m. and 2 p.m. for $65, which is renewable. NYU alumni can join for $400 a year.
- **Manhattan Plaza Swim and Health Club**, 482 West 43rd Street at

Tenth Avenue, 212-563-7001; the handsome, verdant, glass-enclosed 40' by 75' pool with four lap lanes is the main lure here, but there is also a gym and sauna. Annual membership, $850, renewal is $700.

- **Riverbank State Park**, 679 Riverside Drive at 145th Street, 212-694-3600; this glorious facility atop a waste treatment plant over the Hudson River is a treasure for Uptowners. Recreational swim sessions in the Olympic-size (50 meters) indoor pool cost $2 for evening and week-end sessions; daytime and evening lap swim sessions cost $2. There are a host of water classes and activities between sessions, and the outdoor pool is open in the summer. Call for hours.
- **Trinity School Swim Club**, 91st Street, between Columbus and Amsterdam avenues, 212-873-1650; the 45' by 75' pool is available to members for swimming six nights a week. Membership is for a summer session and for a winter session that corresponds to the academic year (and therefore includes fall and spring). Currently, there's a long waiting list.

If a dip for a day is all you require, try the **Asphalt Green Aqua Center**, under **Health Clubs**, or one of these West Side hotel pools:

- **Days Inn**, Eighth Avenue at 48th Street, 212-581-7000; 20' by 30' out-door rooftop pool, call for seasonally changing hours, $25 a day week-ends, $20 weekdays.
- **Sheraton City Squire**, 790 Seventh Avenue at 52nd Street, 212-581-3300; covered 20' by 40' pool with outdoor sunning area, open 7:30 a.m. to 8 p.m., $25 a day.
- **Club La Raquette**, 119 West 56th Street off Avenue of the Americas, in the Hotel Meridien, 212-245-1144, lets you use their fitness area and swim in their pool for $40 per day.

TENNIS

The Department of Parks Permit Office in each borough issues tennis per-mits for city courts. Manhattan permit particulars are detailed under Central Park—Tennis. Of the city's 535 public courts, more than 100 are located in Manhattan at nine sites. The largest single concentration, 30 courts, is in Central Park off 96th Street. Seven of the other locations are north of 96th Street, and the eighth is at East River Park at Broome Street on the Lower East Side.

In Brooklyn, permits are sold at the Brooklyn Borough Parks Department office in Litchfield Mansion, 95 Prospect Park West off Fifth Street, 718-965-8900, Monday-Friday 9 a.m. to 4 p.m. The ten city courts located at the Parade Grounds, Coney Island and Parkside avenues, open from April through November, are probably those most popular with tennis permit holders. The same courts are covered with a bubble and run as a concession in the winter. Call 718-236-7045 for hours and rates.

Eight private clubs with four or more courts in Manhattan, Roosevelt Island and across the East River in Queens are listed below. Check the Yellow Pages for other facilities near you.

- **Crosstown Tennis**, 14 West 31st Street, 212-947-5780, four indoor courts; hourly and seasonal rates.
- **East River Tennis Club**, 44-02 Vernon Boulevard, Long Island City (located on the East River; courtesy minibus service leaves hourly on the half-hour from 57th Street and Third Avenue), 718-937-2381, 20 courts, under bubble in winter; membership.
- **Harlem Tennis Center**, 40 West 143rd Street in Harlem, 212-283-4028, has eight courts in a former armory near Lenox Avenue. Hourly and seasonal rates. Open 7 a.m. to 11 p.m., with a variety of classes for children and adults. Call for a reservation.
- **Manhattan Plaza Racquet Club**, 450 West 43rd Street, 212-594-0554, five courts, two racquetball courts and swimming pool privileges; membership, hourly and seasonal rates.
- **Midtown Tennis Club**, 341 Eighth Avenue at 27th Street, 212-989-8572, eight courts; hourly and seasonal rates.
- **Roosevelt Island Racquet Club**, 281 Main Street, Roosevelt Island, 212-935-0250, twelve clay courts indoors, league play, a Seniors' Club and babysitting; membership, hourly rates.
- **Tennisport**, Borden Avenue and Second Street, Long Island City (opposite Manhattan on the East River near Midtown Tunnel exit), 718-392-1880, 16 indoor, 13 outdoor courts; membership.
- **Trinity School**, 91st Street between Columbus and Amsterdam Avenues, 212-873-1650, has two outdoor courts open April 1 through December 1 and one indoor court open September through May; seasonal memberships.
- **West Side Tennis Club**, 1 Tennis Place, Forest Hills, Queens, 718-268-2300, has 43 outdoor courts, including grass, clay Deco-Turf and four Har Tru courts under a bubble in cold weather. A membership club on the former site of the US Open and home to some 800 members, West Side hosts a variety of tennis programs and tournaments and includes on the premises a fitness room, platform tennis, basketball and a new outdoor pool complex. Membership dues vary depending on age and family status. Lessons with a pro are available at extra charge.

WINDSURFING

- **Island Windsurfing**, 1623 York Avenue, 212-744-2000, this full-service shop provides everything from boards to wetsuits. They can arrange lessons at and transportation to either of their two Long Island locations. In summer they run day trips to both; call for current rates. The Manhattan store is open year-round, and has ski gear and snowboards as well.

- **Olympic Windsurfing**, 475 Port Washington Boulevard, Port Washington, Long Island, 516-883-8207, call during the season for information.

YOGA

Not a sport really, but since so many health and fitness clubs now include it along with aerobics, free weights and Nautilus, we include yoga here. It's the unsport in sports. Listed below are just some of the many sites other than health clubs where yoga, in one form or another, is taught and practiced.

- **Integral Yoga Institute**, 227 West 13th Street between 7th and 8th avenues, 212-929-0585, with classes on the Upper West Side and Lower East Side as well. The main location offers open classes in Hatha I, beginners, intermediate and advanced Hatha, pre-natal and post-partum classes, extra gentle, Hatha in Spanish and for HIV participants. They operate an adjacent health food store and a vitamin store nearby. The Integral Yoga Teaching Center at 200 West 72nd Street and Broadway, 212-721-0400, offers a similar roster of classes as well as yoga for mobility and private lessons in yoga and meditation. Classes are also offered at the Interfaith League at 25 First Avenue between First and Second avenues, 212-473-0370, where there is a vegetarian restaurant, The Sanctuary, on the first floor.
- **Om Yoga Center**, 135 West 14th Street between 6th and 7th avenues, second floor, 212-229-0267, with Hatha Yoga classes at all levels, partner Yoga, breathing workshop and meditation courses.
- **Prana Studio**, 5 West 19th Street between 5th and 6th avenues, 212-666-5816, www.thepranastudio.com, specializes in Ashtanga Yoga.
- **Sivananda** Yoga Vedanta Center, 243 West 24th Street between 7th and 8th avenues, 212-255-4560, offering multi-level yoga for all ages, classes and workshops on meditation, philosophy and vegetarian cooking. They also offer yoga retreats at their ranch in the Catskills.
- **White Cloud Studio**, 50 West 65th Street between Columbus Avenue and Central Park West, 212-579-6825, this studio offers yoga, exercise and movement classes for dancers and non-dancers and teacher training as well. Private sessions are available.
- **White Street Center**, 43 White Street between Broadway and Church Street downtown, 212-966-9005; yoga classes, personal trainers, body work and massage therapy.
- **The Yoga Asana Center of Dharma Mittra**, 297 Third Avenue at

23rd Street, 212-889-8160, offers classical yoga, meditation, work-shops and retreats, as well as massage, breathing courses, psychic development and certification programs.
- **Yoga for Health**, 40 Central Park South, 212-752-4225; classes in Yoga Asana and Prana Yama, as well as teacher training, pre-natal class-es, and weekend retreats.
- **Yoga Studio**, 351 East 89th Street, 212- 988-9474; classical yoga, meditation and workshops.
- **Yoga Zone**, 160 East 56th Street between Lexington and Third avenues, 12th floor, 212-935-9642, and 138 Fifth Avenue, 212-647-9642; classes in all levels of Ishta yoga. Orientation classes are offered monthly.

HEALTH CLUBS, YMCAS, YWCAS, AND YMHAS

Health and fitness clubs have proliferated in the city at an astonishing rate. Beyond offering personal trainers and customized fitness regimes most health clubs offer various classes, ranging from kick-boxing and spinning to yoga and fencing. Facilities go from bare bones weight rooms to ubiqui-tous all-purpose spas where you set your own pace using the most appeal-ing facilities. These often include a pool (varying from postage stamp to Olympic in size), exercise equipment (aerobic and weight), steam-rooms, whirlpools and saunas. Hospitals have gotten into the act as well by offer-ing low-key but well-equipped exercise facilities for patients and others affiliated with a hospital; contact the hospital nearest you to find out what may be available. To indicate the amenities offered, a few of the dozens of health facilities located here are described.
- **Asphalt Green**, 1750 York Avenue at 90th Street, 212-369-8890; two gyms, indoor and outdoor running tracks, state-of-the-art cardiovascu-lar and weight-training equipment at this community-oriented, not-for-profit 5.5-acre sports and fitness complex. But the centerpiece is its AquaCenter, a spectacular 50-meter Olympic-standard pool. Membership is on a monthly, semi-annual or annual basis. Non-mem-bers can purchase a day pass for $20 for use of the pool, $25 for full access to the facility.
- **Bally Sports**, 330 East 61st Street, 212-355-5100, is that glamorous seven-story building you see when entering Manhattan on the 59th Street Bridge from Queens: lots of tinted glass, gleaming chrome and lithe-looking figures back-lit and working out. The big club accommo-dates a 20' by 40' pool, exercise machines, squash and racquetball courts, an indoor track, sun deck, restaurant and juice bar, among other amenities. Other locations: 335 Madison Avenue, 212-983-5320; 351 West 49th Street, 212-265-9400.
- **Bally's Jack LaLanne Fitness Center**, www.ballyfitness.com; this fit-

ness mass merchant has more than 40 locations in New York and New Jersey, 800-695-8111. In Manhattan: Broadway at 75th Street, 212-877-1111; Lexington Avenue at 86th Street, 212-722-7371; Fifth Avenue at 53rd Street (women only), 212-759-6406; Madison Avenue and 55th Street, 212-688-6630; 233 Broadway near Wall Street, 212-227-5977; four locations in Brooklyn; three locations in Queens; one Bronx location. Bally's is one of the few New York City clubs that does not require a full year's payment up front but allows you to pay on a monthly basis. Includes Universal and Lifecycle exercise machines, free weights and daily aerobics classes. Warning: the downtown location is cramped. Some membership packages provide for use of other Bally centers throughout the country.

- **Battery Park Swim & Fitness Club**, 375 South End Avenue, 212-321-1117, swim in a glass-enclosed pool with a patio that opens out onto the Hudson River in summer. Swim classes and aquacize are offered, as well as free weights, Cybex and Nautilus, StairMasters, treadmills and Lifecycles. A host of classes, whirlpool, saunas and steam rooms complete the facility.

- **Cardio-Fitness Centers** at: 79 Maiden Lane, 212-943-1510; 345 Park Avenue at 53rd Street, 212-838-4570; 1221 Sixth Avenue at 48th Street, 212-840-8240; 200 Park Avenue at 45th Street, 212-682-4440; and 9 West 57th Street, 212-753-3980. Some corporations pay part or all of their employees' fees for the individualized, instructor-designed exercise programs at the Cardio-Fitness Centers (members can use the clubs interchangeably). Saunas are in place, as are elliptical and cross training machines, bikes, and treadmills. A medical history is required and a stress test as well for those over 35.

- **Crunch Fitness**, www.crunch.com, is proliferating, with five locations in Manhattan: 152 Christopher Street, 212-366-3725; 404 Lafayette Street, 212-614-0120; 1109 Second Avenue between 58th and 59th streets, 212-758-3434; 54 East 13th Street near Fifth Avenue, 212-475-2018; and 160 West 83rd Street, 212-875-1902. Crunch packs 'em in with catchy ads, an exercise program on ESPN2, and fairly outlandish exercise classes, which appeal to a mostly young crowd. Call it entertaining fitness. The Lafayette Street location is open 24 hours on weekends, but you can generally work out as early as 5 or 6 a.m. or as late as 10 p.m. at any Crunch.

- **Dolphin Fitness Clubs**, www.dolphinfitness.com, might be your neighborhood workout, with all the basics including muscle toning and aerobic classes, Nautilus equipment, personal trainers, weight training, cardiovascular equipment and pools and racquetball courts at some locations. In Manhattan at 242 East 14th Street between Second and Third avenues, 212-614-0390; 330 East 59th Street between First and Second avenues, 212-486-6966; 201 East 23rd Street at Third Avenue,

212-679-7300; 1781 Second Avenue at 93rd Street, 212-426-0909; 155 East Third Street at Avenue A, 212-533-0090; 110 Greenwich Street, 212-233-0700; and 700 Columbus Avenue at 95th Street, 212-865-5454. There are clubs in all the boroughs, Westchester and New Jersey as well.

- **Downtown Athletic Club**, 19 West Street, 212-425-7000, occupies a 35-story building housing numerous dining rooms, hotel rooms on 15 floors, and sports and fitness facilities on 13 floors. These include a 30' by 75' pool, two handball and/or racquetball courts, ten squash courts, a basketball court, Nautilus and Universal exercise machines, saunas, steam-baths and a whirlpool. You must be proposed by a current member.

- **Equinox Fitness Club**, www.equinoxnyc.com, ten locations among them: 897 Broadway at 19th Street, 212-780-9300; 344 Amsterdam Avenue at West 76th Street, 212-721-4200; Broadway at 92nd Street, 212-799-1818; 140 East 63rd Street at Lexington Avenue, 212-750-4900; 205 East 85th Street, 212-439-8500, and 14 Wall Street at Nassau, 212-964-6688. Certified personal trainers and some 200 classes, from high and low impact to Aerobox to pre- and post-natal exercise to yoga and meditation fill out the day. Besides up-to-date equipment, the club boasts boxing circuit training, one-on-one boxing (for women too) and cardio/theater television with the cardiovascular workout equipment. A nutritionist supervises personal weight-loss programs. At the Amsterdam Avenue location a physiology lab offers comprehensive metabolic testing for a fee, to non-members as well as members. No boxing uptown.

- **Lucille Roberts**, www.lucilleroberts.com, operates at three Manhattan locations: 2700 Broadway at 103rd Street, 212-961-0500; 143 Fulton Street, 212-267-3730; and 80 East Fifth Avenue at 14th Street; plus more gyms in Brooklyn, Queens, The Bronx, and Staten Island. Focusing on the lower- and middle-income fitness seeker, this chain occupies a special niche in the field. Forget the sauna, the personal trainers and bring your own towel. Plus, it's always ladies' day at Lucille Roberts. Classes are the draw, including one called "butt and gut." In some neighborhoods there are classes in Spanish. The cost of membership, comparatively low, varies by location, as do hours. Individual gyms have occasional sales promotions, when it's cheaper to join; they're worth checking out.

- **New York Health and Racquet Club**, www.hrcbest.com, 212-986-3100, has six locations. Rates go down considerably in the summer (watch for ads offering discounts, and ask about corporate discounts). Membership includes use (for a fee) of the club's tennis court in the Village and admission to any of its locations: 20 East 50th Street, 18' by

50' pool; 1433 York Avenue at 76th Street, 30' by 35' pool; 24 East 13th Street, 20' by 35' pool; 132 East 45th Street, 18' by 50' pool; 110 West 56th Street, 20' by 60' pool; and 39 Whitehall Street, Olympic-sized pool. Other facilities include tennis courts downtown, a yacht and the midtown Kimberly Hotel.

- **New York Sports Clubs**, www.nysc.com, over 20 locations, among them: 30 Cliff Street (Seaport), 212-349-7700; 541 Lexington Avenue at 50th, 212-838-2102; 404 Fifth Avenue at 37th, 212-549-3120; Madison Avenue at 46th, 212-983-0303; 61 West 62nd Street, 212-265-0995; 1601 Broadway, 212-977-8880; 151 East 86th Street, 212-860-8630; 614 Second Avenue, 212-213-5999; 110 Boerum Place, Brooklyn, 718-643-4400; 151 Reade Street (Tribeca), 212-571-1000. Eagle and Nautilus circuits, Lifecycles, StairMasters, Gravitron and other equipment are available in all clubs. Most have one-on-one training, pools, squash courts, whirlpools and saunas. Membership includes entrance to all clubs and access to tennis courts (additional court fee) in Brooklyn. Fees vary with locations. This is one of the few clubs that does not require payment for a full year up front but will bill you monthly.
- **The Printing House Fitness and Racquetball Center**, 421 Hudson Street at Leroy, 212-243-7600. On the first floor are five squash courts; on the ninth floor four kinds of gym machines, treadmills, locker rooms and a sauna, a steam room and whirlpool as well as a cardiovascular fitness center, two dance studios and a full-service salon. On the roof above is a seasonal 20' by 30' heated outdoor pool. There are three different membership rates here, depending on whether you want to use just the racquetball and squash courts, just the gym, or everything. Call for specifics.
- **Reebok Sports Club/NY**, 160 Columbus Avenue at 67th Street, 212-362-6800, is an upscale, landscaped urban country club. This 140,000-square foot facility on six floors features a 45-foot climbing wall, a rooftop in-line skating and running track, swimming pool with underwater sound, a virtual reality sports simulator for skiing, wind-surfing and golf, a bar, health food cafe, and a bistro.
- **Sports Center at Chelsea Piers**, 23rd Street and Hudson River, www.chelseapiers.com, 212-336-6000; this 150,000 square foot pier houses a 4-lane, 1/4-mile running track, competition track, three basketball courts, a 100-foot climbing wall and a bouldering wall, a six-lane, 25-yard swimming pool with an outdoor sunning deck, cardiovascular, circuit and strength training equipment, a boxing ring, aerobic studios and an infield for volleyball, sand volleyball and touch football. Also training, sports medicine, spa facilities and a physiology lab available. Members have the use of all the other Pier facilities at a 10% discount. Day passes for non-members cost $50.

- **Sports Therapy Institute**, 575 Lexington Avenue, Second Floor, 212-752-7111, specializes in one-on-one, personalized training on Nautilus, Universal, Orthotron and Cybex machines. Besides their strengthening regime, one that has kept numerous sports figures in the best of health, the institute offers aerobic equipment, including Nordic skis, Sitron bicycles and rowing machines, a mat-covered area and a stretch class every 15 minutes.
- **92nd Street YMHA**, 1395 Lexington Avenue, 212-415-5709, the cost of Athletic Membership is $995 annually, with one month free if you pay in full up front. The program provides indoor jogging, weight training, volleyball and handball as well as fitness programs and use of the 50' by 75' pool.
- **Brooklyn YWCA**, 30 Third Avenue between State Street and Atlantic Avenue, Brooklyn, 718-875-1190, for a reasonably priced $395 Athletic Membership plus a $35 Y membership, both men and women can work out on the Universal machines, punching bags, the large basketball court, jogging track and in the 20' by 60' swimming pool, as well as relax in the sauna.
- **Harlem YMCA**, 135th Street and Lenox Avenue, 212-281-4100, offers two pools (for adults and children); Nautilus and weights; a track; basketball courts; table tennis; aerobics, yoga and karate classes; athletic membership (for men and women) costs $432 per year, or $36 per month, plus $125 initiation fee.
- **McBurney YMCA**, 215 West 23rd Street, 212-741-9210, this Y has a carefully developed children's after-school program as well as adult gymnastics, adult lap and recreational swimming, full-court basketball, indoor jogging track, fencing, handball, volleyball and weight lifting room. Annual adult membership costs $792 or $66 per month, for those over eighteen, with a $75 joiner's fee for the first year.
- **Vanderbilt YMCA**, 224 East 47th Street, 212-756-9600, offers yoga, handball and paddleball, along with swimming, basketball, volleyball, indoor jogging, Nautilus and aerobics. Regular memberships cost $936, with a joiner's fee of $125, and include use of the gym, 20' by 60' swimming pool, a 40' by 75' lap pool and other sports facilities. Annual dues for the Businessman's Club and the men's Athletic Club are higher.
- **The West Side YMCA**, 5 West 63rd Street, 212-875-4100, is justifiably proud of its Sports Fitness Department, which keeps both men and women members in the very best of shape. The seven-story building houses two pools, a wrestling room, indoor running track, handball, squash and racquetball courts, Universal exercise machines and numerous other facilities. Annual adult membership is $780, plus a $125 initiation fee.

A S THE RAINFOREST IS TO THE EARTH, SO ITS PARKS ARE TO THIS rushed and hard-edged city. In these verdant oases, New Yorkers breathe, relax, play... and smile. From the smallest community garden on a vacant lot in a dense neighborhood, where neighbors lovingly tend an iris bed and a riotous morning glory, to green bands streaked with runners, bladers, and cyclers along its watery borders, to Manhattan's great lush centerpiece, Central Park, and its sister, Prospect Park, in Brooklyn, New Yorkers use and cherish their parks. Beyond these groomed and cultivated parks familiar to most, there are almost 9,000 acres of urban wilderness in the domain of the city's Parks Department, where the nature lover can wander wooded paths, meadows, and marshlands alone and silent among swans, egrets, herons, turtles, muskrats and rabbits. For the price of a subway ride, one can spend the day in a national park, Gateway National Recreation Area, a birder's paradise, parts of which are within the city. And the city's beaches, seaside parks of a sort, guarantee sandy access to the Atlantic Ocean and Long Island Sound.

There are 1,650 parks and playgrounds throughout the 28,000 acres maintained by the Department of Parks and Recreation in the five boroughs. These range from vest-pocket neighborhood playgrounds to the 2,700-acre Pelham Bay Park in The Bronx. Suffice it to say we can't describe or even list them all. Rather, this chapter focuses on the major parks in each borough, with brief descriptive mention of some others and, finally, a look at the city's beaches. For further information about parks in general or a particular park call 800-201-PARK or 888-NY-PARKS for a tape of upcoming events throughout the five boroughs; go online to www.nycparks.org. A dandy book, *Nature Walks in and Around New York City* by Sheila Buff, leads the reader through a detailed stroll around Central Park and some 40 other parks and preserves in the metropolitan area.

Open from dawn to 1 a.m., all city parks are free and accessible by public transportation. Statistically speaking, the parks are very safe. That said, it is well to remember these are urban parks; common sense tells you it's not a good idea to stroll or jog through a wooded park area alone after dark. Dogs must be on leashes, and you are expected to clean up after your dog. It's the law.

PARKS

MANHATTAN

In 1858 Frederick Law Olmsted and Calvert Vaux won a design competition for the construction of the first public park to be built in America. It was to occupy swampy land inhabited by poor squatters, bone-boiling mills and swill mills, an area described in one report as "a pestilential spot where miasmic odors taint every breath of air." The inhabitants were removed, buildings torn down, swamps drained, tons of earth moved and Manhattan schist blasted away. Following plans for a picturesque landscape of glades alternating with copses, water and outcroppings, and threaded with drives, footpaths and bridle paths, over a period of 20 years the park emerged from wasteland. What Olmsted and Vaux had named Greensward became **Central Park**, 840 acres of man-made romantic landscape stretching rectangularly from 59th Street north to 110th Street, and from Fifth Avenue west to Central Park West (Eighth Avenue): the green jewel in the middle of Manhattan.

Today the park is managed, under contract with the city, by the Central Park Conservancy, a non-profit organization responsible for extensive restoration of the park. Recent work occurred at the Harlem Meer and the surrounding northern portion of the park. Most heavily visited is the southern portion of the park, especially along its outer verges and the area around the ever-popular Central Park Zoo. The northern portion beyond the Reservoir, with its heavily-used jogging track, contains both the wildest terrain, including the Ravine area with its waterfall and the 1814 Blockhouse, as well as the only formal garden in the park, the elegant Conservatory Garden at 105th Street and Fifth Avenue. The Charles A. Dana Discovery Center, 212-860-1370, in the northeast corner of the park, features ecologically oriented exhibits and programs for all ages on a regular basis, and has fishing poles for use at the adjacent Harlem Meer. Throughout the park the Conservancy offers free seasonal events, including bird-watching walks and ecological activities. Pick up the Conservancy's excellent *Central Park Map and Guide* at the Dairy, just north of Wollman Rink near the 65th Street Transverse, open Tuesday-Sunday, 11 a.m. to 5 p.m. To find out what's happening this week in Central Park call 212-408-0204 for a menu of recorded messages. New Yorkers use Central Park: for sports, from croquet to horseback riding to league softball (see the chapter on **Sports and Recreation**); for cultural events such as Shakespeare In the Park, outdoor performances by the Metropolitan Opera and the New York Philharmonic; for children's recreation in its numerous playgrounds, for storytelling sessions, kite-flying and carousel riding, and organized nature activities; for sunbathing on its rocky outcroppings or on bucolic Sheep Meadow; for bird-watching in the Ramble, especially during the annual spring warbler migration; for boating in The Lake or floating beneath Bow Bridge in a Venetian gondola; for weddings. And it's used for daydreaming. In fact, sometimes just knowing it is there is enough.

Central Park is open from a half-hour before dawn to 1 a.m. As in the other large city parks, it is best visited in daylight or at night in the well-lighted areas along the edges and with companions. Check www.centralpark.org for an invigorating virtual visit. This excellent, non-official web site offers a colorful virtual tour, park history, sports and groups, a listing of park events, and links to other park-related sites.

Having completed Central Park, Olmsted and Vaux focused their attention on the banks of the Hudson River and designed most of what is now **Riverside Park**. This elongated ribbon of green, stretching along the river from 72nd Street to 152nd Street and bisected lengthwise by the Henry Hudson Parkway, is particularly beautiful in the spring when daffodils dot the grassy banks and swarms of flowering trees create a haze of pink and white. Riverside Drive winds among great trees along the upper terrace, and the mighty Hudson, nearly a mile wide here, sweeps along past cyclists and joggers on the riverfront promenade. Sailboats and a few houseboats at the 79th Street boat basin bob at anchor, and in good weather reasonably priced sailing lessons are to be had here (see **Sports and Recreation**). Tennis, handball, soccer, and volleyball are played here, and a facility for bladers and boarders, with ramps and half-pipes at 108th Street, draws youthful enthusiasts. Soaring Riverside Church and Grant's Tomb add to the appeal of Riverside Park. For more information call the park administrator's office at 212-408-0264. Further along at 145th Street and Riverside Drive an iron-gate gives access to **Riverbank State Park**, 212-694-3600, built atop a waste treatment plant, where ice skating, swimming and other athletic activities can be pursued at way-below-health-club rates.

Fort Tryon Park in Washington Heights stands atop a ridge of Manhattan schist at the highest natural point in Manhattan. The site of one of the earliest Revolutionary War battles (we lost), this land was purchased in 1917 by John D. Rockefeller Jr. He hired Frederick Law Olmsted, Jr. to design a park here, reserving four acres at the northern end of the 67 acres for a museum of medieval art, The Cloisters—a fortuitous pairing, those juniors. Taking advantage of the sweeping Hudson view at this 250-foot elevation, Olmsted designed a series of terraces with stone parapets and retaining walls, the whole threaded with eight miles of paths. But the centerpiece of the park is the three-acre Heather Garden, including heaths and brooms and thousands of bulbs, which bloom from January through autumn. Further along the Promenade, a leafy Linden Terrace, and then **The Cloisters**, with its three medieval gardens. A branch of Metropolitan Museum of Art, The Cloisters is not to be missed. For more information call Fort Tryon Park General Information, 212-408-0100; Fort Tryon Park Garden Information, 212-795-1388; or The Cloisters, 212-923-3700.

Just north of Fort Tryon Park at the very top of Manhattan, little-known **Inwood Hill Park** contains the last remaining natural woodland in Manhattan, not to mention arresting views of the Hudson River and the Jersey Palisades beyond. Interesting geology on the wooded ridge, which is criss-crossed with paved and graveled paths, includes glacial potholes and cliffs with a hodge-podge of blocky gray rocks, the Indian Rock Shelters, which once sheltered Algonquin Indians. From these rocky cliffs paths descend to playing fields, grassy parkland, and marshland along swift Spuyten Duyvil Creek, across which the Henry Hudson Bridge soars to The Bronx. There is an excellent Urban Ecology Center here, open Thursday-Monday, from 11 a.m. to 4 p.m., and staffed by Urban Park Rangers. They lead occasional walks and canoe trips into the Hudson. For information call 212-304-2365 or the Inwood Hill Park Administrator at 212-408-0264.

South of Central Park, green space is measured out in smaller portions. **Bryant Park** behind the Beaux Arts main branch of the New York Public Library at 42nd Street, between Fifth and Sixth avenues, for example, is too small to encourage sports much more strenuous than chess. But it is green space with a rather European feel, and those who work in the neighborhood are grateful for its elegant air of civility. Further downtown at the foot of Fifth Avenue, **Washington Square Park** is not much larger, but it is the green space in Greenwich Village and SoHo. Nearly surrounded by New York University, which threatens to engulf it entirely, Washington Square Park has managed to retain a sense of its history, which has included being a potter's field, the site of the hangman's tree, a military parade ground, and an elegant park for the wealthy. Its Village location and the presence of college students keep it lively and fairly colorful. To the east, **Tompkins Square Park**, truly a people's park with an English provenance and great old trees that have always made it a shady haven in the summer for a working class population, is the front yard for the East Village. The population is changing as gentrification sets in, but the park is no less used. Dogs in the dog run there come in more exotic breeds now. Way downtown, where **Battery Park City** was built on landfill from the construction of the World Trade Center, land along the river was reserved for imaginatively designed parks. These parks are connected by a sinuous, elegant **Esplanade** spacious enough to accommodate joggers, cyclists, bladers, walkers, and baby strollers moving at their own pace within sight of the Statue of Liberty and Ellis Island.

Students from nearby Stuyvesant High School toss frisbees about in the off-shore breeze and children romp and climb in a fanciful playground. The landscape at the south end was designed to resemble the original shoreline. Just to the south, at the very foot of the island is **Battery Park**, once part of New York Harbor with Castle Clinton surrounded by water rather than grass. This inviting, grassy stretch looks out on the harbor, the statue, Staten Island, and invites a hop onto the free Staten Island Ferry.

BROOKLYN

Who but Calvert Vaux and Frederick Law Olmsted could have designed **Prospect Park**, sister to Central Park and younger by just a few years? In fact, its designers considered it their masterpiece. Free of Manhattan's grid, it is irregularly shaped in a somewhat elongated ovoid, smaller at 526 acres, and unlike Central Park, undisturbed by vehicular traffic. Prospect Park was designed for strolling along a network of paths: on vast Long Meadow, the park's magnificent centerpiece, around Prospect Lake and the Lullwater, through The Ravine and the Midwood Forest, and by The Pools. Sounds English? It is. Olmsted and Vaux incorporated the natural terrain into their design, including water, magnificent old trees and geological features such as glacial kettle ponds, one of which became the charming Vale of Cashmere. To these features they added rustic bridges, a waterfall and lakes, the final effect of which is vistas, surprising nooks and glades, and hilltop prospects. There's even a Quaker cemetery, among whose residents is the actor Montgomery Clift, and an elegant, Palladian-style boathouse. This is not to say that strolling is the sole Prospect Park activity. A small zoo occupies another glacial kettle; there's a Wollman Rink here too for ice-skating; birding is excellent in the park; jogging, tennis, softball, kite flying and soccer flourish here; and on summer weekends the Bandshell at 9th Street and Prospect Park West features music, from calypso to jazz to klezmer and new urban Latin grooves. For more information and for upcoming events in the park call the Prospect Park Administrator at Litchfield Villa, Prospect Park, 718-965-8900, or check with Prospect Park Alliance, 95 Prospect Park West, Brooklyn 11215, 718-965-8951.

Across Flatbush Avenue from Prospect Park, and behind the Brooklyn Central Library and the Brooklyn Musuem, the **Brooklyn Botanic Garden**, 718-622-4433, contains within its compact 52 acres an extraordinary variety of greenery and flora, beautifully landscaped so as never to seem crowded. The Cherry Esplanade, said to be the finest in America, draws crowds in May when the cherry trees are in exquisite bloom. Don't miss it, but come early and on a weekday if possible. There's a rock garden, water-lily ponds, and a lilac collection, offering intoxicating blooms each spring. An herb garden is arranged as an Elizabethan knot, and the stunning Japanese garden evocatively laid out around a lovely pond is a perennial favorite. Year-round, the gently undulating terrain invites wandering, beginning in February, when the witch hazel blooms and the snowdrops begin to come up. Call it midwinter botanical balm. Before you bliss out, don't miss the original Palm House. You may decide to get married there, as many have.

Green-Wood Cemetery, with its main entrance on Fifth Avenue at 25th Street, is at once a cemetery and one of the most beautiful, not to mention unusual, parks in the city. You will not play soccer here, and jogging its winding, hilly drives would be a challenge. What you do do, if not on a cemetery-related mission, is walk, bird watch, identify exotic trees, of which there are many, and look for the graves of the once-famous, including Lola Montez, Boss Tweed, Peter Cooper and Samuel F.B. Morse, to name but a few. Opened in 1840, before Prospect Park was conceived, on 478 acres of glacial terminal moraine, and overlooking New York Harbor from the highest point in Brooklyn, its developers promoted it as an idyllic spot for strolling among the hills, ponds, superb vistas and plantings. It was, de facto, the city's first park. The extraordinary mausoleums, obelisks, temples, pyramids and rustic grave markers make it something of a museum of Victoriana and a draw for occasional guided tours. The main gate building, designed by Richard Upjohn, is a Gothic Revival extravaganza, housing the office where you pick up a pass, brochure, and a map of the cemetery. The office is open Monday-Friday, 8 a.m. to 4 p.m., 718-768-7300. If you wish to roam the cemetery on the weekend you should pick up a pass in advance. It's worth the trouble. Or join one of John Cashman's Sunday walking tours (April-June and September-November), which last about two hours starting at 1 p.m.; call 718-469-5277 for directions. The tours cost $6.

Stepping out of the car at the **Marine Park** parking lot on Avenue U, just west of Flatbush Avenue, you'll find yourself in a landscape of salt marsh and meadow somewhat reminiscent of Holland. This 798-acre park, most of it saltwater wetlands surrounding Marine Park Creek, north of Sheepshead Bay, contains playing fields, tennis courts, a running track and a golf course, 718-338-7149, in addition to a watery urban wilderness. From the parking lot you can hike the Gerritson Creek Nature Trail for about a mile, through grasses, sedges and reeds with glimpses, perhaps, of diamond-back terrapin, horseshoe crabs, cottontails, marsh hens, myrtle warblers, cormorants and peregrine falcons. It's hard to believe you're in New York City. For more information call 718-965-8900. Golfers note the 18-hole public golf course across Flatbush Avenue; call 718-965-8900 for information or seven days in advance for a reservation.

Even more unbelievable, and not known to many New Yorkers, is the presence of a 26,000-acre national park, **Gateway National Recreation Area**, www.nps.gov/gate, which encompasses most of Jamaica Bay in Brooklyn and Queens, and part of the Rockaways in Queens, a long stretch of the southern shore of Staten Island, and parts of the Jersey shore. Besides Jacob Riis Park, an ocean beach with a boardwalk (see **Beaches**, below), the best known point of interest in the area is the **Jamaica Bay Wildlife Refuge**, 718-318-4340, a prime birding preserve with salt water marshes, upland fields and woods, where land and shore birds stop during migration. After obtaining a permit at the visitor center on Crossbay Boulevard in Broad Channel, Queens, visitors can explore diverse habitats by hiking an extensive trail system. Insect repellent in summer is strongly advised. Rangers give interpretive talks and lead nature walks; evening walks, workshops and other programs are offered on a seasonal basis. Floyd Bennett Field, 718-338-3799, the city's first municipal airfield, contains the North 40 Nature Trail, miles of runways for cycling or blading, and Hangar Row, where outdoor concerts and special events are held. Across Flatbush Avenue from the Field, Dead Horse Bay is a popular fishing area with a nature trail. Canarsie Pier just off the Beltway in Brooklyn, 718-763-2202, is the site of summer concerts, excellent fishing, a children's playground, and a commercial restaurant. Fishing is also popular, along with bird watching, at Breezy Point Tip on the Rockaway Peninsula and at Fort Tilden, a 317-acre former Army base, 718-318-4300, where visitors can also hike and explore a military past, participate in organized athletics or attend special events. On the south shore of Staten Island, Great Kills Park, 718-987-6790, offers ocean beaches, nature trails, a model airplane field, and fishing areas. Ranger walks at Miller Field, 718-351-6970, a former Army Air Corps defense station, and at Fort Wadsworth, 718-354-4500, dating from the 18th century, appeal to military buffs and children.

Admission to all portions of Gateway, except Sandy Point, NJ, is free. For the latest information on concerts, special programs and ranger-led activities visit Gateway on the web at www.nps.gov/gate. Or contact the National Park Service, Gateway National Recreation Area, Floyd Bennett Field, Building 69, Brooklyn 11234, 718-338-3799, for a seasonal program guide, which includes transportation directions to all parts of the Area.

QUEENS

At long last **Flushing Meadows-Corona Park**, 718-760-6562, is coming into its own, becoming the grand park originally envisioned when the 1939 World's Fair was held there, and again at the time of the 1964 World's Fair. Built on what was once a garbage heap on Northern Boulevard, between Grand Central Parkway and Van Wyck Expressway, both fairs were to pay for park construction, but neither made money and the great park limped along with World Fair leftovers and a baseball stadium, Shea. The Unisphere, the signature attraction of the 1,255-acre park, and its grassy surrounds have been renovated, and extensive landscaping and planting have beautified the central portion of the park, which also hosts the New York Hall of

Science and the Queens Museum in former fair buildings. Soon the park's entire waterfront along Flushing Bay will be distinguished by an elegant promenade with shade and ornamental trees, shrubs and flowers along a curved ornamental railing. From reproduction cast iron benches visitors will be able to people watch, view the flowerbeds, or watch boats bobbing in the World's Fair Marina. Elsewhere in the park are the Queens Theater and Queens Zoo, the US Tennis Association's National Tennis Center, an ice-skating rink, running trails, and two large lakes lying to the south of the Long Island Expressway, one, Meadow Lake, with a boathouse.

Alley Pond Park, 718-229-4000, sprawls and meanders south from Little Neck Bay to Union Turnpike. Despite being sliced by numerous park-ways, it encompasses forests, meadows, salt marshes and wetlands, making it an ideal environment for a network of nature trails from which one can observe muskrats, bullfrogs, salamanders and hawks. Up on the northern end, by Alley Creek, an Environmental Center offers a variety of education-al classes and workshops.

Southwest of Flushing Meadows Corona Park, bisected laterally by Interborough Parkway and edging Forest Hills, **Forest Park**, 718-235-4100, offers golfing greens, playing fields, and a magnificent 150-year old oak for-est honeycombed with picturesque nature trails. Call for upcoming events. On the other side of Flushing Meadow the **Kissena Park Corridor** con-tains the **Queens Botanical Gardens and Arboretum** and connects up with greater **Kissena Park**, 718-520-5359, a gracious green space sur-rounding a lake and meandering stream. There's a bicycle track for the sportif. To the east, adjacent to Cross Island Parkway and Hempstead Turnpike, **Belmont Park** is famous for its exceedingly beautiful racetrack, where thoroughbreds compete annually for the Belmont Cup. But you don't have to be a horse-lover to enjoy the park. And finally, or first and foremost, Queens is home to much of **Gateway National Park**, described above.

THE BRONX

Up in the northeast corner of The Bronx, sprawling alongside and into Long Island Sound, is the city's largest park, 2,700 acres of it. **Pelham Bay Park**, 718-430-1890, has it all: a city beach, two golf courses, miniature golf and a driving range, a stable, tennis courts, baseball diamonds, picnic grounds and a historic mansion-museum, not to mention a range of habi-tats—the most diverse of any of the city parks. Just off-shore and connect-ed to the park by a bridge, City Island dangles like a fish on a line. The largest portion of the park lies on the north side of the Hutchinson River and Eastchester Bay, Split Rock Golf Course and Pelham Bay Golf Course (see **Sports and Recreation**) scenically occupying the northernmost part. There too on Shore Road is Pelham Bay Riding (again, **Sports and**

Recreation), extensive bridle trails, and the **Thomas Pell Wildlife Refuge and Sanctuary** nearby, home to a variety of owls, wild turkeys and deer. Just to the north and east, off Shore Road, the Barton-Pell Mansion and Museum, dating from 1675 with alterations done in the 19th century, is the single manor house remaining of 28 country estates which once comprised the park area. It is well worth a visit. Orchard Beach (see **Beaches** below) cuts a great sandy arc on Long Island Sound. At its far end is the Environmental Center, where you can pick up literature and a guide booklet to the Kazimiroff Nature Trail, which winds through the adjoining Hunter Island sanctuary, perhaps the most beautiful section of the park. Mature woodlands give way to salt marsh, where, in the fall, migrating hawks and ospreys are to be spotted, and a profusion of water birds year round. The great rounded boulders off-shore in the Sound are glacial erratics, and the gray bedrock visible here is the southernmost extension of the ancient bedrock which forms most of the New England coast.

Directly to the west, abutting Riverdale and Yonkers, **Van Cortland Park**, 718-430-1890, also contains playing fields, two golf courses, a riding stable and trails, and a historic mansion museum. Heavily used for recreation and once the site of an extensive Native American village, the Parade Ground is also home to weekend cricket competitions by largely West Indian teams. Nearby, you can visit the Van Cortland Mansion and Museum, 718-543-3344, the oldest house in the Bronx (1748) and a lovely example of vernacular Georgian architecture. To the north, where the Henry Hudson Parkway crosses Broadway and slices through the park, the Riverdale Equestrian Centre rents horses for trail rides and offers lessons (see **Sports and Recreation**). The Van Cortland Golf Course, the oldest municipal links in the country, surrounds much of long, narrow Van Cortland Lake, while the Mosholu Golf Course lies in the southeast corner of the park (see **Sports and Recreation**). Birders and nature lovers seek out two popular trails: the forested Cass Gallagher Trail with its dramatic rock outcroppings in the northwest portion of the park, and the John Kieran Nature Trail in the southern portion. The latter, which skirts freshwater wetlands and the Tibbetts Brook area esteemed by bird watchers, follows a former rail corridor, along which deer, wild turkeys and coyotes are seen occasionally, and swings down along the lake, where egrets and great blue herons are to be found. There's an Urban Forest Ecology Center, 718-548-7070, with restrooms and information at the southern end of the Parade Ground. Urban Park Rangers offer nature walks and programs out of this facility throughout the year.

Bronx Park in the center of the north Bronx is comprised entirely of the **New York Botanical Garden** and the **International Wildlife Conservation Park** (Bronx Zoo), neither of which, properly speaking, is a park. Separated by Fordham Road and each bisected by the scenic Bronx River, they bear mentioning here because of their natural beauty, their accessibility, and their popularity. The Botanical Garden, 718-817-8700, on the north, is at once an internationally recognized botanical research facility and an extraordinary Victorian Conservatory, with gardens and educational programs on 250 acres of geologically interesting virgin forest and a variety of landscaped gardens, all accessible by pathways and tram. Two cafes and picnic areas make it possible to spend the day here. Leave the dogs home and please don't pick the daisies. **Note**: The Garden operates a shuttle between it and the American Museum of Natural History and the Metropolitan Museum of Art in Manhattan weekends and Monday holidays, March-November. The Zoo, 718-367-1010, on similar wooded terrain with rock outcroppings and wonderfully varied flora, would be a great place to spend the day even without the animals. But it is, of course, a world-class zoo, where you can wander out of the northeast woods into a rainforest, a savannah or a Himalayan mountain enclave.

Another green space that bears mention, though it is not a park at all, is **Woodlawn Cemetery**, 718-920-0500, just east of Van Cortland Park, between the Bronx River and Jerome Avenue. Less spectacular in terrain than Green-Wood in Brooklyn, Woodlawn is nevertheless a splendiferous array of mausoleums, memorials and tombstones, in a richly planted, peaceful setting. Stop by the office at the Webster Avenue entrance at 233rd Street for a map and brochure. You can drive or walk around the terminal mansions of Jay Gould, the Woolworths, Herman Melville and Fiorello ("The Little Flower") LaGuardia, whose modest tombstone bears a simply carved little flower. The cemetery is open daily, 9 a.m. to 4:30 p.m.

STATEN ISLAND

Well into the middle of the 20th century most of Staten Island remained something of a sleepy backwater of woods, meadows and farms. Unbridled suburban sprawl threatened to sweep that away until community action resulted in the preservation of significant chunks of remaining natural lands in the center of the island—their designation: the **Staten Island Greenbelt**. Twelve individual parks strung together by narrow corridors form the 2,500-acre greenbelt, encompassing five distinct vegetative zones and an astonishing variety of terrain. The Wisconsin glacier stopped here some 10,000 years ago, which accounts for the rocky ridges and kettle ponds. Two trails traverse the area: the 8.5-mile Blue Trail, running roughly east-west, and the 4-mile White Trail, running roughly north-south—the two cross at Bucks Hollow in Latourette Park.

One of the parks in the Greenbelt, **High Rock Park** on Todt Hill, which happens to be the highest coastal point in the East south of Acadia National Park in Maine, maintains a Conservation Center, 718-667-2165, which is also the administrative office for the Greenbelt. Trails crisscross the

90-acre park, which was once a Girl Scout campground, winding in and out of woods, along the Richmond Country Club golf course and freshwater wetlands, and down steep slopes to glacial kettle holes. It's a bird watcher's paradise, with woodcock, indigo buntings, northern orioles and other birds, which generally shun urban areas. From the highest point on a clear day one can see the Atlantic Ocean. For information and directions, call or write the Conservation Center at 200 Nevada Avenue, Staten Island 10306.

Clay Pit Ponds State Park Preserve, 718-967-1976, near the southwest shore of the island is the only state park preserve in the city, and its 260 acres preserve a remnant of Staten Island's rural past, its bogs, meadows, ponds, sand barrens, woodlands and swamps. Some 160 acres are designated state freshwater wetlands and unique natural areas, and as such are closed to visitors. But the remainder has much to offer. Two interesting walking trails, with bridges and boardwalks through the wet areas, are easily hiked, even for children, who will marvel at the amphibians to be glimpsed along the way: black racer snakes, box turtles, frogs, lizards and red-backed salamanders. One trail goes through part of one of the designated natural areas. A former pasture is now a meadow full of wildflowers and butterflies. An observation platform overlooks Abraham's Pond, a former clay pit abandoned in the 1920s. Look for muskrats, red-winged blackbirds and painted turtles here. The park is free, open daily from dawn to dusk, but the headquarters and restrooms are open weekdays, 9 a.m. to 5 p.m. No dogs allowed.

And, of course, there's Miller Field and Great Kills Park, Staten Island's share of **Gateway National Recreation Area** described above under **Brooklyn**.

BEACHES

It's July, hot. You think, "Gotta get in some saltwater, stretch out on the sand, smell a salt breeze, eat a hotdog." Grab your suit, your MetroCard, and hop on the subway. New York's got it. There are city-run saltwater beaches in every borough but Manhattan, all one fare away—except for Jones Beach on Long Island, which is not a city beach but is included here because it is wonderful and many prefer it to the more crowded city beaches.

City strands traditionally open on Memorial Day and close the day after Labor Day. Managed by national, state and city park departments, all the beaches mentioned below are staffed by lifeguards. For information on beaches open to the general public, as opposed to residents with permits in Nassau and Suffolk counties, call the Long Island Tourism and Convention Commission, 631-951-3440. We begin with the northernmost beach, in the Bronx, and wind up on Long Island:

• **Orchard Beach**, 718-885-3273, on a long, sandy crescent on Long

Island Sound in The Bronx with all of Pelham Bay Park at its back, is exceptionally popular, so much so you'll need to get there early on weekends if you're driving. Parking can be difficult.

- **Coney Island**, 718-946-1350, Coney Island Avenue and West 8th Street, is a state of mind and an icon. The vast, sandy beach and the long boardwalk reaching from near the tip of the "island" to the Esplanade at Manhattan Beach is a scene for sure on summer weekends. You've seen the pictures, now try the beach. While you're there, don't miss the New York Aquarium, which is excellent, the Cyclone roller-coaster and Astroland, another scene, and a hotdog at famous Nathan's.
- **Brighton Beach**, 718-946-1350, at Brighton Court and Brighton Second Street, in the heart of heavily Russian Little Odessa, makes for exotic people watching along the long, broad boardwalk. Stock up on Russian gourmet specialties and incredibly cheap produce at the stands along Brighton Beach Avenue before taking the subway home.
- **Manhattan Beach**, 718-946-1350, just east of Brighton Beach off Oriental Boulevard in Brooklyn, is a forty-acre public park and beach area with parking, a sandy beach, ball-field and concession stand, a favorite with families. Best reached by car. After a day in the water you can eat at one of Sheepshead Bay's popular restaurants and perhaps catch an outdoor concert at nearby Kingsborough Community College.
- **Jacob Riis Park**, 718-318-4300, in Gateway National Recreation Area on the Rockaway Peninsula in Queens, with a 13,000-car parking lot, a mile of wide, sandy beach with boardwalk and handsome, WPA-era buildings, is perhaps the pre-eminent city beach. Besides swimming and tanning, there's handball, paddle tennis and shuffleboard. It is here that Polar Bear Club members take their winter water frolics. Lifeguards come on duty here June 20. While admission is free, parking costs $3.25 for the day.
- **Great Kills Park**, 718-987-6790, open June 20 in the Gateway National Recreation Area on Staten Island's south shore, boasts miles of trails for jogging and walking, a model airplane field, athletic fields, a fishing area and marina as well as the guarded beach.
- **Jones Beach State Park**, 516-785-2420, is six and a half miles long, wide and beautiful, well worth the drive or the bus ride from the Port Authority Bus Terminal, or the train from Penn Station to Freeport, where there's a shuttle bus to the beach. Field 6, the most popular, attracts a peaceful mix of seniors, families and gays, and on summer weekends the parking lot fills up early. Field 5 is sheltered from waves, good for kids. West End 2 allows fishing and surfing and is the most peaceful. Weekend traffic on the Long Island Expressway is daunting.

For information or travel directions to any of these beaches call your preferred beach directly or the Transit Authority, 718-330-1234 for directions.

IF YOU CAME FROM A SMALL TOWN, YOU MAY HAVE GONE TO *THE* Methodist church, *the* Catholic church, or *the* synagogue. No problem. But there are an estimated 2,300 churches (not counting storefront Pentecostals) and some 650 synagogues in New York City. You'll find some, but by no means all, of them listed by denomination in the Yellow Pages. Finding a suitable church or synagogue may be as simple as that or the suggestion of an acquaintance. Or it may be as intensely personal and complex as choosing a spouse. The houses of worship listed below alphabetically were chosen specifically for their possible appeal to newcomers. It's a place to start.

BAHA'I

- **Baha'l Faith**, 53 East 11th Street, NYC 10003, 212-674-8998, www.bahainyc.org, conducts devotions and discussion Sunday at 11 a.m.

BUDDHIST

- **New York Buddhist Church**, 331-332 Riverside Drive at 105th Street, NYC 10025, 212-678-0305; a stunning bronze statue of Shinran-Shonin in front of this landmarked building marks the presence of this Shin Buddhist Temple. Regular Dharma Service in English at 11:30 a.m. Sunday is occasionally preceded at 10:30 by a service in Japanese. In addition there are regularly scheduled Dharma study classes for adults and for children, meditation sessions, and classes in Japanese calligraphy, drumming, martial arts, yoga, and brush technique.
- **Soka Gakkai International—USA**, 7 East 15th Street, NYC 10003, 212-727-7715, fills the six-story, landmarked former YWCA with lectures, discussions, and group chants for some 5,000 area members who

practice the Buddhism of Nichiren Daishonin. It's a warm and accepting community in a harmonious Romanesque revival building.

CHRISTIAN

ROMAN CATHOLIC CHURCHES

Most Catholics attend Mass near their home or office. But there are a few churches, which, for one reason or another, attract worshipers from beyond the parish confines. One of these may suit you.

- **Cathedral-Basilica of St. James**, 230 Cathedral Place (at Jay Street near Tillary Street), Brooklyn Heights 11201, 718-852-4005, was built in 1822 and restored in recent years to a Georgian brick elegance befitting its prominence. St. James is Brooklyn's cathedral, a bishop's church, but it is also a non-territorial parish, and is especially popular among young professionals in the area, for whom the daily business communion at 12:10 is a special convenience. Mass here is traditional, and the music quite wonderful.
- **Church of the Epiphany**, Second Avenue and 22nd Street, NYC 10010, 212-475-1966, is at once striking and modest, an unusually successful modern structure of rounded verticals in brown brick. It's a family church, with a traditional Mass at 11:15 a.m. and a popular family mass to guitar accompaniment at 10 a.m. But there's a difference, for one thing, altar girls. Nuns are involved in work traditionally done by priests, and women's issues are addressed. The church is popular with young professionals in the community, and there is a social action group.
- **Church of St. Agnes**, 141 East 43rd Street at Lexington Avenue, NYC 10017, 212-682-5722, convenient to Grand Central Station was once a family parish, then a bustling commuter church until it burned in 1992. But it remains a busy church with multiple daily Masses in the chapel of a former boys' high school at 158 East 44th Street at Lexington Avenue. St. Agnes will rise again, and it continues to be one of two churches in Manhattan offering a Latin Mass, Sundays at 10:30 a.m. (The other, less conveniently located, is St. Ann's Armenian Catholic Cathedral at 110 East 12th Street, 212-477-2030, where the Latin Mass is at 2 p.m. Saturdays.)
- **Church of St. Thomas More**, 65 East 89th Street between Park and Lexington avenues, NYC 10028, 212-876-7718; stone Victorian Gothic, was built as an Episcopal Church and still feels a bit like one, with its intimately peaceful, fragrant interior beneath a timbered ceiling. Ever so decorous. You can linger for coffee in the Rochester Room after 10 o'clock Mass.
- **Holy Trinity Chapel**, 58 Washington Square South, NYC 10012, 212-674-7236, is the Catholic chapel at New York University, but its congre-

gants are by no means all students. A moderately liberal intellectual approach and active social life attract a committed band of Catholics from the surrounding Village and beyond to this modest but appealing modern brick structure. Communicants run the Monday soup kitchen, deliver food to homebound AIDS victims, tutor and provide legal advice to the homeless. A women's group meets regularly, and there are sessions of silent Christian meditation.

- **St. Francis Xavier**, 46 West 16th Street, NYC 10011, 212-627-2100; this hulking, gray stone Jesuit presence dominates the block between Fifth and Sixth avenues. The style here is rather less formal than you might expect, perhaps because the congregation covers such a broad social spectrum: Hispanics, knowledgeable Catholic activists, and young professionals. Actively involved in the community, the church shelters the homeless and serves 1,000 meals a week. It's equally busy on the spiritual front, with lay spirituality group retreats, healing Masses, and discussion groups for a fiercely devoted following.

- **St. Ignatius Loyola**, Park Avenue at 84th Street, NYC 10028, 212-288-3588; this solidly limestone Italian Baroque structure is definitely high church and upscale: incense, ornate vestments, and a fine professional choir at the traditionally sung morning High Mass. But the rigorous Jesuit approach is apparent in a strongly social and economic outlook from the pulpit. At 11 a.m. you can attend a folk Mass in the undercroft (Wallace Hall) and linger over coffee. Young adults meet monthly in the Rectory. The church is also known for its series of formal musical programs featuring the fine choir and organist as well as visiting musicians.

- **St. John's**, 210 West 31st Street, NYC 10001, 212-564-9070, as a distinct sideline to its normal parish activities, is host to the Catholic charismatic movement in Manhattan. There are seminars, prayer meetings and a monthly charismatic Mass.

- **St. Joseph's**, 371 Avenue of the Americas at Washington Place, NYC 10014, 212-741-1274; in the heart of Greenwich Village, appeals to a variety of Catholics in the neighborhood and even outside the city. At once a bustling family church and an aesthetic experience, with professional musicians performing at formal, traditional Masses and at evening concerts. Distinctly high church. The lovely stone and stucco Greek Revival structure, resplendent inside with creamy plaster, crystal chandeliers and wide, carved balconies, is the oldest Catholic Church in the city (1833), and the first to open a shelter for homeless men.

- **St. Paul's Chapel** at Columbia University, 116th Street and Broadway, NYC 10027, 212-854-6242 (Catholic Campus Ministry Office), is an architecturally stunning Episcopal chapel but other denominations hold services here. The 5 p.m. Sunday Catholic Mass, with its modern liturgy, lay participation and challenging intellectual content, attracts communicants from beyond campus. In addition to the Sunday Mass while school is in session, there is a daily Mass at 12:15.

PROTESTANT CHURCHES

BAPTIST

- **Calvary**, 123 West 57th Street between Sixth and Seventh avenues, NYC 10019, 212-975-0170, across from Carnegie Hall, is probably the largest Baptist Church in Manhattan. You might begin a typical Sunday at the 9:30 Young Professionals' topical Bible study and fellowship, followed by traditional worship service at 11 a.m. along with some 1,400 other fellow Baptists, mostly young educated singles, and then coffee in Fellowship Hall downstairs. The Worship Team (singers) might perform at the 6 p.m. service. Young Adult Ministries offers occasional weekend retreats, and there are outreach programs to the prison population, the poor and welfare hotel children.

EPISCOPAL

- **Cathedral of St. John the Divine**, 1045 Amsterdam Avenue at 112th Street, NYC 10025, 212-316-7540, www.stjohndivine.org, dwarfs its rather shabby surroundings even as it awaits completion of its stone towers. The largest cathedral in the world, at once Byzantine, Romanesque, and Gothic, it is truly awesome, especially inside, where spectacular stained glass windows light the vast dark vaults and music echoes ethereally. It is also a bustling and exciting community church, a leader in the movement to feed and house the poor. And the performing arts flourish here almost around the clock.
- **Church of the Ascension**, 36 Fifth Avenue at 10th Street, NYC 10011, 212-254-8620; its communicants find this church especially pleasing aesthetically. A LaFarge altar fresco and a St. Gaudens altar relief enliven the quietly tasteful interior, and liturgical music of the highest quality is performed by an exceptional choir Sundays and at special evening concerts.
- **Church of the Heavenly Rest**, 2 East 90th Street at Fifth Avenue, NYC 10128, 212-289-3400, sits confidently but un-ostentatiously— stripped contemporary Gothic in pale gray stone—facing Central Park. It's an upscale, neighborhood family church, where the congregants linger casually for coffee after the morning service while the children play decorously about the door.
- **Grace Church**, 802 Broadway at East 10th Street, NYC 10003, 212-254-2000, www.graceinny@aol.com, despite its rather patrician, lacy English Gothic elegance, is relatively low church. Worship is traditional, however, with wonderful music, especially on holy days. The congrega-

tion runs to young families and a variety of artists. Pastoral counseling is available as well as adult classes on a variety of topics, and there are outreach groups to college students and AIDS victims, programs for children and families, and a thrice-yearly Alpha Course, a 10-week introduction to Christianity.

- **St. Bartholomew's**, Park Avenue at 51st Street, NYC 10022, 212-378-0200, www.stbarts.com; this landmarked Romanesque-Byzantine church houses a friendly, welcoming community numbering about 1,000 worshipers each Sunday. Lay participation in all aspects of church life is encouraged. Sundays feature a stimulating Rector's Forum and Sunday School, in addition to several services, and Bible studies are offered during the week. Several adult social clubs offer a wide variety of social, athletic and theatrical activities, among them St. Bart's Players, "the longest running off-Broadway theater group in the city." Communicants and non-members alike volunteer at the homeless shelter and the feeding program operated by the church.
- **St. James'**, 865 Madison Avenue at 71st Street, NYC 10021, 212-774-4200; distinctly Upper East Side, this trim brownstone is a warm, neighborhood family church which is also decidedly activist in the community and beyond: feeding, mentoring, supporting, and sometimes even demonstrating. Despite its rather liberal bent, St. James' is moderately high church. Its education programs for adults and children are worthy of note.

LATTER-DAY SAINTS/MORMON

- **The Church of Jesus Christ of Latter-Day Saints** (the Mormon church) in Manhattan, is located at 125 Columbus Avenue at 65th Street (across from Lincoln Center), 212-724-0539 or 212-799-6090; several different congregations (called "wards" and "branches") conduct worship services every Sunday in three-hour blocks, beginning at 9 a.m. These include two English-speaking "family" wards, one English-speaking ward for single adults, two Spanish-speaking wards, and one deaf branch. Also, each congregation offers social and musical activities during the week.

LUTHERAN

- **Holy Trinity**, Central Park West at 65th Street, NYC 10023, 212-877-6815, www.holytrinitynyc.org, offers challenging preaching at traditional, rigorously Lutheran services. But it is music, at the regular services and at the Sunday vespers featuring Bach cantatas with professional musicians, for which Holy Trinity is widely known. The sturdy

Gothic revival church is the setting for frequent evening concerts as well.

- **St. Peter's**, 619 Lexington Avenue at 54th Street, NYC 10022, 212-935-2200, www.stpeters.org, nestles, sleek and angular like a modern stone tent, beneath the towering Citicorp Center. A large Louise Nevelson sculpture punctuates the stark, light interior, scene of a sung Mass with traditional liturgy in the morning and Jazz Vespers with jazz as the sermon Sunday afternoons. Classical and jazz concerts, often free, theater and provocative adult-forum lectures attract an ecumenical following, to say the least.

METHODIST

- **Christ Church**, 520 Park Avenue at 60th Street, NYC 10021, 212-838-3036, is sedately Byzantine outside, dazzlingly so inside, every inch covered with mosaics in blazing blues, greens and gold. It's a wonderful setting for the religious music-dramas occasionally performed here. The congregation, though relatively small, supports a weekly soup kitchen and excellent pastoral counseling.
- **John Street**, 44 John Street between Broadway and William Street, NYC 10038, 212-269-0014; to step into this landmarked little Italianate brownstone church (1841) among the towering monoliths of the financial district is to step out of place and time into a peaceful haven of creamy modest proportions and brass sconces. It's the oldest Methodist society in the US, and few know about it. Inquire about the occasional Wednesday noon hymn-sings.
- **Park Avenue**, 106 East 86th Street, NYC 10028, 212-427-5421, www.parkavemethodist.org; a mixed and growing congregation, mostly young families and singles, is attracted by the moderately liberal approach and active social scene at this smallish, restfully intimate, Moorish-looking church. Adult Bible study precedes and a coffee hour follows the traditional Sunday service with volunteer choir. Weekday activities include a Tuesday evening gathering for informal sharing and a Wednesday evening service of prayer and meditation. An adult fellowship group organizes social activities.

PRESBYTERIAN

- **Brick Church**, Park Avenue at 91st Street, NYC 10128, 212-289-4400; staid neo-Georgian with a rather ornate interior, is distinctly Park Avenue. But the welcome is friendly, including a popular coffee hour after the Sunday service. Adult Bible study Tuesday mornings and "Mid-Week at Brick" religious studies Wednesday evenings are intellectually meaty. The church's day school is prestigious.

- **Fifth Avenue**, Fifth Avenue at 55th Street, NYC 10019, 212-247-0490, www.fapc.org; the city's largest Presbyterian Church has a warm, woody interior behind its otherwise undistinguished brownstone facade. A variety of social adult fellowship groups attract large numbers of youngish adults to the traditional services. Activities of these groups include Sunday night church suppers, after-church brunch, movies, and ski retreats, as well as monthly dinner meetings with outside speakers at the Women's Roundtable for business women and the Men's Fellowship. The church's Center for Christian Studies offers challenging five-week courses with outside lecturers on several levels of Christian thought. Fees are minimal, and non-members are welcome.
- **Madison Avenue**, 921 Madison Avenue at 73rd Street, NYC 10021, 212-288-8920, www.mapc.com, has a cozy, Scottish feel, with its Gothic-timbered white walls, carved pews and galleries. The music program is strong, including a volunteer choir and frequent Sunday afternoon concerts. The adult education program at 10 a.m. is sandwiched between the two Sunday services. A young adult fellowship group meets regularly for Bible study, discussion, and socializing.
- **Redeemer**, church office at 271 Madison Avenue, Suite 1600, NYC 10016, 212-808-4460; this recently organized and rapidly growing congregation of the PCA holds two Sunday services in the Hunter College Auditorium, 69th Street between Park and Lexington avenues. The scripture-based emphasis is on preaching, which is intellectually engaging, and there is an array of spiritual, social, and outreach activities.

UNITARIAN

- **All Souls**, 1157 Lexington Avenue at 80th Street, NYC 10021, 212-535-5530, www.allsoulsnyc.org; New England simple and elegant, this Federal-style brick church looks Unitarian. As might be expected here, the busy church calendar tends toward activism on a variety of fronts and a fairly intellectual approach to adult education, which features book groups, films, and lectures. Music is stressed. Social activities are many and varied, including a Career Networking Group.

INTERDENOMINATIONAL

- **Judson Memorial** (Baptist-United Church of Christ), 55 Washington Square South, NYC 10012, 212-477-0351; worldly young adults and seminarians are attracted to this ornate Romanesque church designed by Stanford White and its fairly traditional Protestant liturgy with progressive elements, including a monthly Agape Meal. There is a consumer health library and support for AIDS victims.

- **Riverside**, 490 Riverside Drive at 120th Street, NYC 10027, 212-870-6700, www.riversidechurchny.org; this towering Gothic gift of John D. Rockefeller, Jr. dominates the heights overlooking the Hudson River. Inspired by Chartres, it boasts spectacular stained glass and beautifully carved stone in the large but simple nave and chancel and about the entrance. Activist concerns under the leadership of the Rev. Dr. James Forbes, Jr. are dizzying, as are the opportunities for involvement in activities musical, intellectual and social, not to mention spiritual.
- **Chelsea Community Church**, 346 West 20th Street, NYC 10011, 212-886-5463, is a non-denominational Christian church welcoming "persons of all faiths and of uncertain faith" at its lay-led Sunday services at 11:45 a.m. in historic St. Peter's Church.

HINDU

- **Ramakrishna Vivekananda Center**, 17 East 94th Street, NYC 10128, 212-534-9445, www.ramakrishna.org, is a Vedanta Hindu Temple of universal worship with a Sunday lecture service at 11 a.m. Tuesday evenings at 8 are devoted to the reading and discussion of the gospel of Sri Ramakrishna; Thursday at 8 there is a more formal scripture class.
- **Vedanta Society**, 34 West 71st Street, NYC 10023, 212-877-9197, is affiliated with the Ramakrishna Math and Mission in India. The shrine room is open for meditation daily from 9 a.m. to 6 p.m. There is a lecture Sunday at 11 a.m. and classes Tuesday and Friday evenings at 8 p.m. Devotional sings are held Saturday and Sunday at 6 p.m.

ISLAM

MOSQUES

- **The Mosque of New York**, in the Islamic Cultural Center, 1711 Third Avenue, NYC 10029, 212-722-5234; this imposing structure, the gift of a group of Islamic countries, houses the largest of some 80 mosques in the city. The design is modern, with numerous references to traditional elements of Muslim architecture. The effect is at once peaceful and spiritual. In addition to the weekly congregational prayer service, the Mosque is open for daily prayer at the five prescribed times. Classes for children and adults, held Saturdays from 11 a.m. to 1 p.m. and Sundays from 10 a.m. to 1 p.m., cover a range of Islamic topics. There are Saturday classes for women only.
- **The Muslim Center of New York**, 137-58 Geranium Avenue off Kissena Boulevard, Flushing, NY 11355, 718-460-3000, serves the

growing Muslim community in Queens and Long Island. In a modest neighborhood an octagonal minaret rises from the polished rose quartz structure. Congregational prayers Friday at 1:15 p.m. are followed by Koranic studies. There is a Sunday school and afternoon religious school for children weekdays. Call for hours.

JEWISH

REFORM SYNAGOGUES

- **Brooklyn Heights Synagogue**, 131 Remsen Street, Brooklyn 11201, 718-522-2070, moved up the street from its brownstone home of 20 years to the larger brownstone formerly housing the Brooklyn Club, in order to accommodate its after-school religious school for children and extensive adult education classes. Services here are characterized by a greater use of Hebrew and more congregational singing than is generally found in reform synagogues. The warmth and friendliness of this relatively small (some 260 families) congregation and their purposeful inclusiveness makes this a particularly appealing synagogue for newcomers. Congregants come from all the boroughs, and their numbers swell sufficiently on the high holy days that these services are held in the (Protestant) Plymouth Church nearby.
- **Central**, 123 East 55th Street, NYC 10022, 212-838-5122, is the oldest Jewish house of worship (1872) in continuous use in New York. The Moorish brownstone structure with its interior richly stenciled in red, blue, and gold suffered extensive damage from a fire in 1998. While restoration proceeded, services were held across the street in the Community House Beir Chapel. Services resumed in the reconstructed synagogue in the fall of 2001. Traditional in orientation and ritual, the temple tends to the manifold interests, worldly as well as spiritual, of its 1,400-member congregation in groups and classes ranging from Hebrew and Yiddish to Bible to bridge, teens' and singles' groups, and 7:30 a.m. Central Women's Focus speakers for working women.
- **Temple Emanu-El**, 1 East 65th Street, corner of Fifth Avenue, NYC 10021, 212-744-1400, is perhaps a little less traditional, nevertheless classical Reform in approach, and it is the largest Reform temple in the US, with over 3,000 members. The landmarked limestone Moorish-Romanesque temple facing Central Park seats 2,500 beneath a high, colorfully painted wood ceiling and stunning stained glass windows. The temple has a large staff to run its many facilities, classes and community outreach programs, as well as a large religious school. Services are broadcast every Friday evening at 5:30 over WQXR (1560 AM, 96.3 FM).

CONSERVATIVE SYNAGOGUES

- **Ansche Chesed**, 251 West 100th Street at West End Avenue, NYC 10025, 212-865-9588, houses four separate congregations, each with a different approach to Conservative Judaism, in one medium-sized, squat, brick building. Alternatives within a framework of Jewish tradition are stressed at this much-talked-about West Side synagogue, which offers an adult beginners' service, courses on a wide range of Jewish topics, and social action projects aiding elderly Jews.
- **Baith Israel Anschei Emes/Kane Street**, 236 Kane Street at Tompkins Place in Cobble Hill, Brooklyn 11231, 718-875-1550, has grown considerably in recent years, partly, perhaps, because of the emphasis on egalitarianism in its observances. Vibrant and involved, with challenging study groups, it is regularly packed with congregants, mainly young, from Cobble Hill and nearby Brooklyn Heights.
- **B'Nai Jeshurun**, 257 West 88th Street between Broadway and West End Avenue, NYC 10024, 212-787-7600; under the charismatic leadership of the late Rabbi Marshall Meyer, "BJ," as it is affectionately known, bursts its ornately Byzantine/Romanesque seams. Successor rabbis, his former students, continue to hold traditionally musical services in the larger Methodist Church of St. Paul and St. Andrew, 86th Street and West End Avenue, as well as in the more intimate, richly colorful home temple. Emphasis is on study, with a wide variety of adult courses and lectures as well as a Hebrew school for children. And the diverse congregation thinks of itself as a community, with a strong commitment to social action, *Tikkun Olam*, in the wider Jewish and non-Jewish community beyond. Plan to come early for services, which tend to fill up fast; non-members will want to call about high holy days.
- **Brotherhood**, 28 Gramercy Park South, NYC 10003, 212-674-5750, occupies a landmarked (1859) Friends' Meeting House, starkly beautiful in Italianate brownstone and overlooking lovely Gramercy Park. About its courtyards are housed a shelter for the homeless, a religious school, adult education, an educational program for the developmentally disabled, and facilities to aid Jewish immigrants.
- **Park Avenue**, 50 East 87th Street at Madison Avenue, NYC 10128, 212-369-2600, is the city's largest Conservative temple and an East Side Moorish landmark in carved golden stone. The rich interior boasts fine stained glass, sculpture and paintings, and the traditional services are distinctly formal, with organ and choir. There are many programs for children, singles, young marrieds and seniors, and a food pantry for the neighborhood's hungry.
- **Shaare Zedek**, 212 West 93rd Street between Broadway and Amsterdam

Avenue, NYC 10025, 212-874-7005; this congregation, founded 160 years ago on the Lower East Side and housed now in a gray stone Greek revival temple, has experienced a revival in the mid-1990s with an infusion of college students and young professionals. Friday evening services, usually downstairs in the social halls, can be especially busy, and once a month there is a post-worship dinner. Bridge Club, occasional seders, and special events fill out the social calendar.

- **Tifereth Israel/Town and Village**, 334 East 14th Street between First and Second avenues, NYC 10003, 212-677-8090, stresses sexual egalitarianism in its informally innovative, traditional services and attracts an involved family congregation, largely from the adjacent community, including Stuyvesant Town and Peter Cooper Village. Adult education and a young marrieds group are popular. The Sol Goldman YW-YMHA of the Educational Alliance next door, with whom it shares a Hebrew school, offers members the advantages of a social center with pool, gym, and classes.

- **United Synagogue of Hoboken**, 830 Hudson Street at Ninth, Hoboken 07030, 201-659-4000, is one congregation with two temples, the other being at 115 Park Avenue, a tan brick structure with copper onion domes. Friday evening and Sabbath services are in the converted Victorian brownstone Hudson Street temple, the last of many serving the predominantly German Jewish community here at the turn of the century. The small but growing egalitarian congregation is youngish and welcoming. Extensive adult education courses include Hebrew reading and Jewish history, a Hebrew discussion group, a book club, Jewish women's and men's discussion groups, karate, adult bar and bat mitzvah instruction. There is also a Hebrew school for children.

ORTHODOX SYNAGOGUES

- **Civic Center**, 49 White Street west of Broadway, NYC 10013, 212-966-7141, occupies a small, award-winning, modern structure scrunched among cast iron manufacturing lofts and loading docks. Its flame-shaped interior houses a membership of about 100 families with about 1,000 supporters, including elderly members of long standing as well as artists and young professionals from surrounding Tribeca, Independence Plaza, and Battery Park. There are both Hebrew and adult education classes, as well as parenting sessions conducted by Educational Alliance West.

- **Kehilath Jeshurun**, 125 East 85th Street between Lexington and Park Avenues, NYC 10028, 212-774-8000; though old and rich and housed in classical Romanesque gray stone, this is probably the most progressive of the Orthodox congregations. Its size makes possible a host of activities for singles, couples, and children, recreational facilities, and an educational program including the Ramaz School and "Lunch and Learn" classes. Emphasis is placed on outreach to beginners and singles, with classes, special services and Friday night dinners for them.

- **Shearith Israel**, 8 West 70th Street at Central Park West, NYC 10023, 212-873-0300, known as the Spanish and Portuguese synagogue, is the oldest Jewish congregation in the US, dating from 1655, when a group of Sephardic Jews arrived from Brazil. In the formal sanctuary scholarly rabbis conduct very formal services, which offer the best opportunity to observe Sephardic tradition and music. Excellent adult education explores Sephardic and Ashkenazic culture and tradition, with visiting scholars leading seminars. There are special educational and social events for young adults.

- **Lincoln Square**, 200 Amsterdam Avenue at 69th Street, NYC 10023, 212-874-6100, sometimes referred to as "the hip synagogue," might be described physically as synagogue-modern. Its nickname and popularity among the young professionals who pack four Saturday services is due in large part to the charm and zealous outreach efforts of Rabbi Ephraim Buchwald, who hosts the 9:15 "Learners' Minyan," which is followed by wine and cookies and, if you like, lunch with an experienced family. There are courses at all levels on Jewish law and thought as well as singles and youth groups.

OTHER

- **Society for the Advancement of Judaism**, 15 West 86th Street off Central Park West, NYC 10024, 212-724-7000; known as the SAJ, this is the original Reconstructionist synagogue. Reconstructionism, which attempts to reconcile traditional Conservatism with modern life, views Judaism as evolving rather than divinely inspired. The Torah is observed, and services are largely traditional but egalitarian. The approach here is distinctly intellectual, not social.

- **West End**, 190 Amsterdam Avenue at 69th Street, NYC 10023, 212-579-0777, is a popular Reconstructionist congregation flourishing with a slightly more emotional, interpersonal emphasis and monthly Shabbat dinners as well as concerts, debates, and social action programs.

- **Young Israel of Fifth Avenue**, 3 West 16th Street at Fifth Avenue, NYC 10011, 212-255-4826, is one of three such temples in Manhattan. Young Israel can be defined as modern Orthodoxy, observing all the Orthodox forms, including separate seating of the sexes, but emphasizing programs serving the entire family. This includes communal singing and participation, youth and singles programs, outreach, adult education, and attention to community needs.

- **Congregation Beth Simchat Torah**, 57 Bethune Street in the Westbeth complex, NYC 10014, 212-929-9498; with some 800 members the largest gay and lesbian Jewish congregation in the world, celebrated its 25th anniversary in 1999. The rabbi is Reconstructionist, the community liberal and the services traditional, with egalitarian minyans rotating between traditional, liberal, tot shabat, junior congregation, family minyan, and Hebrew egalitarian Saturdays at 10 a.m. Friday evening services at 8:30 are so heavily attended the congregation moves to the Church of the Holy Apostles on Ninth Avenue at 28th Street. For High Holidays it moves to the Javits Center, where some 3,000 or more come to pray.

DESPITE THE CITY'S RAPID PACE AND ANONYMITY, OR PERHAPS because of it, New Yorkers by the thousands volunteer their services to hundreds of worthy causes. Motivations are as varied as the tasks. So are the rewards.

A mind-boggling array of public, private, and non-profit organizations will gladly put to use whatever talents or interests you have. Experience is not necessarily required; most institutions provide training. What kinds of jobs are available where? Read on. We've also listed the names of agencies that refer volunteers to other organizations and included a few alternative suggestions as well.

HOW YOU CAN HELP

THE HUNGRY AND THE HOMELESS

Scores of volunteers concern themselves with shelter for the city's homeless. Jobs include: monitoring and organizing the shelters, providing legal help, ministering to psychiatric, medical, and social needs, raising money, manning phones, and caring for children in the shelters. Many people solicit, organize, cook, and serve food to the destitute at sites throughout the city. Still others deliver meals to the homeless and the homebound.

CHILDREN

If involvement with children is especially appealing you can: tutor in and out of schools, cuddle a foundling, be a big brother or sister, teach music and sports in shelters, parks, and hospitals, and accompany kids on weekend outings.

HOSPITALS

The need for volunteers in both city-run and private hospitals is manifold: chaplain's aides, interpreters, laboratory personnel, admitting and nursing aides are required; assistants in crisis medical areas—emergency rooms, intensive care units and the like—are wanted; so are ambulance drivers, and volunteers to work with victims of sexual abuse.

THE DISABLED AND THE ELDERLY

You can read to the blind, help teach the deaf, work to prevent birth defects, help the retarded and developmentally disabled, among others. You can also make regular visits to the homebound elderly, deliver them hot meals, and teach everything from nutrition to arts and crafts in senior centers and nursing homes.

EXTREME CARE SITUATIONS

Helping with cancer, suicide prevention, Alzheimer's and AIDS patients, rape victims, and abused children is a special category demanding a high level of commitment—not to mention emotional reserves.

THE CULTURE SCENE

Unpaid stamp-lickers and benefit chairmen keep the city's cultural institutions afloat. Consider guiding tours, raising funds or assisting the staff at your favorite museum, library or ballet company.

THE COMMUNITY

Work in your neighborhood. Block associations and community gardens are run strictly by volunteers. You can help out at the local school, nursing home, settlement house or animal shelter.

WHERE YOU CAN HELP

SPECIFIC-NEED ORGANIZATIONS

The organizations in New York City that address a major disease, disability or social problem are legion. For example, there's the Memorial Sloan-Kettering Cancer Center, The Coalition for the Homeless, Volunteer Services for Children, New York Association for the Blind (The Lighthouse),

Literacy Volunteers of New York, Volunteers in the Schools, the Gay Men's Health Alliance, Women in Need, and City Harvest, which collects and distributes food to the hungry.

INSTITUTIONS

New York's health, education and, some would say, its very civilization rest upon the city's institutions. Hospitals, museums, libraries, schools, animal shelters, opera and ballet companies are mostly under-funded and rely on a veritable army of volunteers to survive.

THE RELIGIOUS CONNECTION

Individual churches and synagogues (in particular, those serving the homeless and the needy), and church federations such as the Federation of Protestant Welfare Agencies, the Catholic Charities, and the UJA-Federation of Jewish Philanthropies use volunteers for a variety of activities.

THE COMMUNITY

More than 5,000 block associations and neighborhood-wide organizations, such as Greenwich House in the Village and Yorkville's Civic Council, can use your talents. Citywide there is a need for volunteers in the schools, parks, shelters, and in consumer affairs.

MULTI-SERVICE ORGANIZATIONS

Don't forget such well-known groups as the Salvation Army, American Red Cross and the Visiting Nurse Service (which is not just nurses).

THE CORPORATE CONNECTION

Corporations encourage employee voluntarism through company-supported projects such as literacy programs, pro-bono work, and management aid to non-profit groups. Check with the company personnel or public relations department to see if your firm is involved in any specific project. Many corporations have set up programs with the help of Corporation Volunteers of New York, 17 John Street, NYC 10007, 212-696-2442.

REFERRAL SERVICES

If you don't know which way to turn, try one of several umbrella organizations that find volunteers for affiliated agencies. At these referral services, staff members will help you determine the tasks you would be interested in doing, where and when. Your interviewer will make specific suggestions and appointments at the places that sound appealing. Interview at several sites if you wish, and return to the referral agency until you find something you want to undertake.

- **Catholic Charities of New York**, 1011 First Avenue, 212-371-1000, are affiliated with more than 100 different agencies dealing with shelters, food kitchens and the homeless. An interview may be requested.
- **The Federation of Protestant Welfare Agencies**, 281 Park Avenue South, 212-777-4800, open 8:30 a.m. to 6 p.m., Monday-Friday. This ecumenical group, with connections to some 800 agencies in the metropolitan area, finds jobs for volunteers of any religious persuasion.
- **The Mayor's Voluntary Action Center**, 49-51 Chambers Street, NYC 10007, 12th floor, 212-788-7550, open 9 a.m. to 5 p.m., Monday-Friday, to 7 p.m. Wednesday. The city's largest referral agency has 5,000 volunteer job openings in some 3,000 public and private non-profit organizations. This enormous clearing-house can place just about anyone in a useful job, especially in the human services, educational and cultural areas.
- **New York Cares**, 116 East 16th Street, NYC 10011, 212-228-5000, www.ny.cares.org, is a favorite volunteer organization among busy young professionals who are discouraged by the time commitments required by other organizations. New York Cares lets its 8,000 volunteers choose from a monthly calendar of events set up with the more than fifty not-for-profit organizations they serve. These projects include reading with homeless children, serving brunch at soup kitchens, cleaning public parks and visiting elderly homebound. Call to attend one of two weekly orientation meetings.
- **The United Jewish Appeal-Federation of Jewish Philanthropies**, 130 East 59th Street, NYC 10022, 212-980-1000, open 9 a.m. to 5 p.m., Monday-Friday. The Jewish Information Referral Service sends callers a catalog describing nearly 200 agencies and projects. Programs include revitalizing old neighborhoods and synagogues as well as working with children, immigrants, the elderly and the homeless.
- **The Volunteer Referral Center**, 161 Madison Avenue, NYC 10016, 212-889-4805, interviews by appointment, 11 a.m. to 3 p.m., Tuesday-Thursday, and 5:30 p.m. to 7 p.m. Tuesday and Wednesday. The Center can place adult and student volunteers at some 350 not-for-profit agencies throughout Manhattan.

OTHER CONNECTIONS

- Check bulletin boards at your office, church, neighborhood grocery store, Laundromat and school.

- **WBAI-FM** (99.5 FM) discusses, and occasionally stimulates, volunteer projects, especially those involving the homeless and the hungry.
- **The Yellow Pages**, under "Social and Human Services," contains more than five pages of organizations and institutions—in categories from Abortion Alternatives Counseling to Youth Services—many of which welcome volunteers. It's a great source of ideas, as well as a tool for follow-through.
- **www.volunteermatch.org**, offers a searchable database of volunteer options for the undecided.
- *Volunteering in New York City* by Richard Mintzer is a useful reference. Published by Walker & Company.

GETTING AROUND

BY SUBWAY

The subway is still the quickest way to get around New York City. All city subway lines are administered by the New York City Transit Authority, and recently they've been considerably improved. Subway crime is down, the graffiti plague has been all but eradicated, and many stations have been handsomely renovated. In 1999 commuters welcomed the opening of Grand Central North, an underground extension from Manhattan's Grand Central Terminal, which allows commuters to enter and exit as far north as 48th Street. In fact, Grand Central is once again an elegant destination in itself, with fine dining, boutique shopping and gourmet food shops worth a detour.

For train information call 718-330-1234 or stop by one of the Authority's Information Booths, open from 7 a.m. to 11 p.m. at Pennsylvania or Grand Central Station. Subway and bus maps for all five boroughs are readily available there. In theory, token booths at the subway stops also distribute maps, but in practice they are often out of stock. Alternatively, the excellent Metropolitan Transit Authority web site, www.mta.nyc.ny.us, offers a complete subway map as well as information on local bridges and tunnels and more.

Subway/bus tokens cost $1.50 at this writing, but the **MetroCard** is the way to go. The plastic debit card, available at token booths and machines (accepting cash, credit and debit cards) in subway stations for $3 or $15 and up, can be used in all stations and on all city buses; you can also order the card in any denomination online at www.metrocard.citysearch.com. Swipe it through the turnstile slot, and one fare is subtracted. When the card is empty it can be refilled by up to $80 and is good for one year. Pay $15, and you get a free ride—11 on the card instead of 10. Seniors and persons with disabilities are eligible for half-fare cards (call 212-878-7294). Two-zone transfers means riders with the MetroCard can move from subway to a bus (and vice versa) without paying another fare.

Delis and convenience stores all over the city sell a $4 MetroCard **Fun Pass**, good for unlimited travel all one day until 3 a.m., handy if you're escorting Uncle Ezra around town on a visit. These are not sold in subway booths. However, they do sell cards good for unlimited travel for one week at $17, for a month at $63, and for Express Bus/subway for one month at $120. Express Buses connecting Manhattan to the other boroughs cost $3 a ride.

Children under 44 inches in height travel free. School children are issued free passes if they attend a public or private school that is a specified distance from their home.

Subway trains operate 24-hours a day, but service slows appreciably after 11 p.m., when it is generally best to take a cab or bus anyway. Subway entrances with red lights have no token booths; avoid them.

For your immediate reference we have provided a subway map at the back of this book.

BY PATH

The PATH (for Port Authority Trans-Hudson) tubes provide clean and efficient service connecting Manhattan with Hoboken, Jersey City, and Newark for $1.50 around the clock. Trains leaving 33rd Street at Avenue of the Americas (Sixth Avenue) go to Hoboken or Jersey City, with stops along the way at 23rd, 14th, 9th and Christopher streets. From the World Trade Center in Lower Manhattan trains leave for Hoboken and for Newark by way of Jersey City. Schedules are available in most stations, or call 800-234-7284.

BY BUS

Independent bus lines found mainly in boroughs other than Manhattan co-exist with those run by the New York City Transit Authority. Call 718-330-1234 for Transit Authority information as well as telephone numbers for the independents. Also, you can now get up to date NYC Transit information on the MTA web site: www.mta.nyc.ny.us.

Maps are sometimes available from drivers but are always stocked at the Information Booths mentioned under **Subways** above.

Buses cost $1.50. Transfers to other buses or subway trains are free. Exact change is required for buses, but the MetroCard and tokens are also accepted.

BY FERRY

Time was, before the advent of the auto, when some 125 passenger-boats plied 50 different routes across the Hudson and East rivers. With the closing of the Hoboken Ferry in 1967, only the Staten Island Ferry remained, both a commuter necessity for Staten Islanders and an excursion delight for Manhattanites and tourists alike.

The water commute is once again a reality on more than a dozen privately operated routes connecting Manhattan with New Jersey, Brooklyn, and Queens. And the Hoboken Ferry is back, faster than ever and landing this time at a floating terminal with a canvas marquee at the World Financial Center in Battery Park City. The new ferries cruise at 35 miles per hour, twice as fast as the Staten Island Ferry. In increasing numbers commuters are choosing this alternative to traffic gridlock, exorbitant parking fees and expressway dementia, especially during the oppressive heat of summer. As more passengers take to the water, increased service comes on line.

- **Staten Island Ferry**, is free, and definitely New York's best deal in transportation (and entertainment). It leaves the South Ferry Terminal at Whitehall in Battery Park for St. George, Staten Island, every half hour between 6:30 a.m. and 11:30 p.m., and every hour between 11:30 p.m. and 6:30 a.m. Car service runs between 6 a.m. and 11 p.m. and costs $3. Call 718-815-2628 for information.
- **Mariners Harbor/Bayonne Ferry**, operated weekdays by Harbor Shuttle, 888-254-RIDE, departs from Mariners Harbor, Staten Island and from Brady's Dock at East First Avenue, Bayonne, NJ, hourly between 6 and 8 a.m., and between 4:30 and 7:30 p.m. in return. Arrival is at Pier 11 on the East River at Wall Street. The fare is $5.
- **New Jersey passenger ferries** are dominated now by NY Waterway, 800-533-3779, www.nywaterway.com, which operates the Hoboken Ferry, running weekdays every 5 minutes during rush hours between 6:15 a.m. and 10 p.m., every 15 minutes off peak. The fare is $2 each way. Service is every half-hour on weekends, 10 a.m. to 10 p.m., with a stop at Jersey City.

The firm also operates service between Port Imperial, Weehawken, and Pier 78 at 38th Street and Twelfth Avenue and to Whitehall next to the Staten Island Ferry in Battery Park. Boats run every 15 minutes from 6:45 a.m. to midnight, Friday and Saturday from 8 a.m. to 1 a.m., Sunday 9 a.m. to midnight. The five-minute ride costs $5 each way to midtown and $6 to Whitehall, including mini-bus service in Manhattan. Parking on the Jersey side is extra ($6 per day).

Their weekday ferry between the World Financial Center and Exchange Place and Harborside in Jersey City runs every 15 minutes between 6 a.m. and 11:45 p.m. The five-minute ride costs $4 round trip. Weekends, the ferry travels a triangular route from Hoboken to Jersey City to the World Financial Center and back to Hoboken, same fare. Weekday ferries from Port Liberte to Wall Street are less frequent and cost $5.

- **Seastreak** operates commuter ferries from Highlands and Atlantic Highlands, NJ, to Pier 11 at the foot of Wall Street and to 34th Street on the East River. Hours are weekdays between 5:30 a.m. and 9:30 p.m. for $19 to $32 round trip, depending on the time, and weekends 9:30 a.m. to 5:30 p.m. for $22 round trip; 12-minute service between the Brooklyn Army Terminal and Wall Street daily, 6:45 a.m. to 6:50 p.m. costs $5 one way. Call 800-B-O-A-T-R-I-D-E or go to www.seastreakusa.com for schedules.
- **Yankee Clipper and Mets Express**, operated by NY Waterway, 800-53-FERRY, departs Weehawken, South Street Seaport, East 34th Street, and East 90th Street for night games at Yankee Stadium and Shea Stadium respectively, Monday-Friday and for weekend day games. Round trip costs $14 from any point to either stadium.

BY BIKE

As street surfaces have improved and auto traffic has thickened to a near standstill, New Yorkers in increasing numbers are mounting bicycles as a means of city transportation. Just how many no one really knows because bicycles are not registered in the city. The virtues of the bicycle are obvious: speed and economy. The down side? Vulnerability in city traffic: 35 bikers were killed on city streets in 1999, and more were seriously injured. Besides alert, defensive riding, there are precautions which will improve the bicyclist's odds: be visible, ride on the right when there are no bike lanes, don't weave in traffic, use hand signals, watch for drivers exiting from parked cars—a car door opening into a bike's path can be lethal—and always wear a helmet!

Many of the **city laws** governing bicyclists also contribute to their safety:
- Bicycles are allowed on all city streets, but not on highways unless signs permit.
- Always ride with traffic and never on sidewalks.
- Traffic rules apply to bicycles as well as to cars. Riders must use hand signals.
- Bicycles must use bike lanes where they are provided.
- Bicycles must be equipped with a bell or horn, brakes, a headlight and taillight.
- Accidents resulting in injury must be reported to the police.
- A rider may not wear more than one earphone to an audio player.

Bicycles are permitted on subways, but a few gates limit entry/exit. MetroNorth and the Long Island Railroad require one-time purchase of a $5 permit to carry a bike on a train, except during rush hours and on weekends, when they are not allowed. Call the Transit Authority at 212-532-4900 or go to Window 27 in Grand Central Station to purchase a permit. Call the LIRR at 718-558-8228 for their permit. Jersey Transit requires no permit on its trains, but bicycles are not allowed during rush hours and on weekends. The same rules apply on the PATH tubes.

There are 107.5 miles of bike lanes in the city streets and 75 miles of greenway. Cycling maps for the five boroughs are available at the Department of City Planning, 22 Reade Street, NYC 10007-1216, 212-720-3300, and online at www.nyc.gov. City biking laws and safe riding tips are outlined on the city's Department of Transportation page, www.ci.nyc.ny.us.

Transportation Alternatives, 115 West 30th Street, 12th floor, 212-629-8080, is a member-supported non-profit citizens' group for the promotion of biking, hiking, and public transportation. Their encyclopedic web site, www.transalt.org, provides up-to-date news of interest to bikers and hikers, links to biking organizations in the metropolitan area, lists of shops offering discounts to members and information on the annual September Bike Tour, as well as other tour rides which they sponsor. Where to buy a used bike after your mountain bike was stolen, a heavy lock, and the wall rack to hang it on in your cramped studio? Look here first.

For more concerning biking in the city, see **Bicycling** in the **Sports and Recreation** chapter.

BY CAR

For the most part New Yorkers don't get around the city by car, except when they're in a cab. Why? Because on-street parking is so limited and off-street parking so expensive. So what are all those cars causing the periodic gridlock? Cabs, car services, and we did say "for the most part?" Some suburbanites even commute to the city by car, despite the availability of mass transit. Those living in the city may own a car or rent a car occasionally. Those in the suburbs certainly own at least one car and may drive into the city now and then. We'll continue with a few things you need to know about driving in and out of the city. (See also **Parking**, **Auto Services and Repair**, and **Traffic Tickets and Towing** in the chapter **Getting Settled**.)

New York drivers are aggressive, cabbies especially. Get used to it, but it is not a required trait. New York pedestrians do not follow the rules: they cross against the light and mid-block when they feel like it; watch out for them. Gridlock is a way of life here, at least occasionally. "Don't block the box," means don't enter the intersection unless you are sure you can cross it before the light changes. Failure to heed this command causes gridlock and can cost you points on your license. If you can, avoid entering or leaving the city during rush hour traffic (roughly 7 to 10 a.m. and 4 to 7 p.m.). Friday and Sunday evenings are especially bad.

Because of the logical street grid covering most of the island and because traffic is so slow, driving in Manhattan is easier than you might think. The north-south avenues for the most part are one-way, generally in an alternating pattern: hence, First Avenue runs uptown, and Second Avenue runs downtown. But Park Avenue is two-way. The east-west streets for the most part are one way, with the even-numbered streets running east (remember, even-east), and odd-numbered streets running west, the exceptions being major cross-town streets: Houston, 14th, 23rd, 34th, 42nd, and 57th streets, for example, which are two-way. For driving in the other boroughs you'll need a map: AAA members get them free; Hagstrom maps are sold at book stores and newspaper/magazine shops all over the city.

Manhattan is bracketed by two major north-south arteries, **The West Side Highway/Henry Hudson Parkway** (Rte. 9A) along the Hudson River on the west side, and **FDR Drive** along the East River on the east side. At the southernmost tip of the island the **Brooklyn Battery Tunnel** (toll) runs under the harbor to Brooklyn, where it connects to the **Brooklyn-Queens Expressway** (BQE), Rte. 278, which arcs around the Brooklyn shoreline and into Queens on either end. The BQE also connects with the **Verrazano Bridge** (toll) to the **Staten Island Expressway** across the Goethals Bridge to New Jersey. On the FDR Drive three bridges cross the East River to Brooklyn: south to north, the **Brooklyn Bridge**, the **Manhattan Bridge**, and the **Williamsburg Bridge**. At 34th Street the **Queens Midtown Tunnel** (toll) shoots under the river to Queens and the **Long Island Expressway** running east on Long Island. The **Queensborough Bridge** crosses from 59th Street into Long Island City, and the **Triborough Bridge** (toll) at 125th Street crosses into Queens and The Bronx. From the West Side Highway the **Holland Tunnel** (toll) at Canal Street goes under the Hudson to Jersey City, and the **Lincoln Tunnel** (toll) at 38th Street crosses to Weehawken, both connecting to the Jersey Turnpike (I95) and routes 78 and 22 west into New Jersey and the Garden State Parkway. Further north the **George Washington Bridge** (toll) sweeps across the Hudson River to connect with the **Palisades Parkway** (I9) north along the west bank of the Hudson, the Jersey Turnpike and I80 west. The **Cross Bronx Expressway**, which runs onto the bridge, also runs (crawls is sometimes more like it) east, connecting with I95 north into Connecticut, I87 north into Yonkers and upstate, and the Bronx River Parkway north. From the northernmost tip of Manhattan the **Henry Hudson Bridge** (toll) soars into Riverdale north on the Henry Hudson Parkway to Rte. 87 and other routes north into New England.

Tolls on the bridges and tunnels rose to $6 in 2001. But drivers with the E-Z Pass pay only $5 at peak times, $4 off-peak. Besides saving money, the pass saves time; drive slowly though tollbooths while a sensor reads an electronic tag attached to the car. To get the E-Z Pass, which also works on the New York State Thruway and in neighboring states, go to www.ezpassny.com and apply online, or call 800-333-TOLL for an application. The pass works like a debit card, subtracting the toll from your balance with each use; you can pay to keep the pass filled by check or money order, but if you pay by credit card the pass is automatically filled as necessary. Your monthly statement keeps you apprised of your toll spending.

TAXI AND CAR SERVICES

All car services in New York City, unlicensed as well as licensed, come under the jurisdiction of the Taxi and Limousine Commission (TLC: 212- 676-1000 for questions or complaints; 212-302-8294 for lost and found), www.ci.nyc.ny.us.

Licensed cabs in New York City tend to be reliable and safe, although in 1994, for the first time, the TLC required licensed cabs to install Plexiglas shields between driver and passenger. This is intended more for the driver's safety, however. The TLC licenses chauffeur-driven stretch limos as well as three types of cabs:

- **Yellow cabs**, or "medallion"—for the emblem affixed to the hood—cabs, are the only taxis authorized to pick up passengers on the street. There are 12,187 of these charging $2 for the first 1/5th of a mile, 30¢ for each additional 1/5th of a mile, and 20¢ for each 90 seconds waiting time. A 50¢ surcharge is collected between 8 p.m. and 6 a.m. No legal surcharge for luggage. Tips in the 15% to 20% range are expected. If you're going cross-town, especially mid-day in the crush of midtown traffic, it pays to take a cross-town bus. Better yet, walk; it's faster.
- **Black cars**, the trade term for those high-quality (somewhat limousine-like), radio-dispatched fleet cars you see around, aren't licensed to stop for street hails. Corporations and private charges account for most of the "black car" business. In theory, these meterless "voucher cabs" (which charge by zone or by mileage registered on the odometer) will respond to telephone requests from "charge-accountless" individuals; in practice few do.
- **Car services** are licensed to work only from a telephone base and can't legally pick up passengers on the street. The vehicles, of which there are some 36,000 licensed, range from the less-than-lovely to the pristine-upscale, but they are never yellow. Each vehicle, as proof of licensing, must display the blue decal of the Taxi and Limousine Commission on the passenger side of the front windshield. Especially useful to residents of the outer boroughs, where cabs rarely cruise, and to baggage-laden wayfarers, these for-hire vehicles charge flat rates per trip, sometimes less than the cost of a metered cab. In fact, with two or three sharing a car, it may be cheaper and more pleasant to go out of town, to Washington or Philadelphia, say, by car service than to fly.

It pays to shop around by phone. Some rides can be reserved 20 minutes before departure, others require a day's notice. Rates and features vary; you may wish to pay a few dollars extra for a station wagon or for a Lincoln Town Car, and you may wish to arrange to have the car wait for you for the return trip from out of town, for which some services charge only half fare. In any case, be sure the service is licensed, and don't hesitate to ask how much liability insurance they carry for passenger injury; they should carry a minimum of $1 million.

The car lurching to your side looks a wreck, and there's no decal? Then it's probably an unlicensed **gypsy cab**, in which you'll ride at your own risk without recourse in case of bad service.

LIMOUSINE SERVICE

For those occasions when you wish to ride in style or have a car and driver at your beck and call, consider hiring a limousine. Many car services also operate limousines; rates are usually on a per hour basis, although some firms set flat rates for trips to airports or for dinner-and-theater evenings. White, 40-foot-long strrrretches such as those operated by Amex Limousine Service, 212-696-4088, are the current ultimate. These block-long beauties carry 14 people, including two in the rumble seat; the garden-variety stretch limos offer stereos, color TV and a stocked bar with ice for five or six. One day's notice is usually required, though cars (but not necessarily your first choice) are sometimes available on short notice. Most firms accept major credit cards, but check when you call. Below are some representative rates. Add 15% gratuity for the driver.

- **All-State Car and Limousine Service, Inc.**, 446 Hudson Street, 212-333-3333; this service requires a two-hour minimum plus gratuity when you rent a sedan at $20 an hour or stretch limo at $45 an hour plus 20% gratuity. All-State also offers good rates to LaGuardia ($20 plus toll and gratuity), JFK ($30 plus toll and gratuity) and Newark ($32 plus toll and gratuity). A stretch to LaGuardia is $75, to Newark or JFK $90, each plus tolls and a 20% gratuity.
- **Carey Limousine**, 62-07 Woodside Avenue, Woodside, Queens, 212-599-1122; Cadillac sedans cost $50 per hour, limousines $70 per hour, starting from the time the car leaves the garage on 34th Street, Manhattan, until it returns. You pay tolls or parking fees plus 10% service charge.
- **Communicar Ltd.**, 129-02 Northern Boulevard, Corona, Queens 11368, 718-418-1500; call 15 minutes ahead of time to have an unmetered maroon Oldsmobile at your door. Flat rates depend on pickup point and destination (fees are listed in a book). East Side to LaGuardia

Airport is $31, to JFK $43. Cars are available hourly at $30 per and can be reserved one day in advance at an additional $4.

- **Dav-El Livery**, Pier 62, North River at 23rd Street, 212-645-4242; sedans cost $49 per hour or $1.75 per mile and stretch limos cost $63 per hour or $2.10 per mile, beginning when the car leaves the garage. Add a 15% gratuity for sedans, 20% for limos. A trip to or from all airports is charged at the two-hour rate. There is a one-and-a-half-hour minimum before 6 p.m., two-hour minimum after 6.

- **Fugazy International Corp.**, 212-661-0100; sedan town cars for $54 per hour, beginning at the scheduled pickup time. Stretch limos at $66 per hour, $86 for super-stretch, with a two-hour minimum, from the time of prearranged pickup.

- **Tel Aviv Car and Limousine Service**, 139 First Avenue near Eighth Street, 212-777-7777, out of town 800-222-9888, www.telavivlimo.com; this courteous outfit will take you around town or to the airport and they'll pick you up on your return at no extra charge if you reserve, even checking your flight to be sure it's on time. Rides around town are at $25 per hour, with a two-hour minimum in Manhattan, $10 elsewhere. The fare to LaGuardia is $25, plus tolls and 15% tip; to JFK and Newark, $35 plus tolls and tip. Usually a call 15 minutes in advance is enough, 20 to 25 minutes during rush hour. The full line of limo service is also available. *New York* magazine called Tel Aviv "the best ride in town."

CAR RENTALS

If you let your fingers do the walking through the 19 yellow pages of car rental firms in the **Manhattan Telephone Directory**, you will undoubtedly come up with the best rate for your particular needs. National and local companies rent everything from the latest model cars in all sizes to sub-compacts, station wagons, vans and "oldies." Prices vary widely from firm to firm, and special rates (for a weekend, say, or midweek) are common; call around for cost comparisons. Keep in mind that companies located just outside the city may have low enough rates to more than compensate for the lack of convenience. In White Plains, NY, for example, a half-hour by train from Grand Central, the Hertz office is across the street from the train station. And rates are lower there than in Manhattan. Pick up a book and leave the toughest part of exiting Manhattan to Metro-North.

Be sure to ask if there is a charge for leaving the car at another location, if that is your plan. Some other helpful hints: Manhattan car rental companies run out of availability quickly, especially before summer and holiday weekends. *Do not wait until the last minute!* Calling early may also get you a better discount. You may be able to get discount packages through your employer's company policy. When you do book your reservation, ask for a confirmation number so you can be sure to get the rate you were quoted when you reserved the car.

Finally, becoming a member of New York City's AAA, 212-757-2000, even if you do not own a car, is a good idea. Aside from access to good discount rental rates, you're guaranteed the protection you might not otherwise get from a small rental company. Other benefits: free travelers' checks, maps, travel guides, and trip planning services, travel discounts and travel agents. At $55 to join and $45 annually thereafter, it's a best bet.

Here are some of the largest companies:

- **Avis**: in New York City call 212-308-2727 for information and reservations; elsewhere call 800-331-1212, www.avis.com. Eleven locations in Manhattan; cars available at John F. Kennedy International Airport, LaGuardia Airport and Newark International Airport.
- **Budget**, 800-527-0700, www.drivebudget.com; nine locations in Manhattan and at all three airports
- **Dollar**, 800-800-4000, www.dollar.com; three locations in Manhattan and at all three airports
- **Enterprise**, 800-566-9249, www.ententerprise.com; ten locations in the city and in all three airports
- **Hertz**, 800-654-3131, www.hertz.com; eleven locations in Manhattan and at all three airports
- **National**, 800-227-7368, www.nationalcar.com; nine locations in Manhattan and at all three airports
- **Thrifty**, 800-THRIFTY, www.thrifty.com; five locations in Brooklyn

COMMUTER AND NATIONAL RAIL SERVICE

Pennsylvania Station, between 31st and 33rd streets and Seventh and Eighth avenues, with the Long Island Railroad Station adjacent, between 33rd and 34th streets, and Grand Central Station at 42nd Street, between Vanderbilt and Lexington avenues at Park, are the railroad hubs in New York City. Grand Central has been restored to its former glory, its gray stone walls cleaned and the spectacular azure vaulted ceiling with gilded constellations uncovered, in celebration of the grand old station's 85th birthday. It is once again truly a destination worthy of its calling. The once dim and dirty passageways now house a spiffy mall: a seductive food court, fine restaurants, Godiva, Starbucks and more. The Oyster Bar downstairs, unbelievably, is one of New York's best restaurants. Penn Station, on the other hand remains a work in progress.

- **Amtrak** trains, www.amtrak.com, call 212-582-6875 for information and reservations, leave Pennsylvania Station for the Northeast Corridor—between Washington and Boston—and for destinations throughout most of the country and to Canada. In late 2000 Amtrak inaugurated high-speed Acela Express service with a sleek bullet train shooting along the Northeast Corridor between Boston and New York at speeds peaking at 150 mph, cutting travel time by a third. As more of the trains are put on, service will extend to Washington, D.C. Both Acela Express and the less expensive, and slower, Acela Regional come in two classes, first and business. For Metroliner service between New York and Washington call 800-872-7245 for information and reservations. Look for "rail sale" entries online, where discounts are available offering savings up to 60% on long-distance coach train tickets.

- **Metro-North** trains, 212-532-4900, leave from Grand Central Station and include the Hudson Line to Poughkeepsie, NY; the Harlem Line to Brewster, NY; and the New Haven Line to New Haven, CT. Find up-to-date Metro-North information on the MTA web site: www.mta.nyc.ny.us.
- **The New Jersey Transit Information Center**, 973-762-5100 and 800-772-2222, is the place to call for Penn Station-New Jersey train schedules.
- **Long Island Railroad** trains, 718-217-5477, leave from their own station next to Penn Station. Find up-to-date LIRR information on the MTA web site: www.mta.nyc.ny.us.

COMMUTER AND NATIONAL BUS SERVICE

- The **Port Authority Bus Terminal**, between 40th and 42nd streets and Eighth and Ninth avenues, 212-564-8484, handsomely modernized and enlarged, is the center for almost all inter-city bus traffic. The exceptions are inter-borough expresses, which have designated pickup points at certain Manhattan intersections, and buses, mostly from New Jersey, that arrive and leave from the Port Authority Bus Station at the George Washington Bridge, 800-221-9903.
- **Greyhound Bus Lines**, 800-231-2222, www.greyhound.com, has its principal ticket offices in the Port Authority Terminal, and their buses arrive and depart from the Lower Level of the North Wing with entrances on both 41st and 42nd streets.
- **Peter Pan Trailways**, 800-343-9999, www.adirondacktrailways.com, uses Adirondack Trailways as its local ticket agent in the Port Authority Terminal. Its buses also arrive at and depart from the Lower Level of the North Wing.

AIRLINES

The Port Authority of New York and New Jersey manages John F. Kennedy, LaGuardia, and Newark airports, and strives mightily to upgrade airport transportation and services and to disseminate information to the public about the facilities. To this end, they distribute particularly helpful materials and staff several telephone information numbers.

Since deregulation, the 90-plus airlines serving the three airports seem to be perpetually changing flight schedules, destinations, and names, to say nothing of fares. To order this chaos, the Port Authority publishes the *International and Domestic Consolidated Airline Schedule*, a pocket-sized quarterly useful for finding the flight to fit one's needs.

The Port Authority also publishes the *Airport Map/Guides*—one each for JFK, LaGuardia, and Newark—illustrating the locations of parking lots, airlines, access routes and other services. Call the 800 number listed below or write or phone the Aviation Public Service Division, Room 65N, One World Trade Center, NYC 10048, 212-435-7000, for copies of either series.

Call **800-A-I-R-R-I-D-E**, 9 a.m. to 5 p.m. weekdays for a menu of recorded information. Better yet, go online to www.panynj.gov for information about airport transportation, parking, and other concerns.

AIRPORT TRANSPORTATION

At $1.50, the cheapest route (and one of the slowest) to JFK is the **A train** (destination Rockaways, not Lefferts Blvd.) to the Howard Beach station, from which a free yellow, white, and blue shuttle bus leaves for all stops at JFK. Allow an hour and a half or more.

You can, of course, **drive** to the airport and park there for up to 30 days at Kennedy International, LaGuardia or Newark (tab: $240). Short-term parking at all airports is closer to the terminal and more expensive, $48 per day after the first day, for example, at Newark. Remember that Fridays and holiday periods most lots are full. Business travelers fill short-term lots on Wednesdays. Arrive at the lot before 3 p.m. most days to be sure of a parking spot, and don't expect to find a space at LaGuardia Sunday night.

For up-to-date information on transportation to any of the three airports go online to the Port Authority's web site, www.panynj.gov, or call the individual airport, below.

Every half-hour, between 6 a.m. and 10 p.m., **New York Airport Service Express**, 718-875-8200, www.panymj.gov, offers **Inter-Airport Service**, a shuttle bus that loops between the passenger terminals at Kennedy to LaGuardia, taking about 45 minutes at a fare of $11. In the opposite direction, same fare, service is from 7 a.m. to 10 p.m. If you are traveling with a companion, or can find someone to share with, it is probably worth taking a taxi. The fare is about $12 to $15 without tip.

New York Airport Service Express also provides transportation from these airports to the Air Trans Center at the Port Authority Bus Terminal round the clock. Just change at the Air Trans Center to **Olympia Airport Express**, 212-964-6233, or vice versa. The fares remain the same: $11 from Newark to New York, $10 from New York to LaGuardia, $13 to Kennedy.

JOHN F. KENNEDY INTERNATIONAL AIRPORT

JFK, which has been shedding its various skins for a few years now, is expected to finish rebuilding itself handsomely by 2006, complete with a new light rail system, AirTrain, which will loop the eight terminals and link up with the Long Island Railroad, subways, and buses at Jamaica Station and at Howard Beach. When completed (ETA 2003), the traveler will zip from midtown to JFK in 45 minutes. For more information about AirTrain go to www.panynj.gov/airtrain. Call 718-244-4444 for airport information, 718-244-4225 for lost and found, and 718-244-4168 for parking.

- **Taxis** from midtown cost about $35 to $40 not including tolls and tip. From JFK to Manhattan there is a flat rate of $30 plus tolls and tip; if there is a second person going beyond the first stop in Manhattan, the meter is started after the first stop and this passenger pays the metered rate. Allow 40-60 minutes or more, depending on time of day.

- **New York Airport Service Express Bus**, 718-875-8200, www.panynj.gov; buses leave from Jamaica Station, Queens, Grand Central, Penn Station and the Port Authority Bus Terminal every 15 to 30 minutes. The trip takes 45 to 60 minutes or more, depending on time of day, and the fare is $11 ($5 from Jamaica Station).

- **Express Shuttle USA** (also known as Grey Line); call 212-315-3006 for information and reservation, also online at www.greylinenewyork.com. Minibus service operates 5 a.m. to 9 p.m. to the airport, and 7 a.m. to 11:30 p.m. from the airport to major Manhattan hotels for $19 per person. Book service also at the Grey Line desk in a hotel lobby and at the airport at the Grey Line Air Shuttle courtesy phone near baggage claim.

- **SuperShuttle (Blue Van)**, call 212-258-3826 on your departure day, 800-BLUEVAN from out of town or to reserve in advance of your travel date, www.supershuttle.com, operates 24-hours a day shuttling passengers from home, office or hotel to each of the three major airports. You will be notified at the time of your reservation if delays of more than 15 minutes are expected. Arrivals at JFK go to the ground transport desk in the baggage claim area to order a Blue Van; pickup takes about 15 minutes. Fare is $15 to $19.

- **Bus**; if you're frugal and subway-phobic, take the Q60 bus from 60th Street and Second Avenue to the last stop in Kew Gardens and transfer there to the Q10 to Kennedy, where it circles the airport, stopping at each airline terminal; one fare.

LAGUARDIA AIRPORT

Call 718-533-3400 for airport information; 718-533-3988 for lost and found; and 718-533-3850 for parking.

- **Taxis** to and from midtown cost about $16 to $26, plus tolls and tip. If you can find a friendly fellow Manhattan (or wherever you are going) bound traveler you can split the fare.
- **New York Airport Service Express Bus**, 718-875-8200, www.panynj.gov; buses leave from Jamaica Station, Queens, Grand Central, Penn Station and the port Authority Bus Terminal every 15 to 30 minutes. The trip takes about 30 minutes, more during rush hours, and costs $10 ($5 from Jamaica Station.)
- **Express Shuttle USA**, (also known as Grey Line); call 212-315-3006 for information and reservation, also online at www.greylinenewyork.com. Minibus service operates 5 a.m. to 9 p.m. to the airport, and 7 a.m. to 11:30 p.m. from the airport to major Manhattan hotels for **$16**. Book service also at the Grey Line desk in a hotel lobby and at the airport at the Grey Line courtesy phone near baggage claim.
- **SuperShuttle** (**Blue Van**); call 212-258-3826 on your departure day, 800-BLUEVAN from out of town or to reserve in advance of your travel date, www.supershuttle.com, operates 24 hours a day shuttling passengers from home, office or hotel to each of the three major airports. If pickup is going to take more than 15 minutes after they receive your call, they will say so. Arrivals at LaGuardia go to the ground transport desk in the baggage claim area to order a Blue Van; pickup takes about 15 minutes. Fare is $15.
- **Public Subway and Bus**; call the Transit Authority, 718-330-1234, and Triborough Coast Line, 718-335-1000, for information. Take the E or F train to the Roosevelt station in Queens and change to the Q33 bus, which runs to LaGuardia every 15 minutes 24 hours a day. Total cost $1.50 one way using a MetroCard. If you're leaving from the Upper West Side and have 45-60 minutes to spare, take the **M60 bus** from Broadway and 106th Street, or anywhere along Broadway north to 125 Street to Second Avenue before midnight. It goes to LaGuardia for one fare.
- **LaGuardia "Q.T."** (**Quick Trip**) leaves from all LaGuardia terminals and the Marine Air Terminal every 20 minutes from 6:35 a.m. to 11 p.m. The express bus leaves you at 21st Street and 41st Avenue in Long Island City, where you can catch the B or Q into Manhattan. Total cost is $5 in exact change or tokens.

NEWARK INTERNATIONAL AIRPORT

Call 973-961-6000 for airport information; 973-961-6230 for lost and found; 973-961-4751 for parking.

The Port Authority, which runs all three NYC area airports, supervises efficient, inexpensive transportation to and from Newark.

- **Taxis** can legally add $10 and tolls to the meter rate, and the trip from midtown to Newark Airport costs about $40 without tolls and tips. Returning to Manhattan, New Jersey cabs are limited to fixed fares determined by location, for example $30 to the West Side between the Battery and 59th Street. Share and Save rates for groups of up to four passengers cut costs by almost half and are available between 8 a.m. and midnight. Check with the dispatcher at the terminal's hack stand.

- **Olympia Airport Express** uses a special air-conditioned airport departure lounge, the Air Trans Center, in the North Wing of the terminal at 42nd Street and Eighth Avenue. Call 212-964-6233 for information, or www.panynj.gov. Buses leave about every 15 minutes during rush hours from the terminal and from 125 Park Avenue, between 40th and 41st streets, across from Grand Central, from Penn Station at 34th Street and Eighth Avenue, and from One World Trade Center on West Street, arriving at Newark Airport some 30 minutes later. The cost is $11 one way.

- **Express Shuttle USA** (also known as Grey Line); call 212-315-3006 for information and reservation, or go online to www.greyline-newyork.com. Minibus service operates from major Manhattan hotels from 5 a.m. to 9 p.m. and from the airport to the city 7 a.m. to 11:30 p.m. for $19 per person. At the airport book return service at the Grey Line service phone near baggage claim.

- **SuperShuttle** (**Blue Van**), 212-258-3826 on day of departure, 800-BLUEVAN from out of town or to reserve before day of departure, www.supershuttle.com, operates 24-hours a day shuttling passengers from home, office or hotel to the three major airports. If pickup is going to take more than 15 minutes after they receive your call, they will say so. Arrivals go to the ground transport desk in the baggage claim area to order a Blue Van; pickup takes about 15 minutes. The fare is $19.

- **Rail**, 800-772-2222 in New Jersey, 973-762-5100 from New York, www.njtransit.com. Late in 2001 a rail connection is scheduled to open to the airport from New York City and other points on Jersey Transit's Northeast Corridor via train. Passengers will leave Penn Station, checking their luggage for the appropriate terminal, and transfer at Pennsylvania Station, Newark, to the monorail, which loops the terminals at Newark Airport.

SATELLITE AIRPORTS

Three airports outside the city offer an attractive alternative to the JFK-LaGuardia-Newark axis: un-crowded access roads, easy parking and fewer delays all around for domestic flights.

- **MacArthur Airport** in Islip, Long Island, is served by American Airlines and USAir, plus the commuter lines of Continental, Delta, Northwest, and United, with direct flights to ten cities in the East. In 1999, Southwest Airlines initiated low-fare, one-class service to 34 cities, including Los Angeles and Houston. One to two hours' drive from Manhattan, this is more of a boon to Long Islanders than to Manhatanites. Call 516-467-3210 for information.

- **Stewart Airport**, a former Air Force base 60 miles north of the city in Newburgh, NY, at the juncture of I-87 and I-84, opened for commercial service in 1990 and offers flights by American and USAir and the commuter lines American Eagle and United Express to five cities and Kennedy Airport. Call 914-564-2100 for information.

- **Westchester County Airport** in White Plains, 914-285-4860, is served by American, Carnival, Northwest, USAir, and United as well as by commuter service of the same lines and Delta. The airport boasts a new terminal, completed in 1995, and ample parking in a three-story lot. Lacking a car, take the Harlem Line out of Grand Central to White Plains, and the Bee Line #12 bus to the airport.

SUMMER ACCOMMODATIONS IN UNIVERSITY DORMS, Ys, CHURCH-run women's residences, hotels, and even B & Bs provide temporary shelter en route to a permanent living situation. Later, there may be the occasional visiting aunt and uncle whom you cannot squeeze into your cramped one bedroom. Descriptions of these varied lodgings are offered, together with a selection of hotels categorized by price and location.

A few generalizations: rates are often negotiable; weekends and the summer months offer the best opportunity for lodging bargains; holidays and the fall months are usually the priciest times to stay in the city.

The rates quoted are from 2001. Increases during the year are a good bet, particularly in the case of hotels, which traditionally hike prices in April or September. To avoid sticker shock at checkout, note that New York hotel rooms are subject to 13.25% tax, plus a flat $2 room tax. Prices quoted in this chapter do not include tax.

SUMMER ONLY

Dorm accommodations and other special situations include:

- **Barnard College**, contact the director, Summer Program, 2009 Broadway, NYC 10027, 212-854-8021, www.barnard.edu/sumprog. During the summer, Barnard opens the doors of its dorm and student apartment rooms to men and women students, parents and summer interns and associates. 2001 rates: $140-$196 single, $130-$147 double per week, one-week minimum. Meal plans are extra.
- **International House** (near Columbia University), 500 Riverside Drive at 123rd Street, NYC 10027, 212-316-8400; you don't have to matriculate at Columbia to be eligible for one of the approximately 700 dorm rooms and suites available to students, interns, and other visitors from late May to mid-August on a first-come, first-served basis. Rates are $540

to $1,400 a month, depending on amenities; for short stays, $100 a night. Write or call for information or to reserve. These bargain accommodations are sometimes available during the school year as well.

- **New York University Dormitories**, c/o New York University, Office of Summer Housing, 14A Washington Place, NYC 10003, 212-998-4621; there is a three-week minimum stay requirement at the NYU dorms, which are open to other students, age 17 or older, and June graduates from early May through early August. However, priority is given to enrolled summer students. Non-student rates range from $170-$260 a week for a double to $225-$260 per week for a single, meals included. Rates for enrolled students are lower. All rooms are contained within shared suites; halls are co-ed, rooms and suites are single sex. Apply early.

See also **Sublets** and **Sharing** in the **Finding a Place to Live** chapter.

TRANSIENT YMCAS

Two Ys in Manhattan, one in Brooklyn and one in Queens offer accommodations for both men and women; all rent rooms on a daily basis only and all subscribe to the "Y's Way" central booking office. Anyone (member or no) can write or call the "Y's Way" booking office located at the Vanderbilt YMCA, 224 East 47th Street, NYC 10017, 212-756-9600, to obtain confirmed reservations at the five YMCAs listed below. "Y's Way" rates range from $85 single and $95 double in Manhattan to $50 single and $70 double in Flushing, and $46 single and $56 double in Greenpoint. In all cases the room rates includes use of all athletic facilities on the premises (see **YMCAs** in **Sports and Recreation**).

- **Vanderbilt YMCA**, 224 East 47th Street, NYC 10017, 212-756-9600; 370 rooms
- **West Side YMCA**, 5 West 63rd Street, NYC 10023, 212-875-4100; 530 rooms
- **Flushing YMCA**, 138-46 Northern Boulevard, Flushing 11354, 718-961-6880; 130 rooms
- **Greenpoint YMCA**, 99 Meserole Avenue, Brooklyn 11222, 718-389-3700, 100 rooms

RESIDENCES

Daily transients are not accepted by any of the residences noted below, which, with the exception of the 92nd Street Y, are for women only. Weekly rates are the norm and many include two meals a day in the price. Full occupancy is the rule at most of these places, as is the requirement for a personal interview, and you should therefore make arrangements for a room well in advance of arrival. Some have special house rules, such as curfews, so inquire about these before booking. For further listings, call or write for **A Temporary Place to Live**, published by the Open Housing Center, 594 Broadway, Suite 608, NYC 10012, 212-941-6101. The cost at this writing was $5.

- **92nd Street YM-YWHA**, 1395 Lexington Avenue, NYC 10128, 212-415-5650; co-ed, for men and women ages 18 and older, with 400 rooms, $690 to $835 a month for a minimum (by application only) stay of one month. Must be working full time or going to school; $995/single and $805 per person, double.

- **Brandon Residence for Women**, 340 West 85th Street between Riverside Drive and West End Avenue, NYC 10024, 212-496-6901; with 120 single rooms, shared baths, a handsome lobby and 24-hour security. Applicants who will be working or students must apply in advance, with approval pending an interview. Rates: $691 to $824 per month single, includes breakfast and dinner.

- **Markle Residence** (Salvation Army), 123 West 13th Street, NYC 10014, 212-242-2400; $230 a week for private room and bath includes two meals a day. Four-week minimum stay.

- **Parkside Evangeline Residence** (Salvation Army), 18 Gramercy Park South, NYC 10003, 212-677-6200; about 200 rooms, $200 a week including two meals a day. Requires $700 refundable security deposit and a $15 non-refundable registration fee. Three months minimum, but they're flexible.

- **St. Mary's Residence** (Daughters of the Divine Charity), 225 East 72nd Street, NYC 10021, 212-249-6850; $200 a week for private rooms with shared baths and facilities. No minimum stay but a long waiting list to get in.

- **Webster Apartments**, 419 West 34th Street between Ninth and Tenth avenues, NYC 10001, 212-967-9000; call well in advance to reserve for a minimum of four weeks at this attractive establishment, which features gardens, a library, and maid service in its 373 rooms. An interview is required of applicants in the area; out-of-towners write directly for an application. Current weekly rates: students, interns/trainees, $200; working residents, $300-$600, depending on weekly gross income. You must provide proof of enrollment in a school, a letter of proof of internship or four consecutive pay stubs with application.

BED AND BREAKFASTS

In Manhattan? Yes! Many a resourceful New Yorker has let out that extra room and thrown a Continental breakfast into the bargain. It's even possible to have the whole apartment, in a charming brownstone or a high tech high rise, to yourself, which is to say un-hosted. In any case, it will be cheaper than comparable digs in a hotel, but the visitor may give up something in privacy, service or convenience. However, don't look for hand lettered shingles advertising availability because owners require anonymity and an agency acts as intermediary.

This cottage industry is unregulated, though reputable agencies inspect the properties they represent and attempt to monitor the quality of service and accommodations on an ongoing basis through visitor critique cards. Shop around by phone; be as specific as you can be about preferred location, likes and dislikes, allergies and other restrictions. There is usually a two-night minimum stay, but there may be exceptions off-season. For the best choice, book well in advance (reasonable B&Bs have gotten as scarce as affordable hotel rooms) and expect to pay a 25% deposit or more. The commission is included in the fee. Many accept credit cards. Expect to pay 8.25% sales tax above the given room price.

- **Abode Bed and Breakfast**, P.O. Box 20022, NYC 10021, 212-472-2000 (800-835-8880 for out-of-state callers only), represents about 200 hosted and un-hosted apartments, mostly in Manhattan, a few in Brooklyn, and some long-term locations. They request business references from guests. Three-night minimum, $135 to $400 a night for a studio
- **Bed and Breakfast and Books**, 35 West 92nd Street, NYC 10025, 212-865-8740, so named because the owners also operate a book business; attracts a fairly bookish clientele, not surprisingly. One of the more established agencies, they handle about 35 apartments, mostly hosted, all over Manhattan and a couple in Brooklyn. In telephone interviews they attempt to match the visitors' background, age and preferences to the location. Prices range from $80 to $110 for a hosted single, to $150-plus for an un-hosted one-bedroom apartment. Two-night minimum; some long-term stays available.
- **Bed and Breakfast Network**, 130 Barrow Street, NYC 10014, 212-645-8134, lists 700 places, hosted and un-hosted, and suggests a few weeks' advance notice. Rates range from $80 to $90 single, $90 to $150 double, and $115 to $250 for an un-hosted apartment. There is a two-night minimum in most cases.
- **City Lights Bed and Breakfast**, P.O. Box 20355, Cherokee Station, NYC 10021, 212-737-7049, lists several hundred rooms and apartments, hosted and un-hosted, all in Manhattan. Rates are $90 to $300 per night, depending on the accommodation, with a two-night minimum.
- **Manhattan Lodgings, Inc.**, 70 East 10th Street, NYC 10003, 212-677-7616, www.manhattanlodgings.com, offers 200 furnished, luxury short-stay apartments in Manhattan. Three-night minimum; two week advance notice required, $100 to $300 per night.
- **New World Bed and Breakfast**, 150 Fifth Avenue, Suite 711, NYC 10011, 212-675-5600, or 800-443-3800 from out of town, represents

about 120 apartments, all in Manhattan. Perhaps because the owner is a woman, the agency tends to attract working women. Rates for hosted rooms range from $80 to $85 single, $90 double with a two-night minimum. Furnished apartments with kitchens cost $90 to $165 for a studio, $140 to $240 for one bedroom per night. Discounts for longer stays.

EXTENDED STAY HOTELS

A number of hotels, particularly smaller neighborhood properties equipped with kitchenettes, quote weekly and monthly, as well as daily, rates. You'll find several listed under **Inexpensive Hotels** below. The late 1990s saw the proliferation of high-end, all-suite hotels for extended stays only, sometimes in apartment buildings, sometimes within transient hotels, but all designed primarily for the business person, offering hotel services and amenities along with fax machines and multi-line telephones. There is also a group that offers monthly rates in ten apartment hotels located in some of New York's nicest neighborhoods:

- **Bristol Plaza**, 210 East 65th Street, 212-753-2081, has 167 apartments and a rooftop health club with a 50-foot swimming pool. Monthly rates range from $5,200 to $14,000.
- **Envoy Club**, 377 East 33rd Street near First Avenue, 212-481-4600, with 60 suites occupies the first five floors of a new rental building. Minimum stay is one month, costing $6,000 or more, and the management will give a lease for as long as a year. Plans are in place to open two more Envoy Clubs on Fifth Avenue and on First Avenue.
- **Hotel Olcott**, 27 West 72nd Street, NYC 10023, 212-877-4200, nicely located between Lincoln Center and Central Park, tends to attract musicians and actors to its homey confines. Rates by the week are $750 plus tax for a studio, $875 for one bedroom.
- **Manhattan East Hotels**, call 800-637-8483, represents the Shelburne (Murray Hill), Eastgate Tower (fringes of Murray Hill), Beekman Tower (near Sutton Place), Plaza 50, The Benjamin, Dumont Plaza and Lyden House (Midtown East), The Surrey and Lyden Gardens (Upper East Side) and Southgate Tower (Penn Station area). The least expensive rental, a studio in Southgate Tower, costs $5,600 a month; a one-bedroom apartment in the more prestigious, Beekman Tower, goes for $7,780 and up.
- **Marmara-Manhattan**, 301 East 94th Street, 212-427-3100, has 107 apartments that were formerly condominiums. Amenities include an exercise room and a daily buffet breakfast (charged extra). The tariff here ranges from $4,500 to $13,000 monthly.
- **The Phillips Club**, 1965 Broadway at 67th Street, NYC 10023, 212-835-8800, at the high end and designed for the corporate traveler, is discreetly tucked into four floors of a sleek 32-floor building just north of

Lincoln Center. Decor in the 96 furnished suites, ranging from studio to two-bedroom apartments in soothing beige, cream and taupe, is somewhat corporate, and a minimum stay of one month ranges from $6,300 to $13,000.

HOTELS

There are about 70,000 hotel rooms in New York City. The average price for one of them in 2001 was a stunning $237. Prices and occupancy rates fluctuate seasonally depending on location. The friendly, and sometimes frenetic, first-class commercial establishments along Central Park West and Lexington and Park avenues in the East 40s and 50s are impossibly full weekdays in the fall, winter and spring, but both occupancy and prices languish during the summer dog days. This is the season, however, when the comparatively feisty West Side tourist class hotels sprinkled around the Broadway theaters in the West 40s cost the most and are the fullest. Low rates are never in season at the town's justifiably famous deluxe hotels, be they large and extravagant, quietly posh or smoothly contemporary—but many do have weekend plans.

Anyone who wants to lessen the blow of oppressive hotel prices should know where to find the lower rates at various times of the year (or week), and some generalizations are included here. *The rates quoted are for two people in a room, weeknights, not including tax.*

Weekend rates are almost always lower than prices charged during the week. However, flossy "weekend packages" with champagne, flowers and free brunches for two don't represent the best values. Ask about the no-frills prices available Friday, Saturday and sometimes Sunday nights. Weekend rates are, in effect, contingency plans to fill the house. If full occupancy looms, off they go.

Unadvertised discounts; even with the surge of tourists visiting New York City, the occupancy rate of some hotels is erratic, with the result that accommodating, unadvertised prices are occasionally available. After you've been quoted the standard rates, ask for information about any special deals. Better yet, go to the web site of the **New York Convention and Visitors Bureau,** www.nycvisit.com, or drop in to their Visitors Information Center at 810 Seventh Avenue at 53rd Street, 212-397-8200, for an extensive listing of discounted hotel rooms today and in future. This useful site includes pictures, hotel descriptions and ratings, listed by date of availability, number of nights and number of beds; and you can book the room on line here. There is also a listing of special summer rates for members of American Express, which sponsors the site.

Hotel discounters buy blocks of rooms from hotels at volume discounts and pass savings, some as high as 60%, on to consumers. Visit their web site or call to have their lists mailed or faxed to you, then you call as early as possible for rates and to reserve. You must give a credit card number to hold your room, and payment is at the hotel when you check out. There is no fee for the service, and you should save about 25% on the cost of a room. Cancellations must be made 24 to 72 hours in advance; be sure to check on cancellation policy. **Central Reservation Services**, 800-548-3311, www.reservation-services.com, for example, is especially good at getting mid- to low-priced rooms in New York and in about a dozen other cities. **Express Reservations**, 800-356-1123, www.express.res.com, books into 25 hotels in mid-town Manhattan and one in SoHo at rates generally ranging from $105 to $250 a night. **Hotel Reservations Network**, 800-964-6835, www.hoteldiscount.com, has a particularly useful web site, providing online comparison of properties and direct booking online. They offer accommodations in 17 cities in the US and Europe as well as New York. At **Quikbook**, 800-789-9887, www.quikbook.com, you are connected with a reservation agent who can reserve rooms at dozens of moderate to deluxe hotels all over Manhattan (and more than 30 other cities). Prices are discounted from the hotels' regularly quoted rates. And a few more: **Expedia.com**, 800-397-3342; **Hotwire.com**, 888-362-1234; **Priceline.com**, 800-774-2345; **Travelocity.com**, 877-439-0980.

INEXPENSIVE HOTELS

Doubles for $100 to $195 not including tax may not seem cheap, but that's the range separating New York's hotel bargain category from the rest of the flock this year.

- **Habitat Hotel**, (formerly the Allerton Hotel for Women, and marketed largely to Europeans) 130 East 57th Street, NYC 10022, 212-753-8841 www.habitat-ny.com; the commendable location of this somewhat spartan hotel keeps the place full to overflowing in spite of the fact the rooms are small and occasionally unkempt. $130 double with private bath ($75 single without bath), taxes included.
- **Best Western Seaport Inn**, 33 Peck Slip, NYC 10038, 212-766-6600; a pleasingly restored 19th century building one block from the waterfront at the very lower tip of Manhattan. Doubles start at $169 per weeknight, a bargain if you get one of the upper floor rooms with great views of the Brooklyn Bridge.
- **Excelsior**, 45 West 81st Street, NYC 10024, 212-362-9200; a landmarked building in a great location facing the Museum of Natural History and Central Park compensates for occasionally grungy rooms. $179 single or double, $209-$219 for a one-bedroom suite, $369 for a two-bedroom suite.
- **Hudson**, 356 West 58th Street, NYC 10019, 212-554-6000, opened

in 2000 with 1,000 small rooms behind a bland brick façade. Inside, however, hotelier Ian Schreger and designer Philippe Starck have fashioned a fascinating interior, which includes a public library with pool table, a lobby-as-town-square and a witty garden. Doubles start at $125, suites at $150.

- **Herald Square**, 19 West 31st Street, NYC 10001, 212-279-4017, with a handsome beaux-arts facade is a favorite with European travelers looking for value. Rates begin at the bargain-price of $55 for a small, one-person room and run up to $150 for four.
- **Off SoHo Suites**, 11 Rivington Street, off the Bowery, NYC 10002, 800-OFF-SOHO, is technically on the edge of the old Lower East Side, a short walk from SoHo and Chinatown and a location which may not be for everybody. But the accommodations are clean and comfortable, and a bargain especially for a family or a group of four. The economy suites for two include kitchen and marble bath, which may be shared, for $97; suites for four, with private kitchen and bath, are $179. There is a cafe on site and 24-hour parking for $15.
- **Paramount**, 235 West 46th Street, NYC 10036, 212-764-5500; the designer of the avant-garde Royalton, Philippe Starck, turned his charms on a lower-priced venue. This whimsical effort aimed at the young, hip, and financially challenged offers amenities including a $1 screening room with penny candy, a 24-hour day-care center designed by the Pee Wee Playhouse people, and a Dean & Deluca store. Rates are between $235 for a double, with special weekend rates from $195 to $255.
- **Pickwick Arms**, 230 East 51st Street between Second and Third avenues, NYC 10022, 212-355-0300; clean, randomly-sized rooms, some without baths, and a roof-top garden attracts fans to this slightly flaky place with its East 50s location and doubles for $120 with shower.
- **Quality Hotel** on Fifth, 3 East 40th Street between Fifth and Madison avenues, NYC 10016, 212-447-1500; reasonably priced and centrally located, this midtown newcomer offers spacious, no-frills comfort. You can walk to Grand Central Station and the glorious Morgan Library. Single: $179; double: $250; weekend rate: $159.
- **Radisson Empire**, 44 West 63rd Street, NYC 10023, 212-265-7400; the major selling point for the basic but cheerfully furnished 507-room Empire is its location next to Lincoln Center and near Columbus Circle. $155 to $600 double
- **Westpark**, 308 West 58th Street, NYC 10019, 212-445-0200; with a grand location facing Columbus Circle and Central Park and tidily-renovated rooms—those 16 (out of 99) with park views are especially nice. La Place on the Park, a jazz and rhythm and blues club with bistro food on the lobby level, is another draw. At $95, the Westpark is an especially good buy for a single, doubles $110, $180 for a suite.

WEST SIDE TOURIST HOTELS

The cheapest rates for reliable, if far from classy, rooms are found in the tourist hotels along Eighth Avenue and in the West 40s surrounding the theater district. Better deals are offered here in the winter than in the summer.

- **Hotel Edison**, 228 West 47th Street, NYC 10036, 212-840-5000; 900 rooms convenient to the theater and reasonable: $125 single, $140 double. Doubles represent good value, having two double beds.
- **Howard Johnson's Motor Lodge**, Eighth Avenue and 51st Street, NYC 10019, 212-581-4100; a HoJo's is a HoJo's, even in New York: clean, decent and about $189 to $215 for two, with parking at a rate of $15 for every 24 hours.
- **Ramada Milford Plaza**, Eighth Avenue and 45th Street, NYC 10036, 212-536-2200, is big, basic, and sometimes exceedingly reasonable. Rates: $140 to $200 single, $150 to $220 double.
- **Days Hotel**, Eighth Avenue and 48th Street, NYC 10019, 212-581-7000; the nicest motel in town. An in-house swimming pool makes this a good buy for $177 to $230 double, high season. Parking is $15 per day.

FIRST-CLASS COMMERCIAL OR DELUXE HOTELS

Manhattan is known for its grand and luxurious hotels, among which a handful are legendary: the Pierre, the Plaza, the Carlyle, the Plaza Athenee, the Ritz Carlton, the Waldorf Astoria. To these have recently been added I.M. Pei's marble Four Seasons, the Righa, and the Peninsula, to name but several—deluxe hotels all. We've chosen to list a few which are perhaps less well-known, on the basis of glamour and singularity, as well as fair prices, when they can be found. As said, discounts and good weekend values in these hotels are generally available only in the summertime.

- **Omni Berkshire Place**, 21 East 52nd Street at Madison Avenue, NYC 10022, 212-753-5800, carefully created bouquets frame the elegant marble lobby and provide a backdrop for the toney (in a low key) tea and cocktail area on the far side of the flowers. An accommodating concierge caters to clients with dispatch in this bijou hotel, where the only major drawbacks are the smallish rooms and higher than average prices: $359 to $429.
- **Swisshotel: The Drake**, 440 Park Avenue at 56th Street, NYC 10022, 212-421-0900, glowingly updated in the continental manner complete with attractive lobby bar, the Drake is now owned by Swissair's hotel division. Doubles cost $265 to $385 weekdays. Summer rates are lower.
- **Grand Hyatt New York**, 42nd Street and Lexington Avenue at Grand Central Station, NYC 10017, 212-883-1234, fast paced and glitzy with

a terrific lobby, especially when the fountains are splashing, and a dramatic bar cantilevered over 42nd Street. Rooms, 1,407 of them updated in 1996, with a penthouse health club and other features to appeal to business travelers, $225 to $375 for two. Weekends are cheaper: $199 per night.

- **The Mark**, 25 East 77th Street at Madison Avenue, NYC 10021, 212-744-4300, or 800-T-H-E-M-A-R-K from out of town. Your Frette linens are tended to twice daily in this handsome, sophisticated late arrival in Carlyle country. Dining is on a par with its "glorious" rooms, which run $400 to $3,000 for the Presidential Suite, $315 weekends.

- **Michelangelo**, at the Equitable Center, 152 West 51st Street at Seventh Avenue, NYC 10019, 212-765-1900; this is the old Taft Hotel resurrected in Eurostyle "neoclassical" elegance to which well-designed rooms and great baths attract a glitzy crowd. Bring the kids, but avoid the slow, overpriced room service. Doubles run $325 to $635 for a suite. Corporate rates available.

- **Middletowne Helmsley**, 148 East 48th Street near Third Avenue, NYC 10017, 212-755-3000; one-, two- and three-room suites all with kitchenettes and cheerful flowered decor. A favorite of UN personnel when the General Assembly's in session. Weekdays a double is $190 to $250, $430 for a suite.

- **The Millenium Hilton**, 55 Church Street, NYC 10007, 212-693-2001; classy and convenient (if you're visiting Wall Street), the Millenium offers stunning views as well as first-class amenities such as computers and a health club with an attractive pool. Service too is top-notch. Singles can be had here for $350, doubles start at $380 per night. Weekends all rooms are discounted.

- **Morgan's**, 237 Madison Avenue between 37th and 38th streets, NYC 10016, 212-686-0300; an upstart on New York's rather traditional hotel scene, this narrow, vertical little place around the corner from the staid Morgan Library, has been re-decorated and toned down from its original sleek and swinging look to a softer, earth-toned feel. Small but nicely appointed rooms. Rates are $290 single and $290 for a weekday double.

- **Royalton**, 44 West 44th Street off Fifth Avenue (lately become chic hotel row), NYC 10036, 212-869-4400; with mahogany beds, Danish faucets, French and Italian furniture, Ian Schreger (see Morgan's) has fashioned a swinging silk purse out of a sow's ear. You can have a gym, a computer and a fireplace too in your room, which will run about $295 to $400 for a double, singles for $275 to $375.

- **SoHo Grand**, 310 West Broadway between Grand and Canal Streets, NYC 10013, 212-965-3000, until recently the only hotel in SoHo, offers 367 rooms with amenities to suit the businessman as well as tourists. Located in the midst of the art galleries, boutiques and cafes that fill the formerly industrial buildings of this landmarked cast-iron district. Doubles $334 to $414

- **San Carlos**, 150 East 50th Street, between Lexington and Third avenues, NYC 10022, 212-755-1800; quiet, small hotel with pleasantly spacious rooms and kitchenettes. $170 to $190 for a single, $180 to $195 for a double
- **St. Regis**, 2 East 55th Street at Fifth Avenue, NYC 10022, 212-753-4500; this grande dame of Fifth Avenue reopened in all her Beaux Arts glory, and then some, after a multi-million dollar restoration in 1991. A continental hotel in the old style with no modern convenience overlooked. And, yes, you can still dance on the St. Regis Roof. Doubles $520 to $640
- **The Stanhope**, 995 Fifth Avenue at 81st Street, NYC 10028, 212-774-1234; quiet, discrete, old-world luxury is what the Stanhope achieved with its $30-million facelift. It's all French antiques, crystal ashtrays, Egyptian cotton sheets, fresh flowers, that sort of thing, not to mention unrivaled views of Central Park and the Metropolitan Museum. Superb food and impeccable service gild the lily at $395 to $900 for a large suite.
- **United Nations Plaza**, 44th Street and First Avenue, NYC 10017, 212-758-1234; superior service and sensational views from every room because they begin on the 28th Floor. A good-sized pool, health club, tennis court and free limousine rides to Wall Street make this classically modern hotel unique. Doubles start at $350; $199 weekends.

SOME FAVORITES

Small, charming, personal hotels are not the city's forte, but there are seven fairly priced, medium-sized hotels in other Manhattan areas that deserve special mention:

- **Algonquin**, 59 West 44th Street, NYC 10036, 212-840-6800; little has changed under Japanese ownership. All muted rose, green and burnished wood, the famous lobby bar combines with anachronistic elevators and smallish, genteel rooms to make you feel welcome, secure and part of a pleasantly elite and talented group. Singles: $270; doubles: $290; suites from $350 to $525.
- **Doubletree Guest Suites**, 1568 Broadway, NYC 212-719-1600; overlooking Times Square; this recently renovated hotel rents suites (sitting room and bedroom) rather than single rooms, at the reasonable rate of $279 to $359 for a double. Corporate accounts available.
- **Lowell**, 28 East 63rd Street, NYC 10021, 212-838-1400; once the haunt of independent parents come to visit their well-established Upper East Side children, the Lowell has been totally refurbished and now lets

only a quarter of its 60 rooms to transients. But the more-attractive-than-ever Art Deco hotel remains intimate and friendly. Doubles start at $445.

- **Salisbury**, 123 West 57th Street, NYC 10019, 212-246-1300, or 888-692-5757 from out of town; pleasant, pastel rooms in a relatively intimate setting attract a high percentage of women travelers. $239 for a single, $329 for a double

- **Sheraton Park Avenue**, 45 Park Avenue at 37th Street, NYC 10016, 212-685-7676; the wood-paneled, book-lined lobby (perfect for tea after 3) and the agreeable welcome complement carefully decorated rooms, and the incomparable Morgan Library is just around the corner. Don't miss it. Singles $330; doubles $360. Weekends lower

- **Wales**, 1295 Madison Avenue corner of 92nd Street, NYC 10028, 212-876-6000, was long an annex for guests of Upper East Siders with too-small apartments. Clean and cheerful, the Wales represents good value with doubles for $209 a night, including breakfast and an evening dessert buffet to a harp accompaniment. Chamber music Sunday evenings is a nice touch. Suites are $339.

- **Wyndham**, 42 West 58th Street, NYC 10019, 212-753-3500; small, attentively managed and nicely furnished, the Wyndham is home to numerous theatrical luminaries whenever they're in town and is one of the best buys around at $130 to $145 for a single, $145 to $160 for a double, and $190 to $230 for a one-bedroom suite.

The hotels mentioned here reflect a purely personal taste and are not meant to be an all-city catalog of lodgings.

NEW YORK CITY FAIRLY CRACKLES WITH EVENTS: PARADES, FESTIVALS, celebrations, ethnic holidays, shows, feasts, and tournaments. Imperceptible at first to the newcomer, there is, in fact, a rhythm to this endless round of activity; many of these events occur annually at about the same time, and New Yorkers look forward to them. The calendar below lists them by month. Watch *The Times, New York* magazine, *Time Out New York*, or *The New Yorker* for specific dates and details. Or stop by the New York Convention & Visitors Bureau at 810 Seventh Avenue at 53rd Street, 212-484-1222, www.nycvisit.com, to pick up brochures and a complete seasonal calendar of events. Or call the Department of Transportation, Public Events, at 212-225-5368. For more information on the web go to the city's web site, www.nyclink.org, www.nytoday.com, or www.allianceforarts.org.

JANUARY

- **Big Apple Circus**, Lincoln Center
- **Three Kings Parade**, 5th Avenue, 104th to 116th streets
- **Winter Festival**, Central Park
- **NY Coliseum Antiques Show**
- **NY National Boat Show**
- **Winter Antiques Show at the Seventh Regiment Armory**

FEBRUARY

- **Chinese New Year celebrations**
- **Westminster Kennel Club Dog Show**, Madison Square Garden
- **Black History Month**, citywide events
- **NY International Children's Film Festival**

MARCH

- **International Cat Show**, Madison Square Garden
- **St. Patrick's Day Parade**, Fifth Avenue, 44th to 86th streets
- **Circus Animal Walk to Madison Square Garden**
- **Greek Independence Day Parade**, Fifth Avenue, 44th to 59th streets
- **New York Flower Show**

APRIL

- **Easter Parade**, Fifth Avenue near 50th Street
- **Spring Flower Show**, Brooklyn International Botanic Garden
- **Mets and Yankees baseball season**
- **Rockefeller Center Flower and Garden Show**
- **Cherry Blossom Festival**, Brooklyn International Botanic Garden
- **Greater NY International Auto Show**

MAY

- **Prospect Park Carousel opening**
- **9th Avenue International Food Festival**, 37th to 57th streets
- **You Gotta Have Park celebration**, Central Park
- **Washington Square Outdoor Art Exhibit**
- **Promenade Art Show**, Brooklyn Heights
- **Bike New York**: The Great Five Boroughs Bike Tour
- **Fleet Week**
- **Lower East Side Festival of the Arts**

JUNE

- **Summer Stage concerts**, Central Park
- **Puerto Rican Day Parade**, 5th Avenue, 44th to 86th streets
- **Welcome Back to Brooklyn Festival**, Grand Army Plaza
- **Museum Mile Festival**, 5th Avenue, 82nd to 102nd streets
- **Queens Festival**, Flushing Meadows Corona Park
- **Feast of St. Anthony of Padua**, Sullivan Street below Houston
- **Annual Lesbian and Gay Pride March**
- **Midsummer Nights Swing at Lincoln Center**
- **New York Jazz Festival**
- **Salute to Israel Parade**, Fifth Avenue, 52nd to 79th streets

JULY

- **Free Shakespeare in Central Park**, Delacorte Theatre
- **Macy's Fireworks**, Lower Hudson River
- **Summergarden free concerts**, Museum of Modern Art
- **Washington Square Music Festival**, Washington Square Park
- **Bryant Park Summer Film Festival**, Monday nights, Bryant Park

AUGUST

- **Mostly Mozart Festival**, Lincoln Center
- **NY Philharmonic free parks concerts**, all boroughs
- **US Open Tennis Tournament**, Flushing, Queens
- **African-American and Hispanic Festival**, Harlem
- **Fringe Festival**, theater, music, dance and whatever from outside the mainstream, throughout the Lower East Side; www.fringenyc.org
- **Brooklyn Puerto Rican Day Parade**
- **Brooklyn County Fair**
- **Bronx Puerto Rican Day Parade**, East Tremont Avenue to East 161st Street

SEPTEMBER

- **Lincoln Center Out-of-Doors Festival**
- **Labor Day Parade**, Fifth Avenue, 33rd to 72nd streets
- **African-American Day Parade**, Adam Clayton Powell Blvd., 111th to 142nd Street to Fifth Avenue
- **African-American/Caribbean Parade**, Bronx, Tremont Avenue to 161st Street
- **Greenwich Village Jazz Festival**, around the Village and in Washington Square Park
- **Metropolitan Opera season begins**, Lincoln Center
- **Washington Square Outdoor Art Exhibit**
- **NY Film Festival**, Lincoln Center
- **San Gennaro Festival**, Mulberry Street, Little Italy
- **West Indian Carnival**, Labor Day Weekend
- **New York is Book Country**, Fifth Avenue, 48th to 59th streets
- **Van Steuben Day Parade**, Fifth Avenue, 61st to 86th streets
- **Wigstock**, Pier 54, 13th Street and Hudson River

OCTOBER

- **Ice Skating**, Rockefeller Center and Central Park
- **Columbus Day Parade**, Fifth Avenue, 44th to 86th streets
- **Pulaski Day Parade**, Fifth Avenue, 26th to 52nd streets
- **Hispanic Day Parade**, Fifth Avenue, 44th to 72nd streets
- **Next Wave Festival**, Brooklyn Academy of Music
- **Promenade Art Show**, Brooklyn Heights
- **Greenwich Village Halloween Parade**, 6th Avenue, Spring to 23rd streets

NOVEMBER

- **New York City Marathon**, all five boroughs
- **Veterans Day Parade**, Fifth Avenue, 39th to 24th streets
- **NY City Ballet**, winter season, Lincoln Center
- **Virginia Slims Tennis Tournament**, Madison Square Garden
- **Christmas Spectacular stage show**, Radio City Music Hall
- **Thanksgiving Day Parade**, 77th Street to Herald Square
- **NY Knicks basketball season**, Madison Square Garden

DECEMBER

- **Christmas Tree Lighting**, Rockefeller Center
- **New Year's Eve Celebration**, Times Square
- **Fireworks**, South Street Seaport; Grand Army Plaza, Brooklyn
- **Midnight Run**, Central Park
- **First Night events throughout city**
- **New Year's Eve concert**, NY Philharmonic, Lincoln Center

B ELOW, WE LIST A FEW BOOKS THAT THE NEWCOMER MAY FIND
helpful, enlightening, or just entertaining.

GUIDES

- *AIA Guide to New York City* by Elliot Willensky and Norval White; *the* guide and reference book for anyone fascinated by urban architecture and history. Includes maps, drawings and directions to neighborhoods throughout the five boroughs. Encyclopedic and fascinating.
- *Away for the Weekend, New York* by Eleanor Berman; includes 52 weekend excursions less than 250 miles from New York, some possible without a car.
- *Don't Even Think of Parking Here* by Paul Trapido and Barbara Ensor; keeping a car in the city, it's not all parking.
- *Mr. Cheap's New York* by Mark Waldstein; suggests cheap eats and things to do, bargains, factory outlets, off-price and discount stores, interesting things to do in the city for little or nothing.
- *Nature Walks in and Around New York City* by Sheila Buff; just the thing to get you out of the apartment for a walk in the woods, the fields, the wetlands—all in New York City.
- *The New York Times' Weekends: 46 Fabulous Ways to Slow Down and Get Back in Touch Within Easy Reach of New York City* by *Times* writers; includes maps, precise travel details, where to eat and stay.
- *New York's 50 Best Places to Go Birding In and Around the Big Apple* by John Thaxton and Alan Messer
- *NYC for Free* by Christopher Sulavik; museums, lectures, concerts, festivals, tours, shows and more, even in the outer boroughs, all free.
- *Take Charge! The Complete Guide to Senior Living in New York City* by John Vinton; encyclopedic how-to manual for seniors and gonna-bees.
- *Volunteering in New York City* by Richard Mintzer; where to, how to, tips on 300 listings in five boroughs.

- ***Where to Go: A Guide to Manhattan's Toilets*** by Vicki Rovere; don't laugh. In a city with a dearth of public toilets this can be a life-saver—well, a dignity saver.
- ***The WPA Guide to New York City: The Federal Writers' Project Guide to the 1930s New York***; what was the city like in the 1930s? Mapped, photographed, illustrated and described in this classic. Among the writers, the young John Cheever.

PETS

- ***The Dog's Guide to New York City, with Jack, the City Dog*** by Jan Rohman; keeping a dog in the city. Cute.
- ***The Great New York Dog Book*** by Deborah Loven; you *can* keep a dog here, and here's how.

HISTORY

- ***The Encyclopedia of New York City*** edited by Kenneth T. Jackson; from A&P to Zukofsky, Louis this unwieldy literary monument will delight any Gotham-lover.
- ***Glanton's Guide to the African American New York*** by Latrice Glanton-Chandler
- ***Gotham*** by Edwin G. Burrows and Mike Wallace; New York City to 1898, the best and most comprehensive history, with volume two yet to come.

PARENTS/STUDENTS

- ***The Grownup's Guide to Living with Kids in Manhattan*** by Diane Chernoff-Rosen and Lisa Levinson; a comprehensive guide and resource book for parents of kids aged one to twelve.
- ***How to Find the Best Doctors New York Metropolitan Area*** by John Castle and John Connolly
- ***The New Ultra Cool Parents' Guide to All of New York*** by Alfred Gingold and Helen Rogan; this may be the one to reach for when you hear, "But what are we going to do today, Dad?"
- ***The New York Parents' Book*** by Lois Gilman; covers everything from having the baby to care to entertainment.
- ***The Parents' Guide to the Best Public Elementary Schools in New York City*** by Clara Hemphill; the last word on the city's public schools, how to choose and get into good ones.
- ***Public Middle Schools: New York City's Best*** by Clara Hemphill; the sequel to the above, with descriptions and ratings of middle schools, district by district.

WHILE THERE IS CLEARLY NO SUBSTITUTE FOR CONDUCTING most newcomer business in person, a significant portion of preparatory work can be done by phone or online. Whether it is researching available apartment rentals, determining the nearest library in your neighborhood, or discovering which train to take from your friend's apartment in Brooklyn to your office on the first day on the job, much of the information you need may be gathered even before you arrive here.

What follows is a partial listing of web sites that cover a variety of services. In addition to the listings below there are many others embedded throughout the book. Check in your section of interest for additional sites.

ALCOHOL AND DRUG DEPENDENCY

- Al-Anon Family Intergroup, 212-254-7230
- Alcoholics Anonymous 24-hour Help Line, 212-431-4640
- Alcoholics Anonymous Grapevine, 212-8703400
- Cocaine Anonymous, 212-929-7300/7302
- Narcotics Anonymous, Inc., 212-929-6262
- Narcotics Anonymous 24-hour Help Line, 212-431-4640
- National Council on Alcoholism and Drug Dependency, 212-206-6770

ANIMALS

- ASPCA, American Society for the Prevention of Cruelty to Animals, 212-876-7700
- Animal bites, Bureau of Animal Affairs, NYC Department of Health, 212-676-2483
- Animal Medical Center, 212-838-8100; open 24-hours; phone calls 9 a.m. to 11 p.m.

- Bureau of Animal Affairs, NYC Department of Health, 212-442-9666
- Center for Animal Care and Control, 212-722-3620, www.nycacc.org

BIRTH/DEATH CERTIFICATES

- New York City, 212-788-4520; TTY, 212-442-9038

CONSUMER COMPLAINTS AND SERVICES

- Automobile Dealer (used) Complaints, 212-487-4444
- Better Business Bureau, 212-533-6200, www.newyork.bbb.org
- Federal Trade Commission, 212-607-2829
- Licensing and Insurance System of the Federal Highway Administration's (FHWA) Office of Motor Carriers, 212-264-1070, or check www.fmcsa.dot.gov
- NYC Office of Telecommunications, 800-342-3330
- NYC Department of Consumer Affairs, 212-487-4444; TTY, 212-487-4465
- NY State Attorney General, 800-771-7755, complaint line
- NY State Consumer Frauds and Protection Bureau, 518-474-1471, www.consumer.state.ny.us
- NY State Department of Transportation, 800-786-5368, www.dot.state.ny.us
- NY State Department of Insurance, complaints and inquiries, 212-480-6400
- NY State Governor's Consumer Hotline, 800-697-1220
- US Consumer Product Safety Commission, 800-638-2772, www.cpsc.gov

CRIME

- Crime in Progress, 911
- Crime Victims, 800-771-7755
- Police Headquarters, 212-374-5000: 24-hour number for precinct referrals

CRISIS HOTLINES

- Ambulance, 911
- Arson Hot Line, 718-403-1300
- Boys Town National Hotline, 800-448-3000
- Housing complaints, 24-hours, 212-960-4800; TTY, 212-316-8295
- Rape/Battered Persons Crisis Center, 800-621-4673
- Sex Crimes Unit, Police Department, 212-267-7273, 24-hour service staffed by female NYPD detectives

- Suicide Hotline, 212-673-3000
- Youth Line, 800-246-4646; TTY 800-246-4699

CHILD ABUSE & FAMILY VIOLENCE
- Abducted, Abused and Exploited Children, 800-248-8020
- Battered Women Domestic Violence Program, 24-hour, 800-621-4673
- Child Abuse and Neglect Reports, 800-342-3720; TTY, 800-638-5163
- Emergency Children's Services, 212-966-8000

CULTURAL LIFE

- Arts on Line, www.allianceforarts.org
- Big Onion Walking Tours, 212-439-1090, www.bigonion.com
- Broadway Show Line, 888-292-9667
- City Search, www.newyork.citysearch.com
- City Web Site, www.nyclink.org
- NYC/OnStage, 212-768-1818
- New York Convention and Visitors Bureau, 212-484-1222, www.nycvisit.com
- *New York* magazine, www.newyorkmag.com
- *New York Times*, www.nytimes.com
- *New York Today*, www.nytoday.com
- Tele-Charge, 212-239-6200, www.telecharge.com
- Theatre Development Fund tickets, www.tdf.org
- Ticketmaster, 212-307-7171, www.ticketmaster.com
- *Time Out New York*, www.timeoutny.com
- Times Square Visitor's Center, 212-869-5667, www.timessquarebid.org
- *Village Voice*, www.villagevoice.com

DISCRIMINATION

- NYC Commission on Human Rights, 212-306-7450; TTY, 212-306-7686
- State Commission on Human Rights, 212-417-5041, 212-961-8650
- US Department of Fair Housing & Discrimination Hotline, 800-424-8590

EDUCATION

- Board of Education, 718-935-2000, www.nycenet.org

ELECTIONS

- Board of Elections, 212-868-3692

EMERGENCY

- FEMA Disaster Assistance Information, 800-525-0321
- Fire, police, medical, 911
- Poison Control Center, 24 hours, 212-764-7667

GOVERNMENT

State and local government listings for all profiled communities are on the net at www.piperinfo.com/index.

NEW YORK CITY
- Bronx Borough President, 718-590-3500
- Brooklyn Borough President, 718-802-3900
- City Council, 212-788-7100, www.nyclink.org
- Manhattan Borough President, 212-669-8300
- Mayor's office, 212-788-3000, www.nyclink.org
- Official New York City web site, www.nyc.gov
- Public Advocate, 212-669-7200, www.pubadvocate.nyc.gov
- Queens Borough President, 718-286-3000
- Staten Island Borough President, 718-816-2200

NEW YORK STATE
- Attorney General, 212-416-8000; TTY, 800-780-9898, www.oag.state.ny.us
- Governor's Office, 22-681-4580, www.state.ny.us/governor
- State Assembly, www.assembly.state.ny.us
- State Senate, www.senate.state.ny.us

FEDERAL
- Federal Government Information Center, 800-688-9889
- Social Security Administration, 800-772-1213, www.ssa.gov

HEALTH AND MEDICAL CARE

- AIDS Hotline, 212-676-2550, 212- 447-8200
- Ambulance Emergency Number, 911
- Dental Emergencies, First District Dental Society, 212-573-9502
- Department of Health Central Complaint Bureau, 212-442-9666
- Doctors on Call, 212-737-2333, 718-238-2100
- Doctors-on-Call, private group, 718-745-5900; 24 hour house-call service
- Lead Poisoning Prevention Program, 212-676-6100

- Medicaid Fraud Control Unit, Attorney General's Office, 212-417-5397
- New York County Medical Society, AMA, 212-684-4670
- New York Public Advocate, www.pubadvocate.nyc.gov
- Poison Control Center, 24-hours, 212-764-7667
- US Department of Health and Human Services, 800-336-4797

HOSPITALS
- Bayley-Seton Hospital, Staten Island, 718-354-6000, www.schsi.org
- Bellevue Hospital Center, 212-562-4141, www.nyc.gov
- Beth Israel Medical Center, 212-420-2000, www.bethisraelny.org
- Calvary Hospital, Bronx, 718-863-6900, www.calvaryhospital.org
- Columbia-Presbyterian Medical Center, 212-305-2500, cpmcnet.columbia.edu
- Harlem Hospital Center, 212-939-1000, www.nyc.gov
- Jacoby Medical Center, Bronx, 718-918-5000, www.nyc.gov
- Jamaica Hospital and Medical Center, Queens, 718-206-6000, www.jamaica-hospital.org
- Kings County Hospital Center, Brooklyn, 718-245-3131, www.nyc.gov
- Lenox Hill Hospital, 212-434-2000, www.lenoxhillhospital.org
- Mount Sinai Hospital, 212-241-6500, www.mountsinai.org
- New York Downtown Hospital, 212-312-5000, www.nyudh.org
- New York University Medical Center, 212-263-7300, www.med.nyu.edu
- St. Luke's Roosevelt Hospital Center, 212-523-4000, www.slrhc.org
- St. Vincent's Catholic Medical Center, 212-604-7000, www.stvin.org
- St. Vincent's Catholic Medical Center, Staten Island, 718-876-1234, www.schsi.org
- Woodhall Medical Center, Brooklyn, 718-963-8000, www.nyc.gov

HOUSING

- Department of Environmental Protection, 718-337-4337
- Division of Housing and Community Renewal, 212-480-6732
- Fair Housing Information Clearinghouse, 800-343-3442
- Metropolitan Council on Housing, 212-693-0550
- New York City Rent Guidelines Board, 212-385-2934, www.housingnyc.com
- Rent Administration Info line, 718-739-6400
- Rent Stabilization Assn. (Owners), 212-214-9200
- TenantNet, www.tenantnet.net
- Tenants and Neighbors Coalition, 212-695-8922
- US Department of Fair Housing and Discrimination, 800-477-5977, www.fairhousing.com/fhsc

LIBRARIES

- Bronx Reference Service, 718-579-4257
- Brooklyn Reference Service, 718-780-7700, www.brooklynpubliclibrary.org
- Manhattan Reference Service, 212-340-0849
- New York Public Library Information, 212-340-0849, www.nypl.org
- New York Public Library, Staten Island, 718-442-8562, www.nypl.org
- Queens Public Library, 718-990-0700, www.queenslibrary.org
- Branch libraries, see **Neighborhoods** chapter

MARRIAGE LICENSES

- NYC Marriage License Bureau, 212-669-2400

MOTOR VEHICLES/PARKING

- Alternate Side Parking, NYC Bureau of Traffic Operations, 212-225-5368, www.nyc.gov/html.dot
- American Automobile Association, 212-586-1166, www.aaany.com
- Auto pound, 212-TOW-AWAY
- Automobile Dealer (used) Complaints, 212-487-4444
- Licenses and Registration Information, State Motor Vehicle Dept., 212-645-5550, 7:30 a.m. to 4 p.m.
- NYC Dept. of Highways, 212-442-7090, 24 hour service; calls tow trucks for highway (not street) breakdowns
- Parking in New York City, City Department of Finance Parking Violations Operations, www.ci.nyc.ny.us/finance
- Parking Violations Hotline, NYC Department of Transportation, 718-422-7800, www.nyc.gov
- State Department of Motor Vehicles, 212- 645-5550, www.nydmv.state.ny.us
- Towed away cars, NYPD Towing, 212-971-0773; 7 a.m. to 10 p.m. daily

PARKS AND RECREATION

- General information, including special events, 888-NY-PARKS, www.nyparks.org
- See **Sports and Recreation** and **Greenspace and Beaches** chapters

POLICE

- For all police emergencies dial 911
- State police troop, NYC, 718-319-5100
- See **Neighborhood** chapter for precinct stations

POST OFFICE

- General Information, 212-967-8585, 8 a.m. to 8 p.m., Saturday 8 a.m. to 4 p.m., closed Sunday
- US Postal Service, 800-275-8777, www.usps.com

SANITATION AND GARBAGE

- NYC Department of Sanitation, 212-219-8090, www.nyc.link.org
- Environmental Action Coalition, 212-825-3367, www.eacnyc.org

SENIORS

- NYC Deptartment for the Aging, 212-442-1000, www.ci.nyc.us/aging
- New York Foundation for Senior Citizens, 212-962-7559
- Social Security and Medicare Eligibility Information, 800-772-1213, www.ssa.gov

STREET MAINTENANCE

- Potholes, NYC Bureau of Highways, 212-768-4653; after 4:30 p.m. and weekends, 212-442-7090
- Streetlights, NYC Bureau of Electrical Control, 212-669-8353
- Water mains and sewers, NYC Dept. of Environmental Protection, 718-699-9811; 24-hour service

SPORTS

PARTICIPANT SPORTS AND ACTIVITIES
- New York City Parks and Recreation, www.nyc.gov/parks
- Brooklyn, 718-965-6980
- Bronx, 718-430-1858
- Manhattan, 212-408-0205
- Queens, 718-520-5936
- Staten Island, 718- 816-6172
- Central Park Conservancy, 212-310-6600, www.centralparknyc.org

- Gateway National Recreation Area, 718-338-3799, www.nps.gov/gate
- President's Council on Physical Fitness and Sports, 202-690-9000

PROFESSIONAL
- New Jersey Nets, 800-7NJ-NETS, www.nba.com/teams
- New York Giants, 201-935-3900, www.nygiants.org
- New York Jets, 516-560-8200, www.newyorkjets.com
- New York Knicks, 212-465-5867, www.nba.com/knicks
- New York Liberty, 212-564-9622, www.wnba.com/liberty
- New York Mets, 718-507-8499, www.mets.com
- New York Rangers, 212-465-6000, www.newyorkrangers.com
- Sports Phone scores and schedules, 212-976-1313
- Sports Phone supplemental, 212-976-2525

TAXES

CITY
- NYC Department of Finance, 718-935-6000, www.nyclink.org

FEDERAL
- Internal Revenue Service, 800-829-4477, www.irs.gov

STATE
- NYS Department of Taxation and Revenue, 800-225-5829, TTY, 800-634-2110, www.state.ny.us

TAXIS

- Complaints, Taxi and Limousine Commission, 212-676-1000
- Lost & Found, Taxi and Limousine Commission, 212-302-8294

TELEPHONE

- AT&T, 800-222-0300, www.att.com
- MCI WorldCom, 800-950-5555, www.wcom.com
- RCN, 800-RING-RCN, www.rcn.com
- Sprint, 800-425-0982, www.sprint.com
- Verizon, 212-890-1550, www.verizon.com

TIME/TEMPERATURE, 212-976-1616

TRANSPORTATION

- NY State Department of Transportation, 718-482-4594, www.dot.state.ny.us
- Port Authority of New York & New Jersey, 800-A-I-R-R-I-D-E, www.panynj.gov
- US Department of Transportation, 212-264-8701, www.dot.gov

AIRPORTS
- John F. Kennedy International, 718-244-4444, www.panynj.gov; parking information, 718-244-4168
- LaGuardia, 718-533-3400, wwwpanynj.gov; parking information, 718-533-3850
- Newark, 973-961-6230, www.panynj.gov; parking information, 973-961-4751
- Port Authority of New York & New Jersey, 800-A-I-R-R-I-D-E, www.panynj.gov

BUSES
- Adirondack Trailways, 212-967-2900
- George Washington Bridge Bus Terminal Information, 800-201-9903, www.panynj.gov
- Greyhound Bus Lines, 800-231-2222, www.greyhound.com
- Peter Pan/Trailways, 800-343-9999
- Port Authority Bus Terminal Information, 212-564-8484, www.panynj.gov

FERRIES
- Mariner's Harbor/Bayonne Ferry, 888-254-R-I-D-E
- New York Waterway, 800-533-3779, www.nywaterway.com
- Seastreak, 800-B-O-A-T-R-I-D-E, www.seastreak.usa.com
- Staten Island Ferry, 718-815-2628, www.mta.nyc.ny.us

RAIL
- Amtrak (Penn Station), 800-872-7245, www.amtrak.com
- Long Island Railroad (Penn Station), 718-217-5477; TTY, 718-558-3022, www.mta.nyc.ny.us
- Metro-North (Grand Central), 212-532-4900; TTY, 800-724-3322, www.mta.nyc.ny.us
- New Jersey Transit (Penn Station), 973-762-5100, www.njtransit.com
- Staten Island Rapid Transit, 718-966-7478, www.mta.nyc.ny.us

SUBWAYS AND CITY BUSES
- Complaints about service, 718-330-3322
- Lost & Found (NYC Transit Authority), 212-712-4500

- PATH service to New Jersey, 800-234-7284, www.panynj.gov
- Subway and Bus Schedules (NYC Transit Authority), 718-330-1234, www.mta.nyc.ny.us

TAXIS, LIMOUSINES
- Taxi and Limousine Commission, www.ci.nyc.ny.us, 212- 676-1000, questions or complaints; 212-302-8294, lost and found

TOURISM AND TRAVEL

- National Park Service, www.nps.gov
- New York Convention and Visitors Bureau, 212-397-8200, www.nycvisit.com
- New York State Division of Tourism, 800-CALL-NYS, www.iloveny.com
- US Passport Agency, 212-206-3500
- Vacation Information, 800-225-5697; Recording after 5 p.m.

UTILITY EMERGENCIES

- Electrical emergencies, Con Edison, 212-683-0862
- Gas leaks, Con Edison, 212-683-8830
- Heat complaints, NYC Housing Preservation and Development, 212-960-4800

WEATHER, 212-976-1212

ZIP CODE INFORMATION

- USPS zip codes request, 800-275-8777, www.usps.com

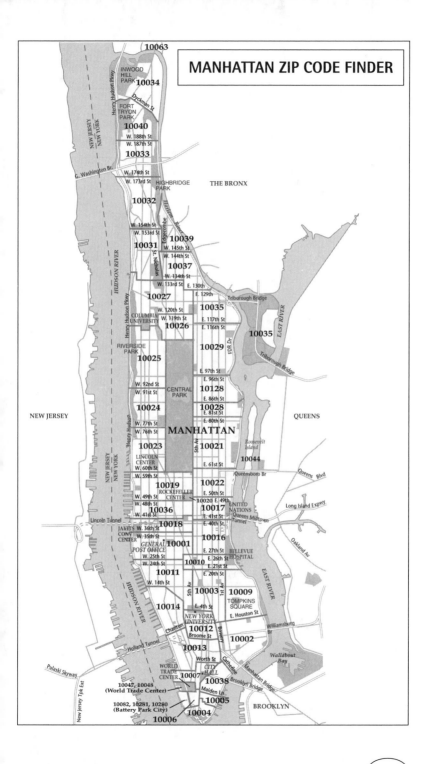

MANHATTAN ZIP CODE FINDER

INDEX

BELDEN RANDOLPH MERIMS was a newcomer to New York longer ago than she wants to remember. A researcher at *Newsweek* then, she married a native and stayed to raise a family in Greenwich Village. After some 40 years here as an occasional editor and writer, she still finds the city endlessly fascinating, exciting and, yes, beautiful.

READER RESPONSE FORM

We would appreciate your comments regarding this nineteenth edition of the *Newcomer's Handbook*® *for Moving to New York City.* If you've found any mistakes or omissions or if you would just like to express your opinion about the guide, please let us know. We will consider any suggestions for possible inclusion in our next edition, and if we use your comments, we'll send you a *free* copy of our next edition. Please send this response form to:

Reader Response Department
First Books
6750 SW Franklin, Suite A
Portland, OR 97223 USA

Comments:

_____

_____

_____

_____

_____

_____

_____

_____

Name: _____

Address _____

_____

_____

Telephone (_____) _____

6750 SW Franklin, Suite A
Portland, OR 97223
503-968-6777
www.firstbooks.com

FIRST BOOKS

NEWCOMER'S ORDER FORM HANDBOOK®

THE ORIGINAL, ALWAYS UPDATED, ABSOLUTELY INVALUABLE GUIDES FOR PEOPLE MOVING TO A CITY!

Find out about neigborhoods, apartment and house hunting, money matters, deposits/leases, getting settled, helpful services, shopping for the home, places of worship, cultural life, sports/recreation, vounteering, green space, schools and education, transportation, temporary lodgings and useful telephone numbers!

	# COPIES	TOTAL
Newcomer's Handbook® for Atlanta	_____ x $17.95	$_____
Newcomer's Handbook® for Boston	_____ x $18.95	$_____
Newcomer's Handbook® for Chicago	_____ x $18.95	$_____
Newcomer's Handbook® for London	_____ x $20.95	$_____
Newcomer's Handbook® for Los Angeles	_____ x $17.95	$_____
Newcomer's Handbook® for Minneapolis-St. Paul	_____ x $20.95	$_____
Newcomer's Handbook® for New York City	_____ x $19.95	$_____
Newcomer's Handbook® for San Francisco	_____ x $20.95	$_____
Newcomer's Handbook® for Seattle	_____ x $18.95	$_____
Newcomer's Handbook® for Washington D.C.	_____ x $19.95	$_____
	SUBTOTAL	$_____
POSTAGE & HANDLING (*$7.00 first book, $1.00 each add'l.*)		$_____
	TOTAL	$_____

SHIP TO:

Name _____

Title _____

Company _____

Address _____

City _____ State _____ Zip _____

Phone Number (_____) _____

Send this order form and a check or money order payable to:
First Books

First Books, Mail Order Department
6750 SW Franklin, Suite A, Portland, OR 97223
Allow 1-2 weeks for delivery

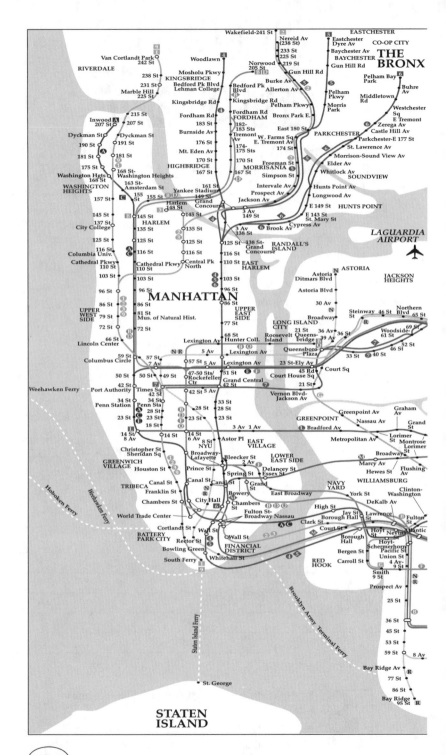

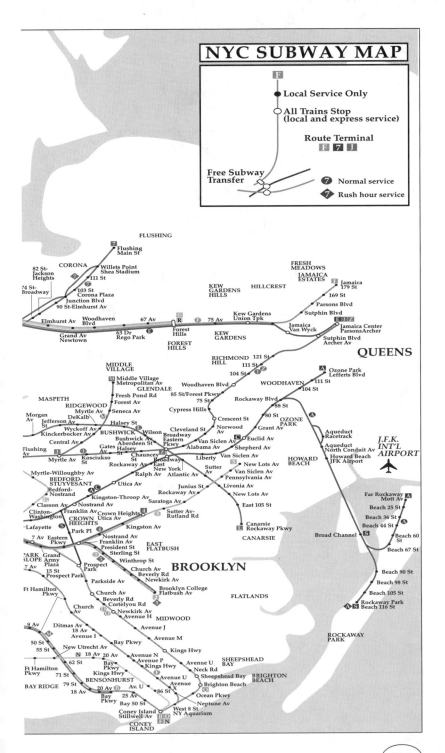

FIRST BOOKS

Visit our web site at

www.firstbooks.com

for a sample of all our books.